TCHAIKOVSKY
AND HIS WORLD

OTHER PRINCETON UNIVERSITY PRESS VOLUMES
PUBLISHED IN CONJUNCTION WITH
THE BARD MUSIC FESTIVAL

Brahms and His World
edited by Walter Frisch (1990)

Mendelssohn and His World
edited by R. Larry Todd (1991)

Richard Strauss and His World
edited by Bryan Gilliam (1992)

Dvořák and His World
edited by Michael Beckerman (1993)

Schumann and His World
edited by R. Larry Todd (1994)

Bartók and His World
edited by Peter Laki (1995)

Charles Ives and His World
edited by J. Peter Burkholder (1996)

Haydn and His World
edited by Elaine R. Sisman (1997)

Tchaikovsky
AND HIS WORLD

EDITED BY LESLIE KEARNEY

PRINCETON UNIVERSITY PRESS
PRINCETON, NEW JERSEY

Copyright © 1998 by Princeton University Press

For permissions information see p. x

Published by Princeton University Press, 41 William Street,
Princeton, New Jersey 08540
In the United Kingdom: Princeton University Press,
Chichester, West Sussex

Library of Congress Cataloging-in-Publication Data

Tchaikovsky and his world /edited by Leslie Kearney.
p. cm.—(The Bard Music Festival)
Includes bibliographical references and index.
ISBN 0-691-00429-3 (cloth: alk. paper).—ISBN 0-691-00430-7 (pbk.: alk. paper)
1. Tchaikovsky, Peter Ilich, 1840–1893—Criticism and interpretation.
I. Kearney, Leslie.   II. Series: Bard Music Festival series.
ML410.C4T36 1998
780'.92—dc21   98-25777

This publication has been produced by the Bard College Publications Office:
Ginger Shore, Director
Juliet Meyers, Art Director

This book has been composed in Baskerville
by Juliet Meyers

Music typeset by Don Giller

Princeton University Press books are printed on acid-free paper and meet the
guidelines for permanence and durability of the Committee on Production
Guidelines for Book Longevity of the Council on Library Resources

http://pup.princeton.edu

Printed in the United States of America

1 3 5 7 9 10 8 6 4 2

1 3 5 7 9 10 8 6 4 2
(Pbk.)

Designed by Juliet Meyers

FOR REINHARD STROHM,
DOUGLAS JOHNSON,
AND WALTER SOKEL
AND
IN MEMORY OF ARTHUR LEFF

Contents

Contents

PART III
THEORETICAL WRITINGS

Acknowledgments

First and foremost, I would like to thank Leon Botstein for choosing to focus this year's festival on a person, time and place dear to my heart and, I believe, to his as well. I would also like to thank Richard Taruskin for his support of my work, which has led to this and other rewarding opportunities. Mark Loftin and Robert Martin have been endlessly patient, helpful and good natured, as have the Bard Publication staff and Paul De Angelis.

All the contributors have been a sheer joy to work with; even though we are unfortunately separated by great geographical distances, we have created a community that I hope will endure. I would like to give special thanks to Thomas Kohlhase for permission to translate and reprint three articles from his excellent volume *Cajkovskij-Studien I;* Marina Kostalevsky for her invaluable experience and advice; and Alice Dampman Humel for performing above and beyond the call in an impossible situation. Alexander Poznansky's contribution to the present volume, in terms of insight, comprehensive knowledge, perspective, sense of humor, and sensitivity for the subject cannot be exaggerated.

I would like to thank four scholars who, although not directly involved in this project, are always present in my work and to whom I will be forever indebted: Douglas Johnson, Professor of Music History, Rutgers University; Walter Sokel, Professor Emeritus of German, University of Virginia; the late Arthur Leff, Southmayd Professor of Law, Yale Law School; and Reinhard Strohm, Heather Professor of Music, University of Oxford. This book is dedicated to them.

Finally I would like to thank Eric Onore.

—L.K.

Permissions

The images appearing in the essay by Richard Wortman were printed with the permission of Special Collections Office, Room 316, The Research Libraries, New York Public Library, Fifth Avenue at 42nd Street, New York, NY 10018-3423.

The articles by Susanne Dahmann, Kadja Grönke, and Arkadii Klimovitsky originally were published in German in *Čajkovskij-Studien I: Internationales Čajkovskij-Symposium Tübingen 1993* (Schott, 1995), and appear here in translation by kind permission of the editor, Thomas Kohlhase.

Caryl Emerson's article is reprinted, with permission, from the Metropolitan Opera's *Stagebill* of March 1997.

We gratefully acknowledge the following publications, from which images of artworks have been reproduced: *The Tretyakov Gallery Moscow: A Panorama of Russian and Soviet Art* (Aurora Art Publishers, Leningrad); *Valentin Serov: Paintings, Graphic Works, Scenography* (Aurora Art Publishers, Leningrad); *Three Centuries of Russian Painting; The Russian Experiment in Art, 1863–1922* (Thames and Hudson); ЛЕВИТАН; ИВАН ШИШКИН; and *Ilja Repin: Malerei Graphik* (Aurora-Kunstverlag, Leningrad).

Preface

Tchaikovsky experienced the old Chinese curse of living in interesting times. In the mid 1860s he witnessed the most dramatic social reorganization that had taken place in Russia to that time, the Great Reforms, which centered on the emancipation of the serfs, and affected the legal, educational, and military systems as well. During these volatile times the Russian literary language saw unprecedented development, as did the production, dissemination, and societal function of art and literature in general. Tchaikovsky got in on the ground floor of organized musical education in his country, becoming a member of the Petersburg Conservatory's first graduating class in 1865, and one of Russia's first music pedagogues. Other than that, the degree to which he seems to have remained untouched by the monumental changes going on around him is remarkable.

Tchaikovsky and his Russian contemporaries occupy an odd place in music history. The very exoticism and sense of "otherness" that attracts the imagination to Russia has likewise often engendered fanciful, even outlandish views of both Russian artists and their work. This situation has of course been complicated by the fact that information concerning Russian matters has not always been readily available or reliable. Thus, only recently has music scholarship possessed the means and the inclination to move beyond a perception of Musorgsky as *idiot savant*, for example, or Tchaikovsky as a suicidal, tortured crackpot. Similarly the music of these composers has often received only vague and subjective treatment. Ironically, precisely at the time when music analysis had developed and refined to a point where it appeared capable of elucidating this music, the interest of musicology turned toward issues which, if anything, often hindered and obscured such elucidation.

The present volume aspires to address a number of these problems. First, it attempts to rectify certain factual information about Tchaikovsky's life and attitudes. In the case of a figure like Tchaikovsky, in whose personal life posterity cannot seem to resist meddling, it is particularly important to allow him to speak for himself to the fullest extent possible, and to hear accurately what he has to say. Alexander Poznansky's translations and interpretations of previously censored archival material are of inestimable value in this endeavor, bringing human dimension to a personality that has so often slipped into caricature in the past.

Through the inclusion of translations of three essays from *Čajkovskij-Studien I*, the proceedings of the 1993 Tübingen conference on the centenary of his death, heretofore unavailable in English, this volume also offers a balance among American, Russian and West European views of Tchaikovsky and his work, views which are complementary but decidedly different. For example, Susanne Dammann's understanding of the Fourth Symphony in the context of nationalist composition and German "universalism" presents an interesting counterpoint to Natalia Minibayeva's explication of the same symphony in the context of the First Suite for Orchestra. Likewise, both Arkadii Klimovitsky and I identify references to Wagner's *Tristan* in *Iolanta* and *The Maid of Orleans* respectively, operas Tchaikovsky composed thirteen years apart, and which seem to point in sharply different directions in spite of the common association with Wagner's work. Kadja Grönke and Caryl Emerson contribute analyses of perhaps the two most complex and successful characters Tchaikovsky created, Gremin and Tatiana, both from *Eugene Onegin.*

Russian arts are not only inseparable from their social and political environment, but are also intensely interconnected. The cross-disciplinary essays contained in this volume, by Richard Wortman, Rosamund Bartlett, Janet Kennedy, Leon Botstein, and again Klimovitsky, place Tchaikovsky's work in a creative context that will be new to readers accustomed to understanding him as a part of the Western canon, and suggest the many levels of meaning his work contains.

Finally, an obligatory word about transliteration of Russian proper names. In the course of working on this volume, I have, no doubt, only come to the same conclusion as have countless before me—that there is no one good answer. The choices I have made attempt to address a number of admittedly conflicting needs. In general I find the Library of Congress system to be the best and most accurate. Unfortunately, applying this system to the name of the subject of this particular study confronts us with the following spelling: Pëtr Il'ich Chaikovskii. To avoid the cognitive dissonance this would undoubtedly cause the non-specialist reader, we have opted for the spelling with which English speakers are probably familiar through the Grove Dictionary: Pyotr Tchaikovsky. The spelling of the patronymic, Ilich, reflects a rather recent and sensible convention of omitting soft signs from proper names. In order to maintain some consistency, we have retained the common convention of ending last names with a "y"—for example Tolstoy, Musorgsky, etc. Other names, including first names, we have tried to render as accurately as possible, with exceptions for historic or artistic figures whom readers may expect to see in a particular spelling—thus you will find in these pages Alexander I, II and III, (not Aleksandr) as well as Scriabin, Balanchine etc. In endnote and other references to works employing different systems of transliteration, we have either preserved the spelling they used or tried to transliterate all words as accurately as possible, including soft signs, in an effort to facilitate access to sources.

Dates of events in Russia are given according to the Julian calendar in use there until 1918. When two dates appear, the first represents the old style, the second the Western Gregorian calendar.

—Leslie Kearney
New Haven, 1998

Part I
Biographical Works

Tchaikovsky: A Life Reconsidered

ALEXANDER POZNANSKY

Toward the end of his fairly short life Tchaikovsky's inner and outer circumstances appeared perfectly splendid. After completing his triumphal tour of America and receiving an honorary doctorate at Cambridge University, he was accepted as a world figure, a national composer of universal significance. In 1891 a Carnegie Hall program proclaimed Tchaikovsky, Brahms and Saint-Saëns as the three greatest living composers, and music critics praised Tchaikovsky as "a modern music lord."

Within Russia he became even more than that—he was considered a national treasure, his music admired and adored by all strata of society. He enjoyed the favor of the Imperial court, where he had a number of influential protectors, including two Grand Dukes, and the personal patronage of Tsar Alexander III, who had granted him a handsome government pension. Despite his homosexuality, which had in Russia become a matter of public knowledge, it cannot be said that Tchaikovsky's inner life had suffered any prolonged frustration; on the contrary, his emotional involvement during this period with his beloved nephew Vladimir [Bob] Davydov proved a source of stability and spiritual enjoyment.

Towards the end of the century, however, rumors of Tchaikovsky's homosexuality spread beyond Russia's borders, and this caused a change in attitude toward his work within Western musicological circles. His music began to be criticized as sentimental, romantically excessive, and charged with many imperfections, even pathology.

It was Oscar Wilde's trial of 1895 that created an enormous resonance in the English-speaking world, heightening negative tendencies in the reception and critical judgment of Tchaikovsky's art. As Richard Taruskin has noted, Wilde's trial became a "major watershed in the essentialization—and pathologization—of homosexuality around the turn of the century. . . . The homosexual was now defined not by his acts but by his character, a character that was certified to be diseased, hence necessarily alien to that of healthy, 'normal' people."[1]

From that moment on, the essentialist curse began to claim Tchaikovsky. Almost everything written about his work in American and especially English criticism has been substantially affected by this single fact of his personal life. Students of the composer's biography and music more often than not chose to dwell on his "abnormal" sexuality, employing their own standards of sexual morality and health to color their fundamental interpretation of his music.[2]

For most of our century Tchaikovsky was portrayed as a sort of fictionalized figure, an embodiment of romantic grief and turbid eroticism supposed by many to have commited suicide as a logical end to his sexual lifestyle. This image, which constantly lurked in the inflamed imagination of the lay audience, fails even remotely to resemble a real man with real concerns.

It is time to change this fallacious perception of Tchaikovsky's personality and his art by putting the record straight. Because Tchaikovsky's archives in Russia have recently been made accessible to students of his life and music, we now know much more about him and his environment than we ever did before.

I

Pyotr Ilich Tchaikovsky was born on 25 April/7 May 1840 at Votkinsk, in Viatka Province, which is located in the Urals 600 miles east of Moscow. He was the second son of Ilia Petrovich Tchaikovsky, a mining engineer and manager of the Kamsko-Votkinsk iron works, and Aleksandra Andreievna Tchaikovsky (née Assier).

On his father's side, Tchaikovsky's origin may be traced to the Ukrainian village Nikolaevka in the Poltava region. His great-grandfather was an eighteenth-century Ukrainian Cossack named Fëdor Chaika. Later the family name was changed to Chaikovskii, which is usually spelled in English according to the French transliteration. At first Chaika's son Pyotr studied in a seminary in Kiev, but he later received medical training in St. Petersburg. From 1770 to 1777 he served as a physician's assistant in the army. Eventually he found himself in the Ural region and there, in 1776, married Anastasiia Posokhova. In 1785 he was included (as a member of the landless gentry) in the register of nobility instituted by Catherine the Great. He resigned from his medical service and ended his life as city governor of Glazov in Viatka Province. Pyotr Chaikovskii had nine children, one of whom was the composer's father Ilia (1795–1880). After graduating from the College of Mines in St. Petersburg with a silver medal, he held several teaching and administrative posts, some of the latter in the northeast of Russia.

In 1837 Ilia became a factory manager in Votkinsk. This city was famous for its ironworks, which had been founded in 1758, and by 1820 it could boast the first hearth furnace in all Russia. As manager of the ironworks Ilia Tchaikovsky enjoyed broad authority within the Ekaterinburg region—from governing local factories to repealing the decisions of local courts. In 1827 he had married Mariia Kaiser, who died in 1830, leaving him with a daughter, Zinaida.[3]

Tchaikovsky's mother Aleksandra (1812–54) was the younger daughter of Andrei Assier (1790–1832), who was descended from a French émigré family. According to the version preferred by Tchaikovsky himself, the d'Assiers were Protestants who left France after the revocation of the Edict of Nantes in 1685; another, more reliable version maintains that the d'Assiers left in the wake of the French Revolution in 1789. At first Michel d'Assier lived with his family in German lands. Around 1795 they moved to Russia and, by an oath of allegiance, officially became subjects of the Imperial Crown. Michel's son Andrei, owing to his social connections and excellent knowledge of almost every European language, came to occupy a distinguished position within the bureaucracy in St. Petersburg, where he served in the Customs Department. He received government honors and was twice married. From his first marriage to Ekaterina Popova he had four children, including Aleksandra, the composer's mother. After the divorce of her parents and the death of her mother in 1816, Aleksandra was placed in the so-called Patriotic Institute, the government-sponsored school for orphaned girls from noble families, where she received a fine education. In 1833 she met Ilia Tchaikovsky and married him.

Apart from his stepsister Zinaida (1829–78) and elder brother Nikolai (1838–1911), after Pyotr's birth in 1840 the Tchaikovskys would have a daughter, Aleksandra (1841–91), and three more sons: Ippolit (1843–1927), and the fraternal twins Anatolii (1850–1915) and Modest (1850–1916). Tchaikovsky was never close to Zinaida, nor was he particularly intimate with his older brother Nikolai, who followed in the steps of their father as mining engineer, nor to a younger one, Ippolit, who became a naval officer. But he dearly loved his sister Aleksandra (or Sasha); and his youngest brothers, the twins Modest and Anatolii, always enjoyed his particular affection. Later in life Anatolii made a prominent career in law, rising by the end of his life to the rank of privy councilor and senator, while Modest became a playwright and educator, as well as the biographer of his famous older brother Pyotr.

Tchaikovsky was a very impressionable child, due in part to the highly emotional atmosphere within his family and to the characters of his parents. These factors could not but influence the specific "familial-erotic" dimension of his developing personality—a dimension later to play a prominent role in his relations with his younger brothers and his nephews.

Tchaikovsky's earliest musical impressions came from the family's orchestrion, with its excerpts from Mozart, Rossini, Bellini, and Donizetti. In September 1844 he made his first documented attempt at composition—"Our Mama in Petersburg," a song written together with Aleksandra. Pyotr became deeply attached to his French governess, Fanny Dürbach, and he also developed a friendship with the son of a neighbor, Venedikt Alekseiev. At the end of 1845 he began taking piano lessons with one Mariia Palchikova and became familiar with the mazurkas of Chopin.

In 1848 Ilia Tchaikovsky resigned his post and the family moved first to Moscow and later, in the expectation of a new appointment, to St. Petersburg. In St. Petersburg, Pyotr and Nikolai were placed in the private Schmelling School, where Pyotr resumed piano lessons. But the appointment in the capital did not materialize, and in May 1849 the family had to return to the Urals, where Ilia Tchaikovsky was appointed manager of an ironworks in Alapaevsk, some 300 miles to the east of Votkinsk. This did not prevent the composer's mother from returning with him to the capital the following autumn, so that he could enroll in the preparatory class of the Imperial School of Jurisprudence. On this occasion Pyotr saw Mikhail Glinka's *A Life for the Tsar (Zhizn' za Tsaria)* at the Alexandrinsky Theater, and it made a lasting impression on him.

During the next couple of years Tchaikovsky's parents moved back and forth between the Urals and St. Petersburg, finally settling in the capital in 1852. By this time Pyotr had successfully passed his entrance exam for the School of Jurisprudence, where he participated in the school choir under the direction of the distinguished Russian choirmaster Gavriil Lomakin. Tchaikovsky later remembered: "My voice was a splendid soprano and for several years in succession I took the first line in the trio which on these occasions was sung by the three boys at the altar at the beginning and end of [the Liturgy]."[4]

The sudden death of Tchaikovsky's mother from cholera on 14 June 1854 was a traumatic event for Pyotr, then a young adolescent.

Earlier that year the Tchaikovsky family was living with the family of Ilia's brother Pyotr (1789–1871), a retired general, in a large apartment on Vasilevsky Island, an arrangement that lasted for three years. After Ilia's eldest daughter Zinaida married Evgeni Olkhovsky and left the capital to live in the Urals, Aleksandra, now fifteen years old and newly graduated from school, took charge of the household and of the twins.

Tchaikovsky spent nine years (1850–59) as a boarding student at the School of Jurisprudence. At that time he also made his first attempts at composition, among which were an opera, *Hyperbole* (now lost), a waltz for piano, and his first published work, the song "Mezza notte." His stay in that institution must have enhanced Tchaikovsky's innate homosexual sensibilities. The School of Jurisprudence, like any boarding school, was never distinguished by high morals of any sort, a fact well known to contemporaries: the School, for instance, could boast an obscene homosexual song composed by its students, and it also produced a number of prominent homosexuals. Of his schoolmates, two loomed large in his life of that period—Aleksei Apukhtin (1841–93), a future poet of renown, and Sergei Kireev (1845–88?), arguably the most passionate of all Tchaikovsky's attachments.[5] As regards Tchaikovsky's relationship with Kireev, Modest Tchaikovsky calls it in his still unpublished autobiography one of the "strongest, most durable and purest amorous infatuations" of Tchaikovsky's life; "it possessed all charms, all sufferings, all depth and force of love, most luminous and sublime," such that, without its passion, the "music of *Romeo and Juliet*, of *The Tempest*, of *Francesca da Rimini* is not entirely comprehensible."[6] I believe that one of Tchaikovsky's first songs, "My genius, my angel, my friend," composed in 1858, was dedicated to Kireev.[7] Outside the School he forged a close friendship with his cousin Anna Tchaikovsky (later Merkling), the daughter of his uncle Pyotr.

In the autumn of 1858 Tchaikovsky's father was named to the coveted directorship of the Technological Institute in St. Petersburg, and his family moved to the director's large apartments. At the end of 1860 Tchaikovsky's sister Aleksandra moved away from the family after marrying Lev Davydov, a well-to-do landowner; the couple settled at his family estate, Kamenka, in Ukraine. A few years later Ilia Tchaikovsky married for a third time, taking as his wife Elizaveta Lipport, who had already been taking care of his household for several years. With the death of his mother, Tchaikovsky became a mother figure for his twin brothers, Anatolii and Modest. Both boys followed in his footsteps to the School of Jurisprudence, where it became clear that Modest was alarmingly similar in character to his elder brother—he too became homosexual.

A month after his graduation on 13 May 1859, Pyotr Tchaikovsky began working as a clerk in the Ministry of Justice. Although he remained there for four years, he quickly found the job ill-suited to his abilities. At the same time he entered the capital's social and cultural milieu as a young man-about-town, spending much of his energy in the pursuit of pleasure, engaging in affairs and amorous adventures with members of his set, until the threat of homosexual scandal, according to an account in Modest's autobiography, sobered him up.[8]

The conflict between his desire for pleasure (sexual pleasure in particular) and his creative aspirations forms the root of his phobia regarding human contact, especially in large crowds, so characteristic of the mature Tchaikovsky. This conflict could not but result in a profound ambivalence with respect to the erotic dimension of his personality.

In the summer of 1861, Tchaikovsky traveled abroad for the first time as secretary and interpreter for a family friend, Vasilii Pisarev. In the course of this trip he visited Berlin, Hamburg, Antwerp, Brussels, London and Paris.

Tchaikovsky's life took an unexpected turn that autumn: he started to attend Nikolai Zaremba's class in thoroughbass offered by the Russian Musical Society, which had recently been founded by Grand Duchess Elena Pavlovna and Anton Rubinstein with the purpose of promoting professional music education in Russia. When the St. Petersburg Conservatory was opened on 8 September 1862, Tchaikovsky was among its first students. Herman Laroche, the future music critic and composer, also enrolled the same year in the Conservatory, and the two soon became friends. Tchaikovsky studied harmony and form with Nikolai Zaremba, and orchestration and composition with Anton Rubinstein.

Having decided to devote his life to music, Tchaikovsky resigned from the Ministry of Justice on 11 April 1863. This decision coincided with the onset of financial hardships for his father Ilia, who by this time had retired from the directorship of the Technological Institute. To support himself, Tchaikovsky began giving private lessons in piano and music theory to students recommended to him by Anton Rubinstein. Tchaikovsky spent almost three years of his life at the St. Petersburg Conservatory. In addition to his study of harmony, strict counterpoint, composition and instrumentation—and despite having been excused from the compulsory piano class—he also decided to study flute and organ.

The leading spirits of the Conservatory from its beginning were Nikolai Zaremba and Anton Rubinstein. Despite Tchaikovsky's enthusiasm for learning, he considered Zaremba just an average instructor, whose dislike of Mozart and Glinka greatly disappointed him, and whose admiration for Beethoven and Mendelssohn the future composer found unbearable.

There is no doubt that, from the beginning, Tchaikovsky's main attraction to the newly founded Conservatory was its director, Anton Rubinstein, who seems to have had the power to stimulate his student's innate abilities, so that Tchaikovsky soon threw off the last traces of dilettantism in pursuit of his goal to become a good composer.

Tchaikovsky never worked as hard as in those years: he faithfully fulfilled his technical assignments and instrumental studies, and tried to master the art of conducting. He was always in the company of fellow student Herman Laroche, who would be the first critic to champion his music, and the two friends attended concerts and operas. Together they made many important connections in St. Petersburg music circles, including to Aleksandr Serov, an ideological opponent of Rubinstein, but the composer of the opera *Judith (Iudif)*, which Tchaikovsky admired.

Summer 1863 Tchaikovsky spent at Apukhtin's estate in Pavlodar. Next summer he stayed at the home of his society friend Prince Aleksei Golitsyn, near Kharkov, where he composed his overture *The Storm (Groza)* to the play by Aleksandr Ostrovsky (later the source of Leoš Janáček's opera *Kat'a Kabanová*). Tchaikovsky also sketched out a program for a descriptive concert overture. Upon completing the music, he sent it to Herman Laroche, with instructions that it be passed along to Rubinstein. The idea of showing the overture to Rubinstein made Tchaikovsky uncomfortable, since he both adored and feared his eminent teacher. This stratagem served him well, for it was the hapless Laroche who received the full force of Rubinstein's anger. Here was not the expected classical exercise, but a remarkably powerful work, a mature attempt at dramatic program music (after the programmatic overtures of Henri Litolff), scored for an orchestra that included some instruments "forbidden" to mere students, such as the harp, English horn and tuba; and also incorporating Russian folk song.[9]

Tchaikovsky was not discouraged by what was to be the first of many such incidents with Rubinstein. Theirs was always an uneasy relationship. Nevertheless, in the summer of 1865, Tchaikovsky found himself fulfilling a promise to Rubinstein to translate for Conservatory students the much needed textbook *Traité général d'instrumentation* by the eminent Belgian theorist François Auguste Gevaert, which had appeared in 1863. This task did not spoil Tchaikovsky's happy vacation spent with younger brothers Anatolii and Modest on the estate of their brother-in-law Lev Davydov at Kamenka, near Kiev in Ukraine. Rubinstein proved to be quite pleased with the completed translation.

While at Kamenka, Tchaikovsky paid close attention to Ukrainian folk songs, gathering material for use in future compositions. Soon after his return to St. Petersburg he learned that Johann Strauss the younger had conducted the newly composed *Characteristic Dances (Kharakternye tantsy)* at an orchestral concert in Pavlovsk in late August 1865; it was the first public performance of any of the young Tchaikovsky's works, and he was extremely pleased.[10]

On 14 November 1865, Tchaikovsky made his debut as a conductor, directing the Conservatory orchestra in a performance of his Overture in F. Two weeks earlier his String Quartet Movement in B-flat was played by a quartet of his fellow students, including the violist Vasilii Bessel.

The Conservatory's graduation concert on 29 December 1865 included a performance of Tchaikovsky's ambitious cantata on the text of Schiller's ode *An die Freude* (which Beethoven had used in the Finale of his Ninth Symphony), which was not Tchaikovsky's choice but Rubinstein's. According to Tchaikovsky's first biographer, his brother Modest, the young composer absented himself because he feared the public examination, much to Rubinstein's annoyance. But the examination commission's records, preserved in the archives of the Conservatory, insist that "all students were present."[11] Still, Rubinstein threatened to withhold Tchaikovsky's diploma and refused to countenance public performance of the cantata unless it was revised.

A number of musical celebrities who were present at the concert, among them Serov and Cui, also disliked it. The final report on Tchaikovsky was, however, very favorable, and two days later he graduated from the Conservatory. Yet it appears that Tchaikovsky's diploma was withheld by Anton Rubinstein after all: the extant copy is dated 30 March 1870. His grades were reported as follows: theory and instrumentation, excellent; organ, good; piano, very good; conducting, satisfactory. To Tchaikovsky's surprise, he also received the silver medal—the highest student award at the Conservatory, since the gold medal was not offered at that time.

II

In September 1865, Anton Rubinstein's brother Nikolai offered Tchaikovsky the post of professor of classes in harmony sponsored by the Moscow branch of the Russian Musical Society, which would shortly become the Moscow Conservatory under the directorship of Nikolai Rubinstein. Tchaikovsky moved to Moscow on 5 January 1866. Nikolai Rubinstein welcomed him, not only providing him with accomodations in his own apartment, but also introducing him to his circle of friends, which included writers, musicians, and publishers. Tchaikovsky found teaching rather a strain, but Nikolai Rubinstein's constant enthusiasm and encouragement were to have the most palliative effect on him. At a concert on 4 March 1866, Rubinstein conducted Tchaikovsky's Overture in F major to great success, which helped the composer have faith in his own potential. He began to work on his first symphony, but found this not an easy matter: he was unable to sleep, and suffered from terrible headaches and depression.

At the end of November, his first symphony, *Winter Daydreams (Zimnie grezy)*, Op. 13, was complete. Nikolai Rubinstein had offered to give the work its first performance, but Tchaikovsky refused because he wanted first to hear the opinions of Zaremba and Anton Rubinstein from St. Petersburg. Apparently they did not like the symphony, and Rubinstein did not conduct the work until February 1868. In March 1867 Tchaikovsky started to work on an opera, *The Voevoda,* to a libretto by the well-known Russian playwright Aleksandr Ostrovsky. Tchaikovsky lost the libretto and, despite Ostrovsky's efforts to reconstruct it, their collaboration ended in failure; Tchaikovsky himself completed the libretto on Ostrovsky's plot.[12]

The summer of 1867 Tchaikovsky spent in Finland and Estonia, where he composed a set of piano pieces *Souvenir de Hapsal (Vospominanie o Gapsale)*, Op. 2. After returning to Moscow, he continued to work on his opera, and in February 1868 he was invited to conduct some selections from it at a charity concert. Music from *The Voevoda* was well received, even by the "Mighty Handful," who were making their presence known in Russian composition at that time. Later that spring Tchaikovsky went to St. Petersburg, where he met members of the Mighty Handful personally and also visited the composer Aleksandr Dargomyzhsky. In January of 1868 he became friendly with their self-appointed leader, Mili Balakirev, to whom he sent a score of his new tone-poem *Fatum*, which was not well received.

Tchaikovsky as a teacher at the Moscow Conservatory (1868) (*The Tchaikovsky State Archive and House Museum, Klin, Russia*).

In the spring of 1866 Tchaikovsky made the acquaintance of the actor and baritone Konstantin de Lazari. A companionable socialite, de Lazari knew everyone in Moscow theatrical circles and introduced his new friend to the actors and their milieu. It was de Lazari who brought Tchaikovsky to the Artistic Circle club, where Tchaikovsky enjoyed spending time, and it was he who brought Tchaikovsky to the home of Vladimir Begichev, director of repertory for the Moscow theaters. Here the young composer was introduced to Begichev's wife

Mariia Shilovsky and her two sons from her first marriage, Konstantin and Vladimir.

According to Modest Tchaikovsky, "the chief interest for our composer in his acquaintance with the Begichevs lay in the personality of the younger of the Shilovsky brothers, Vladimir. He was then a fourteen-year-old boy, weak, sickly, with, as a result, a neglected education, but endowed, as it seemed then, with phenomenal capacity for music. In addition, his appearance was unusually lovely, his manners most originally charming and his mind, despite his poor education, sharp and observant."[13] Vladimir Shilovsky apparently studied music for some time at the Moscow Conservatory, and Tchaikovsky came to be his tutor in music theory. He was bound to his student not only by Shilovsky's talent, but also in great measure "by that love verging on adoration which he instilled in the boy."[14] Though Tchaikovsky's profound attachment to Shilovsky cannot be doubted, the emotional initiative almost always issued from pupil to teacher.

Initially Tchaikovsky appears to have been delighted with his new young friend, but during the following years of their acquaintance their relations deteriorated, becoming stormy and uncomfortable, full of unpleasant scenes and ruptures, due to Shilovsky's intractable character.

During the 1866–67 season Vladimir Shilovsky's compositions were already being performed in public concerts and productions; later he would be commissioned by Tchaikovsky to write the entr'acte for the second act of his opera *Oprichnik*. It was Shilovsky to whom Tchaikovsky dedicated his Third Symphony, and the two piano pieces Op. 10.

On 26 May 1868, Tchaikovsky departed on an extended European vacation in the company of Vladimir Shilovsky, his stepfather Vladimir Begichev, and their mutual friend Konstantin de Lazari. Shilovsky had not only invited Tchaikovsky to join them but also paid all his travel expenses. Returning to St. Petersburg in early August, Tchaikovsky went to visit his brothers in Estonia.

It seems that Tchaikovsky enjoyed life in Vladimir Shilovsky's circle because of their mutual homosexuality. Recent archival studies have revealed that the conventional perception of Tchaikovsky as a person tormented by his sexual difference is unfounded.[15] The perception was based on two largely unsupported assumptions: first, that nineteenth-century Russia was a society characterized by sexual repression; second, that Tchaikovsky consequently developed a particular fear of exposure and tendency to self-hatred. In fact, the Russia of that period happens to have been a society considerably more permissive than, say, Victorian England. Russia had no legal ban on homosexuality until Peter the Great in the early eighteenth-century, and then the ban was only extended to the army. Homosexuality was criminalized in 1832 by Nicholas I, but the law was virtually never enforced. With regard to members of the upper classes, homosexual incidents were covered up by the authorities, the guilty parties at worst being transferred from one official position to another. Among Tchaikovsky's contemporaries one may identify several homosexual members of the Imperial family, the most prominent of them being Grand Duke Sergei Aleksandrovich, governor of Moscow. One of the most powerful statesmen under Alexander III and Nicholas II, Prince Vladimir Meshchersky (who was, incidentally, Tchaikovsky's schoolmate and friend), was repeatedly rescued from disgrace by the two emperors despite his flagrant homosexual activity. One may list many other individuals of similar status in Russian society.[16] Furthermore, even after the emancipation of the serfs in 1861, the deep-rooted tradition of serfdom continued to exert a powerful effect on social behavior in both upper and lower classes. According to established patterns of conduct, socially inferior people were expected to submit to the wishes of the socially superior in every respect, including the gratification of sexual desire. Russian peasants were traditionally tolerant of all varieties of sexual preferences among their masters, and were often prepared to satisfy them on demand. This naturally resulted in boundless "sexploitation," and explains the sexual affairs with servants and other lower class persons so characteristic of Tchaikovsky and his milieu—a sort of hierarchical sex.[17]

As far as Tchaikovsky's own attitude to his sexual situation is concerned, he could not, of course, fully neglect societal convention and, generally speaking, was rather conservative by temperament. In addition, in his youth he was repeatedly pressured to marry, and at some point he thought he could change his sexual orientation and successfully live with a woman in order to ease his own life and mollify his relatives. Even at that stage, however, he considered his homosexual tendencies natural and in no way his own fault.

In the autumn of 1868 Tchaikovsky experienced an altogether new amorous development. This time it was an "affair" with the well-known Belgian mezzo-soprano Désirée Artôt, which, while ultimately and predictably doomed to failure because of Tchaikovsky's homo-sexuality, nevertheless proceeded to the point of betrothal. Artôt, having studied under the famous French singer Pauline Viardot, began singing with the Paris Opera in 1858. In 1868 she arrived in Moscow with a mediocre Italian opera company under the direction of

Merelli. The fact that Artôt belonged wholly to the world of art and music formed the psychological basis of Tchaikovsky's infatuation. It seems the composer fell in love not so much with her as with her voice and her performance, the more so as she was neither very young, being five years Tchaikovsky's senior, nor exceptionally beautiful, according to some contemporary memoirs.

Wishful thinking regarding his own abilities for a heterosexual lifestyle and continuing pressure from his father, who passionately wished to see his son married, led Tchaikovsky to believe that he could marry Désirée Artôt. He met her for the first time very briefly in spring 1868, but her name does not begin to appear in his letters until her autumn performance in Moscow. He admits in his letter of 21 October to his brother Anatolii: "I am now on very friendly terms with Artôt and enjoy her very noticeable favor; rarely have I met a woman so lovely, intelligent and kind."[18]

By the end of December Tchaikovsky's infatuation with Artôt was obvious to all. He wrote some music for her, and even began to discuss marriage plans with his father.

It is likely that Artôt's mother found out about Tchaikovsky's sexual orientation and took control of the situation. At the end of January Tchaikovsky heard that his beloved had married the Spanish baritone Don Mariano Padilla y Ramos in Warsaw. Although he was upset by the news, Tchaikovsky recovered from the disappointment rather quickly, as might be expected.

The premiere of *The Voevoda* took place at the Bolshoi Theater on 11 February 1869. Despite initial success, interest in the opera soon evaporated and it was withdrawn from the repertoire after only five performances. Two weeks after the premiere, Nikolai Rubinstein conducted the first performance of the symphonic poem *Fatum*. Public reaction was favorable, but again, as in case of *The Voevoda*, success was short-lived. After Balakirev's harsh criticism of its St. Petersburg performance, Tchaikovsky refused to allow the work to be published and, a few years later, destroyed the score. It was reconstructed after his death on the basis of some discovered orchestral parts. The same fate befell his opera *The Voevoda,* from which Tchaikovsky decided to retain only the overture, one chorus, an entr'acte, and the dances.

Struggling for recognition, the young composer started work on another opera, based on a Russian translation of Friedrich de la Motte-Fouqué's famous tale *Undine*. On 6 August 1869 he submitted the finished opera to the Opera Directorate of the Imperial Theaters. Two years later the work was formally rejected and, like its predecessor, consigned to the flames by the composer himself. He saved only four pieces from it, which were used later in Symphony No. 2, the ballet *Swan Lake (Lebedinoe ozero)*, and the incidental music to Ostrovsky's play *The Snow Maiden (Snegurochka)*.

In autumn 1869 Tchaikovsky met in Moscow with Balakirev, who encouraged the composer to begin a new tone-poem based on Shakespeare's tragedy *Romeo and Juliet*. The Russian obsession with love and death, themes that permeate the story of the young lovers from Verona, almost immediately fired Tchaikovsky's imagination. After making many revisions and modifications at Balakirev's suggestion, *Romeo and Juliet* was heard for the first time at a concert in Moscow on 4 March 1870 conducted by Nikolai Rubinstein. Tchaikovsky himself held a very high opinion of *Romeo and Juliet* to the end of his life.

It is ironic that the tragic situation so well presented by Tchaikovsky in his tone-poem was reflected in real life. About that time he was involved in a passionate love affair with a student at the Moscow Conservatory, Eduard Sack, which ended in Sack's suicide on 2 November 1873. Fourteen years after the young man's death, Tchaikovsky wrote in his diary: "It seems to me that I have never loved anyone so strongly as him . . . and his memory is sacred to me!"[19]

Tchaikovsky's relationships with young men were starting to cause disconcerting talk and gossip in Moscow musical circles, but despite this he continued to pursue his love affairs. He rushed off to join Vladimir Shilovsky, who had fallen seriously ill in Paris in 1870, and the two traveled together for some time following Shilovsky's recuperation.

On 16 March 1871, a concert at Moscow's Hall of Nobility witnessed a successful performance of the young composer's First String Quartet, as well as a few of his piano pieces and songs.

In autumn 1871, Tchaikovsky finally engaged a small apartment of his own, furnished with a sofa, a few chairs, and two pictures, one a portrait of Anton Rubinstein and the other of Louis XVII, the dauphin who died in the aftermath of the French Revolution and whom Tchaikovsky had worshipped from childhood. He also took on a manservant, Mikhail Sofronov (soon to be replaced by the latter's younger brother Aleksei), a peasant boy from the Klin region near Moscow. Tchaikovsky began to supplement his small income as a Conservatory professor by writing music criticism for the Moscow newspaper *Russian Register (Russkie Vedomosti)*.

In May 1872 he finished his third opera, *The Oprichnik* (adapted from the tragedy by historical novelist Ivan Lazhechnikov, set during the reign of Ivan the Terrible in the sixteenth-century), and, while staying at Kamenka during the summer, began work on his Second

Tchaikovsky in 1874 (*The Tchaikovsky State Archive and House Museum, Klin, Russia*).

Symphony, later dubbed the "Little Russian." The new symphony was received enthusiastically in February 1873. Encouraged, Tchaikovsky proceeded to his next project, incidental music for Ostrovsky's play *The Snow Maiden*. After another vacation in Europe, he spent almost the whole of August at Shilovsky's estate, Usovo, near Kiev, where he sketched out a new symphonic fantasia, *The Tempest* (*Buria*), based on Shakespeare's play. *The Tempest* was a great success at its first performance in Moscow in early December.

On 12 April 1874 *The Oprichnik* was first performed at the Mariinsky Theater in St. Petersburg. Despite some initial success, the opera did not convince the composer's critics. Cesar Cui attacked the music as "barren of ideas" and "without a single outstanding passage or a single happy inspiration."[20] Tchaikovsky found himself agreeing with the critics: "*The Oprichnik* torments me," he confided to his niece Anna Merkling.[21] He went to Italy in the capacity of music critic, but the journey was spoiled by the opera's failure. Seized by an intense desire to prove to himself and others that he was capable of better things than *The Oprichnik*, he returned to Russia. By the middle of June, while staying at the Nizy estate owned by his society friend Nikolai Kondratiev, he started another new opera, this time to a libretto based on Nikolai Gogol's story "Christmas Eve" ("Noch' pered Rozhdestvom").

A few years earlier, the music patron Grand Duchess Elena Pavlovna had commissioned from the poet Iakov Polonski a libretto for an opera based on Gogol's tale. It had been intended for Aleksandr Serov, who died in 1871 without commencing the project. The Grand Duchess decided to offer a prize in Serov's memory for the best setting of the libretto. Upon her own death in 1873, responsibility for the competition passed to the Russian Musical Society. Having learned that Balakirev, Anton Rubinstein, and Rimsky-Korsakov were not competing, and under the impression that the closing date for entry was 1 August 1874, Tchaikovsky finished the new opera within a month, only to discover he would be obliged to wait a full year for the decision. Although Tchaikovsky eventually won first prize, the setting did not impress the public, and the opera, *Vakula the Smith,* was abandoned. Nine years later, the composer radically revised it under a new title, *The Slippers* (*Cherevichki*); in 1895 the same story became the subject for Rimsky-Korsakov's opera *Christmas Eve.*

In November 1874 Tchaikovsky began working on a piano concerto, a complete draft of which he had completed by 24 December, when he played it for Nikolai Rubinstein. Three years later he described Rubinstein's reaction on that occasion in a letter to Mrs. von Meck: "I patiently played the concerto to the end: it was greeted with silence. I got up and asked, 'What do you think of it?' Suddenly a torrent of words gushed from Rubinstein's lips, getting louder and fiercer every minute until he sounded like a thundering Jupiter. According to him my concerto was no good at all, impossible to play, with many awkward passages . . . so poorly composed that it would be impossible to correct them. The composition was vulgar, and I had stolen bits from here, there, and everywhere. . . . I was not only aston-ished but offended by this scene." Stunned, the composer left the room without a word. Presently Rubinstein came to Tchaikovsky and, seeing how upset he was, tried to soften the blow by saying that if Tchaikovsky agreed to revise the piece, he would introduce it at one of his concerts. "I shall not alter a single note," answered Tchaikovsky, "I shall publish the work precisely as it stands!"[22]

The concerto was indeed published exactly as it stood, though eventually Tchaikovsky did make alterations, particularly to the piano part. He decided to dedicate it not to his student at the Moscow Conservatory, the composer Sergei Taneev, as he had originally intended, but to the famous German pianist Hans von Bülow, whom Tchaikovsky had heard in recital at the Bolshoi Theater the previous March. Bülow, highly flattered by the dedication, gave the first suc-cessful performance of the B-flat minor Concerto in Boston 13/25 October 1875. Five days later, Tchaikovsky attended the premiere of the Concerto in St. Petersburg. Despite excellent forces—the pianist was Tchaikovsky's old school friend, Gustav Kross, and the conductor Eduard Nápravník—the reviews were almost all unfavorable. When, later that autumn, Taneev performed the "impossible" work at a con-cert of the Russian Musical Society in Moscow with Nikolai Rubinstein conducting, the concerto was proclaimed an instant success.

Tchaikovsky spent the summer of 1875 with his sister's family at Kamenka, his brother-in-law's estate in Ukraine. Here Tchaikovsky composed his third symphony, this in five movements, two in dance style. The symphony has since been nicknamed *The Polish*, for no more reason than the tempo di polacca marking of the Finale. Performed for the first time on 7 November with Nikolai Rubinstein conducting, the symphony gained almost immediate acclaim.

In August, Tchaikovsky began work on the first of his famed tril-ogy of ballets, *Swan Lake*, commissioned by the Imperial Theaters in Moscow. Throughout the winter months the work progressed steadily and was finished by 10 April 1976. Meanwhile he also accepted a com-mission from the editor of *Nuvellist*, a music magazine, to compose a series of twelve piano pieces, which became popularly known as *The Seasons* (*Vremena goda*).

At the very end of 1875, the composer left Russia together with his brother Modest and Modest's deaf-mute seven-year-old pupil Nikolai Konradi. The two brothers decided to go to Paris via Germany and Switzerland. Modest was planning to study the latest methods of teaching deaf-mutes in a private school at Lyons. While in Paris Tchaikovsky experienced one of the strongest musical impressions in

Tchaikovsky, 24 July 1877 (*The Tchaikovsky State Archive and House Museum, Klin, Russia*).

his entire life, when he attended a performance of Bizet's *Carmen* at the Opéra Comique. He returned to Russia at the end of January, but rejoined Modest in France that June. After about a month there Tchaikovsky traveled to Germany, where he attended the first festival devoted entirely to Wagner's *Der Ring des Niebelungen*, a work that he valued more for its historical significance than its musical content. During his stay he made the acquaintance of Liszt, but failed to meet Wagner himself. Tired by his stay at Bayreuth, Tchaikovsky returned to Kamenka on 11 August.

On 14 October he completed the symphonic fantasia *Francesca da Rimini*, which he claimed to have worked on "with love, and that love, it seems, has come out quite well."[23] At the end of 1876 he was honored by a visit from Leo Tolstoy, whom he greatly admired. The premiere of *Swan Lake* took place on 20 February 1877. It was a dismal failure, owing to terrible choreography and a poor orchestra, and after a few productions it was dropped from the repertoire.

III

Bearing in mind his affair with Désirée Artôt, there is every reason to believe that until the middle of the 1870s Tchaikovsky did not take his homosexuality too seriously and, as is frequently the case, did not allow himself to think that his sexual preference was irreversible or insurmountable. Most probably he thought he could act on his inclinations for as long as possible, and then, when it became absolutely necessary, he could simply abandon his habits.

After travelling with his brother Modest and Nikolai Konradi in early 1876, Tchaikovsky clearly realized that the emotional atmosphere surrounding his brother's relationship with his charge was unhealthy and deeply fraught with potential, even imminent danger. He became conscious of this on a very personal level, since he also felt an erotic attraction to the boy and had always been a role model for his younger brothers. And so the composer resolved to end the crisis in his own way, by making an example of himself.

On 19 August 1876 Tchaikovsky suddenly wrote to his brother: "I have decided to marry. It is inevitable. I must do this, and not only for myself, but also for you and for Anatolii, Aleksandra [their sister] and all whom I love. For you in particular! But you also, Modest, need to think seriously about this. Homosexuality and pedagogy cannot abide in harmony with one another."[24] A month later, in a letter to Modest, he stressed this point further: "A man who, after parting with, so to speak, *his own* (he can be called your own) child falls into the embraces of any passing trash, cannot be the real educator that you want and ought to become."[25] Discussing with Modest the possibility of the three of them living together the following year, the composer touched upon another issue which no doubt had been weighing heavily on his mind: "I do not want evil tongues to wound an innocent child, about whom they would inevitably say that I am preparing him to be my own lover, moreover, *a mute one*, in order to elude idle talk and rumors."[26] Contemptuous though he was of public opinion,

Tchaikovsky found that he could ignore it no longer. He was never a fighter by nature, and in the end he had no choice but to yield. His sudden and impulsive decision to marry was motivated primarily by an emotion more altruistic than selfish—a desire to ensure his relatives' peace of mind and to retain full and mutual understanding with them without need for reticence or deception.

Until this time Tchaikovsky had treated his homosexuality as a morally indifferent phenomenon. Now it suddenly seemed imperative to suppress it and, what is more, to advise his brother to do the same. Indeed, his customary relationship with Modest dictated that Tchaikovsky set an example of behavior to be imitated, one that might save Modest from the danger of scandal without causing him to abandon a pupil who was so deeply loved by both brothers. That he himself would have to make certain sacrifices in this respect must no doubt have flattered the self-esteem of the composer, who may well have seen the decision as an almost heroic gesture. Nevertheless, however vigorous their intent, Tchaikovsky's preparations for marriage did not proceed without some severe setbacks. A few weeks after his somber letters to Modest about marriage, he went to the country estate of his friend Bek-Bulatov, where he discovered a veritable homosexual bordello and found himself infatuated with his coachman.[27]

Tchaikovsky was torn by ambivalent feelings on the subject of sexuality and marriage. In a letter of 28 September 1876, after referring to three homosexual encounters since his last letter, he agreed with his brother that "it is not possible to restrain oneself, despite all one's vows, from one's weaknesses."[28] Moreover, at the end of the same letter he honestly confessed "I shall not enter into any lawful or illicit union with a woman without having fully ensured my own peace and my own freedom."[29] The "freedom" that Tchaikovsky intended to ensure obviously refers to the freedom to indulge in those "weaknesses" that could not be resisted, whatever vows one made.

Some time later, at the end of 1876, he fell deeply in love with his Conservatory student Iosif Kotek. This was a "passion" which, he admitted in letter to Modest on 19 January 1877, assailed him "with unimaginable force":

> I have known him for six years already. I always liked him, and on several occasions I have felt a little bit in love with him. That was like a trial run for my love. Now I have momentum and have *run right into him* in the most decisive fashion. I cannot say that my love is completely pure. When he caresses me

with his hand, when he lies with his head on my chest and I play with his hair and secretly kiss it, when for hours on end I hold his hand in my own and tire in the battle against the urge to fall at his feet and kiss these little feet, passion rages with me with unimaginable force, my voice shakes like that of a youth, and I speak some kind of nonsense. However I am far from desiring physical consummation. I feel that if *that occurred* I would cool to him. I would feel disgusted if this *wonderful youth* stooped to sex with an aged and fat-bellied man. How horrible this would be and how disgusting I would become to myself! It is not called for. . . .

I must tell you that yesterday was the eve of his departure for Kiev, where he is soon to give a concert. After my *confession* he suggested we travel out of town for supper. It was a delightful, moonlit night. I hired a carriage and we flew off. I cannot tell you the thousand details that caused me ineluctable bliss. I wrapped him up, hugged him, guarded him. He complained of the frost on the tip of his *nose*. I held the collar of his fur coat the whole time with my bare hand in order to warm this nosetip, so holy for me. The freezing of my *hand* caused me pain and, at the same time, the sweet thought of knowing that I was suffering for him. . . . [30]

In spring 1877, when Tchaikovsky's passion for Kotek suddenly declined owing to the latter's infidelity and his disfigured finger, and when his close homosexual friend Vladimir Shilovsky was getting married, it happened that Tchaikovsky received several love letters from a former Conservatory student, Antonina Miliukova (1848–1917).[31] Tchaikovsky hardly remembered Antonina, since he met her for the first time in Moscow in late May 1872 at the apartment of her brother, the staff-captain Aleksandr Miliukov (1840–85), whose wife Anastasiia (neé Khvostova) was a close friend of the composer from his days at the School of Jurisprudence in Petersburg.[32]

Antonina later admitted, both in her letters to Tchaikovsky (1880s) and in her recollections (1894), that this first meeting had made an indelible impression on her, resulting in a profound affection that lasted for many years. She lent special meaning to the fact that her love arose from her attraction to Tchaikovsky's appearance and purely human qualities, that she was utterly ignorant of his music and growing fame in cultural circles. At Tchaikovsky's personal invitation, Antonina had attended the premiere of his cantata in honor of the opening of the Polytechnic Exhibition in Moscow on 30 May 1872. Their relationship, however, had not developed in the years after their first meeting, and during Antonina's studies at the Conservatory they saw each other only in passing. As Antonina later wrote, she had loved Tchaikovsky "secretly" for over four years. In late 1876, Antonina received a small inheritance due to the division of the family estate. This potential "dowry" was apparently the immediate incentive for taking active steps toward renewing her acquaintance with the composer.[33]

On 26 March 1877, Antonina sent Tchaikovsky a written confession of her love for him.[34] Both Antonina and Tchaikovsky testify that they "began a correspondence," as a result of which the composer received her offer "of hand and heart" in the early days of May 1877.[35]

On 20 May Tchaikovsky met Antonina. An analysis of Antonina's surviving letters suggests that in all likelihood their personal meeting was initiated by Tchaikovsky himself. The threat of suicide, made in the last letter Antonina wrote before their meeting, cannot be considered a serious factor in Tchaikovsky's eventual decision; in the context of the entire letter, this "threat" seems to be no more than a device in the tradition of sentimental models from so-called letter books that were popular at the time and contained samples of fictional letters for all occasions.[36]

The meeting occurred in the house where Antonina was renting a room, not far from the Conservatory. At the next meeting on 23 May, Tchaikovsky made an official proposal, promising his bride only his "brotherly" love, to which she readily agreed.[37] But Tchaikovsky chose not to mention this meeting in his letter to Modest, written on the same day. He tried to explain his cooling off in regard to Kotek, and even began to see the manifestations of Providence in various recent coincidences:

> You will ask about my love? It has once again fallen off almost to the point of absolute calm. And do you know why? You alone can understand this. Because two or three times I saw his injured finger in all of its ugliness! Sometimes it seems to me that Providence, so blind and unjust in the choice of its protegés, deigns to take care of me. Indeed, sometimes I begin to consider some coincidences to be not mere accidents [Tfu, tfu, tfu].[38]

The marriage took place at St. George's Church on 6 July 1877. The bridegroom's witnesses were his brother Anatolii and his friend Iosif Kotek, the bride's were her close friends Vladimir Vinogradov and Vladimir Malama. They were joined by the priest Dimitri

Razumovsky, who was also professor of the history of church music at the Conservatory.[39]

The majority of biographical works on Tchaikovsky date the beginning of his relationship with Antonina Miliukova to early May 1877, the time of the genesis and first drafts of his opera *Eugene Onegin*. According to the composer's own testimony in his letters to Nadezhda von Meck, an important factor in their rapid intimacy and marriage was Tchaikovsky's fascination with the plot of Pushkin's novel—his sympathy for the heroine and his desire to avoid "repeating" Onegin's cruelty towards a woman who loves him. Another significant factor was Antonina's own insistent requests for meetings, accompanied by threats to commit suicide in case of a refusal. The fact that there remained about two weeks before the idea of the opera *Eugene Onegin* took solid root in Tchaikovsky's mind, after being suggested by the singer Elizaveta Lavrovskaia on May 13, allows one to conclude that the choice of Pushkin's novel as the plot for an opera could well have been stimulated by Tchaikovsky's personal situation: a distant female acquaintance confessing her love in a letter[40]—a splendid example of life influencing art.

From the very beginning of his married life, Tchaikovsky suffered greatly from his new predicament. He quickly realized that he had made a grave mistake. Moreover, he found himself unable to accept the personality and character of his wife and the presence of her family and circle of friends. After twenty days of cohabitation, their marriage was still not consummated.[41] It is uncertain whether Tchaikovsky had confided in his wife at the outset the problem of his homosexuality, or whether she may simply have disregarded such a confession. On July 27, Tchaikovsky left Antonina for one and a half months, traveling to Kamenka to stay with his sister.[42]

After returning to Moscow the composer lived with his wife from September 12 to 24, before leaving her for good. First, he contrived to be summoned to St. Petersburg on a fictitious errand, thereupon going abroad for a considerable period of time to recuperate from a nervous breakdown which, as archival documents make clear, was faked.[43] Contrary to popular belief, we have no factual evidence whatsoever that Tchaikovsky attempted suicide after his marriage by wading into the freezing cold Moscow River. The only source for this myth is Nikolai Kashkin's unreliable memoirs, written more than forty years later.

There remains hardly any doubt that his homosexuality, coupled with the psychological incompatibility upon which he insisted in his correspondence, proved the ultimate cause of the breakup of his marriage. The recognition forced Tchaikovsky to admit that he had failed in his plan to enhance his social and personal stability. Even more important, however, his impulsive marriage helped him to realize that his homosexuality could not be changed and had to be accepted as it was. That Tchaikovsky at some point came to think of it as natural follows from his use of that very word in a letter to his brother Anatolii on 13/25 February 1878 from Florence: "Only now, especially after the tale of my marriage, have I finally begun to understand that there is nothing more fruitless than not wanting to be that which I am by nature."[44]

There is not a single document from the rest of his life that can be construed as an expression of self-torment on account of his homosexuality. Some occasional expressions of nostalgia for family life are perfectly understandable in a bachelor, and have nothing to do with sexual orientation. Tchaikovsky's eventual solution in his private life was to accept a dichotomy: while often entertaining passionate and even sublime feeling for young males among his social peers and his pupils, he gratified his physical needs by means of anonymous encounters with members of the lower classes. In between was his manservant Alësha Sofronov, whose status changed over the years from bed mate to valued friend, who eventually married with Tchaikovsky's blessing but stayed in his houshold till the very end. The composer finally succeeded in creating an emotionally satisfying environment through close relationships with his relatives and by surrounding himself with a group of admiring young men, headed by his beloved nephew Bob Davydov.

Tchaikovsky made several attempts to divorce in 1878–80, but without success; for a long time Antonina continued to believe in the possibility of a future "reconciliation," and refused to agree to what her husband proposed, invoking his wrath, accusations of stupidity, suspicions of "blackmail," etc. Only in 1881 did Tchaikovsky finally abandon the idea of divorce. At this time he ceased paying his wife the pension he had promised her (it had fluctuated from 50 to 100 rubles a month), due to her erratic and unpredictable behavior.

Antonina Miliukova's role in Tchaikovsky's life is no longer viewed in one-dimensional terms. It is now impossible to deny that she had a very negative effect on the composer's psychic and physical state, a fact confirmed by Tchaikovsky's own statements in his letters and diaries. Tchaikovsky called his wife a "terrible wound," felt heavily burdened by his legal obligation and sometimes even feared possible "disclosures" by her concerning his homosexual preferences.

Yet he was also deeply concerned over the entire fiasco and felt sincere remorse for his seeming cruelty toward her. Paradoxically, it is precisely the years 1877–80, the most difficult time in Tchaikovsky's marital drama, that stand out as one of his most creative and productive periods. Tchaikovsky was later plagued with pangs of conscience, for instance in his letters to Pyotr Jurgenson (1883 and 1888), wherein he asks his publisher to locate his abandoned spouse in order to help her materially. Tchaikovsky appreciated his wife's musical abilities, which is shown by a series of favorable judgments found in his letters. Yet he often perceived Antonina's personal qualities unfairly, painting a distorted picture of her based on his annoyance at this or that trait of her character (for instance in his letters to his brothers, Nadezhda von Meck, and others). One of Tchaikovsky's more balanced statements in regard to his wife is to be found in the letter to his sister Aleksandra Davydova from Rome 8/20 November 1877: "I give full justice to her sincere desire to be a good wife and friend to me, and . . . it is not her fault that I did not find what I was looking for."[45] The fact remains that, despite her ruined family life and perennial pain, not once did Antonina attempt to avenge herself on her husband. On the contrary, she even embellished slightly the composer's human image in her recollections: "No one, not a single person in the world, can accuse him of any base action."[46]

Until recently, most of Tchaikovsky's biographers have recounted the details of Tchaikovsky's marriage in a superficial and tendentious manner, always with a bias in favor of the composer. Antonina Miliukova's own recollections, which present her side of the story, have been labeled the product of a rash and insane woman, and therefore ignored.[47] Recent archival studies have made it possible to clarify several key details relating to Antonina's origin, the history of the couple's acquaintance, marriage, and further relationship, and her life after their separation.[48]

Following the composer's death, Antonina received a pension of 100 rubles a month, which Tchaikovsky left her in his will. She moved to St. Petersburg and lived near St. Alexander Nevsky Monastery, where he was buried. Antonina's further fate was tragic: soon after Tchaikovsky's death she began to display signs of an emotional disorder (persecution mania). By 1896 the disease worsened and Antonina moved to Kronstadt, where she sought spiritual support and a cure from the renowned miracle worker Father John of Kronstadt. For some unknown reason the priest refused to help her. In October 1896 Antonina Miliukova ended up in the Petersburg Hospital of St. Nicholas the Wonderworker, which cared for the emotionally disturbed. After a partial recovery in February 1900, she was released from the hospital, only to return there in June of 1901 with a diagnosis of *paranoia chronica*. A month later, with the help of Tchaikovsky's brother Anatolii, she was transferred to a more comfortable psychiatric hospital outside the city, the Charitable Home for the Emotionally Disturbed at Udelnaia. The pension of her late husband served as payment for her room and board. Antonina spent the last ten years of her life at this institution more as a "resident" than a patient. The home provided her in her old age with medical supervision, attentive care by the personnel, and full living conveniences. She died of pneumonia on February 16, 1917, and was buried at Uspensky Cemetery in St. Petersburg. Her grave has not survived.

IV

At the end of 1876 a second woman entered Tchaikovsky's life. This was Nadezhda von Meck, the widow of a wealthy railway tycoon. She had heard and admired some of Tchaikovsky's music, and when she found out that he was encountering financial problems, she began to commission pieces from him. Both agreed on one condition—that they should never meet. Their strange relationship, carried out through more than 1200 letters, was to last for almost fourteen years. They met only twice, by accident, and hurried off without greeting each other. When Mrs. von Meck learned what had happened with Tchaikovsky during his abortive marriage, she agreed with his request to arrange for him to receive a regular allowance of 6000 rubles. In this way the composer resolved his permanent financial crisis. Mrs. von Meck's money allowed him to dedicate himself to creative work.

Tchaikovsky's relationship with Nadezhda von Meck, despite its obvious eccentricities, occasional feelings of frustration, and gradual, albeit incremental deterioration, may be argued to have been among the most gratifying experiences of the composer's life. Their silent understanding never to meet endowed their "epistolary friendship" with a particular platonic coloring that was deeply emotional and at times approached ecstasy. In the case of von Meck, the erotic component was very significant (even at the conscious level), though always neutralized through her emphatic sentimentalism. The relationship proved satisfactory to both parties, providing a safe outlet for their feelings by ruling out any obvious manifestation of sexual love. In her correspondence with the composer von Meck displays an exceptional degree of tact, sympathy, and understanding of Tchaikovsky's psy-

chological idiosyncracies. There are reasons to believe that she may
have been aware of Tchaikovsky's homosexuality from the very start
of their friendship, even if in a somewhat vague and inexplicit fashion, in keeping with general attitudes toward the subject.

At the end of 1877 and the beginning of 1878, Tchaikovsky and
his brother Anatolii (later replaced by Modest) proceeded with their
European tour through Switzerland, France, Italy, and Austria, hoping to put the whole disastrous business of Tchaikovsky's marriage
firmly behind them. Iosif Kotek arrived at the end of November in

Nadezhda von Meck, the composer's benefactress and 'the beloved
friend.' (*The Tchaikovsky State Archive and House Museum, Klin, Russia*).

Vienna and spent some time traveling with brothers. By January 1878 Tchaikovsky had finished his Fourth Symphony, the first of his mature symphonic works, which he dedicated to Nadezhda von Meck. The other major work occupying him during the period of his ill-fated marriage was *Eugene Onegin*. At first the opera made little impression on the audience, requiring several years to achieve the public success it deserved. One other masterpiece emerged from this period of self-exile: the Violin Concerto, written in Switzerland, inspired by Iosif Kotek but for practical reasons dedicated to the famous violinist Leopold Auer. Initially, however, the Violin Concerto suffered the same fate as the First Piano Concerto: Auer claimed it was far too difficult and refused to play it. In 1881 another violinist, Adolf Brodsky, gave the first performance in Vienna; the famous critic Eduard Hanslick declared, in his newspaper review, that the music "gave off a bad smell." Like the Piano Concerto, the Violin Concerto is established today as one of the concertos loved best by musicians and audiences alike.

In April 1878 Tchaikovsky returned to Russia, depressed by the prospect of teaching and short of inspiration. Nevertheless he finished some smaller piano pieces, including the popular *Children's Album* (*Detskii al'bom*). Returning to Moscow after his usual summer visit to Kamenka, and also after a visit to Mrs. von Meck's estate Brailov, he took a decisive step: he resigned his teaching job at the Conservatory, and shortly thereafter set off on his travels once again. He was to spend the next few years constantly on the move, avoiding Moscow and St. Petersburg as much as possible.

First he traveled to Florence, then to Paris, and then to Clarens in Switzerland, where he started to work on another opera, *The Maid of Orleans* (*Orleanskaia deva*), not one of his greatest successes. Back in Russia by the autumn, he began the Second Piano Concerto. Later he traveled to Rome, where he composed *Italian Capriccio* (*Ital'ianskoe kaprichio*). Tchaikovsky then returned to his homeland, where he spent much of 1880 in the country; there he completed the Serenade for Strings and the piece most often associated with his name, the *1812 Overture*, a commemoration of the historic Russian defeat of Napoleon's army. Early in 1881, still in Rome, Tchaikovsky learned that the seriously ill Nikolai Rubinstein had gone to Paris for treatment and died there. He rushed to Paris to pay his last respects to Rubinstein, and in December began work on a musical memorial, the piano trio dedicated "To the memory of a great artist" (Op. 50). This trio was first played on 18 October 1882 in Moscow, with Sergei Taneev, Ivan Hřimalý and Wilhelm Fitzenhagen.[49] By now

Tchaikovsky, 17 March 1884 (*The Tchaikovsky State Archive and House Museum, Klin, Russia*).

Tchaikovsky's music was being performed more often, thanks in large degree to the efforts of the late Nikolai Rubinstein, who had played and conducted a Tchaikovsky program at the Paris Exhibition of 1878 and premiered many of his new compositions in Moscow, though rarely with total success.

The main work of 1882–83 was the opera *Mazepa*, based upon Pushkin's epic poem *Poltava*. In the course of its composition his enthusiasm flagged considerably; writing to Mrs. von Meck on 14 September 1882 he admitted, "Never has any important work given me so much trouble as this opera. Perhaps it is the decadence of my powers, or have I become more severe in my self-judgment?"[50] *Mazepa* was performed in both Moscow and St. Petersburg in February 1884, but Tchaikovsky left for Europe without attending the St. Petersburg premiere, since the opera was not very cordially received in Moscow. He had hardly spent three weeks in the French capital before he was summoned back to Russia to appear before Alexander III and receive an official decoration—the Order of St. Vladimir (4th Class).

By the beginning of 1885 the composer was feeling the need to cease his restless wandering and settle down. He found a manor house in Maidanovo, near Klin, in the countryside outside Moscow. This residence also had the advantage of being on the direct line between Moscow and St. Petersburg, and he moved there on February 14. The view from the windows and the quiet and sense of being home delighted him. Soon he settled down to a regular routine: reading, walking in the forest, working in the mornings and afternoons, and playing cards or duets with friends in the evenings. He wrote to his brother, "I am contented, cheerful and at peace."[51] He was occupied at this time with the revision of *Vakula the Smith* (to be reissued under the new title *Cherevichki*), and also with a new opera based on Ippolit Shpazhinsky's play *The Sorceress* (*Charodeika*), a story about an innkeeper's daughter who is courted by two princes—father and son— with predictably disastrous consequences.[52] In May Tchaikovsky began to fulfill a promise made to Balakirev to compose a symphonic work on the subject of Lord Byron's *Manfred*. This task cost Tchaikovsky an immense effort and was finished only in September 1885. The entire autumn he continued work on *The Sorceress* while traveling for days or weeks at a time to Moscow, St. Petersburg and Kamenka.

On 11 March 1886, *Manfred* was successfully performed for the first time in Moscow, conducted by the German conductor and composer Max von Erdmannsdörfer. Tchaikovsky was very pleased. At the end of the month he decided to visit his brothers—Ippolit in Taganrog and Anatolii in Tiflis in the Caucasus. At Tiflis, where he spent the entire month of April, he enjoyed a triumphant reception: a concert was organized on 19 April consisting entirely of his works and conducted by his great admirer, the composer and later professor at both the Moscow and Tiflis Conservatories, Mikhail Ippolitov-Ivanov. The concert was followed by a supper and the presentation of a silver wreath. From the Caucasus Tchaikovsky traveled by sea to France, and in Paris he met the French composers Léo Delibes, Ambroise Thomas, and Gabriel Fauré, and spent almost a month combining professional meetings with entertainment. In the middle of June he returned to Russia to continue work on *The Sorceress.*

At the beginning of October, the composer paid a visit to St. Petersburg in order to be present at the first performance of Eduard Nápravník's *Harold* (*Garol'd*) and to meet fellow composers Nikolai Rimsky-Korsakov, Aleksandr Glazunov and Anatolii Liadov.

The first performance of the new version of *Vakula the Smith,* (*Cherevichki*) took place at the Bolshoi Theater in Moscow on 19 January 1887. It had a far-reaching influence on Tchaikovsky's future, for it marked his first successful attempt as conductor. The work had great success, perhaps due to the composer's presence, but it lasted in repertory for only two seasons. He appeared in the capacity of conductor again on March 5 at a concert of the St. Petersburg Philharmonic Society that was totally devoted to his works. Now Tchaikovsky began to think of venturing abroad on a concert tour. He spent most of the spring at Maidanovo at work on the orchestration of *The Sorcercess.* At the end of May Tchaikovsky set off on another Caucasian journey to visit his brother Anatolii, making a pleasant steamer trip down the Volga from Nizhny Novgorod to Astrakhan and through the Caspian Sea to Baku, then on to Tiflis and Borzhom. In Borzhom he received a telegram from his old friend Nikolai Kondratev, who was dying in Aachen.[53] By July 15 Tchaikovsky had reached Aachen, where he spent over a month thinking about God, life, and death, while watching Kondratev's agonizing end.

On October 20 his new opera *The Sorceress* was produced at the Mariinsky Theater in St. Petersburg. Tchaikovsky conducted again but, in spite of a personal ovation, the opera left audiences cold. On the seventh night the work was sung to a half-empty house, and was soon withdrawn. On November 14, Tchaikovsky conducted in Moscow another very successful concert of his own works, including the premiere of his fourth orchestral suite, *Mozartiana* (Op. 61). At the end of December he set out on his first European tour as a conductor, giving concerts in Leipzig, Berlin, Prague, Hamburg, Paris and London. It was a very successful tour, especially in Prague, Paris and London, where he met several well known composers (among them Brahms, Grieg and Dvořák) and established many good relations with many famous musicians.

In the middle of March 1888 Tchaikovsky returned to Russia and visited his brother Ippolit in Taganrog and his brother Anatolii in Tiflis. He returned home only in the middle of April, moving into a new house in Frolovskoe, a village that, like Maidanovo, is located near the small town of Klin. There he began a new symphony—the

Tchaikovsky and cellist Anatolii Brandukov in Paris, 6/18 March 1888
(*The Tchaikovsky State Archive and House Museum, Klin, Russia*).

Fifth, inspired by the death of his friend Nikolai Kondratev. The Fifth Symphony was first performed under its composer's baton in St. Petersburg on November 5 and was well received, despite discouraging reviews. At the end of November Tchaikovsky traveled to Prague, where he conducted a successful performance of *Eugene Onegin*.

In December he retired to Frolovskoe for six weeks in order to compose a ballet, *The Sleeping Beauty* (*Spiashchaia krasavitsa*) (Op. 66), based on the old French fairy tale and commissioned by the directors of the St. Petersburg Theaters. Tchaikovsky worked with genuine enthusiasm until he was forced to lay the work aside to go on another concert tour at the end of January 1889, appearing on January 31 at a concert in Cologne, whence he traveled to Frankfurt-am-Main, Dresden, Berlin, Leipzig, Geneva and, finally, back north to Hamburg. There he found himself in the same hotel as Brahms who, Tchaikovsky felt gratified to hear, had liked the concert performance of his Fifth Symphony, with the exception of the finale. Before going to London at the end of March, as scheduled, Tchaikovsky spent a few weeks in Paris. He returned to Russia via the Mediterranean, visiting Batum on the Black Sea and seeing his brother Anatolii in Tiflis. The local music society again celebrated his visit with concerts from his works. The summer was spent as usual in his country home, his time occupied by the completion and orchestration of *The Sleeping Beauty*.

Tchaikovsky spent the greater part of the autumn traveling between St. Petersburg and Moscow, conducting concerts of his own works and those of Anton Rubinstein (on the occasion of the latter's Jubilee Festival) and rehearsing his new ballet at the Mariinsky Theater. The first performance of *The Sleeping Beauty* took place on 3 January 1890, in a splendid production choreographed by Marius Petipa. The day before, Alexander III had expressed his approval of the ballet at a gala rehearsal attended by the Imperial court.

On January 14 Tchaikovsky went to Florence, where he began work on another opera, *The Queen of Spades* (Op. 68), the libretto of which had been adapted from Pushkin's novella by his brother Modest. Tchaikovsky composed the opera with an enthusiasm almost without parallel in his career. The entire score was written in a fit of creative frenzy that lasted forty-four days. In the process, as we learn from Tchaikovsky's letters, the composer came to identify with its characters and its action. "I almost totally lost my appetite, my sleep, my cheerful disposition, in a word, all the attributes of health," he wrote to a friend soon after finishing, "but I really performed a heroic deed and wrote a great opera in seven weeks."[54] Elsewhere, Tchaikovsky wrote, "I worked on [the opera] with unbelievable ardor and excitement, and actually experienced everything that happens in the story, at one time even fearing the appearance of the old dame's specter, and I hope that my authorial tumult and absorption will echo in the hearts of the audience."[55]

As was the case with almost each one of Tchaikovsky's major compositions, the immediate public and critical response to *The Queen of Spades*, in the St. Petersburg production first presented on 7 December of 1890, was mixed. While he never doubted the quality of his art, the composer was genuinely modest and sensitive to unfavor-

Tchaikovsky (center) with Nikolai and Medea Mei-Figner, who created the roles of Germani and Liza in *The Queen of Spades*, 7 July 1890 (*The Tchaikovsky State Archive and House Museum, Klin, Russia*).

able feedback. Furthermore, he tended to deprecate his own work and lose interest in it upon completion. It was not so with *The Queen of Spades*. Despite the skepticism of many, he adamantly held to the belief that the music of this opera belonged among the finest in the world. The judgment of posterity has proved him right.

Tchaikovsky spent the entire summer 1890 in Frolovskoe, putting the finishing touches on his opera and composing the sextet *Souvenir de Florence* (Op.70). On December 17, he was present at a very successful production of *The Queen of Spades* in Kiev.

Over these last ten years the pathos and enthusiasm so characteristic of the early days had gradually diminished in Tchaikovsky's correspondence with Nadezhda von Meck. Her financial assistance had continued for more than a decade, and eventually they had so accommodated themselves to one another that they could treat the whole situation as a matter of fact, quietly and prosaically. The intellectual level of their correspondence remained high, however, ranging from theoretical discussions to intimate confessions. Then, in September 1890, Tchaikovsky received a letter from Mrs. von Meck informing him that she was on the brink of ruin and therefore unable to continue his allowance. The suddenness of this news wounded him deeply and depressed him for a long time.

His satisfaction with *The Queen of Spades* led Tchaikovsky to accept two more commissions from the Imperial Theaters, for the opera *Iolanta* and the ballet *The Nutcracker* (*Shchelkunchik*). In the meantime, though, Tchaikovsky accepted an invitation to conduct his own works in America on the occasion of the grand opening of Carnegie Hall in New York. On March 6 he left Frolovskoe for Paris, where he was to conduct one of the Edouard Colonne concerts on March 24. The success of this concert, which consisted entirely of his own works, was marred by the news of his sister Aleksandra's death.

Nevertheless, he went ahead with the tour of America. Tchaikovsky sailed from Le Havre on 6/18 April 1891 and landed in New York on the 14/26th. On the voyage, and throughout his American visit, he kept a diary of his experiences. Tchaikovsky conducted six concerts in which his own works were performed: four in New York, one in Baltimore and one in Philadelphia. He also visited Niagara Falls. The composer was greatly impressed and heartened by the warmth and hospitality of his American hosts and by the enthusiastic reception given his music. On 9/21 May he sailed from New York back to Hamburg feeling fully gratified with his American tour.

Back home, Tchaikovsky returned to the composition of the ballet *The Nutcracker* (Op. 71), based on E. T. A. Hoffman's fantasy story (but in the version by Alexandre Dumas père). He finished it at the end of June, whereupon he immediately commenced work on the one-act opera *Iolanta* (Op. 69), the story of a blind princess, set in medieval Aix-de-Provence. In addition, Tchaikovsky composed a symphonic ballad, *The Voevoda* (Op.78), based on a poem by Pushkin after

Tchaikovsky with his brothers. Left to right: Anatolii, Nikolai, Ippolit, Tchaikovsky and Modest (1890), January 1890 (*The Tchaikovsky State Archive and House Museum, Klin, Russia*).

the Polish poet Adam Mickiewicz. On November 4, Tchaikovsky went to Moscow to be present at the first performance of *The Queen of Spades* at the Bolshoi Theater and to conduct *The Voevoda* in a concert given by the pianist/conductor Aleksandr Siloti. This time the opera enjoyed tremendous success, but after its performance Tchaikovsky developed a strong dislike for *The Voevoda* and actually tore up the score, which was reconstructed only after his death.

At the end of the 1891 we find Tchaikovsky embarking on a new concert tour. This time he visited Kiev and Warsaw before proceeding on to Germany. From Warsaw he went by way of Berlin to Hamburg, in order to be present at a first performance of *Eugene Onegin* conducted by Gustav Mahler. Towards the close of his life Tchaikovsky often felt overcome by the homesickness that attacked him whenever he left Russia. On this occasion he even abandoned a concert for which he had been engaged in Holland, going instead to Paris and then back home. At the end of February Tchaikovsky traveled to St. Petersburg, where he conducted his *Romeo and Juliet* as well as the first performance of the *Nutcracker Suite*, which was received with immense enthusiasm.

On 5 April 1892 Tchaikovsky moved into another new home in the same area around Klin. This time he found a bigger house on the outskirts of the town itself, right next to the Petersburg highway but surrounded by the fields and the woods. At the end of April he successfully conducted Gounod's *Faust*, Anton Rubinstein's *Demon*, and *Eugene Onegin* in Moscow at Ivan Prianishnikov's Private Opera. In May Tchaikovsky began work on a symphony in E-flat, but the sketches he produced to this end—which were in some state of completion by October—did not satisfy him. Almost a year later they were used as the basis for the one-movement Third Piano Concerto (Op.75) and for the Finale for Piano and Orchestra (Op.79), which was reworked by Taneev after the composer's death. At the beginning of June Tchaikovsky went abroad with his nephew Bob Davydov to Vichy (France) for a short cure, and spent some time in Paris.

On July 7 he was back in St. Petersburg and four days later in Klin, where he dealt with the proofs of *The Nutcracker* and *Iolanta*. At the beginning of September 1892 Tchaikovsky planned to conduct a concert in Vienna. However, after he arrived and learned that it was to be played by a scratch orchestra in a restaurant, he took offense and left. His old friend from the Moscow Conservatory, the Austrian pianist Anton Door, who had not seen him since the late 1860s, not surprisingly found him looking older than his years. From Vienna the composer traveled to Tyrol, where he was a guest of the German pianist Sophie Menter at the Castle of Itter, then went to Prague in order to attend the first performance of *The Queen of Spades*. Early in November Tchaikovsky had to return to St. Petersburg to take part in the rehearsals of *Iolanta* and *The Nutcracker*, originally intended as a double bill.

On December 6 both opera and ballet were performed in splendid productions at the Mariinsky Theater in the presence of the Tsar and the court. The opera was conducted by Eduard Nápravník, the ballet by Riccardo Drigo. Alexander III was cordial with respect to both pieces, but it seems that the music of *Iolanta* did not appeal to the public. *The Nutcracker* proved luckier: most critics approved of its music and choreography. Tchaikovsky left the capital on December 12, disappointed at the lukewarm welcome received by his new creations.

This time he traveled to Switzerland, visiting his old governess, Fanny Dürbach. He wrote to his brother Nikolai, "The past rose up so vividly before me that I seemed to breathe the air of Votkinsk and hear mother's voice."[56] The last days of 1892 Tchaikovsky spent in Paris and Brussels. In the Belgian capital on 2 January 1893 he successfully conducted an all-Tchaikovsky concert, then traveled home by way of Odessa.

Tchaikovsky in Kharkov, 14 March 1893 (*The Tchaikovsky State Archive and House Museum, Klin, Russia*).

The composer was fêted in Odessa for almost two weeks. He conducted five all-Tchaikovsky concerts, supervised the production of *The Queen of Spades*, and attended several banquets in his honor. Returning to Klin in early February with renewed confidence and inspiration, Tchaikovsky started work on the Symphony No. 6 in B minor. He worked so vigorously that, in the week after his arrival, the first part of the symphony was already complete and the rest was clearly outlined in his head.

On March 11, Tchaikovsky arrived in Kharkov for a scheduled concert appearance. A great crowd gathered at the train station to greet the famous composer. The response to the concert itself three days later, at which Tchaikovsky conducted his Second Symphony, *The Tempest*, and the *1812 Overture*, surpassed all expectations: the hurrahs and bravos seemed to continue on without end, and as soon as the famous man appeared in the doorway he was lifted up and carried to his coach.

Tchaikovsky returned from Kharkov on 18 March and resumed work on his new symphony. He finished the finale, and only then took up the second movement. Within five days he completed the full sketch of the entire work. After finishing the score in mid-August, he wrote to his publisher Pyotr Jurgenson, "On my word of honor, I have never been so satisfied with myself, so proud, so happy to know that I have done something so good!"[57]

In April Tchaikovsky began to compose the Eighteen Pieces for Piano, Op. 72, commissioned by Jurgenson, and Six Songs, Op. 73, to the text of the poet Daniil Rathaus. In May he traveled to St. Petersburg, Moscow, and Nizhny Novgorod, where he visited his brother Anatolii, now the deputy governor of that city. During his visits to Petersburg Tchaikovsky's meetings with Nikolai Rimsky-Korsakov and the younger generation of composers, such as Aleksandr Glazunov and Anatolii Liadov, grew more frequent and productive.

On May 13 the composer set off for England to receive the honorary degree of Doctor of Music *honoris causa* from Cambridge University, conferred upon him earlier. The London Philharmonic Society intended to give two concerts at which all the foreign composers who had recently received honorary degrees at Cambridge would conduct compositions of their own. At the first of these concerts, on 20 May/1 June, Tchaikovsky was represented by his Fourth Symphony, which appears to have been an enormous success. The festivities at Cambridge, in honor of the Jubilee of the University Musical Society, began on 31 May/12 June with a concert whose program included one work by each of the five doctors of music: Boïto, Saint-Saëns, Bruch, Tchaikovsky and Grieg (the last was not present at the ceremony for reasons of ill health). Tchaikovsky directed the first English performance of *Francesca da Rimini* and then attended a "gala dinner and still more gala reception." The next day saw the ceremony awarding him the honorary doctorate. The composer left London on June 2/14 for Paris, where he could finally relax from three weeks of tension and exhaustion. A few days later he traveled to the Tyrol to spend a week with Sophie Menter and the prominent Russian pianist Vasilii Sapelnikov. By 18 June 1893 Tchaikovsky was back in Russia.

While Tchaikovsky was abroad he received a continuing flood of bad news from Moscow and St. Petersburg: his old Conservatory and society friends Karl Albrecht and Konstantin Shilovsky both passed away, and in late June Vladimir Shilovsky also died. Also, he was led to expect similar news concerning Aleksei Apukhtin and professor Nikolai Zverev.

In late August, Tchaikovsky visited Hamburg briefly to attend a production of *Iolanta* conducted by Gustav Mahler. Upon his return he visited his brother Anatolii and family in Nizhny Novgorod.

Toward the end of August Tchaikovsky finally came up with the title of his new symphony, found in the unpublished letter of September 20 to his publisher Pyotr Jurgenson.[58] The composer decided to call it *Paticheskaia Simfoniia*, which in Russian means roughly the same thing that Beethoven meant when he called his Sonata in F minor, Op. 57, the "Apassionata," that is "impassioned"; it does not posssess the connotations of its better known French equivalent, *Symphonie Pathétique*, "symphony of suffering."

In September he worked on his Third Piano Concerto, and started to consider the possibility of writing a new opera. A few ideas had already occured to him. One was Shakespeare's *Merchant of Venice* and another was *Nal and Damaianti* (adapted from Vasilii Zhukovsky's *Mahabharata*), but he was especially enthralled by the plot of George Eliot's tale "Mr. Gilfil's Love-Story."

His engagement calendar for the forthcoming concert season was extremely full. On October 16, at a concert in St. Petersburg, he planned to conduct his new symphony for the first time. On November 27 Tchaikovsky expected to return to St. Petersburg for a concert; on December 4 he was to appear at a concert in Moscow, although on 15 and 29 January 1894 he had two more engagements in St Petersburg. In March he was to go on tour to Amsterdam, in April to Helsinki, and in May to London. In addition he had invitations from Odessa, Kharkov, Warsaw, Frankfurt-am-Main, and other places.

V

In the beginning of October 1893 the composer finished scoring his Third Piano Concerto. He enjoyed the visits to Klin by two young cellists: his old friend and former pupil Anatolii Brandukov, and a new,

The house at 13 Malaia Morskaia street in St. Petersburg in which the composer spent his final days in October 1893 (*Alexander Poznansky Collection*).

promising young musician, Iulian Poplavsky. On 8 October he went with his guests to Moscow, and from there he proceeded to St. Petersburg on October 9.

Tchaikovsky arrived in St. Petersburg on October 10.[59] He planned to leave in a few days, to be present at a concert at the Russian Music Society in Moscow, and put up temporarily at the apartment of his brother Modest, who shared it with their nephew Bob Davydov. This apartment, located on the corner of Malaia Morskaia and Gorokhovaia streets, had been rented just a few weeks before Tchaikovsky's arrival.

The entire first week of Tchaikovsky's stay in the capital was occupied by rehearsals with the orchestra, and his free time was spent in helping his brother and nephew settle into their new apartment. The days following the premiere he visited relatives and friends, conducted business negotiations and correspondence, and went to theaters and restaurants.

On the night of October 20, after returning from a late dinner at Leiner's restaurant—the one most frequented by the composer and his brother—Tchaikovsky experienced an upset stomach. By morning it had worsened, but it was taken for his usual "indisposition," which as a rule passed quickly. But this time his condition continued to worsen and self-treatment failed to give any positive results. Towards evening Modest was obliged to summon a doctor, the family friend Vasilii Bertenson. Without making a definite diagnosis, but convinced of his patient's extremely dangerous condition (with symptoms of constant diarrhea and vomiting, extreme weakness, chest and abdominal pains), the doctor turned for help to his more experienced elder brother, the renowned Petersburg physician Lev Bertenson.[60]

Upon his arrival Lev Bertenson immediately diagnosed Asiatic cholera in its severe or algid stage. By this time (about 11:00PM) the life of the patient was in immediate danger: he began to experience spasms, his head and extremities turned dark blue, and his temperature fell. Throughout the night the doctor undertook the most energetic measures, such as the constant massaging of the composer's body by several persons at a time, and injections of musk, camphor and other substances recommended by the scientific knowledge of the day. By the morning of October 22 Tchaikovsky's condition had greatly improved; on this morning the police were informed of the composer's illness. An official announcement of the composer's infection with cholera appeared in St. Petersburg's newspapers on the following day.

Vasilii Bertenson, who left Petersburg and participated no further in the treatment of Tchaikovsky, was replaced by two other physicians, Aleksandr Zander and Nikolai Mamonov.[61] They took turns at the bed of the patient between visits of the head doctor, Lev Bertenson. The latter was particularly concerned with the development of the disease because Tchaikovsky's kidneys had ceased to function. Still, he hesitated to use the one method at the time considered effective—namely, immersing the patient in a hot bath—due to a superstitious fear of this treatment shared by Tchaikovsky and his family: his mother had died from cholera precisely as she was taking such a bath.

All other methods failed to achieve results, and though on October 22 Tchaikovsky had considered his life to have been saved, the following morning a crisis in his emotional state became apparent: he had stopped believing in the possibility of recovery. The inactivity of his kidneys (uremia) resulted in the gradual poisoning of his blood. On October 24 his condition became so critical that the doctors finally resorted to giving Tchaikovsky a hot bath. However this belated treatment did not have any effect.

Throughout the day of October 24 Tchaikovsky repeatedly lost consciousness and succumbed to delirium; towards the evening his pulse began to weaken and his breathing became inhibited. After ten o'clock in the evening the patient's state was declared hopeless. Almost without regaining consciousness, the composer passed away at fifteen minutes after three o'clock on the morning of October 25. Immediate cause was edema of the lungs and a weakening of cardiac activity. Present during his final minutes were his brothers Modest and Nikolai Tchaikovsky, his nephew Vladimir Davydov, and the doctor Nikolai Mamonov.

On the morning of October 25, several newspapers printed a short announcement of Tchaikovsky's death. Disinfection measures were taken at the apartment where he died. The body of the deceased lay in state and was made available for homage. Throughout the day the flow of visitors gradually increased. Two memorial services were held at the apartment. After nine o'clock, at the insistence of health officials, the coffin was closed and was not opened for the following two days. During this time hundreds of people came to bid farewell to the composer, dozens of wreaths were laid, and several more memorial services were given.

The papers published reports on Tchaikovsky's illness, interviews with doctors, relatives, and friends of the deceased, and the texts of numerous commiserating telegrams. Already on October 25, Alexander III had indicated that the funeral was to take place in Petersburg, with expenses attendant on the burial being covered by the Tsar's personal treasury. On October 28, after a funeral service at Kazan Cathedral and a grand public procession down Nevsky prospect with the participation of dozens of delegations from various cities, organizations, and institutions, the composer's body was interred at the Tikhvin Cemetery of St. Alexander Nevsky Monastery.

The acute public reaction to Tchaikovsky's death found its primary expression in accusations leveled against the doctors who had treated him. Although cholera was quite a rare condition for members of the privileged class, the very fact that he had been taken ill with the disease, in a city that at the time was one of the centers of a cholera epidemic, did not elicit surprise. The papers reported that the composer was generally susceptible to stomach illnesses, that he had survived a case of cholerine (a mild form of cholera) that very summer, that he had often drunk unboiled water in Petersburg (the usual source of infection), and that on the morning of October 21, as a form of self-treatment, he had mistakenly taken a glass of Hunyadi alkaline water, which had only aided the development of disease-bearing vibrios.

The only question was where Tchaikovsky could have become infected; at Leiner's restaurant or at home, since according to various testimonies he had drunk unboiled water at both places. This question turned out to be of little importance, even amid growing criticism of lax restaurant procedures, since Tchaikovsky's recklessness was self-evident; nor was he alone in ignoring elementary hygienic measures.

The treatment of the patient was another matter. Here all responsibility would be shouldered by specific doctors, who would become the inevitable targets of outraged attacks. Lev Bertenson and his assistants were accused of incompetence, a lack of practical experience in treating cholera, a belated use of the bath, ignorance of modern treatments, and even, given their reluctance to consult with colleagues who had more experience in treating cholera patients, of criminal arrogance.

Modest Tchaikovsky published two explanations in the doctors' defense.[62] In the first he described with great detail the progression of the illness; in the second he declared that everything possible had been done to save his brother, that the family of the deceased had no grievance whatsoever against the doctors who had treated him. Moreover, Modest expressed profound gratitude for their "sincere and irreproachably thorough treatment" of the composer's illness.[63]

A second wave of emotion arose over the new performance of Tchaikovsky's Sixth Symphony at a concert in his memory on 6 November 1893. Stunned by the recent tragedy, the public was especially sensitive to the funereal moods of several of the symphony's passages. It is not surprising that many listeners (including some of the journalists writing about the concert for the press) gained the impression that Tchaikovsky had written a requiem for himself. Shortly after this there appeared the first rumors of the composer's possible self-poisoning, although these existed then only in oral form: not only at this time, but also much later, not a single hint of intentional poisoning was to be found in print.

Tchaikovsky's contemporaries were profoundly shocked by his death. Sorrow over the irreparable loss for Russian and world art was exacerbated by the very time of its occurrence: Tchaikovsky went to his grave full of creative strength and plans, at the height of his glory and artistic successes. Naturally, the causes and circumstances of his death immediately became the subject of heightened public attention. The details of this tragic event were closely recounted in the press, actively elaborated upon in oral rumor in arenas as varied as the Imperial family and merchants' clubs, and later found reflection in memoiristic literature.

Accurate information was supplemented with a series of conflicting accounts that led to the emergence of the most fanciful rumors and conjectures. Some of these became so deeply rooted that in time they began to aspire to the role of "truth in the final instance" that was being allegedly concealed by Tchaikovsky's relatives, the Tsarist regime, the Soviet government, etc. Facts discovered by recent studies, however, allow us to reconstruct Tchaikovsky's last days with a much greater degree of accuracy, and to show decisively both the origin and baselessness of various sensational speculations concerning his end.

Versions of the legend of the composer's voluntary departure from life became more persistent in subsequent years. One can classify them roughly into two theories. The first is the "concealed suicide" theory, according to which Tchaikovsky, tormented by unrequited love, intentionally sought death and often drank unboiled water in the hope of catching cholera, and then, having caught it, delayed summoning doctors until he was sure the disease had progressed too far and there remained no chance of recovery.

Second is the "forced suicide" theory: that under the threat of public scandal (or even criminal trial) caused by the inescapable revelation of his homosexual contacts with a man from the highest royal circles, Tchaikovsky saved his own and his family's honor by taking slow-acting poison with effects similar to the characteristic symptoms of cholera, allowing his doctors and family to explain everything away by death from natural causes, a fatal disease.

One variant of this theory is the popular story that an order for suicide stemmed from Alexander III himself. In the 1980s widespread attention was garnered by another version of the forced suicide theory, according to which the composer fell victim to a court of honor conducted by his former classmates at the School of Jurisprudence, who (under the same presumed threat of homosexual scandal) sentenced him to death by his own hand. This version is essentially a new elaboration grounded in old hearsay, but it received sanction as a scholarly interpretation and was publicized in an English music journal.[64] The main conclusions promoted by that story were in fact so provocative they served to move the question of Tchaikovsky's death from the realm of kitchen gossip and literary fantasy to that of the mainstream and scholarly press, where it became a topic of heated discussion and stimulated a series of special studies.[65]

Since the underlying theses of this new version coincided with traditional arguments for Tchaikovsky's suicide (fear of his criminal habit being revealed, the ignoring of sanitary measures with conflicting testimony on the progression of the illness), scholars were obliged to analyze the supporting testimony. At the same time they undertook a review of the entire spectrum of questions and factual gaps reflected in all diverse legends about Tchaikovsky's death.[66]

Recent studies suggest that, given Russian social attitudes, sexual mores, and criminal practice in the late nineteenth century, as well as Tchaikovsky's elevated social standing and the generally sympathetic attitude towards homosexuality in court circles and the Imperial family, any scandal or repression involving the composer was most improbable. The idea of a poison that could imitate the symptoms of cholera also turned out to be imaginary: not a single one of the toxic substances available at that time fulfilled the necessary requirements.[67]

The Soviet microbiologist Nikolai Blinov has thrown particular light on the medical aspect of the problem. Analyzing contemporary ideas of the nature, prevention, and treatment of cholera in Russia before 1893, Blinov established that Tchaikovsky's doctors acted strictly in accordance with the recommendations of the medical science of their day. They were able to save the patient from cholera itself on the first night, at a stage when, statistically, it causes up to ninety percent of all fatalities. But the treatment was begun late, for reasons outside their control, and the doctors were unable to protect the patient from post-choleric complications, which eventually led to his death. He could only have been saved by modern medical treatments.[68]

Because Tchaikovsky died not from cholera itself (which had been a possibility during the night of October 21–22), but as a result of the illness' inescapable repercussions (ultimately, edema of the lungs and the cessation of cardiac activity), the coffin of the deceased could be left open to the public on October 25, in contradiction to prevailing sanitary principles: it was held that the activity of choleric bacilli had ceased two days before death. In any case, sanitary and disinfective precautions were constantly taken in the apartment during the disease and subsequent farewell to the composer's body (October 25–27). That none of the relatives, servants, or friends who had contact with Tchaikovsky was infected is but another proof of the efficacy of these measures.

With respect to the theoretical possibility of a conspiracy by the treating doctors to conceal the composer's self-poisoning, Blinov undertook a detailed inquiry into the biographies of the physicians who treated Tchaikovsky and of then-prevailing medical ethics and concluded that for these people such a conspiracy was unthinkable.[69]

A close study of newspaper publications and a series of memoirs concerning Tchaikovsky's illness and death permits one to explain any factual contradictions between the testimony of eyewitnesses to the tragedy. Together with objective factors (such as the differences in the doctors' and family members' perceptions of Tchaikovsky's illness, the psychological difference between an immediate evaluation of events and subsequent reconstructions, etc.), one can name a series of subjective factors that caused distrust in the official version (cholera) at the time of the event.

In the first place one must note the media's agitation over the sickness of the famous composer. In its race for "hot" news, the papers allowed inaccuracies, distorted information, and sheer disinformation (the emotional statements of Tchaikovsky's friend, singer Nikolai Figner, were given as "the opinion of Dr. Bertenson"; an interview with Lev Bertenson himself was handled in such a way that the date of Tchaikovsky's death would appear as October 24; etc.).[70]

Then too, the creation of confusion was aided by the writers of memoirs published in later years. In his 1912 memoir, Vasilii Bertenson, who was absent from Petersburg from October 22 (and who only sent a telegram of condolences from Moscow on October 26), presented the whole affair as if he had been at the dying man's bedside throughout his last days. This, despite the fact that he had earlier requested Modest Tchaikovsky to describe details of the event "to refresh my memory" (letter from January 11, 1911).[71]

The composer's nephew Iurii Davydov and the actor Iurii Iurev composed "co-authored" memoirs in the 1940s concerning their presence at Leiner's restaurant with Tchaikovsky, luridly describing details of the "fateful supper" of October 20, while in actuality they had not been present there at all. In both cases the psychological motives of such license find a simple explanation: people close to the great composer found it permissible to distort the truth in order to lend greater weight to their own role as eyewitnesses.[72]

The various rumors concerning "imperial wrath" directed at Tchaikovsky also turn out, upon close analysis, to be nothing but sensational fiction. Alexander III highly revered the composer's talent, and members of the imperial family frequently attended Tchaikovsky's operas and ballets, buying up new editions of Tchaikovsky's music to play at home. Tchaikovsky's outstanding merits as citizen were also appreciated: in addition to a life pension, he was awarded the Order of St. Vladimir, and was presented with a valuable ring as a personal gift from the Tsar. His death, according to Grand Duke Konstantin Konstantinovich's diary entry of 26 October 1893, "grieved the Tsar and Tsarina greatly." "How sorry I am for him and what a disappointment!" wrote the Emperor to the Minister of Court Illarion Vorontsov-Dashkov on October 25, after receiving the news of Tchaikovsky's demise. On that same day he issued a resolution concerning the organization of a state funeral for the composer at his own expense, and then personally revised the plan of the memorial events. It is impossible to imagine that such instances of the Tsar's attention could be bestowed posthumously on a man who had fallen into imperial disfavor during his lifetime.[73]

A series of documents found in recent years present solid evidence against the historical, psychological and medical foundations of the suicide theories, while no new evidence in their support has been discovered. The composer's death from cholera is attested to in a burial certificate from 28 October 1893, preserved in the archive of St. Alexander Nevsky Monastery.[74] Tchaikovsky's brother Nikolai wrote privately on a page alongside a list of memorial wreaths, "Three doctors treated his cholera."[75] In 1898, Vladimir Davydov in a letter to Modest Tchaikovsky (both immediate witnesses to Tchaikovsky's last days) recalled, "After all uncle Pyotr had a terrible catarrh, which by the time I knew him was evidently weaker, but which reached an extreme state and finally served as the breeding-ground of his fatal disease."[76] Vasilii Bertenson also commented in private correspondence on the beginning of Tchaikovsky's illness: "he fell ill only as a result of faults in his diet and drinking bitter-alkaline water on an empty stomach" (letter to Modest Tchaikovsky from June 20, 1905).[77] Modest Tchaikovsky himself, a day before his brother's death (on October 24 at 12:48) sent a telegram on the progress of the illness to Vasilii Bertenson, who had left Petersburg: "The first period passed, full retention of urine, condition is grave."[78] On October 25, Lev Bertenson sent to Modest his condolences as follows: "The dreadful disease that took the life of your unforgettable brother has brought me closer to him, yourself, and all to whom he was dear. I cannot recover from the terrible drama I have lived through, and I am utterly incapable of communicating to you all the torment I am experiencing!"[79] These testimonies alone from the archive of the Tchaikovsky Museum at Klin suffice to put an end to the old rumors and new fantasies generated by the proponents of an unnatural death theory.[80]

An inquiry into the personality of any great artist is imperative if we would deepen and enrich our appreciation of his or her achievement, for it allows us to respond in a more complex and powerful way to the emotional and psychological issues involved in the creative process and in their artistic resolution. In the case of Tchaikovsky, his inner longings, which we cannot fully comprehend without studying the realities of his life, had a bearing on the striking and peculiar emotional poignancy of his music, which today is either extolled or else berated as sentimentalism. In the end, such inquiry will enable us constructively to reconsider the whole set of musicological clichés about Tchaikovsky, and perhaps even reconsider his status in art's pantheon, as well as the relevance of his work to our present day cultural and spiritual concerns.

NOTES

1. Richard Taruskin, "Pathetic Symphonist," *New Republic*, 212 (6 Feb. 1995), 6: 29.

2. Nigel Smith, "Perceptions of Homosexuality in Tchaikovsky Criticism," *Context*, (summer 1992–93), 4: 3–9.

3. On Tchaikovsky's genealogy see further: V. I. Proleeva, *K rodoslovnoi P. I. Chaikovskogo* (Izhevsk, 1990); Marina Kogan, "Rodoslovnaia," *Sovetskaia muzyka* 6 (1990): 83–90.

4. P. I. Chaikovskii *Polnoe sobranie sochinenii: Literaturnye proizvedeniia i perepiska* (Complete collected works: literary works and correspondence), 17 vols. to date (Moscow, 1953–81), 8: 434, (hereinafter *PSS*).

5. For more on Tchaikovsky's life and friendships in the School of Jurisprudence, see Alexander Poznansky, *Tchaikovsky: the Quest for the Inner Man* (New York, 1991), 18–49, (hereinafter *TQM*).

6. Gosudarstvennyi arkhiv doma-muzeia P. I. Chaikovskogo (Tchaikovsky state archive and house museum), Klin (Russia), B2, no. 21, 29, (hereinafter *GDMC*).

7. *TQM*, 48.

8. Alexander Poznansky, *Tchaikovsky's Last Days: A Documentary Study* (Oxford, 1996), 10 (hereinafter *TLD*).

9. The work was published posthumously by Mitrofan Beliaev as Op. 76 (1896).

10. Strauss probably obtained the music of the *Dances* through his friend August Leibrock, the owner of a music shop in St. Petersburg, since Leibrock's daughter was in the same class as Tchaikovsky at the Conservatory.

11. Tsentral'nyi Gosudarstvennyi Istoricheskii Arkhiv (Central state historic archive), St. Petersburg (Russia), TsGIA SPb, f. 361, Op. 11, ed. kh. 370.

12. *The Voevoda* was based on Ostrovsky's play *A Dream on the Volga (Son na Volge)*.

13. M. I. Chaikovskii, *Zhizn' Petra Il'icha Chaikovskogo*, 3 vols. (Moscow-Leipzig, 1900–02), I: 259.

14. Ibid.

15. *TLD*, 1–29.

16. Alexander Poznansky, "Tchaikovsky's Suicide: Myth and Reality," *Nineteenth-Century Music* 11 (1988): 202–06; idem, *Samoubiistvo Chaikovskogo: mif i real'nost'* (Moscow, 1993), 25–41.

17. *TQM*, 463–85; see also Konstantin Rotikov, "Epizod iz zhizni 'golubogo' Peterburga," in *Nevskii arkhiv: istoriko-kraevedcheskii sbornik* (St. Petersburg, 1997), 449–66.

18. *PSS*, 5: 145.

19. P. I. Chaikovskii, *Dnevniki P. I. Chaikovskogo (1873-1891)* (Moscow-Petrograd, 1923), 176–77.

20. Quoted in *TQM*, 159.

21. *PSS*, 5: 353.

22. *PSS*, 7: 64–65.

23. *PSS*, 6: 80.

24. *GDMC*, A 3, no. 1464; *PSS*, 6: 66 (with omissions); *P.I. Chaikovskii: zabytoe i novoe, vospominaniia sovremennikov, novye materialy i dokumenty*, sostaviteli P.E. Vaidman, G. I. Belonovich, (Moscow, 1995), 121 (hereinafter *CZN*).

25. *GDMC*, A 3, no. 1465; *PSS*, 6: 69 (with omissions); *CZN*, 122.

26. *GDMC*, A 3, no. 1490; *PSS*, 7: 263 (with omissions); *CZN*, 122.

27. *GDMC*, A 3, no. 1467; *PSS*, 6: 76 (with omissions); *TLD*, 13; *CZN*, 121.

28. *GDMC*, A 3, no. 1467; *PSS*, 6: 76 (with omissions); P. I. Chaikovskii, *Pis'ma k rodnym* (Moscow, 1940), 260 (hereinafter *PR*); *TLD*, 13; *CZN*, 121.

29. Ibid.

30. *GDMC*, A3, no. 1470; *PSS*, 6:110 (with omissions).

31. All surviving letters of Antonina Miliukova to Tchaikovsky have been published in full; see V. Sokolov, *Antonina Chaikovskaia: istoriia zavytoi zhizni* (Moscow, 1994), 219–51.

32. Ibid, 13–15.

33. Ibid, 16–18.

34. The letter has not been preserved, its date has been established on the basis of circumstantial data, see Sokolov, *Antonina Chaikovskaia*, 19–20.

35. Ibid, 19–24.

36. Ibid, 29–32.

37. Ibid, 33–34.

38. *GDMC*, A 3, no. 1473; *PSS*, 6: 139; *CZN*, 123. See the full text in the section that follows.

39. Sokolov, *Antonina Chaikovskaia*, 34.

40. *TQM*, 211; Sokolov, *Antonina Chaikovskaia*, 31.

41. Sokolov's attempt to prove on the basis of circumstantial evidence that their marriage was consummated is by no means convincing; see Sokolov, *Antonina Chaikovskaia*, 35.

42. For more on Tchaikovsky's marriage, see *TQM*, 204–30; *TLD*, 12–19; Sokolov, *Antonina Chaikovskaia*, 35–56.

43. Sokolov, *Antonina Chaikovskaia*, 40–47.

44. *PR*, 374; see my discussion in *TQM*, pp. 184–85 and *TLD*, pp. 9–22. Cf. similar conclusions independently reached by Sokolov after his own study of the composer's archives in Klin: "It would be a profound mistake to believe that Tchaikovsky all his life suffered from his 'anomaly.' As can be seen in his letters, in the last decades of his life he achieved a happy psychological balance—after fruitless attempts to struggle against his nature," V. S. Sokolov, "Pis'ma P.I. Chaikovskogo bez kupiur: neizvestnye stranitsy epistoliarii," in *CZN*, 121.

45. *PR*, 310; *PSS*, 6: 227.

46. Antonina Chaikovskaia, "Iz vospominanii vdovy P.I. Chaikovskogo," *Peterburgskaia gazeta*, 3 April 1894.

47. N. D. Kashkin, "Iz vospominanii o P. I. Chaikovskom," in *Proshloe russkoi muzyki: materialy i issledovaniia, P. I. Chaikovskii* (Peterburg, 1920), I: 129–31.

48. *TQM*, 195–249; Sokolov, *Antonina Chaikovskaia*. Sokolov's admirable archival study of Miliukova's life creates an idealized image of the composer's wife. Sokolov failed, however, to comprehend the complexities of Tchaikovsky's psychosexuality, which inevitably led him to misinterpret the composer's motives in marrying her and his behavior in the events that followed. The main value of Sokolov's study lay in his archival research on Antonina Miliukova and her family. It was established by Sokolov that Antonina Miliukova was born into a family of the hereditary gentry residing outside Moscow in the Klin region. The family traced its ancestry to the fourteenth century. Antonina's parents separated in 1851, and her childhood was spent in an unfavorable emotional environment. She was brought up in a private Moscow boarding school, and then at her father's Klin estate. Together with her brothers and her elder sister, she received a standard home education, including the study of two foreign languages. From early on, Antonina enjoyed music (her father Ivan Miliukov kept a peasant orchestra). She continued her education at the Moscow Institute of St. Elizabeth, completing the full course of study from 1858 to 1864. Here, apart from the required subjects, she took piano and voice lessons. In the 1873–74 school year she studied at the Moscow Conservatory, where her teacher in piano was Eduard Langer and her teacher in elementary theory was Karl Albrecht. After leaving school, Antonina pursued a career in pedagogy, giving private lessons in Moscow in the 1870s and then teaching at a school attached to the local House of Industry in Kronstadt in 1896; on several occasions she attempted unsuccessfully to become a teacher in various other educational institutions. From 1848 to 1893 she lived in and around Moscow, and from 1893 to her death she lived in Petersburg and its suburbs; in 1887 she had made a trip to Italy.

From 1880 Antonina Tchaikovsky herself lived in a free union with the lawyer Aleksandr Shlykov, to whom she bore three children. Due to her financial vulnerability and semi-legal social situation, as well as the constant illnesses of both herself and her husband, Antonina surrendered her illegitimate children to a Moscow foundling hospital (where they all eventually died). In 1886, after a five-year silence, Antonina Miliukova presented the composer with a request for material assistance and with the suggestion that he adopt and take in her youngest daughter, Antonina. Tchaikovsky readily agreed to support his wife financially and appointed her once again a monthly pension of fifty rubles (later increased to 100, then to 150, then lowered again to 100 rubles). He failed to respond to the idea of adopting her child, although it is known from letters to his brother Modest and to Pyotr Jurgenson that he sharply condemned the fact that Antonina's children were at a foundling hospital. In 1886–89, Antonina regularly wrote Tchaikovsky to thank him for his material support, even sending him a shirt she had sewn as a sign of gratitude; she told him of her life and misfortunes (her civil husband died in 1888), asked him to increase the pension, and offered to join him again. Tchaikovsky reacted painfully not only to Antonina's letters themselves, but also to information concerning her attempts to seek patronage from the Empress and from Anton Rubinstein in finding a permanent teaching position. The composer considered the pension he was paying his wife to be fully adequate for a comfortable existence, and viewed Antonina's "social legitimization" as a threat to his prestige. Throughout these years Pyotr Jurgenson served as mediator between husband and wife, so they could avoid personal contact. They met from time to time at concerts and operatic performances, seeing each other only from a distance. Antonina maintained that their last meeting took place in Moscow in the autumn of 1892 during a stroll in Alexandrovsky Gardens. She recalled that Tchaikovsky walked behind her but "could not make himself speak" to her. This meeting was probably fictitious.

49. Sergei Taneev (1856–1915), composer and pianist, Tchaikovsky's pupil, an opponent of the nationalist school, gave premieres of the Second and Third Piano Concertos;

Ivan Hřimalý (1844–1915), was a violinist and professor at the Moscow Conservatory; Wilhelm Fitzenhagen (1848–1890), was a cellist and professor at the Moscow Conservatory.

50. *PSS*, 11: 216.

51. *PSS*, 13: 33.

52. Ippolit Shpazhinsky (1844–1917), Russian playwright, adapted his play *The Sorceress* as a libretto for Tchaikovsky's opera.

53. Nikolai Kondratev (1837–87), a wealthy landowner, graduate of the School of Jurisprudence, belonged to homosexual circles of Tchaikovsky's friends. On their relationship, see *TQM*, 140–44, 361–63, 476–78.

54. *PSS*, 15b: 107.

55. *PSS*, 15b: 237.

56. *PSS*, 16b: 213.

57. *PSS*, 17: 165.

58. *TLD*, 28, note 64.

59. For more on Tchaikovsky's final stay in St. Petersburg, see *TLD*, 49–191.

60. Lev Bertenson (1850–1929), court physician from 1897, who practiced in St. Petersburg high society; for further information about Bertenson, see N. O. Blinov, *Posledniaia bolezn' i smert' P. I. Chaikovskogo*, (Moscow, 1994), 11–15 (hereinafter *PBC*).

61. Aleksandr Zander (1857–1914), physician, was from 1896 personal doctor of the Grand Duke Mikhail Nikolaevich, also court physician from 1887; Nikolai Mamonov (1869–?), specialist in internal medicine, later became the personal doctor of Anatolii Tchaikovsky; for more on both doctors, see in *PBC*, 18–20.

62. The first explanation or (more precisely) account of the composer's illness was published in *Novoe vremia* and *Novosti i birzhevaia gazeta* on 1 November 1893.

63. Letter to Editor, *Novoe vremia*, 7 November 1893.

64. Aleksandra Orlova, "Tchaikovsky: The Last Chapter," *Music & Letters* 62 (1981): 125–45, and in her book *Tchaikovsky: A Self-Portrait* (Oxford, 1990): 406–14.

65. Poznansky, "Tchaikovsky's Suicide: Myth and Reality," 199–220; idem, *Samoubiistvo Chaikovskogo* ; David Brown, *Tchaikovsky: A Biographical and Critical Study*; 4 vols., (New York, 1978–91); idem, *Tchaikovsky Remembered*, (London, 1993), 207–26; V. Sokolov, "Do i posle tragedii: smert' P. I. Chaikovskogo v dokumentakh," *Znamia* 11 (1993): 144–69; Richard Taruskin, "Pathetic Symphonist," 26–40; *PBC* ; *TLD*.

66. E.g. *PBC* ; *TLD*.

67. Poznansky, "Tchaikovsky's Suicide," 199–220.

68. *PBC*, 31–34.

69. Ibid, 10–28.

70. *TLD*, 94–95, 117–18.

71. *GDMC*, B 10, no. 8, 471.

72. *TLD*, 76–78; *PBC*, 89–90, note; Poznansky, "Tchaikovsky: the Man Behind the Myth," *Musical Times* 4 (1995), 182. Like Iurii Davidov, Sergei Diaghilev also yielded to the temptation of exaggerating his own role in the events in later memoirs, when he "recalled" meeting Tchaikovsky (whom he never met in real life) in the Alexandrinsky Theater, and remembered handling the dead body of the composer together with Rimsky-Korsakov and Nikolai Figner; see Richard Buckle, *Diaghilev* (London, 1969), 23–24 and *TLD*, 134, 139.

73. *TLD*, 125–26, 137.

74. Ibid, 162.

75. *PBC*, 190–91.

76. Ibid, 191–92.

77. *GDMC*, B 10, no. 467; *PBC*, 183.

78. *TLD*, 108.

79. Ibid, 132.

80. The most recent fantasies on this subject can be found in Anthony Holden, *Tchaikovsky* (New York, 1996), 373–400.

Unknown Tchaikovsky:

A Reconstruction of Previously Censored

Letters to His Brothers (1875–1879)

ALEXANDER POZNANSKY

TRANSLATIONS FROM THE RUSSIAN BY

ROBERT BIRD AND ALEXANDER POZNANSKY

On August 13, 1880 Tchaikovsky wrote to his benefactress Nadezhda von Meck, that "the thought that some day I might indeed achieve a crumb of fame, and that interest in my music will generate interest in me personally is very burdensome. It is not that I fear the light of day. With my hand on my heart I can declare that my conscience is clear and that I have nothing to be ashamed of; but the notion that one day people will try to penetrate the intimate world of my feelings and thoughts, everything that all my life I have so carefully hidden from the touch of the crowd, is very sad and unpleasant."[1]

If Tchaikovsky could have foreseen what 20th-century biographers, critics and musicologists have in fact written about him, he would indeed have been horrified. Even though audiences continued to love his masterly compositions, with their unique melodies, and his brilliant orchestration, the image of him in almost every book about him remained for almost a hundred years that of a highly neurotic, self-tormented individual, constantly on the verge of nervous collapse.[2] This, in turn, could not but affect the perception of his music, which is often described as sentimental, fraught with hidden hysteria, and decadent.

The reason for this view was twofold. On the one hand, towards the turn of the century, the rumor of the composer's sexual orientation, long an open secret in Russia, began to spread by word of mouth beyond Russia's borders. During this period, the English-speaking world saw homosexuality as a mental aberration or disease. Consequently, Tchaikovsky emerged in this view as a prime example of a clinical case, and his music as "pathological."[3]

On the other hand, the documentary material on his life and, in particular, his voluminous correspondence, underwent massive censorship since the time of his death, first by the composer's relatives, especially his brother Modest, and later on by the Soviet *apparatchiks*. The first biography of Tchaikovsky, published by Modest in 1900–03 (and in an abridged English version in 1906) was panegyric in character and, owing to the social conventions of the time, left too many aspects of his life (such as his love interests, the failure of his marriage, his relationship with Nadezhda von Meck, and the circumstances of his death) either unexplained, or confused, or both, thus providing room for various lurid or sensational speculations.[4]

As a result, authors in the West took delight in dwelling on Tchaikovsky's "abnormal sexuality" and in allowing their moral or political opinions to color interpretations of his character and music. This attitude created fertile ground for the dissemination, in recent years, of the totally fantastic theory that he was forced to commit suicide by his own former classmates in order to avoid a public homosexual scandal.

In the Soviet Union the figure of Tchaikovsky was constructed, in accordance with the proclaimed principles of "socialist realism," as a blameless and ideologically progressive artist, the servant of his people. Any hint that might contradict this, such as the composer's genuine monarchism, had to be thoroughly avoided. Since the official position of the authorities was that problems regarding sexuality exist only in bourgeois societies, and since homosexuality became a criminal offense from the middle 1930s on, the Tchaikovsky archives in Klin were closed to independent scholars, and no material on him that could even remotely relate to his love life was allowed to see the light of day.[5]

All Soviet editions of the composer's letters, including the so-called *Complete Collected Works (PSS)*, were, in one sense or another, censored and bowdlerized. In the latter edition, 248 letters out of 5,062 had been interfered with; the differing degrees of interference—from the omission of one or several words to the cutting of almost the entire text of the letter—depended on the time of the volume's appearance and the editors involved. Thus the appreciation of Tchaikovsky the man and artist lost its psychological dimension and grew increasingly abstract.

The material that suffered most from the editorial intervention seems to be Tchaikovsky's confidential correspondence with his two younger brothers, rich both in content and in emotional nuance. First it suffered at the hands of the composer's relatives, especially the letters from the period of 1870–77, in which words, sentences, paragraphs and names were often effaced, blotted out, scribbled over, and even in a few instances physically cut out by scissors. This censorship, most likely perpetrated by Tchaikovsky's brothers, was somewhat erratic and inconsistent. Occasionally "innocent" portions (of something we know from extant untouched copies) were removed, while much more telling ones were left untouched. The different styles of interference suggest more than one censor, but identities are difficult to determine. It could hardly have been Modest, the founder of Tchaikovsky's Memorial Museum in Klin and the first biographer of the composer, who himself was homosexual and never minded his brother's tastes. Ippolit, the other brother, who presided over the Archives and the Museum after the Communist takeover, could have been involved, but it was Modest's twin Anatolii who manifested a great concern about the letters. Soon after Tchaikovsky's death, Anatolii wrote to Modest on 6 December 1893: "Regarding Klin, I myself wish that no one except you or me touch any of the remaining papers and letters until those that might in any conceivable degree compromise his memory are destroyed."[6] Furthermore, it appears that most of the blotted-out confidences are found in Tchaikovsky's letters to Anatolii.

Fortunately, all blotted-out parts of these letters are by now reconstructable and readable. Thanks to the arrival of *glasnost'*, the Tchaikovsky Archives were opened to specialists, and it is time now to bring into circulation all missing parts of the composer's correspondence so that a fuller and verifiable portrait of the great composer, far from the earlier stereotypes of "mad Russian" or "homosexual martyr," may become known to the lovers of his music.

The most substantial cuts in Tchaikovsky's letters to his brothers were made for the period of 1876–77, when he was a professor at Moscow Conservatory. This was the period of doubts regarding his homosexual lifestyle that led to his desperate and doomed attempt to create a family by marrying his former student Antonina Miliukova. We selected for this publication seventeen of the most important and revealing letters which have never before been translated into English in full, and which were only recently made available to Russian scholars.[7] The purpose of this selection, which concerns mainly Tchaikovsky's sexual identity, is not sensationalism, but rather the desire to demonstrate how the composer, despite an at times painful and dramatic inner struggle, succeeded in overcoming an emotional crisis, eventually coming to terms with his own psychosexual nature, and thereupon, without further trouble, resumed his creative and social life.[8] As he wrote in a letter to Anatolii on 13/25 February 1878, from Florence: "Only now, especially after the tale of my marriage, have I finally begun to understand that there is nothing more fruitless than not wanting to be that which I am by nature."[9]

The original letters are preserved at the Tchaikovsky House Museum in Klin (near Moscow).[10]

Modest (1850–1916) and Anatolii (1850–1915) were fraternal twins, ten years younger than Tchaikovsky. After the death of their mother from cholera in 1854, Pyotr became their closest friend and confidant. Tchaikovsky's other two brothers, Ippolit (1843–1927) and Nikolai (1838–1911), did not develop such close personal ties with their composer-brother as the younger brothers did. Their sister Sasha (or Aleksandra, 1842–91) married very early and moved to Kamenka in the Ukraine, to the estate of her husband Lev Davydov. All the Tchaikovsky brothers loved their sister and often spent summer together at Kamenka. Modest, like his brother Pyotr, became homosexual, which made the emotional bond of their relationship even closer. Tchaikovsky tried always to be fair in regard to each twin and sought to help them in any possible way. He regularly wrote to them, first when the twins were studying in the School of Jurisprudence in St. Petersburg, and later, when they became civil servants. Tchaikovsky's exceptional candor in this correspondence as regards both himself and the two recipients is remarkable. Anatolii and Modest were aware of Tchaikovsky's homosexuality as early as 1864, and during their stay in Haapsalu (Estonia) in the summer of 1867 the composer openly admitted it to them.

In the painful period of Tchaikovsky's marriage and its aftermath, Anatolii enjoyed greater closeness with him than did Modest, who opposed the very idea of marriage for the composer; later, and for the rest of Tchaikovsky's life, Modest remained the only trusted person, to whom he was able to tell almost everything.[11]

• • •

Dates are given according to the Julian calendar, which remained in effect in Russia until 1918 and which in the nineteenth century lagged twelve days behind the Western Gregorian calendar; for Tchaikovsky's letters written abroad, both the Old and New Styles dates are given. The italics in the text of the letters are Tchaikovsky's.

Anatolii Tchaikovsky, the composer's younger brother (1874) (*The Tchaikovsky State Archive and House Museum, Klin, Russia*).

1. To Anatolii Tchaikovsky

This letter's mood was prompted and colored by Tchaikovsky's disappointment at Nikolai Rubinstein's[12] rejection of his First Piano Concerto two weeks earlier, an obvious blow to his self-esteem. Tchaikovsky's lament about his sexual tastes had more to do with creative psychology than with psychosexuality. Since the letter was occasioned by the lack of approval of his recent composition, which exacerbated his sense of loneliness and alienated him from more successful composers, the mood therein expressed should not be taken entirely at face value.[13]

Moscow
9 January 1875
Perhaps I mixed it up, but it seems to me that you did not respond to the letter wherein I asked you to let me know of your work circumstances. I also thought of you quite often all these days. I cannot bear holidays. On regular days you work at a specified time and everything goes smoothly, like a machine; on holidays the pen falls out of your hand, you want to be with those close to you and unburden your heart to them, and right then comes the awareness (exaggerated though it was) that you are an orphan and alone. But indeed I live in Moscow, strictly speaking, rather as an orphan. Over the holidays a great depression even fell upon me because of this. It is dull at the Davydovs',[14] and with my colleagues from the Conservatory and their wives I am not especially close. In short, I wanted very much to be in Petersburg—but I had little money. Yet besides the fact that there is no one here whom I might call *a friend* in the true sense of the word (even such as Laroche[15] was for me at one time, or as Kondratev[16] is now), I still found myself under the strong impression of a blow that had been dealt to my composer's pride, and by none other than Rubinstein. When drunk he likes to say that he feels a sweet passion for me, but when sober he knows how to irritate me to tears and sleeplessness. I shall tell you personally what happened. And what is more, your Hubert[17] also angered me for the same reason. These gentlemen cannot get out of the habit of seeing me as a beginner in need of their advice, severe comments, and decisive judgments. The matter concerns my piano concerto, which I had been laboring over for two whole months; but this unfortunate composition was not favored with the honor of being liked by Messrs. Rubinstein and Hubert, who expressed their disapprobation in a very unfriendly, offensive manner. If you take into consideration that they are regarded as my friends and that in the whole of Moscow there is no one who might treat my work with love and attention, you will understand that this was very hard on me. An astonishing thing! All these various Cuis, Stasovs and Co.,[18] who sometimes behave nastily to me, often make me feel that they are much more interested in me than my so-called friends. Cui recently wrote me a very charming letter. Today I received a letter from Rimsky-Korsakov that touched me very much.[19] I am very, very lonely here, and if it were not for working constantly I should simply give myself over to melancholy. It is also true that my

damned homosexuality[20] creates an unbridgeable chasm between me and most people. It imparts to my character an estrangement, a fear of people, immoderate timidity, mistrustfulness, in short, a thousand qualities whereby I am growing more and more unsociable. Just imagine, frequently now and at length I dwell on the idea of a monastery or something of the sort. Please, do not imagine that I am not well physically. I am quite well, sleep well, eat even better—this is just a sentimental mood in answer to your letter. Why do you think that I doubt *Utin's*[21] virtues? I do not know him, but I already like him for the reason that you are close with him. I kiss you affectionately.
P. Tchaikovsky.
Poor Velinsky![22] Have you heard that he died?

2. To Modest Tchaikovsky

> The letter describes Tchaikovsky's encounter with a male pros-
> titute in Vienna. Tchaikovsky continued his homosexual activi-
> ties in Moscow and abroad. In this letter he confessed that he
> had an encounter with a young man, whom he calls "she." The
> habit of referring to each other in the feminine gender was
> common among nineteenth-century homosexuals.[23]

Vienna
23 June /5 July 1876
Wednesday, 11 PM
Modia!
I'm stuck in Vienna. I've been staying here for four days already, in anticipation of Sasha's arrival.[24] I arrived here Sunday evening thinking that I would meet them on Monday, and then see them off and leave myself on Tuesday, but that was not to be. On Monday morning I received a telegram from Sasha informing me that she had postponed her departure for a few days. I spent the whole day considering whether or not to wait for her. I do not like Vienna, and to spend several days here by myself seemed the height of tedium. Finally I decided that I would go to the *Carre* circus (which I found interesting because the program was full of old acquaintances, including the *Nagels* family, one member of which—*August*—was very close to my heart ten days ago) with the thought that if I met anyone (at the circus is in Prater) I would stay, and if not, that I would leave the next day for Geneva, at the risk of missing Sasha. Just imagine: I met someone! Right here, even

Modest Tchaikovsky, the composer's younger brother, (1875) (*The Tchaikovsky State Archive and House Museum, Klin, Russia*).

before buying a ticket! We quickly got to know each other (she's very young, fair, and with hands worthy of the brush of a great artist), (oh! how sweet it was to kiss that wonderful hand!!!).[25] We spent the evening together, namely at the circus and in Prater. Yesterday we spent the whole time together, namely we made an excursion far outside of the city. This morning she was with me, then I walked with her around the shops and *equipped* her from head to foot; we again spent the evening together and parted only this minute. Tomorrow . . . but tomorrow Sasha will arrive and I'll spend the entire day with her. But I write this letter with the following aim: bear in mind that Sasha is leaving on *Friday*, but I unfortunately am not, and therefore do not expect me before next week. The thing is that my beauty, a *high-school student*, is due to complete her exams on the 10th. It is impossible for me to leave before that day since she *wants*[26] to accompany me to Munich. For my part I am unable to refuse myself this bliss, since up to this day I had had no *real thing* (namely, an entire night spent together in bed). So I'll leave here together *with her* Monday evening; on Tuesday morning we shall be in Munich, where we shall spend the day and stay the night, consequently only on *Wednesday* shall I leave Munich, directly for *Lyons*, where I hope to enclose you in my embrace. The *Opera* here is open, and performances are given every day, but, as one would expect, they are showing *Troubadour*, *L'Elisir d'Amore*, and other such dirt. On the day of my arrival I heard *Guillaume Tell* in an ideal performance. The day before had been *Aida*, and three days before *Die Meistersinger!* What misfortune for me! So, Modia, I shall see you soon. I shall telegraph you when I'm on my way. Kisses.

P. Tchaikovsky

3. To Modest Tchaikovsky

The letter reveals Tchaikovsky's pondering on the ethical and psychological questions posed by his homosexual brother's association with an eight-year-old deaf-mute boy, Kolia (Nikolai) Konradi (1868–1922), entrusted to his care and education. The experience of living closely in France with his brother, his brother's young pupil, and Konradi's governess Sofia Ershova was still fresh in his mind and led him to draw some disturbing and unexpected conclusions.[27]

Moscow
10/22 September 1876
Dear Modia!

Your silence starts to worry me. In your last letter you wrote that you are sick. Is it true that you fell seriously ill, and, if this is the case, why would you not ask Sofia to let us know? You know that to us, whatever the news, it is always better than uncertainty.

So now it is a month and a half since we parted, but it seems to me that several centuries have gone by. I have done a great deal of thinking during this time about me and about you and about our future. The result of all this pondering is that from today I seriously intend to enter into lawful matrimony, with anyone at all. I find that our *inclinations* are for both of us the greatest and most insurmountable obstacle to happiness, and we must fight our nature with all our strength. I love you very much, I love Kolia very much, and for the good of you both I dearly hope that you never part; but a condition of the durability of your relations is that you no longer be *that* which you have been up till now. This is necessary not for the sake of *qu'en dira-t-on,*[28] but for you yourself, for your peace of mind. A man who, after parting with so to speak *his own* (he can be called your own) child [i.e., Kolia Konradi], falls into the embraces of any passing trash cannot be the real educator that you want and ought to become. At any rate, now I cannot imagine you without horror in Aleksandrovsky Garden walking with Okoneshnikov[29] on your arm. You will say that at your age it is difficult to conquer passions; to this I shall answer that at your age it is easier to turn your tastes in a different direction. Here your religious faith should, I think, be a firm support to you. As for me, I shall do everything possible to marry this very year, but if I should lack the courage for this I am in any event abandoning forever my habits and shall strive to be counted no longer among the company of Gruzinsky and Co.[30] Write me your opinion of this.

Your relationship with the *Konradis* frightens me. I began to think that they are villains.

I spent two marvelous weeks in Verbovka;[31] then I was for several days (*très à contre-coeur*)[32] in *Usovo,*[33] with the purpose of borrowing money from *Shilovsky,* in which I succeeded. Now I live, in my old fashion, in my small apartment. Alësha[34] has grown up and become *inexpressibly* less good-looking, but to my heart he has remained as dear as ever. Whatever happens, I shall never part with him. I still have no news about *the opera [Vakula the Smith]*; I do not know whether it will be produced, but in fact all that is now to me of the least importance. I think exclusively of the eradication of pernicious passions from myself. I kiss you affectionately.
P. Tchaikovsky
I thank you for Kolia's portrait, even though it does not really succeed. Kiss him for his letter. I adore him passionately and think about him every second.
Yours P. T.
Anatolii, who lived with me for about a week, left yesterday.

4. To Modest Tchaikovsky

While the predicament of Modest and his deaf-mute charge was the immediate cause of Tchaikovsky's ruminations, it was by no means the only cause. It is clear that family pressure provided another strong motivation for the composer's decision to marry. His father Ilia dreamed of a devoted wife for his favorite son. Tchaikovsky's main concern at this time, however, pertained to the constant rumors about his homosexuality spreading by word of mouth in Moscow and St. Petersburg. Contemptuous though he was of public opinion, Tchaikovsky found that he could not ignore it. That Tchaikovsky would claim innocence in the very same letter in which he acknowledged three homosexual transgressions need not be seen as contradictory or surprising. His line of reasoning was based on the assumption that he was innocent because he was born homosexual and therefore his inclinations were natural.[35]

Moscow
28 September 1876
Dear Modia!
I have lost your letter and cannot reply point by point to your arguments against marriage. I remember that many of them make no sense, but many, on the other hand, are in complete agreement with my own thoughts. You predict for me a fate like that of Kondratev, Bulatov[36] and *tutti quanti*. Rest assured that, if my plans ever come to realization, I will certainly not be following in the footsteps of those gentlemen. Then, you say that one should spit on *qu'en dira-t-on*. That's true only to a certain degree. There are people who cannot despise me for my vices only because they came to love me when they did not yet suspect that I am in essence a man with a lost reputation. *Sasha*, for instance, is one of these! I know that she guesses *everything* and *forgives* everything. Thus am I treated by very many people whom I love or respect. Do you really think that I am not oppressed by this awareness that *they pity and forgive me*, when in fact I am guilty of nothing! And is it really not dreadful to think that people who love me can ever *be ashamed* of me! But, you see, this has happened a hundred times before and will happen a hundred times again. In a word, I should like by my marriage, or in general an open affair with a woman, to shut the mouth of various contemptible creatures whose opinion I do not value in the least but who can cause pain to the people close to me. In any event, do not be frightened for me, dear Modia. The realization of my plans is not at all as close as you think. I am so set in my habits and tastes that it is not possible to cast them aside all at once, like an old glove. And besides, I am far from possessing an iron will by any means, and after my letters to you I have already given in to the force of my

natural inclinations about three times. Would you imagine! One day I even went to *Bulatov's* country estate, and his house is nothing but a homosexual bordello. As if it were not enough that I had been there, I *fell in love* like a cat with his coachman!!! So you are quite right when you say in your letter that, whatever vows one makes, it is impossible to resist one's own weaknesses. All the same, I am sticking to my intentions, and you can rest assured that I will carry them out one way or another. But I won't do anything suddenly or without careful thought. Whatever happens, I am not going to put a *millstone* round my neck. I shall not enter into a lawful or illicit union with a woman without having fully ensured my own peace and my own freedom. I still have nothing definite in view as yet.

The other day Mrs. Davydov[37] was here. I saw her twice—she is a very nice person. The rehearsals of *Vakula* will start at the beginning of October. On this account I calmed down entirely. Will we see each other? Now, I believe, you may respond to that positively. I cannot but say in conclusion of this letter that I adore Kolia to *the point of insanity, to the point of passion*. Be that as it may, this winter I must see you both. P. Tchaikovsky.

Give my regards to Mme Konradi and Fofa.[38]

5. To Modest Tchaikovsky

This most revealing letter concerns Tchaikovsky's love affair with the twenty-one-year-old Conservatory student Iosif Kotek (1855–85), who in time would develop into a moderately renowned violinist. Though primarily heterosexual, Kotek will play an important part in the composer's emotional attachments in the following years.

Moscow
19 January 1877
Dear Modia!
Thanks for the wonderful letter that I received last week. I sat down to write to you, since I feel a need to pour out my feelings to a sympathetic soul. To whom but you can I entrust the sweet secret of my heart!

I am *in love*, as I haven't been in love for a long time. Can you guess with whom? He is of middle height, fair, with wonderful brown eyes (with a misty gleam characteristic of extremely nearsighted people). He wears a pince-nez, and sometimes *glasses*, which I cannot stand. He dresses with great care and cleanliness, wears a thick golden chain, and always pretty cuff links of noble metal. He has small hands, but utterly ideal in form.[39] They are so delightful that I readily forgive them certain distortions and ugly details that stem from frequent contact of the fingertips with the strings. He speaks with a heavily *nasal* voice, moreover tenderness and sincerity sound in the timbre of his voice. His accent is slightly southern-Russian and even Polish, for he was born and spent his childhood in Polish lands. But in the course of his six-year stay in Moscow this accent has been severely *moscovized*. In sum, i.e., adding this accent to the tenderness of his vocal timbre and charming lips, on which downy-fair whiskers are beginning to grow, the result is something delightful. He is quite smart, very talented in music, and in general blessed with a fine nature, far from any kind of vulgarity and oiliness . . .

I have known him for six years already. I always liked him, and on several occasions I have felt a little bit in love with him. That was like a trial run for my love. Now I have momentum and have *run right into him* in the most decisive fashion. I cannot say that my love is completely pure. When he caresses me with his hand, when he lies with his head on my chest and I play with his hair and secretly kiss it, when for hours on end I hold his hand in my own and tire in the battle against the urge to fall at his feet and kiss these little feet,[40] passion rages in me with unimaginable force, my voice shakes like that of a youth, and I speak some kind of nonsense. However, I am far from desiring physical consummation. I feel that, if *that occurred*, I would cool toward him. I would feel disgusted if this *wonderful youth* stooped to sex with an aged and fat-bellied man. How horrible this would be, and how disgusting I would become to myself! It is not called for.

I need only for him to know that I love him endlessly and for him to be a kind and indulgent despot and idol. It is impossible for me to hide my feelings for him, although I tried hard to do so at first. I saw that he noticed everything and understood me. But then, can you imagine how artful I am in hiding my feelings? My habit of *eating alive* any beloved object always gives me away. Yesterday I gave myself away totally. It happened like this. I was sitting at his place (he takes rooms, very clean, even with some luxury). He was writing out the *andante* from his concerto at his podium. For some reason he needed to reach into the desk, where he found a letter from one of his friends, written last summer. He began to reread it, then he sat at the piano and played some small piece in a minor key that was appended to the letter.

I: What's that? He (smiling): It's a letter from Porubinovsky and an instrumental song of his composition![41] I: I did not think that Porubinovsky could write such dear things? He: Of course. But here he is singing of his love for me. I: Kotek! For God's sake let me read that letter. He (giving me the letter and sitting near me): Go ahead.

I began to read the letter. It was filled with details about the Conservatory and about his sister, who last summer came here to enter the Conservatory. At the end of the letter my attention was especially attracted by the following passage: "*When will you finally get here? I miss you terribly. I have given up all my amorous adventures with women, everything has become disgusting and unbearable for me. I think only of you. I love you as if you were the most charming young maiden. I have expressed my yearning and my love in the appended instrumental song. For God's sake write to me. When I read your last, tender letter, I experienced the greatest happiness that has ever been in my life.*"

I: I did not know that Porubinovsky loves you so. He: Yes. His is such selfless and pure love! (Smiling slyly and stroking my knees with his hand (that's his habit).) *Not like your love!!!* I (delighted to the skies by his recognition of my love): Perhaps my love is selfish, but you can be sure that one-hundred-thousand Porubinovskys could not love you as I do!

And here I burst. I made a *full* confession of love, begging him not to be angry, not to feel constrained if I bored him, etc. All these confessions were met with a thousand various small caresses, strokes on the shoulder, *cheeks*, and strokes across my head. I am incapable of expressing to you the full degree of bliss that I experienced by fully giving myself away.

I must tell you that yesterday was the eve of his departure for Kiev, where he is soon to give a concert. After my *confession* he suggested we travel out of town for supper. It was a delightful, moonlit night. I hired a carriage and we flew off. I cannot tell you the thousand details that caused me ineluctable bliss. I wrapped him up, hugged him, guarded him. He complained of the frost on the tip of his nose. I held the collar of his fur coat the whole time with my bare hand in order to warm this nose tip, so holy for me. The freezing of my *hand* caused me pain and, at the same time, the sweet thought of knowing that I was suffering for him. In *Strelna*, in the winter garden, I met the group of Lenin, Rivol and *tutti quanti*.[42] Lord, how pitiful they all seemed to me in their cynical and ironic debauchery! From there we went to Iar[43] and supped in a private room. After dinner he felt sleepy and lay down on the sofa, using my knees for a pillow. Lord, what utter bliss this was! He tenderly ridiculed my expressions of affection and kept repeating that my love is not the same as that of Porubinovsky. Mine is supposedly selfish and impure. His love in selfless and pure. We spoke of the piece he *ordered* me to write for his Lenten concert.[44] He repeated over and over that he would get angry if I didn't write this piece. We left at three o'clock.

I awoke today with a feeling of unknown happiness and with a complete absence of that emotional sobriety that used to make me repent in the morning for having gone too far the day before. I bore my classes today with extreme ease, was indulgent and tender with my pupils, and to their surprise made witticisms and jokes the whole time, so that they were rolling with laughter. At eleven o'clock he summoned me out of the class so as to pay his farewell. We parted, but I ended class early and flew to the Kursk railway so as to see him once more. He was very tender, merry and dear. At half-past one the train rushed him off. I am not upset that he left. First, he shall soon return. Second, I need to gather my thoughts and calm down. I have done nothing recently and have seen absolutely nobody, apart from those whom he visits. Shilovsky and Kondratev are both angry at me. Third, I am glad that I shall have occasion to write to him and express all that I have not been able to say.

And meanwhile I have begun one very bold enterprise. I want to travel to Paris in March and give a concert there. I have even entered into direct negotiations with Colonne[45] (president of the *Societé des jeunes artistes*) and other officials. But how will I pay for it all! My financial affairs are terrible: I am in debt up to my ears. But I don't care. Modia, I kiss you sincerely. Nikolai and his wife were here;[46] they *really* complained about you for avoiding them recently from fear they will demand you pay your debt for the portrait. Try to pay as soon as possible.

For God's sake don't let Alina catch sight of this letter.[47] I hug Kolia tenderly and sincerely. *Merci* for his wonderful letter.
P. Tchaikovsky

6. To Modest Tchaikovsky

This letter belongs to the time when Tchaikovsky was already in correspondence with the former Conservatory student Antonina Miliukova, who fell in love with him. Nonetheless, as this letter demonstrates, he continued both to feel infatuation for the violinist Kotek and to entertain ties with Moscow's homosexual milieu.

Moscow
4 May 1877
Dear Modia!
Imagine my misfortune! I exhausted my whole supply of small-size paper, and I must write you on a large sheet. It is fearful to imagine that there are four more pages to fill. I sensed very vividly the whole anguish you must have at first felt in Grankino.[48] But at the same time I realize that one can get accustomed to and even find charm in a place where there is much space and few people, since I hope that you have no neighbors. But books are necessary. Even more necessary are the *newspapers*, and on this account I must confess my own perfidy. Imagine, it was only the other day that I remembered Alina's commission regarding *Mosk[ovskie] vedom[osti]*! I hope that by now you already started receiving the newspaper.

My love for a person known to you has ignited with new and unheard-of strength! The reason for this is *jealousy. He has tied himself to Eibozhenko*,[49] and they have sex five and six times a day. At first they hid this from me, but my heart told the truth even earlier. I tried to distance myself from this thought, comforting myself with all sorts of inventions. But one fine day he confessed everything to me. I cannot *tell* you what torture it was for me to learn that my suspicions had basis in fact. I am not even in a state to hide my grief. I have spent several terrible nights. Not that I am angry at him or her, not at all. But suddenly I have felt with unusual force that he is *alien* to me, that this woman is millions of millions of times nearer to him. Then I became accustomed to this terrible thought, but love was ignited stronger than ever before. We still see each other every day, and he was never so tender with me as now. Do you know why I cooled to him this spring? Now I know for sure that it was due to that *disfigured* finger. Isn't that strange?

Donaurov[50] now stays here as a house guest, already for more than a week. He happened to get some from God knows where, and is now spending it mercilessly. Incidentally, about you, he recently uttered that you are his only *debtor!* Meshchersky,[51] who has been here and now has come again, is most displeased with you and told me, with the expression of great grief, some story about some family! Could you tell me please why, being such a good person, you can never be entirely beyond reproach as regards all sorts of money dealings? There is the matter of my nine rubles. I will not pretend that I liked it. You know that it does not relate to nine rubles and that, if you told me that you needed a hundred, I would have got that hundred for you. But to buy things without having money, and then, ten seconds before departure say "I am sorry"—no, this I did not like a bit. Generally speaking, in your case all such dealings are somehow unclean, and you also learned how to lie. Seriously, this simply insults me and grieves me very much.

Shilovsky's wedding took place.[52] Before that he was constantly drunk, howling all day and fainting. Now he is perfectly happy and content. He *has broken in* his wife (that's the utter truth) and spends all day making visits to aristocrats. Yesterday I had dinner with him. His wife's an ugly mug and seems foolish. But she is very *comme il faut.*

Please do not be angry with me because of my reproaching you as above. You know indeed that I love you *very, very, very much.* I kiss you affectionately. I will fulfill all your commissions.
P. Tchaikovsky.
Alësha sends his regards.

7. To Modest Tchaikovsky

On May 23 Tchaikovsky impulsively made an official proposal to Antonina Miliukova, yielding to her requests to marry her but promising his bride only a "brotherly" love, to which she readily agreed.[53] But Tchaikovsky, knowing Modest's opposition to his matrimonial plans, chose not to mention this meeting in his letter to him, written on the same day. Instead he tried to explain why he was temporarily cooling his relations with Kotek, and even began to see the manifestations of Providence in various coincidences that recently occurred.

Moscow
23 May 1877
Dear Modia!
Yesterday I received your letter. It is entirely true that Meshchersky exaggerated everything a hundred times. I accept all your excuses and explanations. Only it is desirable that you would free yourself of that shortcoming, which is the more conspicuous since it stands out against the background of your warm and dear soul. *N'en parlons plus.*[54]

If you like, I am less entitled than anyone to reproach you for that shortcoming, since I am myself infected with it only a little less than you. All my relations with Shilovsky are in essence exploitation, and rather unseemly and humiliating for me. True, he has thrust money at me, but I could simply have not taken it. But, as I have already mentioned: *N'en parlons plus.*

Tchaikovsky with his brothers Modest and Anatolii (standing) and his friend Nikolai Kondratev in Moscow, (1875) (*The Tchaikovsky State Archive and House Museum, Klin, Russia*).

I do not remember whether I wrote you that I chose *Eugene Onegin* as the subject for an opera. What would you say on this?

The examinations are ending and my departure draws nearer, but I do not feel so lighthearted as I have in the past. The thought that I shall again have to endure the same tedious monotony, again the classes, again Bochechkarov,[55] again the various squabbles—all this upsets me and poisons the idea of three free months. I am growing old! At any rate, from here I go for one month to the [Konstantin] Shilovsky's,[56] where I want to do some work on *Onegin*. Then probably to Sasha's, but I must know for certain when you and Kolia will leave for her place. At the end of the summer I want to go either to Caucasus or abroad, depending on the currency rate.

You will ask about my love? It has once again fallen off almost to the point of absolute calm. And do you know why? You alone can understand this. Because two or three times I saw his injured finger in all of its ugliness! But without that I would be in love to the point of madness, which returns anew each time I am able to forget somewhat about his crippled finger. I don't know whether this finger is for the better or worse.

Sometimes it seems to me that Providence, so blind and unjust in the choice of its protégés, deigns to take care of me. Indeed, sometimes I begin to consider some coincidences to be *not mere accidents*.[57] Who knows, maybe this is the beginning of a religiosity that, if it ever takes hold of me, will do so completely, i. e., with Lenten oil, cottonwool from the Iveron icon of the Mother of God, etc.

I send a photograph of myself and Kotek together. It was taken at the very peak of my recent passion. Do not forget to write me at Shilovsky's address: Moscow region, town of *Voskresensk*, village of *Glebovo*. Good-bye, my dear Modia. I embrace Kolia with warmest tenderness. Please give my regards to Alina and her husband. Also to dear Fofa.
Yours P. Tchaikovsky

8. To Anatolii Tchaikovsky

Consumed by the work on his new opera *Eugene Onegin* in Shilovsky's country estate Glebovo, Tchaikovsky was all but oblivious of the proposal he had made to Antonina a month earlier. It is remarkable that Tchaikovsky, having resolved to proceed with so important a step as marriage, made not the slightest mention to his relatives of his decision until this letter. It suggests that in the depth of his heart he hardly took the whole matter seriously. He may have envisioned his future household not unlike that of his married homosexual friends Kondratev, Bulatov or Shilovsky, whose wives tolerated their husbands' homosexual escapades. In the following letter he informs only his brother Anatolii (and their father) of his plans less than two weeks before the wedding.

Glebovo
23 June 1877
Dear Tolia,
You guessed rightly that I was hiding something from you, but you did not guess what. Here is what it is all about. At the end of May an event happened that I wanted to keep secret for some time from you and all the people who are dear and close to me, to prevent you from anxiously wondering how, what, whom, why, am I right, etc. I wanted to finish everything and then make my confession to all of you. *I am going to be*

married. When we meet, I shall tell you how it happened. I made my proposal at the end of May and wanted to arrange the marriage at the beginning of July and announce it to you all afterwards. But your letter made me change my mind. First, I am not going to avoid meeting you, and it would be difficult to play a comedy, to invent reasons why I am not going to Kamenka with you. Second, I decided that to get married without Papa's blessing would not be the thing to do. Give to Papa the enclosed letter. Please, do not worry about me: I have carefully thought over what I am doing and I take this important step in my life quite calmly. This calm must be made obvious to you by the fact that, with my wedding being so close, I was able to write two thirds of my opera. The girl I am marrying is not very young, but quite respectable, and endowed with one main quality: *she is in love with me like a cat*. She has no fortune whatsoever. Her name is *Antonina Miliukova*, and she is a sister of Anastasia Khvostova's husband.[58] So I am not only announcing to you my future marriage, but inviting you to it. You and Kotek will be the only witnesses. Then you will leave for Kamenka, and I will spend about three weeks with *my wife* (what a strange sound does this make!). I negotiated for myself the right of travelling for an entire month. I will be in Kamenka, but I will not stay there for long. I *must have* a medical cure and I *must complete* the opera. All this I will do by leaving for the Caucasus or by going abroad, if I have enough money. My wife, meanwhile, will find and furnish an apartment, so that I will come back to the bosom of *my family*. Thus, so long, my dear best man. I will wait to meet you on the morning of the 6th, in Moscow, Krestovozdvizhensky lane.
Yours P. Tchaikovsky
Ask Papa *to be sure* not to tell anyone; the same applies to you. I shall write myself to Sasha and to our brothers.

9. To Anatolii Tchaikovsky

In this long and candid letter Tchaikovsky described his inner turmoil in the aftermath of the wedding, which took place on 6 July 1877 in the Church of St. George in Moscow.[59] Strikingly, his thoughts and affections seemed centered exclusively on his brother, and not at all on his new bride. Tchaikovsky admitted to Anatolii that he was still by no means accustomed to his new situation.

Tchaikovsky, Modest, Kolia Konrady and his governess Sofia Ershova at Montpellier, France (1876) (*The Tchaikovsky State Archive and House Museum, Klin, Russia*).

St. Petersburg
8 July 1877
Tolia, I should be deceiving you cruelly if I were to assure you that I am already entirely happy and entirely accustomed to my new situation,

etc. After such a terrible day as the 6th of July, after that endless moral torment, it is not possible to recover quickly. But all adversities have also their good side; I suffered unbearably, seeing how distressed you were about me, but at the same time you are responsible for my struggling with my torments with such courage. Tell me, please, what meaning have all our ordeals, failures, adversities when compared with the force of my love for you and your love for me! Whatever may happen to me, I know that in your love I shall always find support and consolation. Even now you do not leave my mind for a second, and your dear image consoles, encourages and supports me. The hope of seeing you again will keep me from losing heart, no matter what.

Now I shall tell you everything in order. When the train started off I was ready to scream from the sobs that were suffocating me. But I had still to engage my wife in conversation until Klin, so as to earn the right to settle down in my own seat in the darkness and be left alone. At the second stop, after Khimki, Meshchersky burst into the car. Seeing him, I felt the sudden need for him to lead me away somewhere as soon as possible. Which he did. Before beginning any sort of conversation with him, I had to give vent to a flood of tears. Meshchersky showed me much tender sympathy and greatly raised my fallen spirits. Upon returning to my wife, after Klin, I was much calmer. Meshchersky arranged for us to be placed in a separate compartment, and after that I slept like a log. The rest of the journey, after I woke up, was not especially difficult. There was not a second that I did not think of you. As I explained above, the thought of you would bring tears to me, but at the same time it heartened and consoled me. Somewhere in the country near *Okulovo* we were delayed about five hours because a goods train had been derailed, and as a result we arrived in St. Petersburg at three instead of ten. Most comforting of all to me was that my wife did not understand and was not aware of my poorly concealed anguish. Even now she appears quite happy and content. *Elle n'est pas difficile.*[60] She agrees with everything and is content with everything.

We stayed at the Europe Hotel: very good, and even luxurious. I went off to the bathhouse, on the way stopped at the telegraph office, and sent telegrams to you and Kotek; the latter should communicate to me how you spent your time after I left. If I know that your mind is at ease and you are well, that will greatly help me attain a normal state of mind. We dined in our room. In the evening we took a carriage to the islands. The weather was quite poor, and it was drizzling. We sat through one part [of a concert] and went home. *As regards defloration,* indeed nothing happened. I made no attempts, since I knew that, until I resume my usual form, nothing will work. But we had conversations that further clarified our mutual relations. *She had agreed with absolutely everything and will never be displeased*. She needs only to cherish and care for me. I had reserved for myself complete freedom of action. After taking a good dose of valerian and prevailing upon my discomfited wife not to be discomfited, I again fell asleep like a log. Such sleep is a great benefactor. I feel the time is not far off when I shall calm down *completely*.

And indeed, why grieve? You and I are both very nervous, and both capable of seeing things in a more somber hue than in fact they are. I have so secured my freedom of action that, as soon as my wife and I have grown accustomed to each other, she will not constrain me in anything. I must not deceive myself: *she is very limited*, but that is even good. I should be afraid of an intelligent woman. But I stand so far above this one, I dominate her to such degree, that at least I do not fear her at all.

The weather today is abominable. All the same, this evening we are going to the Kamennoostrovsky Theater, and tomorrow I want to go to Pavlovsk.

Tolia, if you were here I should smother you right now in my embrace. I do so mentally. You know, it's even a good thing that such days as the 6th of July occur. Only on such days can the love that binds me to you be measured in all its fullness. Be well, play your violin, and do not worry about me. I know that soon everything will be fine.
Yours P. Tchaikovsky

10. To Modest Tchaikovsky

Naturally, Tchaikovsky could not write to Modest—who vehemently opposed his matrimonial experience—in the same vein and with the same candid details as he could write to Anatolii. To reveal to him his miserable perturbations would have meant acknowledging that Modest had been right and he himself wrong. This consideration more than anything else explains the restrained tone of the letter he sent to Modest that same day.

St. Petersburg
8 July 1877
Modia,
I sense that you worried about me and feel I must reassure you. My wedding took place on the 6th of July. Tolia was present. This day was, I'll admit, rather difficult for me, if indeed only because I had to endure

the wedding ceremony, the long wedding party, the departure with everyone seeing us off, etc. I slept beautifully during the journey. Yesterday we spent the day quite pleasantly, in the evening went for a drive and visited some amusement spot on Krestovsky [Island], and the night passed quietly. Defloration did not happen, however, and perhaps will not happen for quite a while. But I asserted myself in a such a manner that there is no need to worry. My wife has one huge merit: she obeys me blindly in everything, she is very accommodating, she is pleased with everything, and desires nothing but to feel happy for providing me with support and consolation. I cannot say yet that I love her, but I already feel that I will love her after we get accustomed to each other.

This is what I would like to ask you, Modia! Until August I will live together with my wife here, in the country at her mother's place, in Moscow, etc. On August 1 I will leave Moscow and go directly to *Sasha*, where in any case I will spend several days. I would so much desire that you prolong your stay there until my arrival, I would so much like to see you! If you are not able to stay longer than for several days, would you consent to come to Sasha's later, and not on July 15 as you planned? Anyway, try to arrange it so you can see me.

I composed the *larger* part of *Onegin* at Glebovo. I would very much wish to complete all the rest by the beginning of the academic year, but I do not know whether I will manage it.

I kiss you tenderly, tenderly; there is nothing to write yet. I love you, and among the petty upheavals I am going through now I direct my thoughts to you with pleasure.

Yours P. Tchaikovsky.

Kiss Kolia for me, and give my regards to Alina, her husband, and dear Sofia.

11. To Anatolii Tchaikovsky

Tchaikovsky desperately wanted to believe that he would eventually grow accustomed to his new situation. Yet more than once he could not bring himself to tell acquaintances in St. Petersburg, whom he would meet accidentally, that the lady with him was his wife. He continued to delude himself about Antonina's desires for the consummation of the marriage and impatiently waited for August 1, when he would be able to leave his wife and come to Kamenka.

Tchaikovsky and violinist Iosif Kotek, (1877) (*The Tchaikovsky State Archive and House Museum, Klin, Russia*).

St. Petersburg
9 July 1877
My dear Tolia!
Yesterday my mood shifted variously from calm to unbearably foul. Anxiety and longing for you tormented me as before, despite Kotek's telegram, which informed me that you left in good spirits.

How cruel and heartless I was when I told you that I will not go to Laroche because I begrudge twenty-five rubles. What egoism on my part! I went to him, and I thank fate that I did. First, he met me as a Jew would meet the Messiah; apparently, he was on the verge of perdition, and seized me as if I were his last chance.[61] I want to be that last chance for him. I must do everything possible to save a perishing friend. Second, he had dinner and spent the entire evening with us; he was very nice with my wife and, most importantly, he disrupted our painful *tête-à-tête*. In fact, it is only I who feels pain: *she* appears perfectly happy and content. In the evening we went to the Kamennoostrovsky Theater, then drank tea and beer (in considerable quantity) at home. His presence greatly cheered me up.

That night the first attack took place. The attack proved weak; it is true, it met no resistance, but in itself it was very weak. However, this first *step* accomplished a lot. It brought me closer to my wife, since I resorted to various manipulations that established intimacy between us. Today I feel in her regard incomparably freer.

The weather is awful. I do not know how we will kill the evening, but at least we will be in Laroche's company. I promised to come to his place at 3 o'clock. I had yesterday two encounters: (1) in the morning, walking with my wife on my arm, I met Niks Litke[62] on Nevsky, spoke with him, but could not bring myself to say (for some reason) that this lady is my wife; (2) in the evening, on the way to the theater—*Konstantinov*,[63] to whom I also said nothing and managed to escape for once in a long time with no more than a loan of five rubles. Money flows like water. It seems to me that August 1 will be the happiest day in my life.

Yours P. Tchaikovsky.

12. To Anatolii Tchaikovsky

In this letter Tchaikovsky continues to describe his miserable experience with his new wife. He took Antonina to Pavlovsk to introduce her to his father and stepmother Lizaveta. His hopes and wishful thinking that somehow the whole situation would resolve favorably developed, by the end of the night, into a sense of repulsion regarding Antonina.

St. Petersburg
11 July 1877
There remain yet about three weeks before we see each other. I live exclusively in the hope of the vacation my wife has allowed me from August 1 till September. Yesterday we were in Pavlovsk. Papa is enchanted with my wife, as was to be expected. Lizaveta was very kind and attentive, but I noticed several times tears in her eyes. This per-

Tchaikovsky and his wife Antonina, (1877) (*The Tchaikovsky State Archive and House Museum, Klin, Russia*).

spicacious and kind stepmother probably guesses that I am going through a critical moment in my life. I confess that all this was very hard for me, i.e., Papa's tenderness and endearments (so opposite to my own coldness to my wife) and the perspicacity of Lizaveta. I am indeed going through a difficult moment in my life; however, I feel that little by little I am growing accustomed to my new situation. [The situation] would be utterly false and unbearable if I had deceived my wife in anything, but I have warned her that she can rely only on my brotherly love. The *attack* was not resumed. After the first attempt, my wife has became *totally repugnant to me in the physical sense*. I am sure that sometime later the attacks will resume and prove more successful. But now any attempts would be useless.

Laroche provides me *with enormous consolation and support*. He is very nice. Yesterday we did not see each other—he went to Peterhof, to attend Rubinstein's concert, and we went to Pavlovsk, but today we will meet. Yesterday morning, while my wife was at bath, I went to Mass at St. Isaac's Cathedral. I felt a need to pray. When I returned, I learned with surprise that Rubinstein (Nikolai) had visited us; he came for his brother's concert. He sat for half an hour, but did not wait for me. My wife was enchanted by his courtesy.

I want to stay here until Wednesday morning and then leave with the express train. If I like it at the estate of the *belle-mère*,[64] I will live there for a few days, and then somehow kill time until August 1 (though I will try to steal a couple of days), at which point I will fly away.[65] I have in mind to spend several days in Kamenka, and then, taking you with me, *indeed to depart to the Caucasus*. It is somehow awkward to live in Kamenka for an entire month. I kiss you tenderly. Yours P. Tchaikovsky.

13. To Anatolii Tchaikovsky

This letter has been preserved only in a copy made by Modest for his House Museum and contains two omissions that cannot be restored, but despite those omissions it is clear that all Tchaikovsky's efforts to establish sexual relations with his wife failed. The letter describes the couple's last day in St. Petersburg, when Tchaikovsky tried to convince himself that the marriage still continued to move in the right direction.

St. Petersburg
13 July 1877
Tolichka, yesterday was perhaps the most difficult day of all since 6 July. It seemed to me in the morning that my life was destroyed forever, and I suffered a fit of despair. By 3 o'clock a multitude of people gathered at our place: Nikolai Rubinstein, his sister Sofia, Malozemova,[66] Karl Davydov,[67] Ivanov,[68] Bessel,[69] Laroche. We had dinner together. In the evening, we first saw Rubinstein off to Moscow, and then Malozemova and Sofia to Peterhof. The most awful moment of the day arrived when, in the evening, I was alone with my

wife. We began to walk in embrace. Suddenly, I felt myself calm and content. . . . I do not understand how it happened! Be that as it may, from that moment on everything around became bright, and I realized that whatever kind of person my wife may be, she is my wife and that this fact is something perfectly normal, as it should be. < . . . > Today I woke for the first time without the sensation of despair and hopelessness. My wife is in no way repugnant to me. I already began to relate to her as any husband who is not in love with his wife. But most important, today I no longer feel awkward with her, do not occupy her with small talk, and I am fully calm. Beginning today the terrible crisis has passed. I am recovering. But the crisis was *terrible, terrible, terrible*; were it not for my love for you and my other dear ones that supported me in the midst of *unbearable mental torments*, it might have ended badly, that is, with illness or madness.

Today we are going straight back to Moscow. My wife received news that the money from the mortgaged forest awaits her. From there, we will go to the country. < . . . > I kiss you affectionately.

Now I give you my word that there is no need to worry about me. I have entirely entered the period of convalescence.

14. To Modest Tchaikovsky

In this letter Tchaikovsky informed Modest about his last days in Kamenka, before he had to leave for Moscow and return to Antonina and to his teaching in the Conservatory. Amid numerous interesting details of his life at Kamenka, he mentioned his "source of delight"—a manservant Evstafy, with whom he fell in love. It testifies to the fact that only a few weeks after his wedding Tchaikovsky resumed his homosexual activity and had no serious intention of becoming a strictly heterosexual man.

Kiev
9 September 1877

Dear Modia!
Yesterday morning I arrived here with Alësha and immediately received your loveliest letter. Your portrayal of the gentleman who boils with rage in public places at any pretext is artistic, which once again confirms my opinion that you are positively endowed with a literary talent you wrongly neglect. If you are too lazy to write whole

novels full of entanglements and disentanglements, you can at least write short stories or sketches like the one you wrote about that man. It would be fresh, and original, and would bring you some money. Think how pleasant your life would be if you could divide it between teaching and literature; how full and rich it would become! I advise you to think seriously about it, as long as you are still young and *le pli du dilettantisme* has not taken hold of you. I know that if I had been in your place I would not have left such ability dormant. Since you left I have read more of *Anna Karenina*. How can you be so excited about this revoltingly vulgar nonsense concealed by pretense of deep psychological analysis? Devil take this analysis, which leaves one with a feeling of emptiness and insignificance, just as if you were present at a conversation between Alexandrine Dolgoruky[70] and Nicolas Kondratev about all sorts of Kittys, Alinas, and Lillys. Also, your episode of waiting at the station is a thousand times more artistic than all those lordly subtleties.

But enough about literature.

After your departure from Kamenka, I felt very sad, and that sadness increased with the passing of the days. These past days I have even suffered from diarrhea caused by that particular sensation of terror characteristic of nervous persons with respect to strong and unpleasant sensations. There were, however, also very pleasant episodes. On Sunday we went hunting in *Zrubanets*.[71] It is a pity that you never had the experience of hunting *partridge*. It is full of unexpected things and very special surprises. It was great fun, very interesting as well as awfully exhausting, since you have to spend the whole time running through the bushes and from one hill to another. At two o'clock we had *dumplings* at *Nikolai's*,[72] and everyone was there, including Alësha. There is my source of delight, about whom I cannot even think without being sexually aroused and whose *boots I would feel happy to clean all my life long*, whose chamber pots I would like to take out, and for whom I am generally ready to lower myself in any way, provided that I could kiss, even *if only rarely, his hands and feet.*[73] Before this hunt I went with Lev for the entire day to Verbovka, and spent about six hours at the lake. The ducks were flying en masse, but not one of them was deprived of its life.

Tania's[74] name day was celebrated with pomp. In the morning—presents; I wrote some verses and presented her with twenty-five rubles. At mid-day there was a short service, and we all drank hot chocolate. In the evening there were a lot of guests, dancing, and a magnificent supper. I have forgotten to tell you that the day before I dined at the Plesskys, and that I had paid them a visit before then.

At 7 o'clock on Wednesday, I left. Naturally I was seen off by everybody, and *Vyshnitsky*[75] was so full of kind feelings that he accompanied me to the Bobrinsky Station, *so it would be more pleasant*, as he expressed it. We arrived in Kiev at noon instead of nine o'clock. Had a bad night, as the train was full. After having had some dinner, I sent Alësha off to [Pechersky] Monastery and went for a walk on my own. In the evening I went to the opera. *Traviata* was performed, with the principal part very well sung by a certain *Pavlovskaia*.[76] The rest was no good. This morning, after a good night, Alësha and I went to St. Sofia's Cathedral, to St. Michel's, the Pechersky Monastery, the Grave of Askold, and then to the delightfully splendid *Vydubetsky* Monastery. *Alësha* once again became extremely nice, tender and affectionate. His heart is wonderful and his nature remarkably delicate.

Today I received a letter from my spouse. She writes that she cannot wait for me to come.[77] I depart tomorrow morning.

I kiss you, dear Modia. I am delighted that everything goes well with you, and, most important, that Kolia's love for you is so strong and firm. Good-bye, my dove. Show the following line to Kolia: *I am awfully fond of Kolia and I am happy that he loves Modia.*
Yours P. Tchaikovsky.
Alësha asked to give you his regards and his *"most humble respect,"* and says that he *"kisses your hands."*

15. To Modest Tchaikovsky

Tchaikovsky came back to Russia after the long stay abroad caused by the matrimonial fiasco on April 11, 1878. This letter sheds new light on Tchaikovsky's homosexual tastes and on the role of his longtime friend in Moscow, Nikolai Bochechkarov.

Moscow
16 September 1878
Only you alone, Modia, can fully understand the emotions I felt yesterday. Due to boredom and unbearable apathy, I gave in to Nikolai's [Bochechkarov] urgings to meet one sweet youth from the peasant class who works as a lackey. Our *rendez-vous* was set for Nikitsky boulevard. My heart moaned sweetly all day, since I am at present quite disposed to falling madly in love with someone. We arrived at the boulevard, introduced ourselves, and I fell in love immediately, just as Tatiana fell in love with Onegin. His face and figure were *un rêve*, the embodiment of a sweet dream. After a walk, during which I fell irrevocably in love

with him, I invited him and Bochechkarov to a tavern. We engaged a private room. He sat next to me on the sofa, took off his gloves . . . and . . . and how horrible! His hands were terrible, small, with small nails, slightly bitten all around, and with a gleam on his fingers next to his nails like Nikolai Rubinstein's! Oh, what a terrible blow this was to my heart! What torment I experienced! However he was so handsome, so dear, charming in all other respects, that with the help of two glasses of vodka I was in love and melting by the end of the evening. I experienced fine, sweet moments capable of reconciling me with the boredom and vulgarity of life. Absolutely nothing happened. Probably I shall gradually reconcile myself to his hands, but this circumstance will prevent *full* happiness from ever coming to be.

Generally speaking, I am in an unprecedentedly strange state of mind and am leading an unprecedented lifestyle. Not that I am experiencing vague yearning or burning feelings of dissatisfaction and craving for another life, not at all! But I am mindlessly bored and view all around me with cold disgust. Moscow is utterly disgusting to me. I cannot remain here; this I have decided and shall act upon, but for the moment I am living *au jour le jour*, hiding myself with great care and avoiding any society. I feel like a guest at the Conservatory; it has become something so alien to me, that I am no longer angry in class and feel only raw disgust towards the male and female students and their works. The respected professors with their servile devotion to the respected Director and their squabbles and petty interests, also seem to me foreigners to whom nothing ties me. Arriving at the Conservatory I go straight to class, and try to leave in such a way that I meet no one! In answer to various exclamations of greeting, such as "Ba!" or "Who is that I see?" I make an angry face and immediately rush aside. Then I regularly walk or ride to Neskuchny Park or Kuntsevo every day for a stroll. I walk for a couple of hours, and then ride home and dine usually with Nikolai Lvovich. In the evening we stroll or go to church. Incidentally, recently I went with him to an All-Night Vigil at the Cathedral of the Dormition, where everyone called him "Your Excellency" or "Your Highness!" Apart from all this I am perfectly healthy, and all of my bodily functions are excellent.

Rubinstein has stayed for another week in Paris, and therefore the resolution of my fate has been postponed. I received your letter and am concerned about the abscess in your armpit. I know from experience how tortuous that is. I await your arrival here with great satisfaction. I am suffering from impecuniousness (sic!!!).
A thousand kisses.
P. Tchaikovsky

16. To Anatolii Tchaikovsky

In this letter Tchaikovsky, while working on his opera *The Maid of Orleans*, describes two curious dreams he had the previous night. The description of the second dream was always supressed in Soviet publications. This material may provide some insight from the psychoanalytical perspective.

Clarens
9/21 January 1879
Even though today is my turn to write not to you, but to Modest, I am still writing to you, moved by the unutterable gratitude for your two wonderful letters, received simultaneously, which are filled with a myriad of interesting details. Modest's letter, to the contrary, is very brief and with no real contents, although I do not reproach him since he explains the reasons why he had no time to write. I assure you, Tolia, that I have read no novel in my life with the same fascination that I read your letters. And this is understandable. All dramatis personae are so close and, even though in different degrees, dear to me. The impression made on me by these letters is mixed. On the one hand, I am frightened, terrified, baffled by the crazy life in which you seem like a speck caught up in a whirlwind. On the other hand, sometimes I feel envious. For instance, I would have loved to have been present at Nikolai's[78] on New Year's Eve in order to watch you all, to see how Tania looks in her ball dress, how Olga[79] hosts the guests, how Georgii Kartsov[80] dances, and so on. But, most importantly, there are moments when I so much want to caress my Tolia a little! What a pity that I cannot stay in Petersburg for long! During my next visit, which will take place in about a month and a half, let's definitely try, on the pretext of working, to go nowhere except to Papa and Kolia. Let us see what will happen.

Your suspicions regarding the loss of your letters makes me love you. None of them was ever lost. From the moment you adopted the diary form in your correspondence, you began to write incomparably more often. You see how convenient it is!

I shall tell you now about today, starting with the night. Because of a slight cold, I had a disturbed night and saw the oddest things in my dreams, which I cannot really describe. One dream was especially interesting, because in it a *play* on words seemed very important. I dreamt that I was present at a *rally*, at which *Renan*[81] was giving a speech that ended with the following curious conclusion: "There exist four things which must be cherished on earth: *France, rêve, tombeau, roi.*"[82] I asked my neighbor what it meant. He replied that Renan was a royalist and had been shot for it, and that was why, after his death, he did not dare speak about it straightforwardly, but spoke instead in word play. These four words mean: "France, dream about thy beautiful king" (*ton beau*). In the dream I was deeply impressed by the ingeniousness of the dead, but speechifying Renan. Right after the speech the barrister Gerke[83] came up to him, and they began drinking beer and speaking German. After this I woke up, and for a long time I admired *Renan's* pun.[84]

Now, the second dream was that Anette Merkling[85] slept with me in the same bed and implored me, sobbing, that I use her. So as not to let her see my nonerect thing, I pretended to sob and said that I felt sorry for her, but despite a passionate desire to satisfy her, I could not bring myself to commit incest. Then she began forcefully to snatch at my shamefully hanging thing, and I awoke in horror and decided to tell both dreams to you or Modia immediately in the very first letter. Isn't it curious?

Finished the first act [of *The Maid of Orleans*]. After another solitary walk (Alësha is still afraid to go out), I found four letters waiting for me at home. Two from you (how glad I was), one from Modia, one from Mrs. von Meck. It is odd, no letters for three days and then four at once. How glad I was to find out from your letter that charming Volodia Zhedrinsky[86] has completely recovered, dances, takes part in theatricals, and so on. Before supper, sat and sweated over the scene between *the King and Dunois* and worried over rhymes. My cold is gone. Am perfectly well. I kiss you.

Yours P. Tchaikovsky

17. To Modest Tchaikovsky

Only the first half of this rather long letter was ever published before. It contains a very vivid description of the composer's feelings during a performance of his Fantasia based upon Shakespeare's drama *The Tempest*, in Paris in March 1879, by the orchestra of Edouard Colonne; and it gives a graphic and uninhibited portrayal of Tchaikovsky's erotic encounter with a homosexual prostitute whom he had met earlier.

Paris
26 February/10 March 1879
Yesterday was a day of very strong agitation. In the morning there was a concert at the *Châtelet* and the performance of *The Tempest*. The torments I experienced were the strongest proof that I should live only in

a village. Even that which was formerly my deepest pleasure, namely listening to my own compositions, has became a source of torture and nothing else. The condition in which I listened to *The Tempest* would seem to have guaranteed my utter calm. But it was not to be. On the evening before the concert, I began to suffer from diarrhea and nausea. My agitation crescendoed right up to the initial chords, and while they played I thought that I would die that very instant, such was the pain in my heart. And this agitation was not at all from a fear of failure, but because for some time each new hearing of any of my compositions has been accompanied by severe disappointment in myself. As if by design, right before *The Tempest* they played Mendelssohn's Reformation Symphony, and despite my terrible emotion I was constantly surprised by his wonderful mastery. I lack *mastery*. To this day I still write like a talented *youth*, from whom one might expect much but who gives quite little. More than anything, I am surprised how poor my orchestra sounds! Of course, my reason tells me that I somewhat exaggerate my faults, but this is cold comfort for me. They performed *The Tempest* quite well, although not in a first-class manner. The tempos were absolutely correct. It seemed as if the musicians were playing diligently, but without delight and love. One of them, to whom my eyes were riveted for some reason, smiled and acted as if exchanging glances with someone, as if saying "Excuse us that we are presenting you with such a strange dish, but we are not guilty: we are told to play and we play!" When the last chords were quite done, there rang out rather feeble applause, then it seemed as if a new salvo was gathering force, but here three or four loud whistles were heard, and then the hall was filled with cries "Oh! Oh!" that signified a favorable protest against the whistling, and then all fell quiet. I bore this without particular grief, but the thought was killing me that *The Tempest*, which I used to consider a brilliant work of mine, is essentially so insignificant! I immediately left. The weather was marvelous, and I walked continuously for a couple of hours, after which I came home and wrote Colonne a note in which I lied and said that I had only been in Paris for a day and therefore could not attend [the concert] personally. The note expressed sincere gratitude, and he really did perform *The Tempest* very well. Here I was considerably calmer, but I decided that I had to spend some time in *pleasures*. Therefore I dined quickly and went to search for *Luisa*. For some time my search was unsuccessful, until suddenly: it was she! I was unimaginably glad, for she really was quite attractive to me. We immediately turned into a deserted street and had an explanation. It turned out that she had not come to the *rendez-vous* that time because she had had a very unpleasant accident. A carriage had struck her on the leg and hurt it considerably. She was in bed for two or three days, and still walks with a slight limp. She suggested we go to her place. She lives immeasurably far away. We walked for a long time, then took an omnibus, then walked some more; moreover I spent the whole time engrossed in her chatter, as if it were the most wonderful music, and in general felt quite in love. Finally we reached *rue de Maine*. That is an area of petty tradesmen. On this and the following street, *de la Goite*, there was a mass of revellers, bar after bar, dancing halls with open windows from which music thundered. In order to get to his *mansarde*[87] it was necessary to enter an *assomoir*,[88] drink *une mante avec de l'eau frappé*, slip through a small door, then climb up a narrow and dark staircase leading to a tiny room with slanted ceiling and a window not in the wall, but in the ceiling!!! All the room contained was a bed, a sorry trunk, a dirty table with candle-stub, several pairs of tattered trousers and shirts hanging on nails, an enormous crystal glass won in the lottery. And nonetheless at that moment I felt that this miserable room was the focus of all human happiness. He (I can't use the feminine pronoun talking about that dear person) immediately showed me passport and diplomas, which fully proved the truth of all he had told me about himself. Then there were various *calinerie*,[89] as he put it, and then I became possessed with amorous happiness and the most improbable pleasure was experienced. With no exaggeration I can say that it has not only been a long time, but that I have almost never been as happy in that sense as yesterday. Then we went to some kind of entertainment: something between a *café chantant and a theater*, then we were in some cafe and drank a lot of beer, then walked for terribly long on foot, again drank beer, and parted at one in the morning. I was so exhausted by the mass of impressions, that I was not able to make it home and engaged a cab. Reaching home I dropped onto the bed and fell dead asleep, leaving Alësha a note in giant letters asking him not to wake me up before ten o'clock.

But I awoke at seven o'clock, with a terrible weight in my head, with tedium, with pangs of conscience, and with a full consciousness of the falsity and exaggerated nature of the happiness I felt yesterday, which, in essence, is nothing but a strong physical attraction founded on the fact that Luisa corresponds to the capricious demands of my taste and on his prettiness in general. However that might be, the youth has much that is fine in the root of his soul. But my God, how pitiful, how profoundly debauched he is! And instead of encouraging his improvement, I only help him to descend further downwards. I shall tell you at our meeting many charming details bearing witness to his naiveté combined with debauchery. Honestly speaking, he really should return to *Lyons*, where his father and mother have a hat shop. But he can't return other than as *a decent young man*, and for this he needs at least five hundred francs. I read his parents' letters, which show that they are decent people. As if by design, I shall have to leave without being in a condition to give him real help, namely send him to *Lyons*. I shall tell you about how radically mistaken I was in some of my calculations, or how Mrs. von Meck was mistaken in hers, but God grant only that I have enough money to get to *Berlin*. I have already written to Jurgenson,[90] asking him to wire me a transfer to a Berlin bank for five hundred marks in order to get to Petersburg.

I must leave quickly, and without delay I am departing the day after tomorrow, on *Wednesday*. As far as the failure of *The Tempest* is concerned, this has faded into the background and depresses me little today. *That is*, I mean the failure it evoked in me. I have reconciled myself to this based on the fact that, after the opera and suite,[91] I shall finally write a model symphonic composition. So, up to my last breath, it seems, I shall only strive for mastery and never achieve it. I lack something, that much I feel, but there's nothing I can do.

My head no longer aches. The weather is marvelous, and I have been walking like crazy. I breakfasted in a stylish restaurant. I send you a newspaper clipping on yesterday's concert. The newspaper is *Paris-Journal*.

Kisses.

Yours P. Tchaikovsky

Show Tolia this letter. I ask his forgiveness that he will have to read of my amorous adventures. Regarding *Abaza*,[92] I resolutely refuse to visit her.

KEY TO ABBREVIATIONS

GDMC Gosudarstvennyi arkhiv doma muzeia P.I. Chaikovskogo [The Tchaikovsky State Archive and House Museum], Klin (Russia)

LF P.I. Tchaikovsky, *Letters to his Family: an Autobiography*, (translated by Galina von Meck with additional annotations by Percy M. Young), (New York, 1981)

PB P.I. Chaikovskii, *Pis'ma k blizkim: izbrannoe* [Letters to his family], redaktsiia i kommentarii V.A. Zhdanova (Moscow, 1955)

PR P.I. Chaikovskii, *Pis'ma k rodnym* [Letters to relatives], redaktsiia i primechaniia V.A. Zhdanova (Moscow, 1940)

PSS P.I. Chaikovskii, *Polnoe sobranie sochinenii: Literaturnye proizvedeniia i perepiska* [Complete Collected Works: Literary Works and Correspondence] (17 vols.; Moscow, 1953-81)

TQM Alexander Poznansky, *Tchaikovsky: The Quest for the Inner Man* (New York, 1991)

TS P.I. Tchaikovsky, *Tchaikovsky: A Self-Portrait*, compiled by Alexandra Orlova; translated by R.M. Davison, (Oxford, 1990)

LETTER REFERENCES

1. To Anatolii Tchaikovsky. Archival reference: *GDMC*, A a3, no. 1088. Published in PR: 213–14 (with omission); *PSS*, 5: 389–90 (with omission); *PB*: 95; *LF*: 93–94 (partially); *TS*: 44 (partially).
2. To Modest Tchaikovsky. Archival reference: *GDMC*, A a3, no.1455. Published in *PSS*, 5: 49–50 (with omissions).
3. To Modest Tchaikovsky. Archival reference: *GDMC*, A a3, no.1465. Published in *PR*: 253–54 (with omissions); *PSS*, 6: 69 (with omissions); *TS*: 57–58 (partially).
4. To Modest Tchaikovsky. Archival reference: *GDMC*, A a3, no. 1467. Published in *PR*: 259–60 (with omission); *PSS*, 6: 75–76 (with omissions); *TS*: 58 (partially).
5. To Modest Tchaikovsky. Archival reference: *GDMC*, A a3, no. 1470. Published in *PSS*, 6: 110–11 (with omissions).
6. To Modest Tchaikovsky. Archival reference: *GDMC*, A a3, no. 1471. Published in *PSS*, 6: 130–31 (with omissions).
7. To Modest Tchaikovsky. Archival reference: *GDMC*, A a3, no. 1473. Published in *PR*: 280–81 (with omissions); *PSS*, 6: 138–39 (with omissions); *TS*: 66 (partially).
8. To Anatolii Tchaikovsky. Archival reference: *GDMC*, Aa3, no. 1109. Published in *PSS*, 6: 143–44.
9. To Anatolii Tchaikovsky. Archival reference: *GDMC*, A a3, no. 1110. Published in *PR*: 286–88 (with omission); *PSS*, 6: 151–52 (with omissions); *TS*: 69–70 (partially).
10. To Modest Tchaikovsky. Archival reference: *GDMC*, A a3, no. 1476. Published in *PR*: 288 (with omission); *PSS*, 6: 153 (with omission).
11. To Anatolii Tchaikovsky. Archival reference: *GDMC*, A a3, no. 1111. Published in *PR*: 289 (with omission); *PSS*, 6: 153–54 (with omissions).
12. To Anatolii Tchaikovsky. Archival reference: *GDMC*, A a3, no. 1112. Published in *PR*: 289–90 (with omission); *TS*: 70 (partially).
13. To Anatolii Tchaikovsky. Archival reference: *GDMC*, A a7, no. 1969. Published in *PSS*, 6: 155 (with omissions).
14. To Modest Tchaikovsky. Archival reference: *GDMC*, A a3, no. 1477. Published in *PR*: 294–95 (with omission); *PSS*, 6: 173–74 (with omission); *PB*: 124–25 (with omission); *LF*: 122–23 (with omission).
15. To Modest Tchaikovsky. Archival reference: *GDMC*, A a3, no. 1509. Published in *PSS*, 7: 401 (with omission).

16. To Anatolii Tchaikovsky. Archival reference: *GDMC*, A a3, no. 1210. Published in *PR*: 507–09 (with omission); *PSS*, 8: 34–35 (with omission); *PB*: 204–05 (with omission); *LF*: 199–200 (partially).

17. To Modest Tchaikovsky. Archival reference: *GDMC*, A a3, no. 1541. Published in *PR*: 547–49 (with omission); *PSS*, 8: 138–39 (with omission); *PB*: 227–28; *LF*: 221–22 (with omission); *TS*: 167 (partially).

NOTES

1. *PSS*, 9: 233–34.

2. E.g., Anthony Holden, *Tchaikovsky* (London, 1995).

3. James Huneker, *Mezzotints in Modern Music: Brahms, Tschaikowsky, Chopin, Richard Strauss, Liszt and Wagner* (New York, 1899): 90.

4. M. I. Chaikovskii,. *Zhizn' Petra Il'icha Chaikovskogo* (3 vols; Moscow-Leipzig, 1900–03); Modest Tchaikovsky, *The Life & Letters of Peter Ilich Tchaikovsky*, edited from the Russian, with an introduction, by Rosa Newmarch (2 vols; London, 1906).

5. The very first and, as it happened, the last time in the Soviet Union that Tchaikovsky's homosexuality was mentioned was in the notes to the first volume of the composer's correspondence with Mrs. von Meck: P. I. Chaikovskii, *Perepiska s N.F. von-Mekk* (3 vols; Moscow, 1934–36), 1:570–72.

6. *GDMC*, b10, no. 6363.

7. V. S. Sokolov, "Pis'ma P.I. Chaikovskogo bez kupiur: neizvestnye stranitsy epistolarii," in: *P.I. Chaikovskii: zabytoe i novoe* (Moscow, 1995): 118–34.

8. See my discussion in *TQM*: 184–85 and in Alexander Poznansky, *Tchaikovsky's Last Days: A Documentary Study* (Oxford, 1996): 9–22. Cf. similar conclusions independently reached by another scholar after his own study of the composer's archives in Klin: "It would be a profound mistake to believe that Tchaikovsky all his life suffered from his 'anomaly.' As can be seen in his letters, in the last decades of his life he achieved a happy psychological balance—after fruitless attempts to struggle against his nature." Sokolov, "Pis'ma P.I. Chaikovskogo bez kupiur," 121.

9. *PR*: 374. We did not include this very long letter in the selection, since its main bulk offers detailed advice to Anatolii on matters that relate exclusively to his circumstances.

10. A total of 972 letters of the composer's original correspondence with the twins are in this museum. Tchaikovsky's original letters to Modest of the period 1866–75 are preserved in the Manuscript Department of the Russian National Library in St. Petersburg.

11. For more on Tchaikovsky's relationships with Modest and Anatolii, see Alexander Poznansky, "Modest Čajkovskij: In his Brother's Shadow," in: *Internationales Čajkovskij-Symposium, Tübingen 1993: Bericht*, herausgegeben von Thomas Kohlhase, (Mainz, 1995): 233–46; *TQM*: 68–82.

12. Nikolai Rubinstein (1835–81) was the founder and the first director of Moscow Conservatory.

13. For more on the concerto crisis, see *TQM*: 161–64.

14. The relatives of his brother-at-law Lev Davydov.

15. Herman Laroche (1845–1904) was a music critic, a friend and fellow student of Tchaikovsky at St. Petersburg Conservatory, and one of the first critics to support the composer.

16. Nikolai Kondratev (1837–87) was a wealthy landowner and married homosexual, and Tchaikovsky's close friend.

17. Nikolai Hubert (1840–88) was professor of musical theory at Moscow Conservatory.

18. Cesar Cui (1835–1918): Russian nationalist composer, member of the Mighty Handful; Vladimir Stasov (1824–1906): prominent Russian music and art critic, supporter of (and coiner of the term) the Mighty Handful. Suggested to Tchaikovsky the program for *The Tempest*.

19. Nikolai Rimsky-Korsakov (1844–1908): this famous Russian composer was also a member of the Mighty Handful.

20. *Moia prokliataia bugromaniia* is the Russian original. The word *bugromaniia*, popular among the Russian homosexuals of that time, is derived from two words: "bugger" and "mania."

21. Anatolii's acquaintance in St. Petersburg.

22. A husband of singer Feodosia Velinskaia.

23. See *TQM*: 131–150.

24. Tchaikovsky had promised Lev Davydov that he would meet his sister Sasha on her way back from Switzerland with the children.

25. For more on Tchaikovsky's obsession with hands, see *TQM*: 310, 467.

26. "I accept her will as law"—Tchaikovsky's note.

27. For more on Tchaikovsky's decision to marry, see *TQM*: 181–92.

28. "What people will say."

29. Pyotr Okoneshnikov was a fellow homosexual in Moscow.

30. Pavel Gruzinsky was another fellow homosexual in Moscow.

31. A village near Kamenka.

32. "Very unwillingly."

33. Vladimir Shilovsky's country estate, near Kiev; Vladimir Shilovsky (1852–93): Tchaikovsky's Conservatory pupil and a fellow homosexual.

34. Tchaikovsky's seventeen-year-old manservant Alexei (Alësha) Sofronov (1859–1925).

35. For more on Tchaikovsky's predicament, see *TQM*: 181–92.

36. Mikhail Bek-Bulatov was a married homosexual in Moscow.

37. Wife of cellist Karl Davydov.

38. Fofa is the nickname of Sofia Ershova.

39. "I say 'but,' because I don't like small hands"—Tchaikovsky's note.

40. "Little and exquisite"—Tchaikovsky's note.

41. Porubinovsky was a student in the Moscow Conservatory.

42. Fellow homosexuals living in Moscow.

43. A fancy restaurant in Moscow.

44. Tchaikovsky fullfilled this request by composing his Violin Concerto in D Major (Op. 35) one year later.

45. Edouard Colonne (1838–1910) was a French violinist, conductor, and concert promoter.

46. Nikolai Tchaikovsky, an older brother.

47. Alina Briullova, Kolia Konradi's mother.

48. Konradi's family country estate, near Poltava in the Ukraine.

49. Kotek's lady friend from the Moscow Conservatory.

50. Sergei Donaurov (1838–97) was a composer and fellow homosexual; for more on Donaurov, see *TQM*:147.

51. Vladimir Meshchersky (1839–1914) was Tchaikovsky's schoolmate and journalist, also a fellow homosexual; for more on Meshchersky, see *TQM*: 366–68.

52. Vladimir Shilovsky married Countess Anna Vasilieva.

53. For more on Antonina Miliukova, see *TQM*: 204–14 and V.S. Sokolov, *Antonina Chaikovskaia: istoriia zabytoi zhizni* (Moscow, 1994).

54. "Let's not speak further about it."

55. Nikolai Bochechkarov (d. 1879): another fellow homosexual, and a close friend of Tchaikovsky in Moscow; for more on him, see *TQM*: 133–35.

56. Konstantin Shilovsky (1849–93): the older brother of Vladimir Shilovsky and an actor with Maly Theater in Moscow.

57. "Tfu, tfu, tfu"—Tchaikovsky's note.

58. Aleksandr Miliukov (1840–85): the elder brother of Antonina; Anastasia Khvostova was a society friend.

59. The most detailed description of the wedding day is found in Antonina's recollections; see A.I. Chaikovskaia, "Iz vospominanii vdovy P.I. Chaikovskogo," *Peterburgskaia gazeta*, 1 April 1894; reprinted in Sokolov, *Antonina Chaikovskaia*, 263–74, and translated into English: *Tchaikovsky through the Others' Eyes*, edited by Alexander Poznansky (Bloomington, 1998), forthcoming.

60. "She is not a difficult person."

61. Laroche suffered from chronic shortage of money and alcoholism.

62. Nikolai (Niks) Litke (1839–87): husband of Amaliia Shobert, Tchaikovsky's cousin.

63. Nikolai Konstantinov (whose stage name was de Lazari) (1838–1904): an actor and a society friend.

64. "Mother-in-law"

65. Tchaikovsky left Antonina on July 27 for one and a half months, traveling to Kamenka to stay with his sister.

66. Sofia Malozemova (1846–1908): pianist and professor at the St. Petersburg Conservatory.

67. Karl Davydov (1838–98): cellist and composer.

68. Mikhail Ivanov (1849–1927): composer and music critic at the newspaper *Novoe vremia* [*New Times*].

69. Vasilii Bessel (1843–1907): violist and music publisher.

70. Alexandrine Dolgoruky was a society friend.

71. A village near Kamenka.

72. Nikolai Davydov, brother of Tchaikovsky's brother-in-law Lev Davydov.

73. For more on the composer's sexual preferences, see *TQM*: 463–73.

74. Tania (or Tatiana) Davydova was Tchaikovsky's niece.

75. Vyshnitsky was Kamenka's acquaintance.

76. Emilia Pavlovskaia (1853–35): soprano.

77. After returning to Moscow the composer lived with his wife from September 12 to 24 only, before leaving her for good. For more on Tchaikovsky's "escape abroad," see *TQM*: 231–49.

78. Nikolai Tchaikovsky, the composer's older brother.

79. Olga Tchaikovsky, Nikolai's wife.

80. Georgii Kartsov, Tchaikovsky's nephew.

81. Ernest Renan (1823–92) was a French religious historian and philologist, author of *Vie de Jésus* (1863).

82. "France, the dream, the grave, the king."

83. August Gerke (1841–1902): Tchaikovsky's schoolmate at the School of Jurisprudence, member of the governing board of the Russian Musical Society.

84. For more on this "bizarre dream," see Henry Zajaczkowski, Tchaikovsky: "The Missing Piece of the Jigsaw Puzzle," *Musical Times, 5* (1990): 238–42.

85. Anna (Anette) Merkling (1830–1911): Tchaikovsky's cousin.

86. Vladimir (Volodia) Zhedrinsky was Anatolii's society friend.

87. "Apartment in the attic."

88. "A tavern."

89. "Tendernesses."

90. Pyotr Jurgenson (1836–1903): Tchaikovsky's music publisher.

91. The opera *The Maid of Orleans*, and The First Suite (Op. 43).

92. Iulia Abaza (d. 1915): a singer and wife of the Russian Finance Minister Alexander Abaza.

Part II
Essays

.

Music as the Language of Psychological Realism: Tchaikovsky and Russian Art

LEON BOTSTEIN

I.

By the early 1890s Tchaikovsky's preeminence as the leading Russian composer of his generation was nearly unquestioned, if not in his native Russia then certainly abroad. Anton Chekhov, in a letter from 1890 to the composer's brother Modest, gave Tchaikovsky second place as Russia's most significant artist after Tolstoy. Third place Chekhov assigned to the painter Ilia Repin.[1] Chekhov's triumvirate linked Repin with Tchaikovsky. Perhaps Chekhov was inspired merely by the great fame of the painter, who was better known abroad than any other Russian painter. As an artist, Repin would have been considered more allied to Musorgsky (whose portrait Repin painted at the very end of Musorgsky's life) and the "Mighty Five" than Tchaikovsky. But in fact Chekhov's pearl of effusive praise implied a somewhat counterintuitive insight—the utility of comparison between the art of Tchaikovsky and of Repin, and beyond Repin, with the character of late-nineteenth-century Russian painting, a comparison that sheds considerable light on the composer's work.

Outside of his native land, Tchaikovsky found more favor than his contemporaries with German, English, and American critics; unlike the music of the Mighty Five, Tchaikovsky's music was understood as offering something beyond another example of Russian exoticism. But during his lifetime, Tchaikovsky's international acclaim was perceived skeptically by some Russians; Tchaikovsky himself was painfully aware of the extent to which he was criticized for not being "Russian" enough by advocates of a strongly nationalist agenda, while at the same time he was often hailed abroad as the greatest distinctively Russian voice in music. The plausibility of the nationalist critique was not helped at home by the terms of Western European critics' appreciation. Karl Storck reiterated in 1904 what had become a cliché among many non-Russian critics, that "of all the Russian composers, only Tchaikovsky is truly at home in non-Russian, and particularly German, musical life."[2] The Viennese critic Gustav Schönaich, writing on the occasion of the first performance of the *Pathétique* in Vienna in 1895, noted, "he has shed the Russian more and more, he has developed to a Western European international musician. Nonetheless, the nationalistic element that remained with him benefited his art."[3] The apparent synthesis of a genuine national element with the presumed compositional norms of Western music led the critic Hermann Kretzschmar to prophesy aptly: "history will name him—despite the strange opposition of his fellow countrymen—as the main representative of the Russian school, not only because of the wealth of original Russian themes and motives in all his works . . . but also because of the indeterminacy of his artistic character."[4]

Tchaikovsky's popularity by the time of his death was indeed formidable, and as the praise given to him by the German critics suggests, the popularity of his orchestral music was not primarily due to its Russian qualities, but rather to the extent to which the Russian element was subsumed by a more apparently mainstream achievement. Tchaikovsky appealed to audiences outside of Russia with an immediacy and directness that were startling even for music, an art form often associated with emotion.[5] In 1913 Philip H. Goepp, the annotator for the Philadelphia Orchestra, called Tchaikovsky the "Byron of music." In his explanation of the Fourth Symphony, Goepp wrote:

> With Tchaikovsky feeling is always highly stressed, never in a certain natural poise. He quite lacks the noble restraint of the masters who, in their symphonic lyrics, wonderfully suggest the still waters that run deep. Feeling with Tchaikovsky was frenzy, violent passion, so that with all abandon there is a touch of the mechanical in his method. Emotion as the content of highest art must be of greater depth and more quiet flow. And it is part or a counterpart of an hysterical manner that it reacts to a cold and impassive mood, such as we feel in the Andante of the Fourth Symphony. The final quality for symphonic art is, after all, less the chance flash of inspiration than a big view, a broad sympathy, a deep well of feeling that comes only with great character. Nay, there is a kind of peril

in the symphony for the poet of uncertain balance from the betrayal of his own temper despite his formal plan. Through all the triumph of a climax as in the first movement of the Fourth Symphony, we may feel a subliminal sadness that proves how subtle is the expression in music of the subjective mood. There is revealed not the feeling the poet is conscious of, but, below this, his present self, and in the whole series of his works, his own personal mettle. What the poet tries to say is very different from what he does say.[6]

Goepp's analysis revealed a quite typical and curious mix of admiration and criticism.[7] Paradoxically, Tchaikovsky's effect on the hearer was explained in part by some implicit reference to artistic and compositional shortcomings. This strategy was similar to that employed by contemporary German critics, who consistently charged Tchaikovsky with apparent structural and formal weakness. They reproached him for an unresolved mixture of the classical and the modern, banality, triviality, and too quick and frequent reliance on coarse and merely coloristic effects.[8] The late-nineteenth-century critique of Tchaikovsky would anticipate a favorite tenet of Schoenberg and his adherents: that popular appeal was not a sufficient criterion of judgment, and that there was a crucial distinction to be made in music between ideas and structures that derive from the transformation of ideas on the one hand, and ornament, decoration, and mere repetition in music on the other. The former represented the essence of musical art and the latter its debasement.[9] Yet Kretzschmar studiously avoided such condescension. He saw the "full importance" of Tchaikovsky reflected in the symphonic music. Kretzschmar considered Tchaikovsky's orchestral music to "resemble atmospherical painting and the descriptions of folk life," and, referring to the later symphonies, he credited Tchaikovsky with offering "full images of life, developed freely, sometimes even dramatically, around psychological contrasts . . . This music has the mark of the truly lived and felt experience."[10]

The vexatious debate in nineteenth-century Western Europe concerning "program music" and the perceived dichotomy between narrative meaning (defined extra-musically) and the abstract and "absolute" character of instrumental music is well known. While audiences of the time embraced Wagnerism (and explicit forms of "realism" in opera, as well as their polar opposites, all side by side), musical taste vacillated between a penchant for extra-musical meaning (which helped fuel the popular demand for nationalist exoticisms from beyond Western Europe). Within the context of an allegiance to the idea that music was a universal language because of its unique non-denotative dimensions, Tchaikovsky's music came to occupy a special position. Not only was Tchaikovsky an enigmatic Russian master, but through his music, as Goepp and Kretzschmar suggested, the listener immediately engaged intense emotions and feeling. The act of listening became a psychological mirror connected to everyday experience, one that reflected on the dynamic nature of the listener's own emotional self. Tchaikovsky's symphonies opened for the listener a vista of emotional and psychological tension and an extremity of feeling that possessed relevance because it seemed reminiscent of one's own "truly lived and felt experience" or one's search for intensity in a deeply personal sense. Goepp directed his readers precisely to the extreme emotion in Tchaikovsky. Beware, subscribers to the Philadelphia Orchestra, Goepp seemed to be warning: with Tchaikovsky you will get more than mere entertainment and distraction!

Tchaikovsky spoke to the listener's imaginative interior life, regardless of nationality. If conservative critics during the mid- and late nineteenth century felt there was something dangerous and unsettling, if not subversive, in Wagner, they also claimed that there was in Tchaikovsky an aspect of violence and "hysteria" that threatened propriety and restraint. Tchaikovsky's music, heard within the highly respectable and dignified arena of the concert hall, attacked the boundaries of conventional aesthetic appreciation—the cultured reception of art as an act of formalist discernment—and the polite engagement with music as amusement. Nadezhda von Meck's enthusiasm for Tchaikovsky was in this sense not as exceptional or extreme as it was perceptive. Her attachment to the Fourth Symphony was not unusual in character. She understood it as reflecting "profound terrifying despair" and inspiring one to "take leave of your senses." This was an apt description of the response of audiences in Tchaikovsky's lifetime, as well as afterwards.[11]

The comparison between Tchaikovsky and Wagner is not a capricious one. Tchaikovsky's attitude toward Wagner was, as Rosamund Bartlett suggests, complex and ambivalent.[12] Wagner was certainly the most important musical innovator of Tchaikovsky's generation, but Tchaikovsky's deep interest in Wagner perhaps even exceeded the more proximate Russian enthusiasm spearheaded by Aleksandr Serov.[13] Tchaikovsky considered Wagner primarily a symphonist *manqué* whose theorizing led him astray, particularly in the arena of opera. Nonetheless, Tchaikovsky's written accounts paid homage to Wagner's greatness, and if the Russian composer maintained a compromised regard for Wagner, it may have been fueled by a mixture of envy and an unspoken sense of affinity. Tchaikovsky objected to what he saw as a predominance of density and incomprehensibility over complexity and meaningful subtlety in Wagner's music. Privately he confessed that he found parts of *The Ring* more boring and protracted than anything he had yet encountered.[14] Yet it is precisely Wagner's use of repetition with harmonic and orchestral coloration in *The Ring* that defines a kinship between Wagner and Tchaikovsky. Both composers managed to maintain elongated structural cohesion (as for example in the first movement of the Fourth Symphony) through the deft use of motivic restatement and emphatic repetition. Despite his criticisms, Tchaikovsky recognized Wagner's importance. He later became an admirer of *Parsifal* in particular, and even occasionally admitted to a Wagnerian influence in his own music.[15] In terms of the character of the musical fabric, Wagner was, like Tchaikovsky, a master of spinning enthralling narrative webs of internal psychological states through music alone, a master of realism (particularly psychological realism).[16] The emotional intensity of Wagner's music and its explicit associations with narratives of courtship, desire, and sexuality suggest a close comparison to Tchaikovsky, especially in light of the views of Goepp and his contemporaries.

Perhaps precisely because of the nearly self-evident psychological and emotional components of Tchaikovsky's music (foremost in orchestral works with overt literary and covert biographical programs, as in the case of *Romeo and Juliet*), much recent Tchaikovsky scholarship has focused on the connection between biography and music. Within the biographical, writers over the last two decades have carried on where Klaus Mann left off in his novel *Symphonie Pathétique*—focusing resolutely on Tchaikovsky's essential loneliness, despair, homosexuality, and failure to achieve lasting intimacy.[17] It has become standard these days not only to analyze the artistic achievements of nineteenth-century homosexual composers as the self-assertion of issues connected to sexual identity, but to deconstruct the critical vocabulary of the late nineteenth century as homophobic.[18] Insofar as Tchaikovsky's homosexuality was widely known (outside of Russia it certainly was not), that approach may be useful as a strategy in understanding the history of reception. However, to distill Tchaikovsky's achievement and success, and for that matter the reactions of his contemporaries to his lifework, into an expression of discomfort with his personal life is to circumscribe his accomplishment in as belittling a way as any type of homophobia. It also assumes that Tchaikovsky's sexual preference, in and beyond Russia, was tacitly or, as Goepp might have put it, subliminally communicated. Historically speaking, this is unlikely. The reaction of Goepp and other critics rather pinpoints something that listeners in the late nineteenth century recognized immediately: that Tchaikovsky's music embodied a drama of internal struggle with issues of intimacy and therefore sexuality, irrespective of sexual orientation. Tchaikovsky's popularity can be ascribed in part to the extent to which his instrumental music succeeded in this respect and indeed created the conventions by which music could conduct an internal dialogue on the part of the listener, regardless of his or her sexual preferences. When foreign critics observed that, unlike his contemporaries, Tchaikovsky transcended his Russian character, they were pointing to Tchaikovsky's adaptation of Western European compositional models to achieve a musical discourse of externalized psychological realism.

For all his hidden private life, Tchaikovsky was unashamedly frank about the internal workings of the heart and mind—particularly with regard to sexuality and love, passion and desire—with his closest correspondents, particularly his brother Modest and Nadezhda von Meck. In a letter to Mme. von Meck of February 17/March 1, 1878, he detailed his program for the Fourth Symphony. Significantly, however, the composer does so only after disputing the presence or importance of any explicit program.

Tchaikovsky begins with a description of the process of composition. He asserts an explicit link between the direct representation of feeling and music by calling his work "the musical confession of a soul in which many things have welled up and which by its very nature is poured out in the form of sounds." He then goes on to use the metaphor of a seed germinating and describes the ecstasy of an idea burgeoning into art: "Everything is forgotten, you become almost demented, everything within you trembles and pulsates." He proceeds to identify the conflict between outside interruptions as well as the "cold, rational, technical process" of composition and the organic consequences of inspiration.[19] Indeed, if one compares the first movement with this description, evidence of the process of composition as the composer described it can be heard in the way the music is structured, inclusive of abrupt shifts and interruptions and resumptions.

In his letter Tchaikovsky talks about a program only after first discussing the challenge of mediating inspiration based on internal states of mind with the stark, compromising necessity of formal compositional demands (in order to find proper means to communicate through music one's emotional experience). Then he proceeds with the now familiar program, which recounts the perception of fate, one's psychological state of mind, and the many permutations of feeling individual experiences. The first two movements, he suggests, are about the unadulterated state of depression.[20] In that context, it is particularly interesting to look at Tchaikovsky's reliance on repetition in those movements. The first movement's use of repetition provides a clue as to the difference in the strategies employed by Tchaikovsky and Wagner. What sets apart repetition in Tchaikovsky's Fourth Symphony—when compared, for example, to Anton Rubinstein's *Ocean Symphony,* whose use of a trumpet fanfare (first movement, 15 measures after letter B) suggests a direct historical link between the two works—is Tchaikovsky's brilliant manipulation of rhythmic displacement and fragmentation. If Wagner relied on repetition mitigated by harmonic inventiveness, Tchaikovsky managed repetition by utilizing subtle but powerful rhythmic variations. The 9/8 meter of the main body of the first movement provided the composer with a myriad of subtle transformations that never mask the repetition but provide each restatement or partial statement with renewed interest and dramatic function (compare, for example, mm. 159–293 to the extended exposition in mm. 28–104 in the first movement of the Fourth Symphony). The displacement of the melodic line, accents, and strong orchestral entrances and the overlays of duple and triple meter are emblematic of Tchaikovsky's manner of repetition. There is nothing comparable in the first movement of the *Ocean Symphony,* even though there is a distinct similarity between Rubinstein's and Tchaikovsky's procedures in bringing together discrete thematic units (compare 17 measures after letter G to letter K of the *Ocean Symphony,* first movement, with mm. 251–283 in Tchaikovsky's Fourth, first movement).

What the two first movements share in common can be further gleaned from their respective reception history. The *Ocean Symphony* was, like the Fourth, immensely popular—an audience favorite. But in Tchaikovsky's case the fundamental strategies of musical communication, including the emphasis on restatement, the use of sequences, and the reliance on thematic unity and coherence, transcend the mundane. Given the basic material and its realization, the encounter with rhythmic tension and variation makes Tchaikovsky's use of repetition not seem tiresome. In Rubinstein, on the other hand, repetition remains static. Tchaikovsky's dynamism, fueled by the deft use of rhythmic alteration and orchestral effect, allowed him to build sequences of intensity and achieve powerful points of arrival and release. This earned him the reputation of being the master of psychological narration through instrumental music—an achievement audible particularly in a less well known but excellent example of

Tachaikovsky's use of music to reveal the psyche, *Hamlet* (Op. 67), a relatively late work from 1888.[21]

The second movement of the Fourth contains little in the way of thematic transformation or variation. Rather, Tchaikovsky creates layers of restatements in which, despite repetition, the character of the foreground and background changes. In the many repetitions of the opening theme different dialogues are created (mm. 78–98, 199–218, 238–304) using the theme as a stable recognizable protagonist, even though it is sometimes relegated to the background. This technique is used also in the famous second movement of the Violin Concerto, written right after the Fourth Symphony. In the Fourth, it may appear that the woodwind writing above the theme is a decorative background, but in fact the fragmentary and novel music above the theme suggests the experience of distraction and daydreaming within the context of a consistent and overwhelming mood. The opening theme that dominates the movement indicates an ever-present and oppressive internal feeling. The second group (mm. 42–75 and 98–117) suggests the externalized reaction to this inner mood of despair. It is then followed by the F major section—a reminder of the external world to which the third and last movements refer, and that section functions as a brief respite. The movement returns to the initial sentiment, carried by the main theme, which once more reestablishes the musical and emotional background.

The experience of hearing provided by the second movement is based on nearly obsessive familiarity created by restatement without diminution. This parallels the real life experience of the listener who can locate through the music the free association of memory that allows one to drift from a dominant mood (e.g. depression) by distraction or connection, as well as to return to its power. The movement uses the "unreal" elapsed time defined by the formal framework of symphonic composition, to create, as in fiction, a realist illusion of a familiar internal psychological experience. That "real" time psychological experience is evoked by and located on the temporal grid of the slow movement of a symphony, just as it might be in a section of a novel. Listening achieves in condensed time what the reading of prose can accomplish in the equally artificial temporal space created by the writer, who effectively controls the pace and structure of narration. Tchaikovsky's brilliant achievement is the use of repetition with only slight variation, the marshaling of overlays of audibly discrete supplementary materials on a common ground, and the effective creation of rhetorical bridges between clearly demarcated sections. Precisely because there is no Brahmsian transformation, the listener is drawn convincingly into the artificially created illusion of the real experience of an emotional state of being. The listener judges the emotions to be as plausible, as intense, and as realistic as those he or she has experienced in real time.

By comparison, Brahms's penchant for the immediate and ongoing development of material and his resistance to unadulterated restatement may explain why Tchaikovsky found Brahms's music strangely cold and unemotional—a view many might today find odd.[22] Indeed, a comparison of the last movements of Brahms's Second Symphony and the finale of the Tchaikovsky Fourth—movements which might be said to share an affirmative extra-musical program—show how Tchaikovsky realized the emotional program, once again utilizing a transparent structure with an emphasis on dramatic restatements.[23] In the Tchaikovsky Fourth, the protagonist of the symphony, whose role is assumed by the listener, finds him- or herself caught in the web of his or her own internal struggle in the first two movements. He or she eventually is forced to turn to the outside world in order to find some exit from despair and finds that, as the composer put it, "it *is* possible to live."[24] The orchestral brilliance and uncomplicated sensibility of the last movement match the first two in a way the finale of the Brahms Second does not quite respond to the melancholy mood of the first two movements of that symphony. Even in so affirmative a moment, Brahms continues to deflect any expectation of regularity and externalized and obvious repetition.

Mme. von Meck's reaction to the Fourth, and Tchaikovsky's explanation of the work, suggest that audiences that for generations have made this work a repertory war-horse understood what was being communicated. Tchaikovsky's real triumph, in fact, was his expression of a disarmingly effective and direct form of psychological realism, using instrumental music. Paradoxically, that novel and unparalleled authentic mirror of the internal workings of one's being was uniquely derivative of the experience faced by Russian artists of Tchaikovsky's generation. When Western Europeans saw in Tchaikovsky an admixture of the universal and the exotic, and when Russian critics saw an inadequate emphasis on the national element, they were identifying, but for different reasons, the singular achievement of Tchaikovsky. That Chekhov should have praised Tchaikovsky is hardly surprising, since Chekhov's art, like Tchaikovsky's, combined the universally appealing and the uniquely local. The Fourth Symphony obviously possesses distinctly Russian features, evident in the last movement. Tchaikovsky was able to extract from the special circumstances faced by Russian artists—censorship, monarchical authoritarianism, an intense quarrel over national identity, ambivalence with regard to the relationship of Western Europe to Russia, enormous social and political movements, as well as the special dimensions of the Russian landscape and legacies of Russian history— a language of musical communication that used Western European models and transcended the particular (i.e., the Russian), without abandoning it.[25]

It is ironic that Carl Dahlhaus's classic study *Realism in Nineteenth-Century Music* does not discuss Tchaikovsky at all.[26] Indeed, Dahlhaus's lack of interest in Tchaikovsky seems to accept unquestioningly the legitimacy of a critque inherent in the extent to which Tchaikovsky became trivialized by his imitators and enthusiasts outside of Russia. Dahlhaus, by placing Tchaikovsky's music in the context of the debasement of his style, implicitly holds the original model responsible for the consequences. But Tchaikovsky may turn out to be the central protagonist of a particular form of realism in instrumental music that has its origin in Russian art and culture and that has turned out to have an overwhelming influence outside of Russia. In his novel *Smoke*, published in 1867, Ivan Turgenev (1818–1883) has the protagonist Potugin expound sarcastically on the absence of a distinctive Russian art. The painter Briullov and the composer Glinka come in for particular scorn.[27] The generation of Tchaikovsky, which followed that of Turgenev, was dominated by a conscious engagement with the creation of a Russian culture independent of but equal to the finest in the rest of Europe. An obvious route was advocated by the critic Vladimir Stasov and his many protégés in music and painting.[28] This approach entailed an explicit distancing from the West and the discovery and embrace of an authentic Russian heritage, which by definition would be more "oriental."

Despite his evident love of his homeland and his intense loyalty to the monarchy, Tchaikovsky resisted such an overt rejection of Western models and traditions. Like Turgenev and Tolstoy—and more to the point, like many of the painters of his own generation born between 1830 and 1845—Tchaikovsky sought to assimilate Western models into the Russian experience and emerge, as it were, back into the West with something that could not have been created there. Tolstoy's debt to the Western European tradition of the novel is well known. Of Chekhov's triumvirate of great Russian artists, both Repin and Tchaikovsky retained lifelong loyalties to Western European models. Despite the desire of Repin's contemporary critics and of later Soviet scholarship to turn him into the model of nationalist and "ideological" realism, Repin's deepest allegiance was to the work of Rembrandt and Velasquez. Repin's Tchaikovsky-like synthesis of the Russian and the Western European led, eventually, to a break with his once-ardent patron and advocate, Stasov.[29] As for Tchaikovsky, whose musical models were not Glinka but Mozart, Beethoven, Liszt and Schumann, Stasov and Cui approached him with skepticism typical of the explicitly nationalist Russian critics.[30] Tchaikovsky's operatic and orchestral music indicates his eclecticism in choice of subject matter and program. It ranged from the folk tale to Russian classical literature, from Schiller and Byron to Dante and Shakespeare.[31] In his own mind, the composer's love of Italy did not compromise his love of Russia, just as writing for the ballet did not. The ballet for which he wrote was not at that time a symbolically nativist Russian art form (though he helped identify it with Russian culture, an association still current among today's audiences).[32] By using his Russian experience within the compositional traditions of Western Europe, Tchaikovsky crafted a unique dimension of musical realism with far-reaching consequences on twentieth century musical culture in both the concert and popular arenas, as Dahlhaus reluctantly implied.

II.

One means of gaining insight into Tchaikovsky's music in both its structure and its effect on listeners is to accept as a hypothetical premise the usefulness of the concept of realism as an overt strategy and ambition on the part of the composer. Tchaikovsky's interest in literature was profound, and it should be noted that he was severely critical of certain forms of realist fiction, particularly that of Emile Zola.[33] Tchaikovsky also had little use for Dostoevsky, though he admired Tolstoy and Chekhov.[34] His distaste for certain species of social realism in literature, however, does not deter one from pursuing the matter of realism, which, as Erich Auerbach has pointed out, is not a unified or singular phenomenon.[35] In the visual arts, Tchaikovsky seems to have had less interest in and limited contact with Russian painters, despite the fact that Ilia Repin was deeply interested in music and like Tchaikovsky was a figure in the artistic and cultural milieu of both Moscow and St. Petersburg. Repin has been most closely identified with the nationalist group, partly because of Stasov's advocacy, and for his portraits of two of the Mighty Five (Musorgsky and Balakirev). But Repin's evolution as a painter in many ways resembled Tchaikovsky's development as a composer. Furthermore, the issues that engaged Russian painters were akin to the ideological and aesthetic debates among musicians. The listener in search of clues to Tchaikovsky's music may find edification not only by suggested links between the work of well-known Russian writers and Russian composers, but in the less obvious but equally important connections between Russian music and Russian painting. Russian painting has suffered more than Russian music and literature in its historical reception by the West because of the overemphasis within art history on the French tradition of the nineteenth and twentieth centuries. If music history is dominated by the seemingly normative universality of the achievements of German-speaking composers from Bach to Webern, the history of painting is equally crippled by a nearly obsessive attachment to the idea that it was French painters from David to Monet who set the course and standard of the visual arts throughout Europe well into the twentieth century.

In Russia the archetype of early nineteenth-century painters was, as Turgenev's novel suggests, Karl Briullov (1799–1852, Fig. 1). Pavel Fedotov (1815–1852) offers a mid-century benchmark from which we may consider two generations of painters whose work overlapped with that of Tchaikovsky. The painters whose examples are discussed here and who were nearly Tchaikovsky's contemporaries are Nikolai Gay (1831–1894), Ivan Shishkin (1832–1898), Vasilii Perov (1834–1882), Ivan Kramskoi (1837–1887), Repin (1844–1930), Vasilii Polenov (1844–1927), Victor Vasnetsov (1848–1926), and Vasilii Surikov (1848–1916). Two painters who followed Tchaikovsky's generation need to be taken into consideration as well: Isaac Levitan (1860–1900), Russia's greatest landscape painter, and Valentin Serov (1865–1911). The issues in Russian art represented by these painters offer a valuable context for an understanding of Russian music. A distinctly Russian contribution to the strategies of realism in art are foregrounded in three genres: portraiture, landscape painting, and historical painting. It is of course reductive to adduce exact generic counterparts between music and painting, but in terms of aesthetic impressions, certain basic correspondences are obvious. For example, if opera and dramatic symphonic music (e.g., the tone poems of Liszt) resemble historical painting in the breadth and elevation of subject matter, then the treatment of landscape similarly suggests large non-programmatic instrumental forms, insofar as the viewer's perspective of the landscape, foreground and background, as determined by the painter, is analogous to the listener's perception of contrasting motives and dominant themes as determined by the composer.[36] Portraiture, in which we may include the sub-genre of domestic and group scenes, suggests parallels to the intimacy and self-reflection encountered in chamber music. In general, looking at art in the nineteenth century may have paralleled, from the vantage point of the viewer, the experience of listening itself. Both were acts of internalized imagination. In the Russian nineteenth-century context, it may be argued that just as reading and listening can be understood as complementary historical phenomena influencing the function and understanding of music, so too must the visual experience be taken into account. In Tchaikovsky's work the role of ballet and opera suggests the significance of the visual. His attachment to real landscapes is well known. Generally, the intense interaction between the visual and musical arts in the generation after Tchaikovsky, the generation of Diaghilev, the *World of Art* movement, Scriabin and Stravinsky, all point to the importance of looking at connections between the visual and musical in Russia from the late 1860s to the early 1890s.[37]

Briullov[38] is significant because he was perhaps the first Russian artist to be known abroad. His *The Last Day of Pompeii* (1830–33) was his most famous work and for future generations embodied the extent to which a great Russian talent seemed to be entirely dependent on

Figure 1

European models, usually French and Italian. Nevertheless, beyond the historical genre, Briullov pointed the way to a more distinctly Russian sensibility in the field of portraiture. His self-portrait (1848; Fig. 1), done eighteen years after *The Last Day of Pompeii*, shows a freeness of brushwork, an intensity of color, and a melancholy psychology that would point out a direction for younger painters. Briullov's portrait needs to be compared to Fedotov's painting of *Nadezhda Zhdanovich at the Piano* (1849; Fig. 2). This is a fine example of Russian figure painting and portraiture of the mid-century in which the life of the privileged classes is depicted in an entirely candid but neutral manner.

Figure 2

From the point of view of the development of Russian realism, it is the work of Nikolai Gay that points toward a genuine breakthrough.[39] In Russian painting, portraiture and historical painting often overlap, partly because of censorship (which recalls how Verdi, for example, used historical plots to express politically subversive contemporary sentiments). In Gay's famous painting depicting Peter the Great and his son Alexei (1871; Fig. 3), the composition of the paint-

Figure 3

ing communicates not only facial expressions but the immediate psychological moment. The center of the painting is marked by the table, which is more brightly illuminated. Time and space are frozen, but with an intensity that is communicated in part by the perspective generated by the checkerboard floor. Rather than a specific historical evocation, the psychology of the two figures is detached from the historical personalities depicted. More than twenty years later Gay painted a shocking portrait of Christ in *Calvary* (1893; Fig. 4); here the horror, terror, and anguish of the son of God burst out of the painting's nearly expressionist surface. If there were a visual equivalent to the *Pathétique,* Symphony No. 6, it might be this painting. Christ becomes the ordinary individual experiencing profound suffering. As in the earlier Gay canvas, the psychological power is not limited to the portraiture but to the composition of the painting as well. The accusatory left hand, for example, undercuts the static character of the scene. The painting assumes a dynamic emotional power that includes a sense of motion towards the center of the canvas: the cluster of three figures surrounding the suffering Christ.

In Gay's generation it was Ivan Kramskoi (see Fig. 5, *Self Portrait,* 1867) who played the most significant historical role in helping Russian artists break away not only from academicism but from Western European models. In 1863 he organized thirteen artists into

Figure 4

the formation known as the Artel Khudozhnikov, the first break with the Academy. This split among Russian artists would eventually generate the most famous and long-lasting association of Russian painters in the nineteenth century, the so-called Wanderers, who found an important patron in P. M. Tretiakov. The tradition of portraiture, nascently visible in Briullov, reappears in Kramskoi, but the emphasis, as in the *Christ in the Wilderness* (1873; Fig. 6), is, like Gay, psychological. One should note here the starkness of the landscape, a characteristic that links Russian portraiture with Russian landscape painting. Whereas the self-portrait of Kramskoi of 1867 shows an affinity with Briullov, the two portraits, *The Unknown Woman* (Fig. 8) and *Portrait of Soloviov* (Fig. 7), 1883 and 1885 respectively, indicate the rapid evolution of Russian realism in portraiture. *The Unknown Woman*, perhaps Kramskoi's most famous painting, has sometimes been employed as a visual representation of Tolstoy's heroine Anna Karenina. The bleak landscape, which is nearly white, contrasts with the beautifully colorful and densely painted dress and hat. The center is the powerful and enigmatic face, painted in a manner that is nearly

Figure 5

Figure 6

Figure 7

Figure 8

hypnotic. There is an almost Mona Lisa-like effect, which permits the viewer to conjure a wide variety of psychological narratives in the act of viewing the canvas, just as he or she might in the act of listening.

Insofar as Russian painting developed an ideological agenda of social criticism beyond the intimate and psychological, Vasilii Perov's *Bachelor-guitarist* from 1865 (Fig. 9) offers a good example of the liberal political sentiments shared by Kramskoi and Perov. Kramskoi believed that painting in Russia needed to advance in the viewer an ethical conscience related to social and political realities. Inspired in part by painters such as Murillo, Perov stresses not so much the tattered garments and reduced status of his subject as his interior resignation.

Painters following Perov incorporated the traditions of politically sensitive portraiture into a larger narrative framework. The greatest examples of this direction are the three painters most directly contemporary with Tchaikovsky: Repin, Surikov, and Vasnetsov. Repin's

Figure 9

Figure 10

two most important paintings in this regard date from the 1880s: *Ivan the Terrible and his Son* and *They Did Not Expect Him*. The *Ivan the Terrible* (1885; Fig. 10) can be compared to the Gay paintings. But in Repin the psychological aspect of the historical drama is put squarely into the center of the painting. The frenzy and hysteria in the music of Tchaikovsky, as it was understood by its contemporary listeners, receive here visual equivalents. The comparison is not necessarily with an operatic scene but with wordless music. The eyes of the father and son, gazing in different directions and framed by streams of blood, made this painting as sensational to its viewers, and in nearly the same critical vocabulary, as Tchaikovsky's Fourth Symphony was to Nadezhda von Meck. The psychological element in this picture, perhaps more than in Gay's painting of Peter the Great, overwhelms any recognition of the historical moment. Viewers without knowledge of Russian history cannot but be drawn into the canvas by the way Repin realizes the figure of the son, his clothing, and the composition of the two figures in the center of the painting. The intensity and trajectory of emotion, suggested from the edge of the painting by the rumpled carpet, reject all placid and motionless tension. As if to pay homage to an earlier example of psychological realism masquerading as histori-cal painting, Repin relegates Gay's checkerboard floor to the back-

Figure 11

ground wall. In Repin's hands, psychological representation assumes a dynamism that is suggestive of musical time, drawing the viewer into the canvas as an active participant.

Repin's masterpiece of psychological realist painting is *They Did Not Expect Him* (1884–88; Fig. 11) in which seven figures convene, each adding to the psychological dynamic in a manner unique to each individual, but in composite creating a charged narrative whose actual events are left undepicted, hidden from the viewer. They can only be inferred. Unlike representations of history, the cause of the astonishment and reaction to the unexpected return of what can only be assumed to be a political prisoner is undisclosed yet clearly significant and explosive. But the political has been tranformed into the personal. The novelistic opportunities characteristic of Tolstoy are created in this magnificent painting; there are four layers of narration: the viewer, the first room, the second room, and the hint of the landscape beyond the house. The family photographs and pictures on the rear wall add yet another dimension to the possibilities of an extensive tale. The contrary motion by the woman in the foreground right, the protagonist to the left, the woman seated at the piano, the maid opening the door, the servant looking over her shoulder, and the two quite different children is almost contrapuntal and symphonic.

Figure 12

Repin's picture creates for the viewer an experience that can be understood as analogous to the act of listening to a large tone-poem or the reading of a novel. What is crucial here is that despite the multiplicity of actors, the painting is nearly monothematic. Each of the viewers in the painting repeats a similar emotion, but in a distinct way. The psychological perspective changes, but a unity is created by the event and by the uniform psychological power generated by the figure of the male protagonist and the way he is perceived and responded to by each of the figures in the painting. Once again, Repin achieves a simultinaeity: a sense of the immediate moment and a sense of elapsed time. As in music, past and future are suggested in the encounter with the immediate sounds of the present moment.

Turning to Repin's extensive work in portraiture: the extent to which his painterly skills are subordinated to the effort to characterize or to suggest the interior workings of the subject is evident in the portraits of Stasov (1883; Fig. 12) and Glazunov (1887; Fig. 13). These examples are chosen explicitly to indicate the eclectic range of Repin's affinities and technical skills. Like Tchaikovsky, Repin refused to be

Figure 13

limited by an ideological agenda. He considered aesthetic questions of form and craftsmanship to be normative and legitimately derived from Western European achievements. Whereas the Musorgsky portrait, like the Stasov, reveals a rough brushwork suggestive of the Russian nationalist celebration of raw power over foreign refinements, the Glazunov portrait has a much more Western European finish and virtuosic patina, one appropriate to Glazunov's emulation of Tchaikovsky's synthesis of the Russian and the European. If the Stasov portrait can be compared to the last movement of the Tchaikovsky Fourth, the Glazunov might be linked to the *Roccoco Variations*. Not surprisingly, it was in the late 1880s that Repin broke most decidedly from Stasov. His magnificent portrait of Mme. von Hildenbandt from 1889 (Fig. 14) suggests Repin's rejection of the nationalist agenda and a return to the style of Kramskoi's 1883 portrait. This full-length portrait reveals how much emphasis is placed on the psychological content, which in this instance is magnificently enhanced by the veil.

Figure 14

Through painterly means and technique clearly associated with Western European traditions, a melancholy, if not dark, psychological sensibility is what confronts the viewer. Compare this, for example, with the Fedotov portrait of four decades earlier.

Among Repin's famous and highly debated paintings is *The Zaporozhye Cossacks* (1880–91; Fig. 15). This picture is especially suggestive of how Russian historical painting, which was a unique extension of European historical painting, can be understood as a phenomenon parallel to Russian music, particularly programmatic symphonic music. Tchaikovsky's contemporaries who were painters mastered the art of complex motion and narrative in their massive historical canvases. In this particular case, Repin spent an inordinate amount of time researching the ethnographic materials. He painted many versions of this scene and had already completed another famous large-scale scene-painting, *The Procession in Kursk* (1880–83). The final version of Repin's depiction of the Cossacks is not strictly historical. Rather it is national, for the event is generic and not specific. It is monothematic in the sense of its subject matter. All the figures, as in *They Did Not Expect Him*, are oriented around the center figure writing the letter. What makes the picture so effective is not so much the composition, the deft manipulation of perspective, or even the obvious realism of the scene. Rather, the psychological characterization of each of the faces—Repin's capacity to evolve personality, mood, and emotional reaction—gives this painting its evident link to music. The subjects act not so much as participants but as listeners. This is a painting of psychological narration that uses slight but distinct alterations of a single mood and event, just as a Tchaikovsky symphony utilizes and re-utilizes motto-like themes and patterns and thereby develops large-scale experiences with clear dramatic anchors.

Figure 15

Two of Repin's favorite contemporaries emulated his example. Among the greatest nineteenth-century Russian paintings is Surikov's *The Boyarina Morosova* (1881–87; Fig.16). Here psychological realism triumphs in the context of a semi-historical narrative. The dynamism of the composition is directional, pulling the viewer forward. This painting is profoundly musical in its evocation of elapsed time. One can imagine the sled visually before it appears on the canvas. The sense of motion is the reverse of what one sees in Repin's *Ivan*. But as in *The*

Figure 16

Zaporozhye Cossacks, the mini-portraits throughout the painting provide the distinctive quality. The central guiding theme and point of energy is, of course, the protagonist. Here the Boyarina's gesture, which may have inspired the hand in Gay's *Calvary*, frames the fearsome depiction of fanaticism that determines the surrounding reactions, the postures of the figures, and therefore envelops the entire canvas. This is perhaps the closest one can come to symphonic portraiture with a Lisztian emphasis on a single unifying motive. Repetition is employed. What makes Surikov's painting analogous to Tchaikovsky is something also evident in Repin's *Cossacks*: the overt employment of evidently Russian materials and their ultimate subordination into the task of revealing non-national and non-specific human experiences. The realist depiction of Russian garb and character types provides the authentic detail for the building up of a large-scale complex composition. Yet there is no evident and overwhelming historical reference point. The national element is not used in the service of an ideology, but transcends it. As in Repin's Hildenbrandt portrait and Kramskoi's *Unknown Woman*, there are unmistakable hints as to the Russian character of the individuals. But as in Gogol and Turgenev, the national becomes a means and not an end. The psychological moment is what is crucially and consistently revealed.

The primacy of psychological narration through painting in late-nineteenth century Russia is underscored by another of Surikov's masterpieces, *Menshikov in Exile* (1883; Fig. 17). The composition is less complex than in Repin's *They Did Not Expect Him*, but the psychological moment generated by the four figures gives the viewer access to the internal workings of each individual in relationship to yet another implied external event. In this canvas Surikov creates the illusion of time moving quite slowly, of a largo or adagio sensibility, quite different from the illusion of rapidity in the *Boyarina Morosova*. Here in painting is what Kretzschmar found in Tchaikovsky: images of life dramatically organized around psychological events in response to truly lived experience.

Even in so blatantly folk-oriented and nationalist a painter as Vasnetsov, the unique capacity of Russian painters to make psychological depiction and narration the central objective of painting becomes evident. His early work, *A Game of Preference* (1879; Fig. 18), is a more daring version of the kind of painting practiced by Fedotov and Perov. This form of genre painting has as its subject multiple psychological reactions. The extent to which Vasnetsov concentrated on portraiture and the human condition is poignantly put forward by *Alionushka* from 1881 (Fig. 19). When one compares this with Kramskoi's *Unknown*

Figure 17

Figure 18

Figure 19

Woman and even his *Christ in the Wilderness,* one can identify a bridge between Russian landscape painting and portraiture. Vasnetsov's protagonist is not only psychologically alluring in the position of the head and body; the painting also suggests the interior musings of the figure by the extent to which her dress evokes the forest and the pond. The juxtaposition of the individual within nature in Russian painting is not limited to the rural environment as the Kramskoi portrait *The Unknown Woman,* set in the city, suggests. Landscape becomes an instrument by which the internal sensibilities of the figure are rendered more visible. When Vasnetsov turns his attention to historical and mythological subjects, as in *Three Princesses of the Underground Kingdom* (1884; Fig. 20) and *Knight at the Crossroads* (1882; Fig. 21), a deceptively simplified but equally compelling psychological narrative becomes the subject again with the aid of a carefully designed landscape. The element of repetition in the *Three Princesses* suggests a Tchaikovsky-like technique of

Figure 20

Figure 21

restatement. Vasnetsov's use of single figures, as in the *Knight* or
Alionushka, is reminiscent of the radical and striking choices in instrumentation by Tchaikovsky in the opening of the *Pathétique* and, for that
matter, his resolution of the work in its closing bars: solo instruments
assume intimate narrative power in the context of a massive structure
and sound texture.

The issue of emotional mood has been understood as central to
Tchaikovsky—his ability to evoke identifiable feelings as if there were

Figure 22

a psychological program or, in the case of the orchestral works based in literature, a mood derived from a single action or event. The large Russian historical or semi-historical narrative canvases, with their distinctive stories, can be compared to *Romeo and Juliet*, *Francesca da Rimini*, and *Manfred*. That Tchaikovsky was profoundly attached to the Russian landscape and to nature is well known. What may have appealed to him about that landscape was its darkness, density, and expanse, all of which seemed uniquely Russian, as was the quality of light. Western European commentators speak of an emotional frenzy and wildness in Tchaikovsky's music; the stark and uncultivated immensity of the Russian landscape permitted Russian landscape painters to generate a comparable emotional intensity through painting. This helped to transform landscape painting into an instrument of psychological realism. In Vasnetsov's *Alionushka* the landscape is subordinate to the narrative of the figure. The inverse of this pattern is Polenov's *Overgrown Pond* (1880; Fig. 22), which might be understood as a visual depiction of Tchaikovsky's own relationship to the Russian landscape. A solitary, hardly distinguishable figure is surrounded by nature, whose uncontrollable power has all but ruined man's effort to define it, to tame it, and to harness it. The great master of landscape painting in Tchaikovsky's time was Ivan Shishkin, who specialized in the depiction of forests and their interior. A great

Figure 23

example is *Sunny Day* (1895; Fig. 23). The thickness of the forest is nearly infinite, the struggle between light and darkness incomplete, and the overall effect is to render the viewer the solitary figure. But the landscape forces the viewer into psychological self-reflection, since the image of the forest is so consistent and so dense as to make the confrontation with it an act of psychological remembrance and exploration.

This unique potential in Russian landscape painting reaches its zenith in the work of Isaac Levitan. Here the painterly technique is an adaptation of Impressionism. Unlike Monet, however, Levitan communicates a nearly overwhelming sense of loneliness and the absence of sentimentality in works such as *On the Volga* (1888; Fig. 24), *Gloomy Day* (1895; Fig. 25), *Evening* (1889; Fig. 26) and even in the *Dilapidated Small Yard* (1888–90; Fig. 27). In *Dilapidated Small Yard*, Levitan uses his technical

Figure 24

Figure 25

Figure 26

Figure 27

virtuosity to create in two dimensions a sense of the almost oppressive insignificance of the human in the context of nature's power. He portrays decay and the process of life collapsing in on itself. The viewer is riveted by the center of the canvas. *Gloomy Day,* however, utilizes the horizon and the seamlessness of sky, water, and earth. Once again the viewer experiences something akin to the intensity of Tchaikovsky's emotionalism, inspired in part by the scale and power of the Russian landscape.

The primacy of psychological realism in Russian nineteenth-century painting can be understood as coming together in Valentin Serov, the son of the composer Aleksandr Serov and the youngest of the painters under consideration (his mother was an important personality acquainted with the Russian intelligentsia of Tchaikovsky's day). The portraits of Mamontov (1887; Fig. 28), Levitan (1893; Fig. 29), Rimsky-Korsakov (1898; Fig. 30), and Glazunov (1899; Fig. 31) imitate and extend a tradition that stems from Briullov. The illustration from *War and Peace* (Fig. 32) and *The Manor House* (1886; Fig. 33) repeat in an

Figure 28

Figure 29

Figure 30

Figure 31

Figure 32

Figure 33

Figure 34

attenuated manner the Russian tradition of psychologizing history and landscape. The adaptation and extension of Western painterly traditions into Russian painting are probably most evident in Serov's *The White Sea* (1894; Fig. 34), in which the self-conscious brushwork is uniformly applied as if to obliterate the realist distinctions between sea, land, and sky. This painterly innovation with its active surface conveys the same kind of overt emotionalism we often encounter in the non-programmatic music of Tchaikovsky.

III.

Nineteenth-century Russian art and music possess a distinctive history when compared to the art and music of European nations during the same period. The rubric of conscious nineteenth-century nationalism, the peculiar circumstances of the Russian intelligentsia and its development through the century, both in Russia and abroad, afford only a partial explanation for Russia's unique position. Certainly, the special character of Russian politics was significant, even for someone like Tchaikovsky, whose political views were quite conservative. The *Coronation Cantata*, however occasional its genesis, is a sincere expression of unabashed patriotism and allegiance to the monarchy. The liberal views of even his beloved nephew's contemporaries left Tchaikovsky somewhat skeptical.

In addition to these broad political factors, the contextual elements that inform the development of Russian painting and music are certainly the landscape, the light, the distinctiveness of the religion, and, from both a Western *and* Russian perspective, the orientalism of Russian history. The contrast between the cultural lives of the cities of Moscow and St. Petersburg is somewhat emblematic of the tug-of-war felt by Russian cosmopolitans between Western European and nativist tendencies. Both Repin and Tchaikovsky struggled without success to find a comfortable place in both communities, and both artists (Tchaikovsky more than Repin) felt continually drawn to travel abroad.

Among the peculiarities in Russian cultural life during Tchaikovsky's lifetime was the unparalleled dominance of a single critical voice, that of Vladimir Stasov. No nineteenth-century Western critic of music exerted as much influence on the visual arts, and no predominant critic of painting ever influenced music so extensively. It was Stasov who brought Musorgsky and Repin together. Indeed, Stasov's influence on Russian painting may have exceeded his influence on music. He was largely responsible for the advocacy of a nationalist, or rather a socially responsible aesthetic agenda. The challenge from Stasov's point of view was to write music that engaged the contemporary world and carried with it a distinct ideological program. That program was more than the vague ethical exhortations of the liberal sort characteristic of the 1860s and early 1870s in Russia. It represented a national objective: the creation of a Russian voice independent of the Western European and linked to the conception of an original folk heritage and history. Tchaikovsky did not think much of the Mighty Five whom Stasov championed. He thought best of Balakirev. Tchaikovsky's resentment of Cui's criticism of his music left Tchaikovsky disinclined to think of Cui's music as any more than superficial. Rimsky-Korsakov was clearly the most impressive member of the group, but like Borodin, whose talents Tchaikovsky recognized, there was something fundamentally uncultivated, raw, and ugly about Rimsky-Korsakov's music.[40] Whatever motivations lurked behind Tchaikovsky's dislike for Musorgsky, the most original of the Five, he was firm in his view that the appeal to truth and authenticity in art (even of a national sort) was not *per se* a sufficient surrogate for craftsmanship. Yet issues of cultivated taste (based in a Western canon), the development of technique, and the consideration of aesthetic criteria of judgment as autonomous of imagery and meaning (or program)— factors we normally consider to be formalist concerning structure, composition, brushwork, handling of form—were considered signs of a Western European bias by the advocates of a nationalist aesthetic. To them, Tchaikovsky's emphasis on craftsmanship revealed an insufficient nationalism and a susceptibility to foreign models. The same criticism would be made of Repin in the late 1880s.

It is a sign of the "cunning of history" that Russia confronted as early as the late nineteenth century an argument concerning the quality of art that the rest of Europe did not encounter until later in the twentieth century. Appeals to normative standards of judgment were deconstructed as flawed appeals to objective criteria of beauty and aesthetic value. When Repin took issue with the crudeness of some of his contemporaries in the Wanderers group, and they defended their aesthetic creations by an appeal to the authenticity of their reflection of the Russian soul and landscape, he was expressing a skepticism reminiscent of Tchaikovsky's doubt about many contemporary Russian composers. Stasov understood the greatness of Tchaikovsky's talent, as he did Repin's. His criticism did not reveal so much about Tchaikovsky as it did Stasov's own defensiveness regarding nationalist composers and his failure to win Tchaikovsky over to the nationalist agenda. Stasov accused Tchaikovsky of poor workmanship, overwriting, and the lack of genuine inspiration, of being the victim of "academic training" and subject to the influence of that notorious Europeanizer, Anton Rubinstein.[41] For Stasov it was not that Tchaikovsky lacked technique, but that he had failed to tap into the only legitimate source of inspiration, the nationalist voice. By using the language of "technique," Stasov rhetorically appropriated the vocabulary that Tchaikovsky himself used against his contemporaries. By asserting that Tchaikovsky lacked the very qualities that the Mighty Five were accused of not having, Stasov deflected the allegation of poor workmanship. Yet Western European critics agreed that it was Tchaikovsky, of all the Russian composers of his generation, who from the European point of view possessed the best technical facility.

At the heart of the conflict between nationalist and academic and Western European influences was not only a definition of beauty or an appeal to a transcendent aesthetic, but a conception of what realism meant as an aesthetic strategy. To what extent were music and painting able to penetrate surface reality and not only mediate overt meaning, but discover hidden meaning in the external world? For Tchaikovsky and Repin, the mere depiction and narration of naturalist truths failed to realize an inherent power in art to pierce the veil of surface realism. The Russia in which Tchaikovsky worked was defined by a rigorous denial of freedom and a fear of absolute and arbitrary state power. Hidden communication in the guise of art was a cultural habit essential for survival. The reality beneath the surface became the proper subject of art.

Impressionism and later Expressionism are explicit engagements with the realist tradition whose claims argue for the special capacity of art to be realistic well beyond the surface of what we might term the photographic or the documentary. In Russia, however, where a simplified conception of realism tied to the national agenda resulted in a kind of immediate and self-consciously primitive authenticity, as in the depiction of peasants on the Russian landscape, a reductive conception of realism, sometimes termed ideological realism, thrived. At the same time, Tchaikovsky and Repin, and later Glazunov and Valentin Serov, who harbored a continuing allegiance to Western canons and standards of technique and craftsmanship and models, found a way to advance to a different definition of realism. Tchaikovsky spent a considerable portion of his career writing opera and explicitly programmatic music. The influence of Liszt is palpable, but Tchaikovsky's achievement transcends the model, particularly in symphonic music. As he well understood from his close study of Mozart and his rigorous academic schooling, music as defined by the traditions of Viennese classicism was not, strictly speaking, a denotative or representative art form. Even with the early Romantics such as Mendelssohn and Schumann, the capacity to deliver a literary or pictorial program through instrumental music to an audience seemed contingent on the command by the composer of purely formalist strategies, such as developing variation, thematic transformation, and a mastery of sonata form. The musical audience in the nineteenth century was already tutored to expect certain patterns of musical discourse, which by definition were artificial and not in any way realistic. This is what fundamentally differentiated the musical audience from the audiences for painting and literature in the nineteenth century. At the same time, listeners and amateurs sought (as much as readers and museum and gallery visitors), a deeper reflective meaning, a transfiguration of the everyday through the manipulation of the illusion of realism by the artist. Imagery or plot were the grid on which a deeper experience could be had. The formal traditions and expectations of concert music offered the same opportunity to Tchaikovsky. What Tchaikovsky and Repin shared was the conviction that the Western European tradition of art could be appropriated and applied in the Russian context and lead to the capacity to penetrate to a different level of realist experience.

Alexander Poznansky, in his biographical study of Tchaikovsky, makes the point repeatedly that the tradition of over-intense expressiveness in letter writing, and in particular Tchaikovsky's almost embarrassingly effusive expression of emotion, are not entirely uncharacteristic of his generation.[42] In a climate of censorship and political unfreedom marked by autocracy, the personal became a screen, if not an indirect forum, for a wider range of emotion than one might expect. In the absence of an effective outlet for political expression, in other words, the intimate became inherently political. Art that seemed only to be about personal emotion and life or even aesthetics became explicitly political, and one of the few tolerated frameworks for public and therefore political discourse. Both Tchaikovsky and Repin used a wide variety of surface realist subject matter, both Russian and non-Russian, to achieve a level of communicative meaning that has as its deeper content the intensity of emotion and psychological insight peculiar to the predicament of Russian artists and writers and their audience. Literature, opera, and painting had more severe limitations because of their susceptibility to facile interpretation and censorship. As in music, however, the expression of feeling in personal letter writing, restricted only to the expression of desire, emotion, and passion, seemed inherently apolitical. Therefore it was a powerful mechanism through which to depict or transmit a level of experience and response to life that was ultimately realistic and true beneath the surface of events. When Tchaikovsky's music traveled beyond the Russian border, its intensity and effectiveness transcended the surface allusions to national tradition and became a language of psychological realism that indelibly changed the fundamental expectations of listeners and the clichés of musical expression and taste.

If early twentieth-century musical modernism was a reaction to the perceived sentimentalities and excesses of Romanticism, it remains the uncomfortable psychological penetration of Tchaikovsky that still continues to irk modernists. Like a narcotic, the apparent accessibility and appeal of Tchaikovsky's music seems to Western European and American modernists just as dangerous, ugly, and coarse as the appeal to national authenticity in nineteenth-century Russia by nationalist artists seemed to Tchaikovsky. As Tchaikovsky's example was turned into a cliché, it inspired many composers to reject the language of late Romanticism and willingly fall prey to the accusation that their music was abstract, cold, and hostile to the audience. In this sense twentieth-century modernism can be seen as a dialectical response to Tchaikovsky's successful penetration of the psyche of his listeners. Ultimately, the twentieth century reaction to the achievements of psychological realism through music was a retreat (or advance) into a high-minded and assertive formalism away from music as a public discourse on intimacy.

Tchaikovsky paved the way, among other things, for the intermediate stage of musical expressionism at the *fin de siècle*. Using the instrumental forms of the Western European tradition, including the tone poem, Tchaikovsky manipulated formal expectations to create instrumental music that has as its subject the narrative of the spectrum of interior emotion and feeling in the encounter with everyday life. In Tchaikovsky's hands, the apex of music as a realist art takes as its subject the individual's inner life.

NOTES

1. Quoted in David Brown, *Tchaikovsky. The Final Years 1885–1893* (New York, London: Norton, 1991), p. 225. It is well known that Tchaikovsky was flattered by Tolstoy's interest in his music. Tolstoy admired Tchaikovsky, particularly the Andante from the String Quartet No. 1, Op. 11, which had brought tears to the writer's eyes, a fact of which the composer was truly proud. See Alexander Poznansky, *Tchaikovsky. The Quest for the Inner Man* (New York: Schirmer, 1991), p. 191. Repin, despite a break with Tolstoy's later views on art, also admired the writer. He visited him and painted him on more than one occasion. See *Ilja Repin. Malerei. Graphik* (Leningrad: Aurora-Kunstverlag, 1985), ill. pp. 147–151, and Elizabeth Kridl Valkenier, *Ilya Repin and the World of Russian Art* (New York: Columbia University Press, 1990), pp. 139–142, 146, 153–154.

2. Karl Storck, *Geschichte der Musik* (Stuttgart: Muth'sche Verlagshandlung, 1910), p. 777.

3. Gustav Schönaich, "Peter Iljitsch Tschaikowsky," *Neue Musikalische Presse* IV/10 (1895): 1–2.

4. Hermann Kretzschmar, *Führer durch den Konzertsaal*, vol. 1 (Leipzig: Breitkopf & Härtel, 1919), p. 600.

5. See for example the attitudes in the many popular biographies which came out in the two decades after the composer's death: "Aus dem Leben Peter Tschaikowskys" in the *Neue Musikzeitung* XXI/21 (1900): 257–258; continued in nos. 22 (272) and 24 (292–294); and Otto Keller, *Tchaikowsky. Ein Lebensbild* (Leipzig: Breitkopf & Härtel, 1914). English enthusiasm for Tchaikovsky reveals the same formula—an embrace of the Russian element with the recognition of the "consummate art" with which the "national element" is expressed. The English also recognized the presence of emotional intensity with sexual overtones. One English critic, Joseph Bennett, writing on the Fourth Symphony, noted that the second movement "came as an expression of pure feeling" that "best vindicated his country's music." Other critics noted the "wild, restless and melancholy" characteristics and praised, as George Bernard Shaw put it (if not ironically, then revealingly, in retrospect), Tchaikovsky's "freedom from the frightful effeminacy of most modern works of the romantic school." See Gerald Morris, *Stanford, The Cambridge Jubilee and Tchaikovsky* (London: David and Charles, 1980), pp. 354–358.

6. Philip H. Goepp, *Symphonies and Their Meaning*, 3rd. vol., *Modern Symphonies* (Philadelphia, London: J.B. Lippincott, 1913), pp. 115–116.

7. See for example the treatment of Tchaikovsky by New York critics Richard Aldrich, the critic for *The New York Times*, and Paul Rosenfeld, the critic of *The Dial*. Rosenfeld, like Goepp, wrote of the composer's "hysteria and energy" (comparing him to Rachmaninoff), and Aldrich commented on the "pathos" and the "feverish" element. Both critics clearly set the composer apart from the Russian nationalists as more of an "intellectualist," as Rosenfeld put it. Richard Aldrich, *Concert Life in New York 1902–1923* (New York: Putnam, 1941), pp. 364–365, and passim, and Paul Rosenfeld, *Musical Portraits* (New York: Harcourt Brace, 1920), pp. 165 and 171 .

8. See Emil Naumann, *Illustrierte Musikgeschichte. Die Entwicklung der Tonkunst von den frühesten Anfängen bis auf die Gegenwart*, vol. 2 (Berlin, Stuttgart: Spemann), p. 1101; Hans Merian, *Geschichte der Musik im Neunzehnten Jahrhundert* (Leipzig: Seemann, 1902), p. 705; and the review of the first Vienna performance of *Eugen*

Onegin by Robert Hirschfeld in the *Neue Musikalische Presse* VI/47 (1897): 2–3. An overview of the topic is provided by Ljudmila Korabel'nikova, "Čajkovskij im Dialog der Zeitgenossen," in Thomas Kohlhase (ed.), *Čajkovskij-Studien I. Bericht des Internationalen* Čajkovskij-Symposiums Tübingen 1993 (Mainz: Schott International, 1995), pp. 187–198.

9. See Arnold Schoenberg, "Criteria for the Evaluation of Music," in *Style and Idea. Selected Writings of Arnold Schoenberg*, Leonard Stein, ed., Leo Black, trans. (London: Faber & Faber, 1975), p. 131. Here Schoenberg takes Tchaikovsky to task for his reliance on repetition. See also Schoenberg's letter to Fritz Stiedry dated August 31, 1940, in which "Tchaikovsky-like" becomes an epithet of contempt, in Josef Rufer, *Das Werk Arnold Schönbergs* (Kassel: Bärenreiter, 1959), p. 20.

10. Kretzschmar, *Führer durch den Konzertsaal*, p. 602.

11. Edward Garden, Nigel Gotteri (eds.), *'To My Best Friend.' Correspondence between Tchaikovsky and Nadezhda von Meck,* Galina von Meck, trans. (Oxford: Clarendon Press, 1993), p. 195.

12. See Rosamund Bartlett, *Wagner & Russia* (Cambridge: Cambridge University Press, 1995), pp. 41–42; and Peter Tschaikovsky, *Musikalische Erinnerungen und Feuilletons* (Berlin: Harmonie Verlagsgesellschaft), p. 124.

13. See Alexander Serow, *Aufsätze zur Musikgeschichte* (Berlin: Aufbau, 1955), pp. 328–329.

14. Letter to his brother Modest, 20 August 1876, quoted in David Brown, *Tchaikovsky. The Crisis Years 1874–1878* (New York, London: Norton, 1983), p. 97; and Bartlett, *Wagner & Russia*, p. 41.

15. For example, he readily admits the influence of the *Nibelungen* on *Francesca da Rimini* in a letter to Taneev (8 April 1878); quoted in Brown, *The Crisis Years*, p. 108; also see Bartlett, *Wagner & Russia*, p. 42.

16. It would be impossible, if not inappropriate, to try to unravel here the many dimensions of the issue of so-called realism in music. Apart from the extensive recent philosophical literature on how music can or cannot represent or describe, one has to take into account the historical context of listening. For example, in the cases of Franz Liszt and certainly Richard Strauss, the use, avoidance, and adaptation of the listener's expectations vis-à-vis sonata form, as well as the explicit reference to past repertoire and to what had emerged as clichés of musical expression, particularly in Beethoven, were essential aspects of the capacity of a piece of music to narrate, for example, as is now the case in film and television music. The extent to which music can signal extra-musical meaning to the listener is historically contingent, well beyond any normative discussion of the "essence" of music. The dependence of advocates of "program" symphonic music on classical compositional traditions was, through the expectations and habits of the listener, as strong as Brahms's debt to the past.

17. See the first unrevised German text of the novel in Klaus Mann, *Symphonie Pathétique. Ein Tschaikowsky-Roman* (Reinbek/Hamburg: Rowohlt, 1996).

18. For an excellent and provocative example of the synthesis of the biographical and the analytical see Timothy Jackson, "Aspects of Sexuality and Structure in the Later Symphonies of Tchaikovsky," *Music Analysis* 14:1 (1995): 3–25; the homosexuality issue is present in Alexandra Orlova, *Tchaikovsky. A Self-Portrait*, R.M. Davison, trans. (Oxford, New York: Oxford University Press, 1990) and Poznansky, *Tchaikovsky. The Quest for the Inner Man.*

19. Garden, Gotteri, *'To My Best Friend,'* p. 184.

20. Ibid., pp. 185–187.

21. The editions used are Peter I. Tchaikovsky, *Symphony No. 4 in F minor, Op. 36* (London: Edition Eulenburg Ltd.); and Anton Rubinstein, *Symphony No. 2 in C major, "Ocean," Op. 42*, reprint of the 1857 version (Boca Raton: Kalmus).

22. See Tchaikovsky, *Musikalische Erinnerungen und Feuilletons*, p. 34.

23. For a detailed discussion allied with this view of Brahms's Second Symphony see Reinhold Brinckmann, *Late Idyll. The Second Symphony of Johannes Brahms*, Peter Palmer, trans. (Cambridge, Mass., London: Harvard University Press, 1995).

24. Garden, Gotteri, '*To My Best Friend*,' p. 187.

25. A discussion of the Fourth Symphony in its historical context is provided, among others, by Susanne Dammann, "Überlegungen zu einer problem-geschichtlichen Untersuchung von Čajkovskijs 4. Sinfonie," in *Čajkovskij-Studien I*, pp. 87–102.

26. Carl Dahlhaus, *Realism in Nineteenth-Century Music*, Mary Whittall, trans. (Cambridge: Cambridge University Press, 1985), p. 101; also Dahlhaus, *Klassische und Romantische Musikästhetik* (Laaber: Laaber, 1988), p. 198.

27. See Ivan Turgenev, *Smoke*, Constance Garnett, trans. (Turtle Point Press, 1995), p. 101. Tchaikovsky read and admired the book. See Brown, *Tchaikovsky. The Early Years 1840–1874* (New York: Norton, 1978), p. 120.

28. See Gerald Abraham, "Vladimir Stasov: Man and Critic," in: Abraham, *Essays on Russian and East European Music* (Oxford: Clarendon Press, 1985), pp. 99–112; as well as Stasov's own writings in Stasov, *Izbrannye sochineniia* (Selected works), 3 vols., P. T. Shchipunov, ed. (Moscow: Iskusstvo, 1952).

29. See Valkenier, *Ilja Repin*, pp. 114–116, 123, 136–137.

30. See Stuart Campbell (ed. and trans.), *Russians on Russian Music 1830–1880* (Cambridge: Cambridge University Press, 1994), p. 250 (Cui) and pp. 196–199, in which Stasov makes a clear distinction between Tchaikovsky and Balakirev and Rimsky-Korsakov. As to Tchaikovsky's debt to Schumann, it may be from him that Tchaikovsky found an example of how rhythm could be used in a subtle but complex manner.

31. It should be noted that in Slavic nations in the late nineteenth century the translation of Shakespeare into native languages permitted Shakespeare to assume an importance as a vehicle of nationalist self-assertion. Balakirev and Dvořák, for exam-ple, wrote music for productions of Shakespeare that carried distinct nationalist over-tones. A "Russian" element can be heard in *Hamlet, The Tempest* and *Romeo and Juliet* just as it can be (as Cui noted) in *Francesca da Rimini*, a work based on Dante. See also James H. Billington, *The Icon and the Axe, An Interpretive History of Russian Culture* (New York: Vintage Books, 1970), pp. 352–358.

32. For the development of Russian ballet see the introductory chapter, "Some Traditions," in Roland J. Wiley, *Tchaikovsky's Ballets. Swan Lake, Sleeping Beauty, Nutcracker* (Oxford: Clarendon Press, 1985), pp. 1–23.

33. Tchaikovsky dismisses Zola's realism wholesale in a letter to Bob Davydov from Paris, quoted in David Brown, *Tchaikovsky. The Final Years 1885–1893* (London, New York: Norton, 1991), pp. 393–394. However, his opinion of Zola varied accord-ing to mood. For example, he considered *Germinal* a "horrifying nightmare" (letter to Modest, quoted in ibid., p. 143) but "admired greatly" *La Débâcle* (letter to Modest, quoted in ibid., p. 394).

34. For his attitude to Russian literature see Rolf D. Kluge, "Čajkovskij und die literarische Kultur Russlands," in *Čajkovskij-Studien I*, pp. 165–175. For his opinion of Dostoevsky see also Brown, *Tchaikovsky. The Years of Wandering 1878–1885* (New York: Norton, 1986), p. 68. As to painting, one curious reference is Tchaikovsky's apparent affection for Gutave Doré's illustration of Dante (letter to Modest Musorgsky. Cited in Brown, *The Crisis Years*, p. 107).

35. See Erich Auerbach, *Mimesis. Dargestellte Wirklichkeit in der Abendländischen Literatur* (Bern, Munich: Francke, 1964).

36. It should be noted that Liszt's *Hunnenschlacht* from 1857, a tone poem for orchestra, was inspired by the work of the historical painter Wilhelm von Kaulbach.

37. See Camilla Gray, *The Russian Experiment in Art 1863–1922*, revised and enlarged by Marian Burleigh-Motley (London: Thames and Hudson, 1986). On the matter of visual listening in the nineteenth century, see Leon Botstein,"Hearing is Seeing: Thoughts on the History of Music and the Imagination," *The Musical Quarterly*, 79:4 (Winter 1995): 581–589.

38. This discussion of Russian painters is based on the following publications: Gray, *The Russian Experiment in Art* (cited above); *Three Centuries of Russian Painting* (St. Petersburg: Kitezh, 1994); *Ilja Repin. Malerei. Graphik* (cited above); I. E. Grabar, *Repin*, 2 vols. (Moscow: Izogiz, 1937); Valkenier, *Ilya Repin and the World of Russian Art* (cited above); Vladimir Petrow, *Isaac Levitan* (St. Petersburg: Khudoshnik Rossii, 1992); A. K. Lazuko, *Victor Vasnetsov* (Leningrad: Chudoshnik RSFSR, 1990); Dmitry Sarabyanov, *Valentin Serov. Paintings. Graphic Works. Scenography* (Leningrad: Aurora, 1982); *Valentin Serov v vospominaniiakh, dnevnikakh i perepiske sovremmenikov* (V. Serov in the reminiscences, diaries, and correspondence of his contemporaries), I. S. Zilbershtein and V. A. Samkov, eds., 2 vols. (Leningrad: Khudozhnik RSFSR, 1971); *Valentin Serov v perepiske, dokumentakh i interv'iu* (V. Serov in correspondence, documents, and interviews), I. S. Zilbershtein and V.A. Samkov, eds. (Leningrad: Khudozhnik RSFSR, 1985); Lev Tolstoy, *Voina i Mir,* 2 vols. (Moscow, Leningrad: 1960); *Ivan Shishkin. 1832–1898* (St. Petersburg: Aurora, 1996); X. Antonova, ed., *The Tretyakov Gallery Moscow: A Panorama of Russian and Soviet Art* (Leningrad: Aurora, 1983).

39. One indication of the importance of Gay in the development of psychological realism as a central achievement of Russian nineteenth-century painting can be gleaned from Nikolai Iaroshenko's 1890 portrait, a powerful evocation the the isolation and loneliness of the artist and the predicament of the Russian artist in relationship to the act of painting and the choice of its subjects. The painter is between an open book and an unfinished canvas. His interior world and ambitions as an artist are only tenuously connected to the external world of politics and career by the strange and alluring walking stick with its shadow leaning against the canvas. See *Three Centuries of Russian Painting* op cit. The painting is in The Russian Museum in St. Petersburg.

40. See Victor I. Seroff, *Das Mächtige Häuflein. Der Ursprung der Russischen Nationalmusik* (Zurich: Atlantis, 1963), pp. 163–164; and Tchaikovsky's letter to Mme. von Meck from December 14, 1877/January 5, 1878 in Garden, Gotteri, *'To My Best Friend'*, p. 121. Tchaikovsky's relationship with the Mighty Five is also discussed in the article by Marek Bobeth, "Čajkovskij und das *Mächtige Häuflein*," in *Čajkovskij-Studien I*, pp. 63–85.

41. Vladimir V. Stasov, "Twenty-five Years of Russian Art: Our Music," in Stasov, *Selected Essays on Music*, Florence Jonas, trans. (London: Barrie & Rockliff, The Cresset Press, 1968), p. 111.

42. See Poznansky, *Tchaikovsky. The Quest for the Inner Man*, pp. XVII, 13, 69.

Line of Succession:

Three Productions of

Tchaikovsky's *Sleeping Beauty*

JANET E. KENNEDY

In November 1921, when Sergei Diaghilev opened his spectacular London production of *Sleeping Beauty*, the souvenir program contained Léon Bakst's account—possibly fictional—of a face-to-face meeting with Tchaikovsky at the dress rehearsal for the ballet's St. Petersburg premiere in 1890. Overwhelmed by Tchaikovsky's presence, Bakst tells us, he managed to utter only a few inarticulate words: "I find the music of *La Belle au bois dormant* excellent." Three decades later he redeemed this youthful awkwardness with a fervid description of that long-ago occasion: "Unforgettable matinée! For three hours I lived in a magic dream, intoxicated by fairies and princesses, by splendid palaces, streaming with gold, by the enchantment of the fairy-tale. . . . All my being was in cadence with those rhythms, with the radiant and fresh waves of beautiful melodies, already my friends." The Mariinsky Theater, thronged with spectators of the highest rank, was itself a fairy tale: an auditorium "draped in beautiful blue velvets, filled with dazzling guards officers, women with low-necked gowns, resplendent, radiant, a perfumed and heterogeneous crowd, in which the red outfits and the white stockings of the valets of court, so proper, so emblazoned with imperial eagles, introduced a solemn note."[1] By means of his program note Bakst deftly succeeded in paying homage to Tchaikovsky while simultaneously establishing his own credentials as privileged participant in the vanished world of tsarist splendor. His bedazzled account of the 1890 dress rehearsal may indeed reflect genuine experience, but it also indicates his hopes for the London production. As designer of the sets and costumes for *Sleeping Princess* (as Diaghilev had rechristened it), Bakst was willing and ready to claim credit for any success.

Alexandre Benois, Bakst's colleague in the Ballets Russes, gave an even more emotional account of the rapture that overcame him when *he* saw *Sleeping Beauty* for the first time:

> I went to the second performance [in January 1890] . . . and left the theatre in a rather hazy state, only feeling that I had just heard and seen something that I was *going* to love. When I try to analyse the feeling that came over me then, it seems to me that I simply could not believe in my own joy. . . . As soon as possible I saw *La Belle au bois dormant* a second time, and then a third and a fourth. The more I listened to the music, the more I seemed to discover in it greater and greater beauty—a beauty that was not universally understood but that was absolutely in harmony with me, that aroused the sweetest langour and an almost celestial joy.[2]

Benois was not embarrassed to use the word *beauty*, though the word had been anathema to the generation of Russian artists who came of age in the 1860s and 1870s. The exception to this rule was, as Richard Taruskin reminds us, Tchaikovsky.[3] By the 1890s, however, Tchaikovsky was not alone, and beauty had recovered some of its privileged status. For Benois and his age group, beauty assumed a near-mystical significance. Beauty was not just an attribute of a work of art, it was a positive force that elevated the human spirit and allowed sensuous pleasure—"the sweetest langour," as Benois put it—to coexist harmoniously with a disinterested "celestial joy." Even at the age of eighty, Benois still longed for the chance to design a production of *Sleeping Beauty*. If this were done properly, he told Sergei Lifar, that is, without any compromises, "then we would stand spotless before Apollo."[4] The participants in such a production would have served the cause of beauty in one of its most radiant incarnations. Alas for Benois, his dream was never realized; there were several near misses, including a planned production at La Scala in 1953, but he never succeeded in designing a full-length version of his favorite ballet.

The events that led up to the St. Petersburg premiere of *Sleeping Beauty* are too well known to need detailed recital here. Ivan Vsevolozhsky, Director of the Imperial Theaters, proposed to Russia's most celebrated composer, Pyotr Ilich Tchaikovsky, a scenario based on Perrault's fairy tale; Tchaikovsky accepted the proposal with more than a little good will, and in composing the music was guided, at least in part, by the requirements of Marius Petipa, longtime choreographer of the Mariinsky Theater. The Italian ballerina Carlotta Brianza danced the part of Aurora, which Petipa created with her in mind. The veteran *danseur noble* Pavel Gerdt appeared as Prince Desiré, and Marie Petipa was the Lilac Fairy. Two established theater designers, Matvei Shishkov and Mikhail Bocharov, designed the stage sets (a magnificent Baroque palace, a forest landscape, and a formal garden reminiscent of Versailles); Vsevolozhsky himself sketched costumes in the Louis XIV style. The stage technicians of the Imperial Theaters created a number of special effects, including a forest that grew up before the spectators' eyes at the end of Act I to hide the castle where Aurora lay sleeping, and a moving panorama for Act II that made the Lilac Fairy's boat appear to sail across the stage. These elaborate stage effects persistently gave trouble in later revivals.

For a number of reasons, *Sleeping Beauty* fared poorly with the St. Petersburg press. Even a respectful viewer like Alexandre Benois found the overall effect ponderous and lacking in poetry. Then, too, all three of the chief performers experienced difficulty during the first performances: Brianza became entangled in the elaborate costumes of her partners; Marie Petipa, though strikingly beautiful, required a "walking" role as the Lilac Fairy; and Gerdt, by then in his mid-forties, was unable to be entirely convincing in the role of young lover.[5] Guardians of the status quo insisted that Tchaikovsky's music was undanceable and too symphonic, the ornate sets and costumes were condemned as tasteless, and the scenario received criticism both for its lack of dramatic content and for its foreignness.[6] Since *Sleeping Beauty* was based on a French fairy tale, with costumes and settings in a French style, how could it satisfy the needs of a Russian music?

On this last count, *Sleeping Beauty* was ably defended by Tchaikovsky's friend Herman Laroche, who gave short shrift to the idea that Russianness could only be identified in peasant costumes and log houses. Was not St. Petersburg, locus of Russian culture from the eighteenth century onwards, as much a part of Russia as the rural hinterland? Although Russia did possess its own unique identity, Laroche argued that this by no means excluded contact with European culture: "It was Peter Ilyich's good fortune that his development coincided with a time . . . when the word 'Russian' was no longer synonymous with 'peasantlike,' and when the 'peasantlike' itself was put in its place, as only a *part* of Russianness."[7]

The familiar mythic structure of *Sleeping Beauty* also escaped national boundaries, Laroche noted. The same pattern of death or deathlike sleep, followed by rebirth, appears in the folklore of nearly every nation. For Wagner, a German, the story was that of Brünnhilde, "one of the innumerable embodiments of the earth, which sleeps during winter and is awakened by the kiss of spring," but analogous myths appear in France and in Russia. Laroche might, indeed, have pointed out that solar mythology and rites of spring are particularly important in Russian folklore, e.g., the reawakening of earth by the sun god Iarilo in Nikolai Rimsky-Korsakov's opera *Snow Maiden*.

Although the scenario of *Sleeping Beauty* conforms to an established mythic pattern, other ingredients have at least equal importance. The seventeenth-century setting —Vsevolozhsky's contribution—was not, for example, an obvious choice. Illustrations to Perrault's tales, like those of Gustave Doré, tended to employ a medieval setting. The Baroque style of the court of King Florestan derived not from fairy tales, but from court spectacles held at Versailles in the time of Louis XIV. From the opening fanfare to the final apotheosis of Apollo as the Sun King, *Sleeping Beauty* pays homage to the institution of monarchy. The real King Louis appeared without embarrassment at Versailles in a production entitled *Le Ballet de la nuit* as an allegorical figure of power and prosperity, bringing wealth, victory, and honor to the people of France. The Russian Emperor, Alexander III, could hardly have breached decorum by appearing on the stage of the Mariinsky Theater, but the implied parallel between past and present must have been satisfying to Vsevolozhsky, a devout monarchist to whom the virtues of a strong, beneficent monarchy were simply not open to question.

Richard Taruskin has given a penetrating account of Tchaikovsky's position as "the last of the court composers" of Europe, a royalist, and a protégé of Tsar Alexander III.[8] Tchaikovsky was, it might be noted, only one instance of the Tsar's surprisingly generous patronage of the arts. Alexander III was determined to enhance Russia's image as a civilized European nation, an image he could burnish through support for the arts.[9] In retrospect his reign has become synonymous with repression; for those members of society not subject to police surveillance or to grinding poverty, however, there was reason to regard this period in a positive light. Alexander had restored stability to a government in disarray after his father's assassination, had avoided conflict with foreign powers, and had lent his considerable authority to developing Russia's economic resources. Given these circumstances, it is not difficult to understand why Benois, Diaghilev, Balanchine, and others looked back upon Alexander III's reign with nostalgia.[10]

Expectations of prosperity were particularly high at the beginning of the 1890s, due to a newly formed Russian alliance with France. In 1894 the French Republic and the Russian Emperor signed an agreement that guaranteed mutual assistance in the event of war with Germany; however, the first signs of rapprochement appeared well before the military agreement. Russian loans floated in Paris at the end of the 1880s shored up Russia's credit, while the French in their turn saw lucrative opportunities for investment in Russian economic development.[11] Recognition of a shared cultural heritage that dated to the seventeenth and eighteenth centuries allowed the two nations to pay graceful diplomatic compliments to each other. In 1890, for example, in conjunction with an exhibition of French art held in Moscow, the French government presented the Russian emperor with an elaborate allegorical plaque decorated in an eighteenth-century style: a beneficent France, seated in the foreground, holds a cornucopia and points toward the distant city of Moscow. Similarly, when Nicholas and Alexandra visited Paris in 1896, they were greeted with temporary structures in a Rococo style—clearly the style of monarchy.[12]

In the context of this rapprochement between Russia and France, the Louis XIV style of *Sleeping Beauty* appears almost natural. It consolidates the image of Russia as a cultured and civilized nation that was already a full-fledged participant in European culture. At the same time, *Sleeping Beauty* pays homage to St. Petersburg, the city in which Russia's European identity was first established. In a series of conversations with Solomon Volkov, George Balanchine attempted to define what he identified as a St. Petersburg style; it was European, but European in a rarefied and distinctive way: "The Russian tsars were so rich that they imported the best architects of Europe to St. Petersburg—from Italy, Austria, France. They paid them enormous sums. And obviously the Romanov dynasty understood beauty. . . . All the buildings are elegant, light—that's the Italian or Austrian style. . . . It's called *Petersburg Empire*—elegant, simple, refined. Without pretension, but majestic."[13] Balanchine saw Tchaikovsky as the preeminent St. Petersburg composer, and of all Tchaikovsky's works, he identified *Sleeping Beauty* as the one that perfectly exemplified the grace, refinement, and beauty of the St. Petersburg environment.

For Alexandre Benois this Petersburg sensibility found living embodiment in the person of Ivan Vsevolozhsky, Director of the Imperial Theaters. Vsevolozhsky's refinement of manner, grace of movement, and propriety of conduct were all, in Benois' view, attributes that belonged to St. Petersburg rather than to crude and backward Muscovy.[14] Of course, even in this turn-of-the-century period the concept of a Petersburg style was already a nostaglic creation. The Imperial grandeur of *Sleeping Beauty* was in fact a thing of the past. Alexander III was Louis XIV neither in position nor in power. Even the city of St. Petersburg was no longer its earlier self. The changes taking place in St. Petersburg's architectural landscape were particularly distressing to Benois, who attributed them to the "vulgar Americanization" (read: "crass commercialism") of late nineteenth-century Russia.

Nonetheless, Benois cherished a passionate conviction that the city of St. Petersburg could serve an educative function for the rest of Russia:

> Our conscious love for our country was closely related to our association with the West . . . our love for our country was united to a desire to serve her absolutely, and the service was somehow to be in the direction which had been given to Russia by her great Reformer [Peter the Great]. In Russia much that was characteristically Russian annoyed us by its coarseness, triviality and unattractive barbarism. It was the coarseness that we longed to fight and to uproot. But the problem had to be solved with the greatest care so as not to harm or break what was really precious; for the good and the bad often lay close together. It was indispensable to save all that was being threatened by the leveling spirit of time, or by false nationalism.[15]

Ballet, in particular, embodied the delicacy, refinement, and sheer beauty of this jealously guarded St. Petersburg style. Petersburg balletomanes were adamant when it came to the superiority of dancers at the Mariinsky Theater over their Moscow counterparts; indeed they were ruthless critics of the unfortunate Muscovites, not sparing even the physical characteristics of the ballerinas ("heavy legs"). In 1897 Petipa generously noted improvements in the Moscow ballet, but added the usual complaint that Moscow dancers lacked "a necessary lightness and grace."[16] Akim Volynsky, a stalwart loyalist of the Mariinsky, sniffed that the Moscow ballerina Ekaterina Geltser lacked subtlety of technique ("Gelster's classical dance shouts"), while André Levinson reacted with a shudder to the 1914 revival of *Sleeping Beauty* in Moscow. The designer of that production, Konstantin Korovin, had committed the unforgivable crime of introducing "crude Muscovite-Oriental luxury" into the quintessential Petersburg ballet.[17]

Guardians of St. Petersburg's ballet tradition also made a point of distinguishing Russian ballet from its Western European competitors. Petipa, for example, described the Russian style of dancing—a style he had done much to create—as vastly superior to the Italian style in grace and subtlety. The Italians were acrobats, but lacked beauty (Petipa even complained about their physical appearance). Carlotta Brianza, the Italian ballerina for whom Petipa created the role of Aurora, was the shining exception. Although Brianza had retained her strong Italian technique, she pleased the St. Petersburg connoisseurs by abandoning Italian acrobatics in favor of the refinement and softness of the St. Petersburg school.[18]

Benois continued to promote his own identity as a European Russian in his first full-length ballet, *Pavillon d'Armide*, based on a story by Théophile Gautier and planned so that the central action takes place in a formal garden in the Louis XIV period: "I wanted it to have all the sparkle, the sumptuousness, the importance, of former ballets." When Michel Fokine decided to choreograph *Pavillon d'Armide* in 1907, Benois wanted Fokine to keep in mind "first-class masterpieces like the scene in the forest and especially the last scene of *La Belle au bois dormant*."[19] After seeing the new ballet, Diaghilev, swept away by enthusiasm, decided to take it to Paris as the centerpiece of a season devoted to Russian ballet. No doubt the scenario and choreography of *Pavillon d'Armide* struck Diaghilev as satisfactory, but the charisma of its two young stars, Anna Pavlova and Vaslav Nijinsky, must also have aroused Diaghilev's enthusiasm.

It was a remarkable gesture to present a French ballet like *Pavillon d'Armide* to a Paris audience. Would it not have been more obvious for Diaghilev to begin his first Paris season of ballet productions with some indisputably Russian choice that would follow upon the spectacular success achieved by his production of Musorgsky's *Boris Godunov* the year before? *Pavillon d'Armide* brought coals to Newcastle. Benois, as might be expected, saw no irony in this, but rather an instructive lesson. *Pavillon d'Armide* "was meant to demonstrate our understanding and interpretation of that 'most French of epochs, the eighteenth century.' . . . *Le Pavillon d'Armide* fulfilled its mission . . . The [Russian] 'barbarians' had not only proved to be up to standard in their own 'barbaric' and wild demonstrations; but had even beaten the 'Athenians' themselves on their own ground."[20]

Pavillon d'Armide received a warm enough reception (it was, after all, Nijinsky's début appearance before a Paris audience), but it failed to match the wild success of other offerings, like Fokine's spectacularly choreographed *Polovtsian Dances* from *Prince Igor*.[21] Obviously it was more profitable to market Russian barbarism and Oriental exoticism than to present the work of a European Russian like Benois. Tchaikovsky's reputation fell victim to the same combination of circumstances. Diaghilev tried including the Second Symphony on the program of his initial concert of Russian music in 1907 and found that Robert Brussel, music critic of *Le Figaro*, could barely control his disgust.[22] He had been warned by French visitors to Russia that Tchaikovsky's music would not be well received in Paris, but he continued to include Tchaikovsky's works on concert programs throughout 1907 and 1908 before finally admitting defeat. During the next few years he occasionally staged excerpts from *Sleeping Beauty*, but only in order to showcase star dancers like Mathilde Kshesinskaia or Vaslav Nijinsky in a particular *pas de deux*.[23] At last, in 1911, he shamelessly went over to the enemy by telling an interviewer from *The Times of London* that *Sleeping Beauty* was an "interminable ballet on a subject taken from a French fable, composed on French themes" and therefore not representative of Russian music.[24]

Consequently it came as a shock to Diaghilev's friends and associates when he announced his intention to revive *Sleeping Beauty* at the Alhambra Theatre in London. Quite possibly he simply hoped to provide his beleaguered company with financial stability. Diaghilev jokingly told Sergei Grigoriev that he wanted to find a ballet production that would have the box office appeal of the long-running musical *Chu Chin Chow*. When Grigoriev suggested *Coppélia*, a full-length Petipa ballet to music by Léo Delibes, Diaghilev countered with his own choice: *Sleeping Beauty*.[25] Probably Igor Stravinsky had a hand in Diaghilev's choice. According to Walter Nouvel, a member of Diaghilev's inner circle, "Stravinsky idolized Tchaikovsky and considered it a necessity to rehabilitate him in the eyes of Europe. He insistently urged Diaghilev to undertake this campaign in the service of a great Russian musician, whom Diaghilev himself had always loved . . . Diaghilev well understood all the significance of the support which Stravinsky's authority, name and prestige gave him. At the same time Diaghilev felt that the public had somewhat tired of modernism." Stravinsky was also concerned that, since the 1917 Revolution, there had been a decided reaction against Tchaikovsky.[26] Certainly Diaghilev shored up his position by invoking Stravinsky's authority: he solicited a testimonial from Stravinsky that argued for the importance of Tchaikovsky's music and arranged for it to appear in *The Times* as well as in the program for *Sleeping Princess*.

Diaghilev's decision to revive a ballet that formed one of the landmarks of classical dance surely also indicates concern for the fate of classical ballet in Bolshevik Russia; numerous dancers had emigrated, while others remained in Russia under conditions of severe hardship. It was perfectly reasonable for Diaghilev to refer to his *Sleeping Princess* as the "last relic of great days of St. Petersburg."[27] *Sleeping Beauty* had been part of a St. Petersburg culture that would never come again. Levinson's introduction to a collection of Bakst designs for *Sleeping Princess*, published soon after the ballet closed, was steeped in royalist nostalgia. Ostensibly describing the 1890 première of *Sleeping Beauty* in St. Petersburg, Levinson used words entirely appropriate to the 1921 production he had just seen: "The fairy tale is the last refuge of the departing gods, of lapsed mythologies, of gracious autocrats now dissolved in smoke, of vanished glories and faded dreams and elemental spirits relegated by triumphant scepticism to an inglorious obscurity." The fate of ballet in Soviet Russia was also on Levinson's mind; not Princess Aurora only, but classical ballet itself had been plunged into deathlike slumber: "*Sleeping Princess* sleeps in a dying land—a sleep from which there can be no awakening."[28]

In preparing his new production, Diaghilev aimed at "authenticity," that is, he made an effort to provide living links between his production and the original. Carlotta Brianza, who had danced the part of Aurora at the St. Petersburg premiere, agreed to appear as Carabosse. Enrico Cechetti, who had appeared as the Blue Bird in 1890, took over the role of Carabosse for one evening—the hundredth performance of *Sleeping Princess*. (Since 1909, Cechetti had been the teacher who traveled with Diaghilev's troupe.) For the role of Aurora, Diaghilev recruited former soloists of the Mariinsky Theater—Vera Trefilova, Liubov Egorova, and Olga Spessivtseva—all of whom had fled to Western Europe. He also obtained the services of Nikolai Sergeev, who had brought his notations of Petipa's choreography with him when he left St. Petersburg. With exquisite thoroughness, Diaghilev even sought out Riccardo Drigo, who had conducted the first performance of *Sleeping Beauty*, but discovered that the aging maestro was barely able to recollect the year 1890. The most poignant allusion to the St. Petersburg past occurred in Bakst's set designs for *Sleeping Princess*. The grandiose Baroque architecture of the Baptism scene derives from an eighteenth-century Italian theater design; however, Bakst added a grand staircase that transformed it into a reasonable facsimile of the Winter Palace in St. Petersburg.[29]

Diaghilev had originally hoped to have the sets and costumes for his new production designed by Benois, an undisputed expert in the Louis XIV period; but since Benois was reluctant to leave Russia without a more secure future than Diaghilev could offer, the commission passed to Bakst, whose fame as a stage designer was well established in Western Europe, thanks to the work he had done for Diaghilev before the First World War. Bakst shrewdly negotiated a contract that allowed him to claim a lion's share of credit for the 1921 production. His name appears twice on the proof copy of the program cover, once as responsible for "the entire production" and further down the page as designer of "Curtain, Scenery, Costumes and Properties." Stravinsky was also prominent. Someone, presumably Diaghilev, had the proof amended so that the names Tchaikovsky and Petipa would appear in larger type than Bakst and Stravinsky.[30]

Fidelity to the original was certainly not of overriding importance for Diaghilev. He ruthlessly made "improvements" in Tchaikovsky's music, deleting anything he considered dull and inserting several dances from *The Nutcracker*. In the interests of audience appeal, he also had Bronislava Nijinska create a Russian peasant dance, the Dance of the Three Ivans, for the finale. This alteration particularly outraged Benois, once he came to hear of it, since it pandered to stereotypical conceptions of Russianness. Not surprisingly, this ethnic inclusion turned out to be one of the most successful moments in the ballet's closing *divertissement*.[31]

Bakst's sets and costumes were sumptuous, "the apotheosis of tangerine . . . orange zig-zags . . . parma violet . . . emerald green," Cecil Beaton raved.[32] Bakst tinkered with the period setting of the original *Sleeping Beauty* so as to mix and match fashions from the reigns of Louis XIV and Louis XV. He diligently studied costume books and historical engravings, but his designs have a marvelous theatrical exaggeration. Even for a relatively minor court dignitary, Bakst devised a swaggering coat in black, gold, deep pink, and blue, to be worn with a cascading wig, two sashes, and enough plumage to equip an entire aviary. The theatricality of Bakst's *Sleeping Princess* is, in fact, so pronounced that it verges on parody. His sketch for the scene of Aurora's awakening is one example: Bakst depicted a canopied bed topped by an Imperial eagle so large and overbearing that its presence is far from reassuring. Bakst also introduced into the costumes a touch of the decadence for which he was renowned. His costume for the Queen is décolleté to the point of indecency. Of course Vera Sudeikina, who appeared as the Queen, did not perform with her breasts exposed, but Bakst's drawing with its outrageously low-cut bodice was proudly featured in the souvenir program for the ballet.

This regal splendor of *Sleeping Princess* was enhanced by the attendance of various representatives of European royalty. The King and Queen of England, the Duke of York, the Queen of Norway, Princess

Victoria, and Princess Mary all saw Diaghilev's ballet. As a celebration of monarchy, however, the ballet was not a success. Despite the unbounded enthusiasm of devotees like Cyril Beaumont and Oswald Sitwell, *Sleeping Princess* was lambasted in the British press. Critics dismissed Tchaikovsky's music and Bakst's designs as a trivial and empty display, little better than popular entertainment. W. J. Turner, writing in *The New Statesman*, laid most of the blame on Tchaikovsky, although his comments implicated Bakst as well: "There was considerable taste in M. Bakst's flamboyancy and great skill in his massing of colours but it was a Tchaikovskian virtuosity, empty of significance, and as I have said, admirably suited to the music."[33] Another reviewer dismissed the entire production as a useless antique: "Last night's Sleeping Beauty was a young lady at the Versailles of 200 years ago. She is, this new 'Sleeping Princess,' the grandest possible relation of our known Sleeping Beauties . . . This new ballet, which out-splendours splendour . . . [conjures up] before our dazzled eyes, all the pomp of dead and done-with kings and emperors—Bourbons and Romanoffs."[34]

In the wake of the First World War, the future of European royalty (those "dead and done-with kings and emperors") was in fact far from secure. In 1918 King George V's advisers gave him the discouraging news that his position was less secure now than it had been in 1914, and the Prince of Wales noted "a regular epidemic of revolutions & abdications."[35] Most poignant of all, in 1917, the King of England had felt himself unable to extend asylum to Nicholas II of Russia and his family, due to anti-Tsarist sentiment among the British working classes. As one historian put it, the Romanovs were sacrificed to ensure the continuation of the Windsors. The Russian Imperial style lived on, but not its originators.

Diaghilev's production of *Sleeping Princess* closed in 1922 after 105 performances. This was not a bad run, but too brief to cover costs; consequently Oswald Stoll, manager of the Alhambra Theatre, had Bakst's sets and costumes seized and put in storage.[36] As Diaghilev sadly remarked, there were no more Grand Dukes to pay the bills for ambitious artistic ventures. *Sleeping Princess* did remain in the repertoire of Diaghilev's company, but only in a sadly diminished form. Diaghilev continued to present Act III of the ballet as *Le Mariage d'Aurore,* using the costumes Alexandre Benois had originally designed for *Pavillon d'Armide.* Ironically, this fragment of *Sleeping Princess* turned out to be precisely the reliable moneymaker that Diaghilev needed.

The Russian Imperial style of *Sleeping Beauty* may not have evoked enthusiasm in 1922, but twenty-five years later London witnessed another, more auspicious recycling of Tchaikovsky's masterpiece. When the Royal Opera House at Covent Garden reopened in 1946 after the Second World War, *Sleeping Beauty* was its first production. A new young star, Margot Fonteyn, danced the part of Aurora, and the Opera House itself was repaired and refurbished for the occasion. The entire event had immense symbolic importance as marking "the beginning of peacetime, as opposed to the mere ending of the war."[37]

The choice of *Sleeping Beauty* as the centerpiece for a national celebration was a conservative one that combined homage to the tradition of classical dance with homage to the tradition of monarchy. Ninette de Valois, who was responsible for the 1946 production, was not opposed to new styles of ballet, but she had dedicated herself to preserving the dance traditions of nineteenth-century classicism. Her goal was to form a state company with a school and theater of its own, in the grand tradition of Russia's Imperial Ballet. De Valois, who had danced in the Diaghilev production of 1921, had already revived *Sleeping Beauty* for her Sadler's Wells company in 1938 under Diaghilev's title *Sleeping Princess*. De Valois engaged the services of Nikolai Sergeev, another veteran of the Diaghilev production; he came daily to teach de Valois' dancers, using choreographic notations he had made in prerevolutionary St. Petersburg. De Valois did not, however, leave everything to Sergeev; she was quite prepared to intervene where she thought it necessary. Among other things, de Valois was convinced that Diaghilev's production had been unsuccessful because of its extravagance: "the costumes so overpowered everything else on stage that the dancing could hardly be seen for plumes and riches. This time the staging would be simple and clean, without feathers or sequins." This policy of restraint resulted in costumes so basic that Margot Fonteyn, the ballet's Aurora, was nearly reduced to tears. She noted that

> bare tutu designs, one peach-coloured, one pale blue and one white and gold, were almost totally unadorned except for some sun-ray points on the skirts. The headdresses were merely cardboard crown shapes covered in plain satin fabrics. Not one sequin or jewel was to be allowed to mar the austerity. . . . I nearly cried when I got home to tell my mother that the costumes would be like 'little cotton house frocks' instead of the rich costumes suitable for a ballerina.[38]

For the grand reopening of the Royal Opera House, such simplicity was set aside. The sets and costumes designed by Oliver Messel were a triumph of muted splendor. The overall color scheme of the production consisted of mauve, burgundy, and gray, with touches of bright red and sky blue. A team of volunteers that included Fonteyn's mother was pressed into service to gather the fabrics and accessories for the ornate costumes: "My mother was delighted to be enlisted as a searcher, and she spent day after day unearthing brocades, feathers, braids, gimps and all kinds of unrationed bits and pieces that could be utilized."[39] Messel's vision scene took place in a lush romantic grotto, and his palace settings combined the Baroque magnificence of Bakst's designs with a pleasing lightness and softness.

Opening night at Covent Garden was literally a royal occasion. The audience included King George VI, the Queen, and the young Princesses Elizabeth and Margaret.[40] Fonteyn wrote, "There were so many 'Royals' present at the opening that, when I came to the last presentation curtsy, I was dizzy from bobbing up and down." (Princess Margaret discreetly offered a steadying hand.) Violetta Prokhorova, recently arrived from the Bolshoi Theater, exclaimed, with a certain lack of historical memory, "You know, is very funny *real* King and Queen will be in audience. In Russia they existed only in fairy tales and ballet."[41] As a concession to postwar austerity, the audience was invited to substitute day clothes for evening dress, but this made little difference: "Last night, when the great curtain went up again at last at the Royal Opera . . . it was more than auspicious; it was festive and it symbolized the rolling back of some of our oppressions from our minds, for the King had come with his family and his Ministers to give their blessing, and we in the audience had done what we could to respond . . . in a sartorial sense to Mr. Oliver Messel's brave and beautiful spectacle upon the stage."[42]

In short, the new production of *Sleeping Beauty* was an elaborate public celebration, conceived with pomp and splendor in spite of, or possibly in compensation for, Britain's postwar austerity. Yet in deciding to reconstitute the regal style of a bygone era, the participants in this 1946 production had to consider a problem that existed in real life, not just on stage. In the years immediately following the Second World War, Britain's monarchy had to consider its image. Even before the war, the Prince of Wales, later Edward VIII, had questioned the wisdom of pursuing an old style monarchy and had launched a campaign to bring the crown closer to the people.[43] In 1946 the importance of determining a future direction presented itself even more acutely. Adherence to the traditional trappings of rank and ceremony posed definite public relations problems in a period of rationing and food shortages. At the beginning of 1946, the King himself had written that "food, clothes and fuel are the main topics of conversation with us all."[44] There was a considerable amount of grumbling over the Royal Family's visit to South Africa in 1947; since it coincided with a cold British winter, the state visit looked too much like a vacation in the sun that no ordinary Briton could enjoy. Later in the same year, further accusations of useless expenditure were directed at the elaborate ceremony that marked the wedding of Princess Elizabeth to Prince Philip of Greece.

Grumbling of this kind did not, of course, come anywhere close to real dissent. Even members of the Labour government that took office in 1945 treated the Royal Family with respect, and the British monarchy continued to function in its symbolic role as guarantors of continuity and stability. On the positive side, there was also a young and attractive princess on whom hopes for the future could focus. The year 1946 saw a striking parallel of fact with fiction. When *Sleeping Beauty* opened at the Royal Opera house, there was already speculation about the marriage prospects of Princess Elizabeth, then aged 19. As future Queen of England and a considerable heiress, Princess Elizabeth was in much the position of Princess Aurora, able to select the suitor of her choice. The young English princess had not, of course, been required to endure a hundred years of deathlike sleep, but she had experienced the strains and, relatively speaking, the privations of a war that overshadowed most of her adolescence. Even her serious-minded father lamented that she had "had no fun." Under these circumstances a royal wedding was more than business as usual; it was the happy ending after an all-too-real period of trial.

Suspense over the Princess's marriage plans ended in 1947, when her engagement was finally announced. Her wedding to Prince Philip took place later that year and was celebrated with all the pomp and circumstance that an ardent royalist could desire. Members of the public made acid remarks about the expense of the ceremony—in particular the Princess' wedding dress, which was worth the equivalent of 300 clothing coupons—but objections gave way to enjoyment as the day of the spectacle approached. "All of us are hungry for colour, romance and adventure," one observer wrote.[45] The fictional celebration of monarchy so spectacularly embodied in *Sleeping Beauty* assumed real-world form in the national celebration that accompanied the royal wedding.

This parallel of fact with fiction could, of course, be seen in a colder light. In 1946 the British monarchy was beginning to assume the role of theater. Significantly, one British newspaper referred to the royal wedding as England's answer to *Oklahoma*, the long-running American musical. Even the loyal Miss Crawford, Princess Elizabeth's governess, remarked that the interior of Buckingham Palace, with its vast rooms decorated in pink and gold , "resembled the setting of a luxurious pantomime."[46] Transformation of monarchy into entertainment reached the point of no return with the Coronation of Queen Elizabeth in 1953. For the first time this solemn ceremonial occasion was broadcast on television, despite some hesitation on the part of the Queen. Media coverage was, in fact, vital in ensuring the Coronation's public success. As one skeptical bystander put it, the journalistic euphoria "reached a level of intensity more comparable with the religious ecstasy of the seventeenth century, when men could still believe in the divine right of kings, than the scientific temper of the twentieth."[47]

The ceremonial events described above indicate the problematic position of the British monarchy in the mid-twentieth century, when it found itself poised between past majesty and a future incarnation as marketable commodity—useful for public occasions, a significant tourist attraction, and an unlimited source of gossip for the pages of tabloid newspapers. By adapting to changed circumstances, the British monarchy has, thus far, survived the rigors of the twentieth century. Tchaikovsky's *Sleeping Beauty*, which graced the declining days of the Russian empire, played a small but telling part in the pattern of events that determined the role of the monarchy in postwar Britain. Of course, the imaginary kingdom of King Florestan has proven quite as adaptable as the British crown. *Sleeping Beauty* has entered the repertoire of popular entertainment in Great Britain, in the United States (where Britain's Royal Ballet reintroduced it to the American public), and, for a time at least, in the workers' paradise of the Soviet Union. Thus, the strange fate of the Russian Imperial style: on at least three occasions— in 1890, in 1921, and in 1946—productions of *Sleeping Beauty* have been closely linked with the fortunes of monarchy, with its rise, fall, and rebirth in a changed form for a modern era.

NOTES

1. Roland John Wiley, *Tchaikovsky's Ballets: Swan Lake, Sleeping Beauty, Nutcracker* (Oxford: Clarendon Press, 1985), p. 164. Charles Spencer suggests that Bakst's account of an encounter with Tchaikovsky was invented, since there is no evidence from other members of Diaghilev's circle to support his claim: Charles Spencer, *Léon Bakst and the Ballets Russes* (London: Academy Editions, 1995), p. 203. It is clear that the members of Diaghilev's group made competing claims of personal contact with Tchaikovsky.

Diaghilev held trumps, since his musical aunt, Aleksandra Panaeva-Kartseva, had taken him to Klin and introduced him to the famous composer. Later Diaghilev boasted of his visit to "Uncle Petia." Benois, always contrary, touted his own restraint in *not* having tried to meet Tchaikovsky: Alexandre Benois, *Reminiscences of the Russian Ballet*, translated by Mary Britnieva (London: Putnam, 1941), p. 125.

2. Benois, *Reminiscences*, pp. 123–24.

3. Richard Taruskin, *Defining Russia Musically: Historical and Hermeneutical Essays* (Princeton, NJ: Princeton University Press, 1997), pp. 254–59.

4. *Sergei Diaghilev i russkoe iskusstvo*, edited by I. S. Zil'bershtein and V. A. Samkov, vol. 2 (Moscow: Izobrazitel'noe iskusstvo, 1982), p. 502.

5. Gennady Smakov, "Marius Petipa and the Creation of *The Sleeping Beauty*," in *100 Years of Russian Ballet 1830–1930*, edited by Nancy Van Norman Baer (New York: Eduard Nakhamkin, 1989), pp. 20–21.

6. For critical reaction to *Sleeping Beauty* see Wiley, *Tchaikovsky's Ballets*, pp. 189–92.

7. German Larosh, *Izbrannye stat'i*, vol. 2 (Leningrad: Muzyka: 1975), p. 143.

8. Taruskin, *Defining Russia Musically*, p. 276. The notion of a "Russian Imperial" style derives from George Balanchine's conversations about Tchaikovsky with Solomon Volkov. Balanchine discoursed at length on Tchaikovsky's relationship to the city of St. Petersburg. In Balanchine's view the music of *Sleeping Beauty* exemplified the "Russian Imperial" in its most perfect form: Solomon Volkov, *Balanchine's Tchaikovsky: Interviews with George Balanchine*, translated by Antonina W. Bouis (New York: Simon and Schuster, 1985), p. 127.

9. John O. Norman, "Alexander III as Art Patron" in *New Perspectives on Russian and Soviet Artistic Culture*, edited by John O. Norman (New York: St. Martin's Press, 1994), pp. 25–40.

10. Dominic Lieven, *Nicholas II: Twilight of the Empire* (New York: St. Martin's Press, 1994), pp. 22–25. In *Balanchine's Tchaikovsky*, Solomon Volkov cites Balanchine's starstruck reaction to the Tsar (in which Balanchine placed himself in the same camp as Tchaikovsky, Diaghilev, and Stravinsky): "Tchaikovsky was stunned when revolutionary terrorists killed Emperor Alexander II. He grew quite close to the new monarch, Alexander III. Diaghilev said to me that Alexander III could be counted among the best Russian tsars. For Russian culture he was, perhaps, really the best of the Russian monarchs. . . . Everything that later made Russia famous began under Alexander III! He was, they told me, a man of enormous height. Stravinsky saw Alexander III a few times when he was a child. The emperor was a real bogatyr, a gigantic warrior, bearded, with a loud voice, and a penetrating glance. But with Tchaikovsky, for example, he was always very simple and gentle." (*Balanchine's Tchaikovsky*, pp. 44–45). In retrospect, Alexander III's imposing physical presence and the strong hand with which he managed affairs of state contrasted favorably with the ineffective rule of his son Nicholas.

11. Georges Michon, *The Franco-Russian Alliance, 1891–1917* (London: George Allen & Unwin, 1929), pp. 13–14.

12. Debora L. Silverman, *Art Nouveau in Fin-de-Siècle France* (Berkeley: University of California Press, 1989), pp. 159–167.

13. Solomon Volkov, *Balanchine's Tchaikovsky*, p. 52.

14. Aleksandr Benua, "I. A. Vsevolozhsky," *Rech'* (November 1, 1909): 2–3.

15. Benois, *Reminiscences of the Russian Ballet*, pp. 182–83.

16. *Marius Petipa: Materialy, vospominaniia, stat'i* (Leningrad: Iskusstvo, 1971), pp. 123–24.

17. M. Konstantinova, *Spiashchaia krasavitsa* (Moscow: Iskusstvo, 1990), pp. 132, 143–144. Some years later Levinson was still ranting against Korovin: "Korovin, of the Imperial Academy, a Muscovite painter, who crushed beneath the weight of cumbersome learning, crude colors and useless bric-à-brac, all that remained of the fragile and elegant dream conceived in the unique atmosphere of Saint-Petersburg" (André Levinson, *The Designs of Léon Bakst for Sleeping Princess* [New York: Benjamin Blom, 1971], p. 11).

18. Aleksandr Pleshcheev, *Peterburgskaia gazeta*, No. 272 (4 October 1890), p. 3. Quoted by Vera M. Krasovskaia, *Russkii baletnyi teatr vtoroi poloviny XIX veka* (Leningrad: Iskusstvo, 1963), pp. 459–60. Also, *Marius Petipa: Materialy, vospominaniia, stat'i*, p. 125.

19. Benois, *Reminiscences*, pp. 225, 252.

20. Benois, *Reminiscences*, p. 292.

21. Prince Peter Lieven, *Birth of the Ballets-Russes*, translated by L. Zarine (New York: Dover 1973), pp. 96–102.

22. Richard Buckle, *Diaghilev* (New York: Atheneum, 1979), pp. 95–97. Tchaikovsky's reputation in France had suffered from the publication of Cesar Cui's propagandistic *La musique en Russie*, which dismissed Tchaikovsky as insufficiently Russian compared with Cui and his allies in the "Kuchka." For the 1909 season of the Ballets Russes, Benois did his best for Tchaikovsky by choosing the finale of his Second Symphony to form part of a ballet divertissement entitled *Le Festin*. Benois had high hopes for success with this venture precisely because of the inclusion of Tchaikovsky's music, but once again the results were disappointing (Aleksandr Benua, *Moi vospominaniia* vol. 2 [Moscow: Nauka, 1990], p. 525).

23. Buckle, *Diaghilev*, pp. 97–101, 162, 211, 241, 243.

24. Alexander Schouvaloff in *Léon Bakst: The Theatre Art* (London: Sotheby's Publications, 1991), p. 201.

25. S. L. Grigoriev, *The Diaghilev Ballet, 1909–1929* (Harmondsworth, Middlesex: Penguin Books, 1960), p. 176.

26. Quoted in *Sergei Diaghilev i russkoe iskusstvo*, vol. 2, p. 438. See also Vera Stravinsky and Robert Craft, *Stravinsky in Pictures and Documents* (New York: Simon and Schuster, 1978), p. 231.

27. Grigoriev, *The Diaghilev Ballet*, p. 182.

28. Levinson, *The Designs of Léon Bakst for Sleeping Princess*, pp. 8, 10. The first printing of Levinson's book was in 1922: André Levinson, *L'Oeuvre de Léon Bakst pour La Belle au Bois Dormant* (Paris: M. de Brunoff, 1922).

29. Deborah Howard identifies the Bibiena source in her article "A Sumptuous Revival: Bakst's Designs for Diaghilev's *Sleeping Princess*," in *Apollo* 91, no. 98 (April 1970), p. 302.

30. A reproduction of the corrected proof appears in Boris Kochno, *Diaghilev and the Ballets Russes*, translated by Adrienne Foulke (New York: Harper and Row, 1970), p. 169.

31. Grigoriev, *The Diaghilev Ballet*, pp. 177–78.

32. Spencer, *Léon Bakst and the Ballets Russes*, p. 213.

33. Howard, "A Sumptuous Revival," p. 301.

34. Nesta Macdonald in *Diaghilev Observed by Critics in England and the United States 1911–1929* (New York, Dance Horizons, 1975), p. 274.

35. Piers Brendon, *Our Own Dear Queen* (London: Secker & Warburg, 1986), p. 107.

36. Some of the costumes were discovered, still in storage, in 1968; for reproductions see *Léon Bakst: Sensualismens triumf* (Stockholm: Dansmuseet, 1993).

37. Alexander Bland, *The Royal Ballet: The First Fifty Years* (New York: Doubleday & Company, 1981), p. 84.

38. Margot Fonteyn, *Margot Fonteyn: Autobiography* (New York: Alfred A. Knopf, 1976), pp. 69–71. The designer for this stripped down production was none other than Nadia Benois, a niece of Alexandre Benois.

39. Fonteyn, *Autobiography*, p. 91.

40. Princess Elizabeth enjoyed *Sleeping Beauty* so much that she returned, incognito, to see a second performance, after which she visited a nightclub and reportedly danced "a rumba, a bahia, a samba and a slow bolero." (Bland, *The Royal Ballet*, p. 85).

41. Fonteyn, *Autobiography*, p. 92

42. "Reopening of Covent Garden: A Royal Occasion," *The Times* (London), 21 February 1946, p. 6.

43. Philip Ziegler, *Crown and People* (New York: Alfred A. Knopf, 1978), p. 34.

44. Elizabeth Longford, *The Queen: The Life of Elizabeth II* (New York: Alfred A. Knopf, 1983), p. 110.

45. Ziegler, *Crown and People*, pp. 80–84.

46. Brendon, *Our Own Dear Queen*, p. 153.

47. Brendon, *Our Own Dear Queen*, p. 160. In deference to the sacredness of the Coronation ceremony, the most solemn religious moments were excluded from television coverage.

Per Aspera Ad Astra:

Symphonic Tradition in Tchaikovsky's

First Suite for Orchestra

NATALIA MINIBAYEVA

Tchaikovsky's First Suite for Orchestra (Op. 43), one of the composer's lesser-known works, has not been comprehensively discussed in musicological literature. Though originally well-received in many European countries, in the twentieth century the work became an object of attack. Ralph Wood proclaimed that "the music is simply not worth detailed study; with the exception of the variations from No. 3 the suites are pretty thoroughly out of the repertoire now."[1] David Brown considered the Suite "rather second-rate, despite some undeniable charm."[2] Several Russian scholars, on the other hand, argued in the work's favor. Daniel Zhitomirsky believed that Tchaikovsky's four orchestral suites "frequently approach the symphony and concerto class. For Tchaikovsky suites were not only a vessel for his favourite lyrical images, but also a pretext for the statement and solution of creative problems."[3] Nadezhda Tumanina and Aleksandr Dolzhansky both observed that the First Suite's Introduction contains a theme that almost exactly repeats the Fate theme of the famous Fourth Symphony;[4] they did not, however, trace the relationship between the two works any further.

The present article notes how speculations about Tchaikovsky have affected our perception of the suites, traces his relationship to that genre, gives a compositional history of the First Suite, and describes its connections to the Fourth Symphony—written during the same period (1877–1879) and, like the Suite, dedicated to the composer's "best friend," Nadezhda Filaretovna von Meck.

In the West, Tchaikovsky's music was for a long time linked inseparably to a distorted image of his personality. Lack of published primary sources, due to censorship of Tchaikovsky's biographical materials in Soviet Russia, the inaccessibility until recent times of certain materials in the composer's archives, and inaccurate or incomplete translations of the available sources, complicated the situation. And so speculations emerged, ranging from undocumented assertions of insanity to descriptions of an egoism exacerbated by homosexuality. Pigeonholing Tchaikovsky as a madman, James Huneker referred to the composer's "unfortunate and undoubted[ly] psychopathic temperament" as a central influence on his "truly pathological" music.[5] Edward Lockspeiser went even further, describing Tchaikovsky's mind as "a text-book illustration of the borderland between genius and insanity."[6] Catherine Drinker Bowen and Barbara von Meck (widow of Nadezhda's grandson, Vladimir von Meck) presented Tchaikovsky as a "passive," "helpless," and "paralyzed" man who was rescued by the "stronger saving hand" of Mme von Meck.[7]

Among those who have commented on his supposed egoism is Gerald Abraham, who criticized Tchaikovsky's operas because their composer "was too self-centered, his music too much the expression of purely personal emotion, for him to think himself into the skins of the various characters."[8] In a similar vein, Lockspeiser noted the "indulgent yearning" in Tchaikovsky's Fourth Symphony and *Eugene Onegin*.[9] Tchaikovsky's harsh self-criticism ("I am very egoistic. . . . I am unable to sacrifice myself for others, even those near and dear to me") enabled Lockspeiser to speculate that Tchaikovsky's music reflects the "whining tone" of his declarations of "self-pity" and "self-hatred."[10]

The issue of Tchaikovsky's homosexuality was at first tactfully avoided or regarded simply as detrimental. At the beginning of the century, Lockspeiser reflected the thinking of his time by describing Tchaikovsky's homosexuality as responsible for "the neurotic elements . . . inseparable from his development as a composer."[11] By 1960, however, John Gee and Elliott Selby took a less judgmental tone, though attributing Tchaikovsky's "divided self" to his homosexuality.[12] A variety of rumors have also been fabricated to link the composer's homosexuality with his psychological state, music, and "mysterious" death.

Perhaps nowhere has the tendency to conflate the composer's biography and music been so marked as in discussions of the symphonies. Of his entire output, these were the most criticized works, despite their tremendous popularity. Malcolm H. Brown suggests that "some lingering Western prejudice against the music of Eastern Europe" might be behind scholarly attacks on Tchaikovsky's music, which in turn may be complicated by "flagrant homophobia on the part of a number of influential critics whose judgements betray the assumption of the essential identity between the artist and his work."[13] Some of these attacks have included Tchaikovsky's presumed inability to develop themes and execute broad symphonic form. Martin Cooper, for example, bluntly declared: "Tchaikovsky was not a symphonist by nature. That is to say, it was not natural for him to express himself in sonata form or to build a full-scale work on a strictly musical plan, without the assistance of those extraneous elements which have come to be loosely called a 'programme.'"[14] Ralph W. Wood made a similar assertion: "Tchaikovsky's conception of himself as above all a symphonist was hopelessly wrong. (No tenable definition of the word 'symphony' seems to have found a place in his stock of ideas)."[15]

Certainly, the Fourth Symphony was a primary locus of such attacks. Eric Blom called it a product "of a pathological state, a nerve crisis." [16] He did not acknowledge Tchaikovsky's competence in symphonic development because the folk theme in the last movement "remains angular and obtrusive, and will not be polished down to formal beauty or utility."[17] Cooper viewed the development section of the first movement as " little more than a free fantasia on the persistent rhythmic figure of the first subject and within [a] restless, hectic emotional atmosphere. Musical growth . . . was virtually unknown to Tchaikovsky."[18]

Given such criticism, it is not surprising that the suites' standing was considered even lower than that of the symphonies. Like them, the suites were said to contain some fine music, but were criticized for not possessing satisfactory unity. In the case of the First Suite, this was attributed to its convoluted compositional history and to Tchaikovsky's general problems with form. Naturally, some critics attempted to posit connections between Tchaikovsky's life and the Suite. David Brown, for instance, speculated about correspondences between letters in Nadezhda Filaretovna von Meck's name and the notes of the fugue subject from the First Suite (first movement).[19] In this attempt, he inconsistently alternates the syllables of two different notational systems. Brown's idea is that the subject of the fugue (a'—d'—e'—f'—a'—d"—f"—e"—d", see Ex. 6) outlines the words *Nadezhda Filaretovna—mily drug* (Nadezhda Filaretovna—beloved friend): [N]*A*—*DE*[zhda] *F*[i]—*La*—*Re*[to]—*F*[na] *Mi*[ly] *D*[rug]. For a', d', e', f', and the last d", Brown uses the German letter names, and in the middle of the second word he switches to the French syllables: la, re, and mi. Moreover, to have the second f" in the word Filaretovna, he changes the written *v* to an *f*, perhaps in the mistaken belief that that is the way the letter is pronounced in Russian.

Recently, some scholars have attempted to reexamine Tchaikovsky's life and works and in some cases to separate them.[20] Alexander Poznansky undertook the difficult task of assembling and analyzing various documentary materials, which enabled him to take a revisionist view on many episodes of Tchaikovsky's life. As to his music, Henry Zajaczkowski argued that, despite the fact that it "certainly did not display the Germanic style of measured, methodical movement," its significance and integrity could nonetheless be discussed in analytical terms.[21] Richard Taruskin also made a significant contribution to Tchaikovsky studies by disputing traditional notions and prejudices. Tchaikovsky's orchestral suites, however, still remain underestimated and relegated to the category of second-rate works. On the other hand, they have generated the same sort of controversy and criticisms as the symphonies, including references to lack of formal unity, structural and developmental faults, and impurity regarding genre. A study of the symphonic aspects of the First Suite suggests that, rather than being second-rate music, the whole genre can be seen as a site of Tchaikovsky's ongoing creative experimentation and quest for solutions to the very problems that concerned both himself and his critics.

The New Harvard Dictionary defines the suite as "a series of disparate instrumental movements with some element of unity, most often to be performed as a single work."[22] By the nineteenth century the suite had essentially lost its popularity in Europe, having been replaced by other multimovement instrumental genres, such as the concerto, sonata, and symphony. Yet the orchestral suite did not disappear completely; rather, it underwent certain modifications. The impetus for the nineteenth-century suite might be a poetic idea or the desire to condense a larger work. Furthermore, David Fuller comments on the lack of distinction between the orchestral program suite and the program symphony, whose designations were often based on little more than the composers' preferences of terminology.[23] In Europe, attempts to revive the suite as an alternative to the sonata or symphony were made in the second half of the nineteenth century by two German composers, Franz Lachner (1803–1890) and Joseph Joachim Raff (1822–1882). They wrote a number of suites, in which they incorporated the old Baroque dances (sarabande, gigue, minuet) and contemporaneous forms (rhapsody, march, *Ländler*, romanze). Fuller remarks that the overall movement structure of these suites often approached that of the sonata (Raff, Op. 162) and symphony (Lachner, no., 1 Op. 113).

In Russia, two types of suite emerged over the course of the nineteenth century. One was related to nonprogrammatic, divertimento music; a second was based on literary sources or programs, or derived from operas and ballets; only a few Russian composers, however, wrote bona fide orchestral suites. Of the first type, there are examples by Cui (*Suite miniature* No. 1, 1882; Suite No. 2, 1887; Suite No. 3 *(In modo populari)*, 1890; Suite No. 4, 1887), Taneev (*Suite de concert*, 1909), and Balakirev (Suite including Préambule, Quasi valse, and Tarantella, 1901–9; Suite on pieces by Chopin, including Préambule, Mazurka, Intermezzo, and Finale, 1909).

The second type of suite may have originated from the programmatic overture, fantasia, and symphonic poem. The programmatic suite seems simply to go a step further in increasing the number of the movements. Rimsky-Korsakov was perhaps the most consistent composer of programmatic orchestral suites, of which the symphonic suite *Sheherazade* (1888) is the most famous. Ironically, the previously discussed argument over the lack of unity in Tchaikovsky's symphonies and suites applies also to Rimsky-Korsakov's suites. Abraham comments on *Sheherazade*'s "brightfully coloured mosaics; although the thematic ideas lack organic cohesion, they are often striking and piquant."[24]

Tchaikovsky considered the orchestral suite eminently suitable for the realization of his own creative tasks. In a letter to Mme von Meck (28 April 1884), Tchaikovsky wrote how the suite "has for some time been particularly attractive to me because of the freedom it affords the composer not to be inhibited by any traditions, by conventional methods and established rules."[25] In the suite, Tchaikovsky was not restrained by Western symphonic requirements and did not have to write up to the grand European level; rather, he could freely realize his creative potential in an orchestral format. Thus it is not surprising that Tchaikovsky significantly contributed to both types of orchestral suite. His nonprogrammatic suites include the Second Suite (1883), the Third Suite (1884), and the Fourth Suite, *Mozartiana*, based on themes from Mozart (1887). The well-known suite from the ballet *Nutcracker* (1892) belongs to the second category, since it is derived from a dramatic work.

Initially it would appear that Tchaikovsky's First Suite for Orchestra illustrates the divertimento-like, nonprogrammatic type of suite; a closer examination of its compositional history and relationship to the Fourth Symphony, however, brings certain qualifications to this understanding.

Tchaikovsky finished his First Suite in August 1879. By that time he had already composed a significant portion of his orchestral works, including the first four symphonies (1866, 1872, 1875, 1878), the symphonic poem *Fatum* (1868), the fantasy overture *Romeo and Juliet* (1869), the symphonic fantasia *Francesca da Rimini* (1876), the *Slavonic March* (1876), and his first ballet, *Swan Lake* (1877). With the First Suite, Tchaikovsky added one more orchestral genre to his compositional repertory.

1877 (two years before the composition of the Suite) brought major changes to Tchaikovsky's life. The circumstances of his disastrous marriage have been described in a variety of literature. It has been argued that the depression Tchaikovsky experienced during that time influenced his artistic work, in particular the composition of the Fourth Symphony. Joseph C. Kraus argues that "most of the sketches for the work were completed by early May 1877, [that is] before the marriage and its subsequent failure."[26] The marriage was evidently not the only cause of Tchaikovsky's depression, however, for he writes "I was down in the dumps last winter when the symphony was in the writing, and it is a faithful echo of what I was going through at that time" (see Fig. 1).[27]

The positive change in Tchaikovsky's life was brought about by the beginning of a friendship with Nadezhda Filaretovna von Meck (née Frolovsky, 1831–1894), who eventually established a yearly pension of six thousand rubles that enabled Tchaikovsky to resign from the Conservatory in September 1878. In this woman of high intelligence, great wealth, and complex character, Tchaikovsky found not only a sponsor, but a friend who felt "an enormous conviction that [they were] one in thought and feeling."[28] This friendship resulted in a correspondence of over 1000 letters, written from 1877 to 1891.

Figure 1. Biographical Events Surrounding the Composition
of the Fourth Symphony and the First Suite

Sketches for the Fourth are completed	May 1877
Marriage	18 July 1877
Presumed suicide attempt (according to Nikolai Kashkin)	October 1877
Leaves Russia	October 1877
Composition of the Fourth Symphony	Winter 1877–78
Fourth Symphony finished	7 January 1878
Moscow premiere of the Fourth	22 February 1878
First Suite conceived	July 1878
First Suite finished	August 1879

In the wake of his divorce and newfound friendship, Tchaikovsky in 1878 conceived the idea of his First Suite. It was his intention to approximate the style of Lachner, to combine the old dances with the new. [29] The first movement composed was the Scherzo, begun with enthusiasm in Brailov, whence he wrote to Mme von Meck: "As I worked, my thoughts were always with you. . . . So it can be dedicated to no one but you. To my best friend; either I shall put it in the heading, as with the Fourth Symphony, or if you prefer, put nothing on it at all, that the dedication may be known to none but ourselves."[30]

Tchaikovsky usually completed his works in short blocks of time (though he might revise them substantially later). With the First Suite, however, his initial conception changed several times. On 28 August 1878, he wrote from Verbovka (a village near Davydov's estate at Kamenka), "In Brailov I composed a Scherzo, here an Introduction and Fugue and an Andante. All this, with an Intermezzo and Rondo, will be part of a Suite. Both of these are germinating in my head."[31] The original plan of August 1878 included five movements: Introduzione e Fuga, Scherzo, Andante, Intermezzo (Echo du bal), and Rondo. [32] The composition of the Suite, however, was interrupted and the initial plan modified several times, as reflected in Fig. 2. On 20 December 1879 the Suite was successfully performed in Moscow under Nikolai Rubinstein. At the time of the premiere, Tchaikovsky was in Rome, but he received a detailed report about the concert from his publisher Jurgenson: "The first movement went off without fervent expressions of delight. The second evidently pleased. The

Figure 2. Summary of the First Suite's Compositional History

Composition of the Scherzo	July 1878	Brailov	
Composition of Introduzione e Fuga and Andante	August 1878	Verbovka	The original plan of the Suite: Introduzione e Fuga,Scherzo, Andante, Intermezzo (Echo du bal), and Rondo
Composition of the last two movements (original names:March of the Lilliputians and Dance of the Giants)	September/ November 1878	Kamenka	The second plan: Introduzione e Fuga, Scherzo, Andante, March of the Lilliputians, Dance of the Giants (the last two are Nos. 4 and 6 in the final version)
Orchestration of the last two movements, the first three movements are considered lost	December 1878	Florence	
The manuscript of the first three movements finally received	16 January 1879	Clarens	
Began to work on the Suite after *The Maid of Orleans*	6 March 1879	Paris	
Finished the score	26 April 1879	Kamenka	
Finished the piano arrangement	6 May 1879	Kamenka	
Decision to replace March with a waltz (a 3/4 movement needed, March seemed to Tchaikovsky "of doubtful merit")*	August 1879	Simaki	
Decision to retain March and replace Andante with a waltz	September 1879	Simaki	The third plan: Introduzione e Fuga, Divertimento (the new 3/4 movement), Scherzo, Marche miniature, Gavotte
Moscow premiere	20 December 1879	Moscow	The final order: Introduzione e Fuga, Divertimento (waltz), Intermezzo (Andante), Marche miniature, Scherzo, Gavotte
St. Petersburg premiere	6 April 1880	St. Petersburg	

*Tchaikovsky, *Polnoe sobranie*, vol. 8, 315. Translated in Brown, *Tchaikovsky*, vol. 3, 20.

Andante pleased very much, but the March drew applause which wouldn't stop until it was repeated. The Scherzo was very well received. The Gavotte found the audience by now fatigued and bursting to get away."[33]

The Suite was frequently performed and enthusiastically received in Russia and in Europe during Tchaikovsky's lifetime. The composer often included it in his concerts, explaining that this piece "has the advantage of generally pleasing the public."[35] Mme von Meck wrote to Tchaikovsky in August 1880 about young Claude Debussy, at the time engaged for her private concerts: "after we had played your suite he was so pleased with the Fugue that he volunteered, 'I've never come across anything so beautiful in all modern fugues.'"[36] In Germany, Clara Schumann wrote in her diary on 3 February 1882, after the Frankfurt performance, "Suite by Tschaikowsky; a good deal of talent and ability."[37] On 3 January 1888, after the concert in Leipzig by the Gewandhaus Orchestra, Tchaikovsky noted that, although Brahms "made no encouraging remarks, I was told he was very pleased by the first movement, but did not praise the rest, especially the 'Marche miniature.'"[38] Grieg left a note appraising the Suite highly after that same concert.[39] In England, the Marche miniature was welcomed the most, called "worthy of H. Berlioz," and the audience demanded it be played twice. After the concert in London (11 April 1889), a critic for *The Musical Times* wrote there was "an absolutely astounding wealth of beautiful ideas. Where other men would use one subject, Tschaikowsky lavishes half a dozen, most of them are remarkably original, all highly attractive, the *soupçon* of triviality attached to a few being altogether nullified by piquant rhythm or harmony, and an orchestration which—for novelty, variety and charm of instrumental effects—defies description."[40]

The rather complicated compositional history of the Suite suggests that the genre indeed was a form of experimentation for Tchaikovsky. The several versions of the Suite that he considered reflect the empirical process of the composer's creative search. The Suite's history helps explain to a degree why certain movements that were composed earlier have greater weight in the Suite than movements composed later, which the composer manipulated for purely prosaic ends.

Written during the same period and dedicated to Mme von Meck, the Fourth Symphony and First Suite share more than mere historical proximity. The two in fact reveal a complex system of interconnections. According to Roland John Wiley, the two main determinants of symphonic procedures include "a sense of balanced architectural pattern" and "a coherent discourse which grows out of the musical ideas themselves, out of the logic of their interaction."[41] The following discussion of the musical similarities reflected in the works' design will reveal the Suite's thematic organization as a "coherent discourse" and the layout of its movements as a vehicle for the growth of musical ideas similar to those of the Fourth Symphony.

Shortly after the Fourth Symphony's Moscow premiere (22 February 1878), Mme von Meck asked Tchaikovsky if it had any program. Her question presumably was prompted by the work's unusual character. Likewise, Sergei Taneev observed that "the first movement is disproportionally longer than the rest of the movements; it gives the effect of a symphonic poem, to which three other movements had been haphazardly added,"[42] a circumstance which could possibly be explained by a program. In reply to Mme von Meck's inquiry, Tchaikovsky wrote "Usually when that question is put to me about one of my symphonic things, I answer: *none whatsoever*."[43] Yet, this time, Tchaikovsky admitted that the Symphony did indeed have a program, and explained its relationship to the music. The main idea, Fate, introduced in the beginning of the first movement, is that "force which prevents the impulse towards happiness from achieving its aim . . ."[44] According to Tchaikovsky's program, attempts to seek happiness in memories of the past (the second movement: "it's both sad yet somehow sweet to immerse yourself in the past") and in dreams (the third movement: "capricious arabesques . . . evanescent images . . . flit past in your imagination"[45]) fail because Fate constantly awakens to reality."

First presented in the Introduction of the Fourth Symphony (Ex. 1a), the Fate theme is one of the work's most striking features. In the above-mentioned letter to Mme von Meck, Tchaikovsky explains its relationship to the Introduction, calling it *Fatum*: "The Introduction is the seed of the whole symphony, without doubt the principal idea. This is *Fate* [Fatum]."[46] Tchaikovsky's use of this theme also resembles Beethoven's approach in his Fifth Symphony. In a reply to Taneev's letter, Tchaikovsky wrote "In fact, my symphony is an imitation of Beethoven's Fifth; i.e. I imitated not the musical ideas but the main concept."[47]

The theme, which is introduced in the beginning, returns in the first movement and Finale and also serves as a source for other themes.[48] The Fate theme fulfills two functions: on the local level (within the movements) it represents a destructive power that "checks our aspirations toward happiness before they reach the goal," and on the larger scale (between the movements) it unifies the composition, serving as a basis for the dramatic action throughout the movements and as a source of thematic ideas. The idea of a Fate theme, also incorporated in Tchaikovsky's Fifth Symphony and Brahms' First Symphony, reflects the nineteenth-century concept of *per aspera ad astra*.[49] It imbues symphonic writing with a dramatic element and, especially in the case of Tchaikovsky's Fourth, contributes to the development of a stronger and more coherent form. The composer treats the idea of conflict with Fate as a true Romantic trying to escape reality, seeking happiness in fantasy. In the Fourth Symphony, however, the solution to this tragic conflict is relatively optimistic (at least in comparison with his Sixth Symphony). In the same letter to Mme von Meck, Tchaikovsky writes about the last movement of the Fourth: "If you can't find reasons for joy within yourself, look at others. Go among the common people. . . . Rejoice in the rejoicing of others. Yes, it is possible to live."[50]

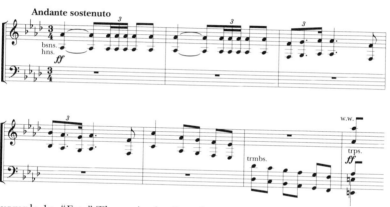

Example 1a. "Fate" Theme in the Fourth Symphony (mm. 1–6)

The program, although not very detailed, influenced the composition of the whole Symphony. The contrasts and the unusual length of the first movement relate to the struggle with Fate, the character of the second and third movements portrays the search for happiness, and the folk tune in the last movement represents one's unity with the people and one's sharing in their simple joys. Further, the program for the Fourth elucidates certain features of its form, structure, thematic character, and development. I shall argue that, if the program for the Fourth Symphony resulted in unusual symphonic procedures and musical forms, it should then be possible for other compositions resembling the Fourth to reveal similar programmatic implications or at least allude to their existence.

Tchaikovsky did not leave a programmatic description for the First Suite as he had for the Symphony. On the surface, there is nothing unusual in the Suite: the movements constitute a variety of genres in related keys within a single composition. On the other hand, the Suite possesses ambiguous qualities that produce a musical logic different from a more typical example of the genre. Introduzione e Fuga, Intermezzo, Scherzo, and Gavotte are of greater length and weight than the other movements. (As will be discussed below, the themes in these four movements are often dramatically opposed and receive some development). Further, the layout of those movements resembles the order typical of the movements in the Symphony (Fig. 3).

Figure 3. The First Suite: Symphonically Derived Movements

---

1. Introduzione e Fuga (Andnte sostenuto. Moderato e con anima), D Minor	I
2. Divertimento (Allegro moderato), B-flat Major	
3. Intermezzo (Andantino semplice), D Minor	II
4. Marche miniature (Moderato con moto), A Major	
5. Scherzo (Allegro con moto), B-flat Major	III
6. Gavotte (Allegro), D Major	IV

In isolating these four movements, it becomes apparent that they are connected by a logic similar to that of the symphony. Full of contrasts and dynamism, Introduzione e Fuga could serve as a first movement, while the reflective and lyrical Intermezzo resembles a second. The dance-like Scherzo could function as a third movement, and the Gavotte is analogous to a Finale.

A principal dramatic agent in the First Suite is the Fate theme, first appearing in the Introduzione (mm. 50-55, see Ex. 1b). The connection between the themes in the Fourth Symphony and in the First Suite is apparent from a similarity of rhythmic ideas (dotted quarter note and sixteenth-note triplets), the distribution of brass in octaves, and persistent repetition. Such similarity, however, is not enough to conclude this theme in the First Suite symbolizes Fate. To address that possibility, it is necessary to trace the two themes as they function on local levels and compare their respective roles in the works. In the Fourth Symphony, the Fate theme appears at the outset of the first movement and returns before the development (m. 193); it also punctuates the development (mm. 253, 263, 278), and makes a parting gesture in the Coda (m. 389). At its initial appearance, the Fate theme announces the drama and warns of future tragedy; every time thereafter it "intrude[s] peremptorily and inexorably, sweeping aside all other material" (Ex. 2).[51]

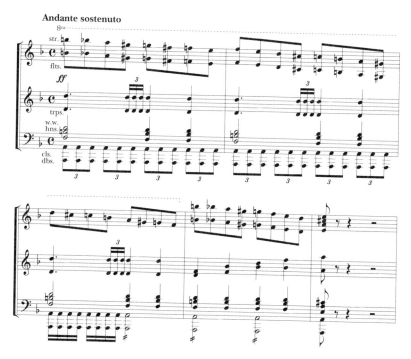

Example 1b. "Fate" Theme in the First Suite (mm. 50–55)

In contrast, in the First Suite the Fate theme is delayed until m. 50 of the Introduzione and is the movement's first climax. As in the Symphony's development, however, it maintains an intrusive quality, challenging the previous unfolding of musical ideas. The theme in the Suite is not presented as a symbol at the beginning of the composition, but rather appears already invested with active power. The unexpected dramatic effect is, therefore, even stronger than in the Symphony, where tragedy is inevitable from the very beginning.

In the rest of the first movement the theme returns only once, in the Fugue (m. 159). Here it again interrupts the unfolding of the form: the polyphonic texture is liquidated in a prolonged diminished seventh chord (mm. 159-61, see Ex. 3), breaking the carefully built fugal process. The fugue subject is changed drastically, rhythm remaining its

Example 2. "Fate" Theme in the Development and Coda, First Movement, Fourth Symphony (mm. 253–257, 389–392)

only recognizable feature. The passage is orchestrated in three distinct
layers: the Fate theme (horns and trumpets), the transformed fugue
subject (cellos, double basses, and bassoons), and harmonic support (the
rest of the orchestra). This section constitutes the first phase of the
movement's climax. The second phase incorporates the fugue subject in
augmentation, also in the brass section. Although the theme occurs only
twice in the first movement of the Suite, each time it effects major
changes in the logic of musical development. If in the Symphony it
repeatedly insists upon tragedy, in the Suite the theme reveals its dramatic qualities through a sparing but powerful impact. Thus the local
function of the theme is similar in both first movements: its sudden
appearance throttles the progression of musical ideas.

Example 3. "Fate" Theme in the Fugue, First Suite, First Movement (mm.
159–163)

A similar comparison can be made regarding the theme's large-scale function. In both works, the theme returns in another movement, serving to unify the composition. In the Symphony it recurs in the last movement, producing "an astonishing melodramatic effect" (Ex. 4).[52]

Example 4. "Fate" Theme in the Finale of the Fourth Symphony (mm. 198–201)

In the Suite, however, a modification of the theme recurs in the third movement, Intermezzo (mm. 180-82), which substitutes for the symphonic slow movement. It is important to note that the recurrence does not come immediately after the first movement, in which the outline of the dramatic conflict is established; rather, its appearance is delayed by the Divertimento, a light, waltz-like movement, which in fact Tchaikovsky composed after the others to break the monotony of the omnipresent duple rhythms. As Tchaikovsky wrote to Mme von Meck, "I did not know how to call the new movement, and chose Divertimento as the first name that turned up. It seemed to me that it was not important among other movements and was attached to the Suite to save it from the monotonous rhythm."[53] Despite the composer's negative assessment, however, the Divertimento postpones the Intermezzo, thus making dramatic contrasts even more compelling.

The Fate theme in the Intermezzo is the culmination of the movement, preparing the way for the final statement of the first theme (Ex. 5). Its appearance is emphasized by an unexpected harmonic change (D Minor to E-flat Major), a sudden tutti, and an abrupt change of texture (the tutti chords alternating with a descending line in the strings). It is clear that the function and dramatic impact of this theme are analogous to those of the Fate theme in the Fourth Symphony. In the Intermezzo, however, the Fate theme does not represent the final stage of drama, as in the Symphony; instead, the Intermezzo is one more stage of the dramatic action, far from any conclusion. Although the Fate theme does not return in any of the following movements, that does not mean the drama is exhausted, for *another* thematic idea comes to the fore, one that also made an appearance in the first movement:

Example 5. "Fate" Theme in Itermezzo (mm. 178–182)

At first sight, the elimination of the Fate theme after the Intermezzo in the Suite seems to signify an approach different from that taken in the Symphony. When we examine Tchaikovsky's approach to thematic transformation, however, further parallels between the two works obtain. In the Symphony, a thematic unit besides the Fate theme connects all four movements, and the first group of the opening movement contains the seed of that unit: the descending minor second. It later appears as the initial interval of the main themes in the second, third, and final movements (Fig. 4).

Figure 4. Main Themes of the Fourth Symphony
(Beginning Pitches)

I	D-flat	C	B	B-flat
II	D-flat	C	B-flat	A
III	F	E	D	C
IV	F	E	D	C

The true significance of this thematic unit, however, lies in its transformations. The emotional expression carried by its themes changes from lyrical and lamenting (the first and second movements) to energetic and joyful (the third and fourth movements), representing a transformation from within. This transformation corresponds to Tchaikovsky's program, according to which one seeks happiness and protection from Fate in unity with the world of simple people. In order to do that, however, one must change oneself. The various guises of the main theme, culminating in a major key, would seem a logical solution to the problem of executing such an idea musically.

In the Suite, Tchaikovsky also conveyed the triumph of positive forces. Instead of showing the gradual transformation of one thematic idea, however, he employed two contrasting thematic units, the first of which (the Fate theme) declines after the Intermezzo and the second of which comes to the fore in the last movement. This second idea is represented by the fugue subject of the first movement of the Suite (Ex. 6).

Example 6. The Fugue Subject in the First Suite (mm. 83–87)

Here it is worth reiterating that the climax of the first movement dramatically opposes these two themes, since the Fate theme (mm. 159-63) is immediately followed by the fugue subject in augmentation (mm. 163–69, see Ex. 7). Thus, these two themes have confronted one another from the start, the former a negative and distracting power, the latter positive and creative (generating a fugue and concluding the whole Suite). At the start it is not obvious which of these powers will eventually prevail. The solution to the conflict appears in the last movement, a Gavotte: the Fate theme now vanquished, the fugue subject symbolizes victory, manifest in its major key (D Major instead of D Minor), its dynamics and orchestration (fortissimo, tutti), and the status it occupies (the final two statements of the Suite).

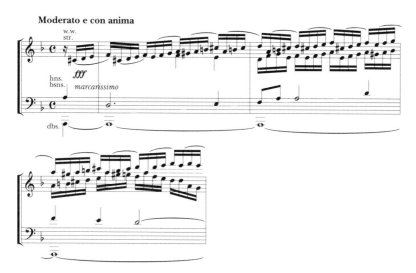

Example 7. The Fugue Subject in Augmentation Second Phase of the First Movement's Climax, First Suite (mm. 163–166)

An additional thematic issue arises in the penultimate movement, Scherzo. Although it is the only symphonically derived movement in the Suite (see Fig. 3) that does *not* include a clear statement of either the Fate theme or the fugue subject, this movement nonetheless is crucial to our understanding of the Suite's underlying logic. As noted earlier, this was the movement with which Tchaikovsky began composition of the Suite, and which includes the variations on a folk theme resembling the Ukrainian tune "Kazachok" (m. 74, see Ex. 8a).[54] As is well known, the culmination of the Fourth Symphony likewise employs a folk tune, "Vo pole bereza stoiala" (In the fields there stood a birch tree; m. 10, see Ex. 8b). There, if we take the composer at his word, it represents a unity with the people that serves as an antidote to tragedy. The return of the Fate theme in the coda, of course, darkens this temporary feeling of brotherhood. In the Suite, the folk-influenced Scherzo prepares for the glorious Finale, in which not a hint of tragedy occurs. We might even conclude that the Suite brings to a victorious conclusion the tragic issues that remained unresolved in the Symphony, completed just a year and a half earlier.

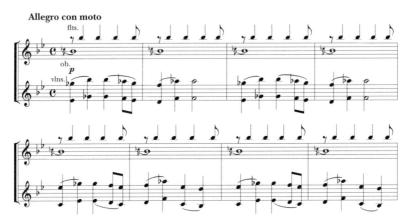

Example 8a. The Folk Tunes in the First Suite and the Fourth Symphony, Scherzo First Suite (mm. 74–81)

Example 8b. The Folk Tunes in the First Suite and the Fourth Symphony, Finale, Fourth Symphony (mm. 10–17)

Further comparisons can be made between the two works. Dramaticism, focused thematic and tonal development, connections on the structural level, and other links between the movements are principles not commonly associated with the suite genre. However, they are frequently present in romantic symphonies, both non-programmatic and programmatic. This is largely due to an overall unity common in the symphony but less so in the suite, with its diversity of movement types. How does the First Suite incorporate these *general* symphonic principles?

Besides the inter-movement thematic connections noted above, the tonal organization of the First Suite is telling. First, tonality links the symphonically derived movements (Introduzione, Intermezzo, Scherzo, and Gavotte). In traditional suites, all the movements are written in the same key, which is in some cases the sole organizational principle. In his First Suite, however, Tchaikovsky did not follow this general rule, for all the movements are in different keys (see Fig. 3); thus he introduced an element of symphonic style, namely, tonal contrast, into the modest genre of the suite. Second, and more important, these four movements create a tonal design that alludes to the organization of the Fourth Symphony (Fig. 5).

The first two movements of both Symphony and Suite are in minor keys, representing the first stage of the drama. The general direction of both works is from minor to major, embodying the optimistic idea of man's unification with people and the common nineteenth-century trope *per aspera ad astra*. This tradition of opposing the minor and major keys in the first and last movements is also reflected in symphonies by Beethoven (the Fifth, the Ninth), Brahms (the First), and Tchaikovsky (the Fifth). In Tchaikovsky's First Suite and Fourth Symphony, minor and major keys are balanced, each being given two movements. In the Symphony the tonic key is given to the last two movements, while in the Suite it is given to the first two.

Figure 5. Tonal Design

Fourth Symphony	*First Suite*	
I. F Minor (i)	D Minor (i)	(Introduzione e Fuga)
II. B-flat Minor (iv)	D Minor (i)	(Intermezzo)
III. F Major (I)	B-flat Major (VI)	(Scherzo)
IV. F Major (I)	D Major (I)	(Gavotte)

In the Suite, of course, the presence of two additional movements (Divertimento and Marche miniature) diffuses this tonal organization. As will be recalled, however, Tchaikovsky had to be persuaded to retain the Marche miniature in the Suite, and the Divertimento was meant to replace Marche miniature only to provide relief from duple meters. Only the performance success of those movements (due to their witty orchestration) prompted Tchaikovsky to leave them in the Suite. In his letter to Jurgenson (5 September 1879), he commented "You write that the Marche miniature ought to be left. . . . Speaking frankly, I would wish to throw out this rubbish altogether. Moreover, I find six movements too many."[55] Thus the Divertimento and Marche miniature did not originally play a major role in the Suite's overall tonal organization and were regarded by the composer as structurally insignificant.

Another general procedure evident in the First Suite is a thematic development and manipulation of the musical ideas that result in broad symphonic structures. Again, we find several parallels with the Fourth Symphony. As noted, Taneev compared the first movement of the Fourth Symphony with a symphonic poem, suggesting that the other three movements were "accidentally" added to make up a symphony. Although he overlooked the role and significance of the rest of the movements, Taneev nonetheless identified one important feature of the Symphony: the unusual length and weight of the first movement. Clearly, this is due to the movement's functions, namely, to introduce the dramatic conflict, to serve as a site for the first collision between the Fate theme and the unfolding of symphonic structure, and to achieve the first dramatic climax. This wealth of events explains its disproportionate length: over seventeen minutes, compared with a little over nine minutes for the second movement, approximately seven minutes for the third, and approximately eight minutes for the last.[56] Likewise, the first movement of the Suite exceeds the rest of its movements in terms of length and density of events. As in the Symphony, this movement includes the exposition of the main ideas (the Fate theme and the fugue subject) and involves the first collision of both powers. It lasts over twelve minutes, almost twice as long as any of the ensuing movements (5:42, 8:01, 1:52, 7:53, and 6:14).[57] Clearly, the dramatic tasks of the first movements and their balance with the subsequent movements are related.

In the Suite, Tchaikovsky managed to convey the unfolding drama in a completely original way. He once wrote to Mme von Meck about the Fourth Symphony, "In certain circumstances, such as a symphony, the form is taken for granted and I keep it—but only as to the large outline and proper sequence of movements. The details can be manipulated as freely as one chooses."[58] If Tchaikovsky admitted such structural freedom in the symphony, the suite would provide even more leeway for his urge to experiment with form. As I have argued, the Suite has a "large outline" and "proper sequence of movements" typical of the symphony. As for "details," Introduzione e Fuga demonstrates how an impression of the symphonic procedure can be achieved even within looser structure. The Fate theme and the fugue subject provide the necessary dramatic element and create the opposition resembling that in the first movement of the Fourth. This opposition results in a structure that is comparable to sonata form (albeit without standard formal attributes).

The Suite's slow introduction furnishes another connection with Tchaikovsky's symphonies, all but the first of which contain slow introductions. The association with the Fourth Symphony is especially apparent, because its introduction also contains the Fate theme. The Introduzione is rather long to be a simple preamble; moreover, it contains a series of thematic statements that contrast in terms of musical character and subsequent development. The first theme (mm. 1–30, Ex. 9) starts with a tense, chromatic motive played by two bassoons, while the rest of the orchestra is silent. This motive ends on A (the fifth scale degree in D Minor), which resembles a typically romantic "motive of question" (similar to the beginning of Schubert's Unfinished Symphony and Chopin's First Ballade for piano).

The second theme (mm. 30–40, Ex. 10) is introduced with a polyphonic imitation of the strings (pianissimo). The Fate theme (Ex. 2b, mm. 50–54, tutti, fortissimo, brass) contradicts the previous musical flow, as noted earlier. The last theme (mm. 55–70, Ex. 11) concludes the Introduzione with the repeated "question motive" of the strings.

The Fuga introduces a new theme (see Ex. 6), characterized by an active ascending melodic line spanning a tenth, and by an energetic rhythm (the first nine notes are all emphasized by accents). Its vigorous spirit and developmental nature serve as a next logical step after the introduction, and it includes several thematic statements.[59] Moreover, the fugue subject consists of two contrasting parts that provide potential for future development. Both parts, the decisive beginning (eighth notes, mm. 83–85) and more neutral dancelike continuation (mm 85–87), become the basis for different sections of the fugue's development.

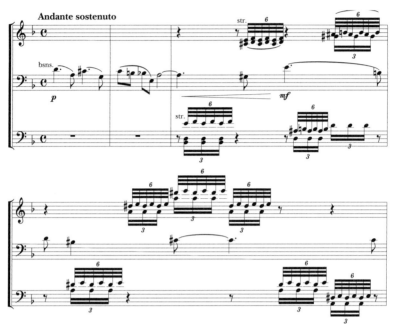

Example 9. The First Theme of Introduzione, First Suite (mm. 1–4)

Example 10. The Second Theme of Introduzione, First Suite (mm. 30–33)

Example 11. The Last Theme of Introduzione, First Suite (mm. 55–58)

At first, the fugue follows a traditional scheme (exposition). The initial statement of the subject (D Minor) is in the alto (clarinet, oboe, and second violins). The tenor (oboe, bassoon, and cellos), bass (bassoon, cellos, and double basses), and soprano (flutes, oboe, and first violins) continue with the tonal plan, A Minor–D Minor–A Minor. After the four-measure episode, serving as a link between the exposition and development, the soprano states the subject in F Major (m. 104), the beginning of the tonal development. The following appearances of the subject in C major (alto, m. 107; bass, m. 116), A Minor (tenor, m. 120), and D Minor (soprano, m. 124) complete the first section. The division of the first and the second sections is significant for several reasons. First, the last two subject entries (A Minor and D Minor) lead the tonal progression back to the initial key, creating a local recapitulation. Second, for the last time before the subject appears in its final augmented form, the A Minor entry states the subject in its complete form (including the two contrasting parts). Third, the D-Minor entry constitutes the first climax and transformation, which turns the subsequent development of the fugue to a different direction.

What is important here is the fact that the intensity of the fugal process surpasses the limits of the traditional polyphonic form and creates development on a symphonic scale. This emerges on several levels in the development section. For example, the second stage of the development contains stretto imitations of the first motive of the subject that were not present in its initial form (mm. 132–46). Only the rhythm and certain motives are preserved. Since only the first part of the subject is being developed (eighth notes), the overall impression is that the motion slows down; yet the orchestral density produced by the large number of stretto entries, dynamics (fortissimo), and articulation (marcato) increases tension. Thus the method of development here approaches that of a symphony, where the most active and effective motives are isolated and developed, producing new combinations. In addition, the fact that the stretto imitations of the subject are not literal serves to highlight Tchaikovsky's departure from traditional fugal processes. Yet these nonliteral imitations are controlled by clear harmonic motion.

Further, the tonal motion in these entries is intensive and directed to distant keys: G Minor (m. 132)–F Major (m. 135)–B-flat Major (m. 137), G Minor (m. 138)–E-flat Major (m. 139)–C Minor (m. 140)–B-flat Major (m. 141)–E-flat Major (m. 143)–C Minor (m. 144)–A-flat Major (m. 145)–F Minor (m. 148). This active harmonic progression resembles symphonic development more than fugal procedure. The second section thus differs remarkably from the previous progress of the fugue. Tchaikovsky limited the traditional polyphonic procedures to the exposition and first section of the development of the fugue and then started a new phase approximating symphonic development. In addition, the fugue subject has been transformed.

The third section of the development returns to the main key (m. 150); it cannot, however, be considered a recapitulation, because the subject appears in an incomplete form and the subsequent tonal motion is directed away from the main key. Rather, this section is a preparation for the first phase of the climax, signified by the appearance of the Fate theme. The fugue subject momentarily loses its strong-willed character (only the rhythm and directions of the motives recall the original theme), signifying the tragic nature of Fate's interference. The texture is transformed also. As noted, the orchestra is divided into three layers: the subject, harmonic figurations outlining a diminished seven-chord, and the Fate theme supported by the chords of the wind instruments (Ex. 3). Thus the two themes, which were first opposed in time (Introduzione versus Fuga), here are combined contrapuntally, indentified by Zajaczkowski as "juxtaposition-then-combination technique," most typical of Tchaikovsky's sonata form in the symphonies.[60] The development of the Fourth Symphony also incorporates this technique, when the motives from the first and second groups alternate in a different order compared to the exposition, revealing a new quality of antagonism.[61]

The subject, which follows in augmentation in D Minor (m. 163), constitutes the highest stage of the climax, with fortissimo horns and a pedal on A (dominant of D Minor). This climax is a result of several preceding stages of the development, and it coincides with the beginning of the real recapitulation (complete subject, D Minor, Ex. 7). A similar design can be found in the first movement of the Fourth Symphony, where the recapitulation was the movement's culmination. The first theme appeared there on the top of the last stage of development, accompanied by the dominant pedal in the orchestra (Ex. 12). Once again, the Symphony and Suite appear related in their design.

Example 12. The Climax of the First Movement, Fourth Symphony (mm. 283–286)

Example 13a. The Themes of Intermezzo, The First Theme (mm. 2–11)

Example 13b. The Themes of Intermezzo, The Second Theme (mm. 38–45)

The Fugue thus approaches the Symphony in several ways. Symphonic methods of tonal and thematic development prevail, in that the fugue subject creates an alternative to the Fate theme and produces an opposition of two powers; this gives impetus to the development. The return of the fugue subject in the last movement, Gavotte, is therefore not simply a means of structural unification but also a conclusion to the long-range, dramatic process initiated in the first movement.

As noted, the third movement, Intermezzo, could be a slow movement of a symphony. It opens with a slow lyrical theme (Ex. 13a; bassoon, flute, violins, and violas) supported by ostinato strings recalling a funeral march. The theme has a vocal quality similar to the Russian nineteenth-century romance; behind its simplicity, however, lies an inner tension realized in the very structure of the theme. The melody slowly climbs to its highest point, which is reached only the second time (m. 20). This resistance in achieving a melodic climax hints at the dramaticism of the music that will be projected throughout the movement. The second theme (m. 38, see Ex. 13b), which represents a warm and dreamlike image (bassoon), provides contrast. Compared to the music of the first movement, the Intermezzo has a more lyrical, tragic character. In the first movement, the dramatic Introduzione was followed by the active fugue with broad development, while in the Intermezzo the two themes are opposed as two invariable poles. The changes occur only within the themes, not between them, rendering the Intermezzo more static than the first movement.

The type of contrast between the first and second themes in the Intermezzo, however, is similar to that in the second movement of the Fourth Symphony (Ex. 14). The feeling of deep and dark melancholy dominates the first theme, expressed by a songlike melody. The theme in F Major is more dynamic, and contrasts with the first theme by virtue of key area and its short motifs (rather than spacious, song-like phrases) that are developed sequentially. The ABABA form of the Intermezzo (which could also be viewed as a sonata form without development) reflects the idea of the endlessness of suffering and the impossibility of reaching happiness. Neither theme receives broad development. The theme conveying the spirit of optimism (the second group) is, in the recapitulation, brutally interrupted by the repeated opening motives of the first theme (fortissimo) and immediately followed by the Fate theme (Ex. 5), and so the unfolding movement is pulled back to its initial melancholic state.

The Scherzo could be seen as a typical dancelike third movement in a symphony, its variations constituting the second section of ternary form. It and the last movement balance the dramatic Introduzione e Fuga and Intermezzo. The return of the fugue subject in the major at the end of the whole Suite provides the "balanced architectural pattern" which, according to Roland Wiley, contributes to the general symphonic procedure.[62]

Having traced the stages of drama in the Suite that affect thematic and tonal correspondence among the Introduzione e Fuga, Intermezzo, Scherzo, and Gavotte, and having compared these processes with the Fourth Symphony, it is apparent that the special symphonic character of the First Suite is due in large part to its relationship to that Symphony's original organization and unity. The

Example 14a. The Themes of the Second Movement, Fourth Symphony, The First Theme (mm. 1–9)

Example 14b. The Themes of the Second Movement, Fourth Symphony, The Theme in the Middle Section

dramatic conflict of musical ideas developed throughout the movements of the Suite affect the transformations of the themes, thematic arches, and active tonal and harmonic development. The suite genre provided Tchaikovsky with more independence from standard organizational principles than did the symphony. In the First Suite, Tchaikovsky managed to achieve an illusion of real symphonic organization (development, drama, transformation, and process) in a genre and form other than the symphony. Yet the drama introduced in the Fourth Symphony is not simply reiterated in the Suite. The first Suite resembles the Fourth Symphony in general concept, just as the Fourth resembles Beethoven's Fifth Symphony. Differences in the development of similar ideas and the working-out of symphonic and dramatic issues assure the specific character of the two Tchaikovsky compositions.

Conclusion

Enthusiastically received in Russia and abroad during Tchaikovsky's lifetime, the First Suite has been relegated in the twentieth century to the category of the composer's "second-rate" works. Its convoluted compositional history explains why certain movements are more significant than others, which were included in the Suite for practical rather than aesthetic purposes. Despite its broadly recognized melodic, harmonic, and orchestral originality, the work has been criticized for insufficient internal unity, lack of cohesion between themes, and uneven organization of the movements. Indeed, similar complaints have been leveled at other nineteenth-century Russian suites and at Tchaikovsky's symphonies. Tchaikovsky once mentioned to Taneev, with regard to the Third Suite, "I meant to write a symphony, but the title is of no importance."[63] Such a comment lends further credence to the suggestion advanced here that the suites, far from being inconsequential works, represent Tchaikovsky's experiments with orchestral style. The suites, in turn, share certain characteristics of Russian orchestral music.

The present study has investigated one aspect of Tchaikovsky's orchestral style, as reflected in the First Suite: the symphonic element.[64] The comparison of the First Suite with the Fourth Symphony shows that these compositions have a similar organization. Both feature the Fate theme (the kernel of each whole composition), which is developed throughout the movements and opposed to themes representing positive power. The latter is manifested in the folk tunes in the final movements of both works. Thematic interconnections among movements are reflected in the Symphony's program, as acknowledged by Tchaikovsky in his letter to Mme von Meck.

Besides the thematic relationship, the four most significant movements of the Suite produce a layout resembling not only the order of the Fourth but of standard symphonic configuration. The first movements in both compositions present the main conflict, resulting in disproportionate lengths. The second movements feature a similar type of contrast between the themes (dark, melancholic, songlike melody opposed to the second, inspired and joyful theme). The last movements convey a joyous atmosphere, reflected in faster dance rhythms and major keys. The overall tonal direction in both works is from the minor in the first two movements to the major in the last movements. In addition, the last movement of the Suite incorporates the fugue subject from the first movement, creating a thematic arch. The transformation of the fugue theme in the coda of the final movement (major key, fortissimo, tutti) reflects the general idea of *per aspera ad astra*, which informs the Fourth Symphony as it continues the symphonic tradition started by Beethoven.

The Suite's balanced architectural structure and development of interacting musical ideas (Wiley's requirements for symphonic style) can be related to the program of the Fourth Symphony because of similarities in their thematic and formal design. The likelihood of programmatic correspondences leads us to a consideration of Tchaikovsky's life. The program of the Fourth, which reflects the composer's philosophical judgments about life, gave rise to a unique musical realization of those very ideas. The Suite, with both chronological proximity and resemblance to the Symphony, is through its medium indirectly related to events in Tchaikovsky's life. Although it would be an exaggeration to declare the Suite programmatic simply on the basis of its relationship to the Symphony, the similarities noted between the works cannot be considered coincidental. The concept reflected in Tchaikovsky's Fourth Symphony also influenced the First Suite, and both works are worthy representatives of nineteenth-century symphonic tradition.

NOTES

1. Ralph W. Wood, "Miscellaneous Orchestral Works," in *The Music of Tchaikovsky*, ed. Gerald Abraham (New York: Norton, 1946), 99.

2. David Brown, *Tchaikovsky: A Biographical and Critical Study*, vol. 3, *The Years of Wandering (1878–1885)* (London: Gollancz, 1978–91), 22.

3. Daniel Zhitomirsky, "Symphonies," in *Russian Symphony: Thoughts about Tchaikovsky* (New York: Philosophical Library, 1947), 126.

4. Nadezhda Tumanina, *Chaikovskii. Velikii master, 1878–1893* (Moscow: Izd. Nauka, 1968), 47; Aleksandr Dolzhansky, *Simfonicheskaia muzyka Chaikovskogo* (Leningrad: Muzyka, Leningradskoe otd-nie, 1981), 103.

5. James Huneker, *Mezzotints in Modern Music* (New York: Scribner, 1922), 86, 91.

6. Edward Lockspeiser, "Tchaikovsky the Man," in *The Music of Tchaikovsky*, ed. Gerald Abraham (New York: Norton, 1946), 12.

7. Catherine D. Bowen and Barbara von Meck, *"Beloved Friend": The Story of Tchaikowsky and Nadejda von Meck* (New York: Random House, 1937), 41.

8. Gerald Abraham, *Tchaikovsky* (London: Novello's Biographies of Great Musicians, 1938), 7–8.

9. Lockspeiser, "Tchaikovsky the Man," 20.

10. Ibid., 22–23.

11. Ibid., 14.

12. John Gee and Elliott Selby, *The Triumph of Tchaikovsky: A Biography* (New York: Vanguard Press, 1960).

13. Malcolm H. Brown, review of *The Quest for the Inner Man*, by Alexander Poznansky, in *Journal for American Musicological Society* 47 (1994): 359.

14. Martin Cooper, "Peter Ilich Tchaikovsky," in *The Symphony*, ed. Ralph Hill (London: Penguin Books, 1954), 261.

15. Wood, "Miscellaneous Orchestral Works," 74.

16. Eric Blom, *Tchaikovsky: Orchestral Works* (London: Oxford University Press, 1927), 26.

17. Ibid., 41.

18. Cooper, "Tchaikovsky," 31.

19. Brown, *Tchaikovsky*, vol. 3, 62.

20. Alexander Poznansky, *Tchaikovsky: The Quest for the Inner Man* (New York: Schirmer, 1991), *Tchaikovsky's Last Days* (Oxford: Oxford University Press, 1993); Henry Zajaczkowski, *Tchaikovsky's Musical Style* (Ann Arbor: UMI Research Press, 1987), "Tchaikovsky's Fourth Symphony," in *The Musical Review* 45 (1984): 265–76; Richard Taruskin, "Pathetic Symphonist: Chaikovsky, Russia, Sexuality and the Study of Music," in *The New Republic* February 6, (1995): 26–40, *Defining Russia Musically* (Princeton, N.J.: Princeton University Press, 1997).

21. Zajaczkowski, *Tchaikovsky's Musical Style*, 1.

22. Bruce Gustafson, "The Suite," in *The New Harvard Dictionary of Music*, ed. Don Michael Randel (Cambridge: Belknap Press of Harvard University Press, 1986), 813.

23. David Fuller, "The Suite," in *The New Grove Dictionary of Music and Musicians*, ed. Stanley Sadie (London: Macmillan, 1980), 18:349.

24. Gerald Abraham, "Rimsky-Korsakov," in *The New Grove Russian Masters*, ed. Stanley Sadie (New York: Norton, 1986), vol. 2, 24.

25. Petr Il'ich Chaikovskii, *Polnoe sobranie sochinenii: literaturnye proizvedeniia i perepiska* (Moscow: Gos. muzykal'noe izd-vo, 1953–), vol. 12, 352. Translated in Brown, *Tchaikovsky*, vol. 3, 22.

26. Joseph C. Kraus, "Tchaikovsky," in *The Nineteenth-Century Symphony*, ed. D. Kern Holoman (New York: Schirmer, 1997), 312.

27. Letter of 1 March 1878, Pyotr Ilich Tchaikovsky, in *'To My Best Friend:' Correspondence between Tchaikovsky and Nadezhda von Meck, 1876–1878*, trans. Galina von Meck, ed. Edward Garden and Nigel Gotteri (Oxford: Oxford University Press, 1993), 187–188.

28. Lawrence and Elisabeth Hanson quoting von Meck, *Tchaikovsky: A New Study of the Man and His Music* (London: Cassell, 1965), 152.

29. In his letter to von Meck of 25 August 1878, Tchaikovsky wrote: "I have written to you already that in Brailov I sketched a Scherzo for orchestra. Right away, a number of orchestral pieces emerged in my head, from which a suite in the style of Lachner should be composed." Chaikovskii, *Polnoe sobranie*, vol. 7, 375.

30. Quoted in Bowen and von Meck, *"Beloved Friend,"* 255.

31. Piotr Ilyich Tchaikovsky, *Letters to His Family: An Autobiography*, trans. Galina von Meck (New York: Stein and Day/Publishers, 1981), 170.

32. Brown, *Tchaikovsky*, vol. 3, 19.

33. Quoted in Brown, ibid., 21.

34. Chaikovskii, *Polnoe sobranie,* vol. 8, 315. Translated in Brown, *Tchaikovsky,* vol. 3, 20.

35. Quoted in Gerald Norris, *Stanford: The Cambridge Jubilee and Tchaikovsky* (Newton Abbot: Devon, 1980), 322.

36. Quoted in Hanson, *Tchaikovsky: A New Study,* 200–201.

37. Quoted in Norris, *The Cambridge Jubilee,* 335.

38. Ibid.

39. John H. Warrack, *Tchaikovsky* (New York: Scribner, 1973), 211.

40. Quoted in Norris, *The Cambridge Jubilee,* 258–59.

41. Roland John Wiley, "The Symphonic Element in *Nutcracker,*" *The Musical Times* 125 (1984): 693.

42. *P. I. Chaikovskii: S. I. Taneev. Pis'ma* (Moscow: Goskul'prosvetizdat, 1951), 32.

43. Letter of 1 March 1878, Tchaikovsky, in Garden, Gotteri, eds. *'To My Best Friend,'* 183–184.

44. Ibid., 185.

45. Ibid., 186–187.

46. Ibid., 185.

47. *P. I. Chaikovskii: S. I. Taneev,* 34.

48. For a discussion about the Fate theme in the Fourth, see Zajaczkowski, "Tchaikovsky's Fourth Symphony."

49. For a discussion of Brahms's approach to the symphonic tradition of *per aspera ad astra* ("through asperity [struggle, severity, harshness] to the stars") see David Brodbeck, *Brahms: Symphony No. 1* (Cambridge: Cambridge University Press, 1997), 2, 31. Brodbeck identifies this trope as a dramatic narrative ("a path from stormy opening movement . . . to triumphant finale") found in Beethoven's Fifth and Brahms's First Symphonies.

50. Tchaikovsky, in Garden, Gotteri, eds. *'To My Best Friend,'* 187.

51. David Brown, "Pyotr Il'yich Tchaikovsky," in *The New Grove Dictionary of Music and Musicians,* ed. Stanley Sadie (London: Macmillan, 1980), 18:616.

52. Blom, *Tchaikovsky: Orchestral Works,* 42.

53. Dolzhansky, *Simfonicheskaia muzyka Chaikovskogo,* 101.

54. Tumanina, *Chaikovskii: Velikii master,* 51.

55. Chaikovskii, *Polnoe sobranie,* vol. 8, 335.

56. P. I. Tchaikovsky, *Symphony No. 4,* Philharmonia Slavonica, Point Classics AG 2670322, 1994.

57. Peter Ilyich Tchaikovsky, *Complete Suites for Orchestra,* New Philharmonia Orchestra, Philips Classics Productions 454 253-2, 1996.

58. Quoted in John Warrack, *Tchaikovsky Symphonies and Concertos* (London: Cox & Wyman Ltd., 1969), 7.

59. Besides the relations of expression and semantics between Introduzione and Fuga, the latter is also prepared by the polyphonic imitations in the second theme (mm. 30–40, see Ex. 10).

60. Zajaczkowski, *Tchaikovsky's Musical Style,* 30.

61. Ibid., 27.

62. Wiley, "The Symphonic Element," *The Musical Times*, 693.

63. Warrack, *Tchaikovsky*, 161.

64. Besides the symphonic aspect, the First Suite could also be discussed in terms of stylistic characteristics typical of the concerto and ballet genres, which furthers the idea of the suites being Tchaikovsky's vehicle for experiments with orchestral writing. These issues, however, deserve a special consideration that exceeds the scope of the present study.

An Examination of Problem History in Tchaikovsky's Fourth Symphony

SUSANNE DAMMANN
TRANSLATED BY ALICE DAMPMAN HUMEL

Despite the popularity and affectionate regard enjoyed by many of P. I. Tchaikovsky's works, the fact that this composer has for many years been largely excluded from serious musicological research in the German language can scarcely be ignored. The reason for this can hardly be sought in the fact that the works most commonly performed today were composed relatively late, which means their reception and effective history first began in the mid 1890s. After all, the First Piano Concerto in Bb minor, Opus 23, and the Violin Concerto in D Major, Opus 35, were both readily absorbed into the standard repertoire of contemporary piano and violin virtuosi. Even the Overture-fantasia *Romeo and Juliet* held its own in German concert halls, Eduard Hanslick's disdainful reviews of it and the Violin Concerto notwithstanding. The didactic condescension with which certain of Tchaikovsky's operas were received by the German music critics on the one hand, and the resounding international acclaim afforded many of the virtuosic concerti by concert-goers on the other, clearly illustrate the yawning chasm between the connoisseur or expert (Kenner) and the aficionado or amateur (Liebhaber), a dichotomy not restricted to the nineteenth century, but existing to the present day.[1]

The Russian reception was also no exception to this situation. The path to Tchaikovsky's popularity was smoothed by different genres in the concert halls of tsarist Russia than in those of Germany. It was, then, the chamber music and the symphonic works that had the earliest public success. V. V. Stasov particularly praised the last movement of the C Minor Symphony, Opus 17 (the 1872 version): "The Finale in C Major is one of the most significant works of the entire

Russian school, in its palette, its masterful voicing and, not least, its humor," [2] and pronounced in retrospect: "Tchaikovsky is by nature an extremely talented symphonic composer."[3] However, the composer first succeeded in making a real breakthrough in 1881 with the successful staging of *Eugene Onegin* in Moscow's Bolshoi Theater.

The often cited dualism between Tchaikovsky on the one hand and the circle of Petersburg composers on the other, and their respective adherence to western cosmopolitanism and national Russian/Slavophilic ideals, all characteristic of the history of ideas, could certainly not have been brought about by Tchaikovsky's instrumental music. It is far more likely that critical assessment by V. V. Stasov and C. A. Cui of Tchaikovsky's musical training and his vocal compositions was responsible for this, as well as for the less than positive response in Russia to Tchaikovsky's entire oeuvre.

First, we need to examine the aesthetic implications of the still tenaciously and commonly held view of the enmity between the Petersburg composers and Tchaikovsky, since this interpretation had a protracted determining effect on the historiographic perspective. After the portrayal of the Russian reception of Tchaikovsky's music, we can discuss the opinions of the German language music critics about specific works, as the Russian and German receptions are more closely related than was previously thought to be the case.

Another factor that contributed to the state of current research is the broad popularity of certain Tchaikovsky compositions. Even as early as the turn of the century, their very familiarity had its negative consequences and eventually weighed on some of them like a verdict, finally causing the dismissal of these particular works into the domain of the planners of internationally successful "pops" concerts.

The reception of the symphonies in the German, as well as in the Anglo-American spheres, occurred in inverse order to their composition, effecting an orientation on the reception and recognition of the B Minor Symphony. The function of "sounding autobiography" and "spiritual confession" ascribed to the *Symphonie Pathétique* spread to the much earlier symphonies in F minor and E minor, through its identification with the life of the composer and the direct expression thereof in the work. Tchaikovsky's last three symphonies, however, continued to be largely excluded from more scholarly discourse, with its emphasis on musical structure and its quest for an understanding of esoteric thematic processes, for various reasons—not the least of which was the assumption, based on the widespread attitude at their reception, that these works were better understood by "sympathetic feeling" than by analytical reflection.

Moreover, Stalinist cultural politics at the end of the 1920s began to claim specific works from Tchaikovsky's oeuvre as "national heritage," which meant that Tchaikovsky and the Petersburg composers alike were inserted into the historical teleology "from critical to socialist realism." Nineteenth century composers were thus judged to be forebears of the realistic art of the twentieth century by reason of their social criticism and their susceptibility to the ideas of the revolutionary democrats. The inexactitude of many Russian language sources and the previous excessive ideological strain in the East, as well as the exclusion of Tchaikovsky from Western research, allowed many prejudices and clichés to be salvaged out of the nineteenth century and carried over into the twentieth.

Tchaikovsky was and is constantly reproached for his emotionalism. Extensive examination of his spiritual disposition encouraged the interpretation that Tchaikovsky had little interest in writing music conceived according to strict compositional principles, but that his marked affinity was instead for gestures so theatrical they bordered on the trivial, and that he tended to them not only for the sake of their effect. And it was strongly felt that these gestures had a cathartic function to fulfill, through which the composer found spiritual relief.

In the following article, we present certain carefully chosen sources that, at the very least, place the above mentioned clichés in a questionable light. To this end, it would be worthwhile, first of all, to undertake certain considerations of Tchaikovsky's Fourth Symphony in F minor, Opus 36, in the context of the "problem history" associated with symphonic composition post-Beethoven. Hans Blumenbergs's consideration of the concept of problem history,[4] a concept embraced by Hans Robert Jauß in his reception theory, has convincingly established that "to take the sources literally" can only lead to an "ahistorical ghost story."[5] "What really transpires lies in the dimension of the problems that found their expression in and throughout the sources . . . . Accordingly, functional interpretation demands the intersection of all available statements concerning these ever acute problems, both in content and in form. . . ."[6] Relating Tchaikovsky's F Minor Symphony to the "circumpolarity theory" (*Zirkumpolaritätsthese*) at the heart of Carl Dahlhaus' representation of the Second Age of the Symphony can—in a modified way—be connected into his view of the history of the problematic. Dahlhaus derives Tchaikovsky's stylistic pretension from, among other things, the introductory theme in the horn and the trumpet. Thus the Fifth and the Sixth Symphonies are excluded from such consideration, as they have no comparable titling gesture that would indicate such an emphatic stylistic pretension. Nevertheless, according to Dahlhaus, it could hardly be claimed that Tchaikovsky could have fulfilled the expectations he himself raised. If one inquires into the reason behind this verdict pronounced on the F Minor Symphony, one finds at the root of the criticism an orientation on the Beethoven legacy, namely, that a symphonic main idea has "on the one hand to be an element of the development reduced to particles, and on the other to be as a complete whole its triumphant end and consequence."[7]Already in 1989, Siegfried Kross spoke of the "ideological dead end"[8] hidden behind a stylization typical of the ideal of the model of the Beethoven symphony in relation to which composers of subsequent generations would have to legitimize themselves. The objection should be considered that one herewith aids a particular form-type to ahistorical validity, in so far as it is to be questioned if—and if so, why—Tchaikovsky sought a confrontation at all with this idea of form.

It remains to discuss Tchaikovsky's aesthetic stance, which should provide a more thorough explanation of the composer's relationship to the genre of the symphony.

I

In the history books, Tchaikovsky was and is still today usually excluded from the so-called "new Russian school," if not indeed juxtaposed to it, although in the nineteenth century he was still numbered among the representatives of the "Russian school," at least as far as his instrumental music was concerned. Even in reports about Russian music in the nineteenth century, very pertinent at the time, one seeks Tchaikovsky's name in vain, as the epithet "Russian" was apparently reserved for the circle around Balakirev.[9]

In his article *La musique en Russie*, C. A. Cui attributes his ambiguous relationship to the works of Tchaikovsky to the undefined position which that composer would take in Russian musical life: "Indeed, Tchaikovsky is far from being a partisan of the new Russian school; he is instead its antagonist. But he could not escape its influence, which has left its visible traces in his lyrical works. What is unfortunate for him is that he did not know how to be entirely of one faction or the other."[10] Despite the *doctrines nouvelles*, that may have left their *traces visibles* on Tchaikovsky's oeuvre, since he belonged to neither one faction nor the other, Cui placed him among the *Antagonistes*. The fact that, with this conclusion, Cui entangled himself in a contradiction in logic changed nothing about his insistence on "correcting"

Tchaikovsky's undefined position by putting him into the opposing faction. Apparently the contradiction was to remain intact, even when one could actually no longer speak of a contradiction as such.

Stasov attributed Tchaikovsky's weaknesses in interesting words and music, in both Romances and the operatic recitatives, to an "uninterrupted scribbling as well as to a deficiency in self-criticism."[11] In this respect, *shkol'noe uchenie* (book learning) had a particularly damaging effect on him. Tchaikovsky was criticized not only for composing bad music, but also for having graduated from the conservatory. After all, as a graduate Tchaikovsky found himself in danger of being labelled a devotee of the "aesthetic of form" described by Hanslick, who, according to Stasov, did not understand the demand of the Zeitgeist for program music. How is this to be explained?

Basically, the polarization in Russian musical life flared up over the question of whether institutionalized formal musical training was useful or harmful. There was a desire to raise the niveau of Russian music with the help of the Conservatory. Stasov's criticism of this idea was that this form of musical training could hardly guarantee "progress" in Russian music.[12] "There was a wonderful musical epoch in Germany before the founding of the conservatory, during which all the great talents acquired their musical training outside the confines of the conservatory . . . ."[13] Before the founding of the conservatory, no one had even bothered to ask exactly what constituted the uniquely Russian in the Russian music. "The intention to develop and promote Russian music was, of course, on the whole a praiseworthy one. But is such a development and promotion of Russian art even necessary when we already have an independent, inventive, and deeply national school beginning to form? In assessing Russian music, the first question should naturally be: what distinguishes our new school, what defines its character and its peculiarity, what is needed for the further development and evolution of just that essential peculiarity?"[14]

Stasov's decidedly outspoken insistence on the necessity of reflecting upon the specifically Russian contribution to European music history had its negative effect on the Russian (and also German) reception of the works from the "novaia russkaia shkola" (new Russian school): "These detractors began to call the representatives of the new Russian school musical 'nihilists,' 'radicals,' 'musical Slavophiles.' They accused them of utterly despising the remainder of musical Europe (which in reality was absolutely not the case), and asserted in the press that our new school was at odds with every other tenet and teaching. It turns its back on a declining Europe in order, purely and simply, to establish exclusively its own works on the ruins of tradition. This is the result of its autodidacticism."[15]

For all that, Stasov in no way advocated the position of a nihilist[16] or even a Slavophile regarding music. As early as 1858[17] he published an article in the *Neue Zeitschrift für Musik*, with the title "About some new forms of contemporary music: A Letter to Dr. Franz Liszt in Weimar and Professor Adolph Bernard Marx in Berlin."[18] A year before the founding of the Russian Music Society (*Russkoe Muzykal'noe Obshchestvo*) Stasov tried to legitimize the aesthetic position of the Russian composer by, among other things, confirming the significance of the church modes and orientalism with the help of a sort of musical pedigree.

This and other writings by Stasov clearly demonstrate his knowledge of the German-language music literature of his time; they also dismiss as mere polemic the accusation of ignorant iconoclasm[19] levelled by the Russian journalists. But above all, the article, written in German, substantiates the "emotional aesthetic" foundation on which the Russian contribution to European music history was supposed to rest: Stasov alludes not only to the "epoch-defining aesthetic" of the pupil of Hegel, Fr. Th. Vischer, but also to the *Compositionslehre* of A. B. Marx,[20] since the church modes were discussed there.[21] Stasov, like A. B. Marx, approved of their use "only in certain isolated cases."[22] Aware that "the art had become *free* in the last centuries,"[23] the composers of the nineteenth century had the "old system . . . for the expression of certain particular moods and emotions"[24] (i.e., of the soul) completely at their disposal. Thus Beethoven's late works pointed to a new way that first Chopin pursued and finally Glinka continued. Stasov's explanations document, in addition, that the pan-European origins resting in the Middle Ages can manifest themselves through the church modes and eastern melodies, be they "Polish or Hungarian, Russian or Spanish (after the Moors), Germanic or Finnish, and so on."[25]

Stasov's plea for the development of Russian music asked not for renunciation of, but rather fusion with European music history.[26] Stasov criticized the unexamined acceptance and assumption of the Conservatory modelled on that in Leipzig or Berlin, not least because he saw the creation of an independent contribution to European music history already underway in Russia. On the other hand, an absolute music was propogated at the Conservatory, which did not allow appropriate regard for the content-laden aesthetic of the Russian composer.

II

As a graduate of the Conservatory, Tchaikovsky ran the risk of being branded a Hanslick disciple, at least by Russian music critics. This was, however, exactly what was *not* expected from the German critics. Hanslick's criticism was aimed directly at Tchaikovsky's expressive forms, which is why he placed him in the camp of the musicians of the future. Similarly he disliked intimations of a national idiom. He remarked on the subject of the Overture-fantasia *Romeo and Juliet*:

> The composer is at the pinnacle of musical young Russia. . . . Tchaikovsky is of course a musician of the future, as is all of young Russia (which Rubinstein called a half-conquered classic) [. . .] The Allegro sounds somewhat too Russian to illustrate the feud of the Veronese families; one hears clearly the blows of the knout in the heavy beats that fall uninhibited by a regular measure. . . . We hardly need expressly mention that Tchaikovsky's 'Romeo'-Overture is on such a grand scale that it is practically expanded into the format of a 'symphonic poem' as used by Liszt.[27]

In contrast to this, Hanslick had nothing but praise for the *Symphonie Pathétique*, since it "betrayed a thoroughly western European character, a noble breeding, and an inner heartfelt devotion."[28] Hanslick's statements document the viewpoint from which in turn the German-language music critics confronted the works of Russian composers. For Hanslick, an original and individual contribution could only consist of the brilliant combination of the national element with the universal tradition.

Carl Dahlhaus asked the crucial question concerning the relationship between the work and the national contribution as early as 1974: "Does the individualistic arise out of the substance of the national or is the national a result of a generalizing interpretation of the individualistic . . . ?"[29] This question has been decided in favor of the latter hypothesis, after having been discussed for almost the past twenty years, with the result that the concept of the national "is subordinated to an artistic expectation of singularity."[30] Herewith the idea of the national "was made subservient to the most effective category in the European aesthetic until 1910, originality."[31] The fact that the thought of the national could even become a problem for a composer can be traced back to the implications of the aesthetics of autonomy. "The change of paradigm from the previous one of a functional restriction of the genres to the idea of an autonomous art must be seen as the generative moment for any attribution whatsoever of a problematic character to the national romantic school. [. . .] On the one hand this way of thinking did not limit itself to the area of its origin, but rather demanded an overlapping validity. On the other hand, it had as a consequence that new art could legitimize itself only to the extent that it was capable of proving itself independent and distinctive."[32] If one wanted to inquire into European music, it could be interpreted "as the result of communication"[33] that "will always be nationally interpreted."[34]

This meant, relative to Hanslick's Tchaikovsky reception, that the motivation to inquire into the original contribution of the Russian composer depended, from that moment, on how that contribution was received beyond its own national borders. Two possibilities existed in this case: either the work could be understood as an original, and integrated into the entirety of tradition if it complied with the canons of the expectations of a German recipient who moved naturally in his history; or a sort of "experience of difference" would set in, whereby the work would be rejected and banished to its regional origins.[35]

For Hanslick, apparently, Tchaikovsky's B Minor Symphony not only fit nicely into the inventory of the traditional, but at the same time had the power to gain an identity as new and original in the face of that tradition. However, the Russian audience could react negatively to the very work that was declared highly individual by the German recipients, simply because the work did not represent the Russian concept of individuality. By making the classical norm more relative, the call for universality derived from Viennese classicism could be "nationalized."[36] So it was not exclusively the Russian recipient who could nationalize the German call for universality. In the same way, the German recipient could nationalize by confining his understanding of works by Russian composers to the realm of the picturesque.

The idea of the embodiment of the "universally human" in art[37] that governed German music criticism demonstrated the continuing legacy of Viennese classicism and its claim to universality. Nevertheless it gives rise to consideration that "this wider use of the concept (i.e. of the classic) [was] systematically established for the first time in Kant's aesthetic: the precepts of genius replace the standard singularity of classical antiquity through a historical plurality of models of the beautiful which, even in their canonization to 'exemplary validity,' did not forfeit their historical dimension."[38] "But the plurality of the exemplary classical dissolves both: the material thinking as well as the Eurocentrism."[39] Domestic and foreign aphorism[40] must be strictly separated from each other in the process of understanding between nations. If one does not wish to relinquish universality as a general concept even in the nineteenth century, it must be taken into consideration that the binding of these categories through the aesthetic of autonomy is relativized. Primarily, universality is procedurally constituted through the course of understanding between nations.

III

As may have become clear in the first section, Stasov's demand for a national contribution meant anything but a national historical "solo flight." It was equally unlikely that Tchaikovsky's course of training would lead to a rejection of expressivity in favor of western schematicism. In fact, the early orchestral compositions often had a tendency toward actual expressive excess in the form of disparate motivic details that threatened to explode the framework of the sonata form Tchaikovsky nonetheless was unwilling to abandon. Yet in 1876 Laroche expressed the opinion that Tchaikovsky was absolutely not to be labelled a traditionalist: "Mr. Tchaikovsky stands matchlessly closer to the *extreme Left* of the musical Parliament than to the moderate Right, and only the misguided depiction that the musical factions in the West think it finds in us can even begin to explain why Mr. Tchaikovsky would ever be represented as a proponent of tradition and classicism."[41]

With all that, in 1872 Tchaikovsky began increasingly to express dissatisfaction with the inadequacies of his early orchestral works and the well-known divergence in them between form and content. Although Tchaikovsky, like Stasov, represented a standpoint of the aesthetic of emotion, Liszt's renunciation of the traditional idea of form still did not set an example for him. Instead he thought of form as a remedy, a way to channel his expressivity. Neither did Tchaikovsky share Laroche's contrary viewpoint, according to which music consisted of "the empty play of chords, rhythms, and modulations."[42] In his opinion, form had its justification even in program music wherein the composer "expresses musically the subject that sparked his inspiration, whether it is a poetic work or impressions of a landscape."[43] To this end Tchaikovsky differentiated between subjective and objective inspiration,[44] always basing the symphony, as "the most lyrical of all musical forms,"[45] solely on the "subjective." "In the first case, he expresses his feelings, such as joy and sorrow, in the music; in a word, he speaks out with his own soul as does a poet. In this case, a program is not only unnecessary, it is impossible."[46] Tchaikovsky most decidedly counted on his symphonies getting along without extramusical supplementation (that is, while spurning the verbal tangibility that was demanded by Stasov).

He relied instead on direct communication by means of a distinct and unequivocal musical structure that addressed the listener, complete with the course it traced. With the assumption that music expresses emotions that can be understood even without language beyond the definition of the tonal structure,[47] Tchaikovsky allied himself with an aesthetic theory of sensitivity (*Empfindsamkeit*) according to which the "sympathetic sharing of the self and self-empathy" materializes directly through an object external to the participating individuals. Thus in Tchaikovsky's mind the theorem that music was to be understood as an art of experience that not only originated in the subjective act of experiencing, but at the same time should be an expression of that same act of experiencing, continued to have its effect. The necessary prerequisite for successful understanding was based thereby on the material power of suggestion of the musical form and the course it took, which therefore also rendered superfluous a program that would lead the listener. Tchaikovsky's perception "that music has at its disposal inequitably more powerful means and an essentially more refined language in order to express the thousand different moments of spiritual experiencing,"[48] thoroughly resisted every subsequent attempt to literalize his works.

Tchaikovsky's discussion of his own works as well as the works of others is also characterized by the language of experience,[49] a perspective which may have been transmitted through the then widely circulated hermeneutic association with Beethoven's works.[50] As is well known, Tchaikovsky also expressed his opinion about his F Minor Symphony in this form. His attempt to display, or rather paraphrase the internalized program ended up generally omitting musical details, since Mrs. von Meck was a musical amateur. Thus far it has not been properly understood that it is not a question of a direct translation of the moods and emotions of the composer: "Anyone who believes that the creative person is capable of expressing what he feels out of a momentary *affect* aided by the means of art, is mistaken.

Melancholy as well as joyous feelings can always be expressed only out of the *Retrospective*. Even if I had no particular reason to be glad, I am still able to be overcome by a joyous, creative state of mind. Conversely, in the midst of happy circumstances, I can create something for which it is necessary for me to be flooded with the most dismal and despairing feelings. In a word, the artist leads a double life: the two segments, the universally human and the artistic, absolutely do not have to be in agreement with each other."[51] (Emphasis in original.) The fact that Tchaikovsky could, upon reflection, transport himself into the state of mind appropriate to the characteristic mood of the music as he composed, handling it in retrospect, leads us to question why one should expect to find enlightenment in the composer's background experience as such. In the end, the subjective experience loses much of its power of expression during the creative process, in the face of the body of facts attesting that the aforementioned states of mind materialize musically during the process of composing. Tchaikovsky emphasized to Mrs. von Meck that the characters of the Fourth Symphony were purely the "echo" (*otgolosok*) of that which he had once experienced. The fact that the echo prominently appears twice must be explained by the retrospection with which the compositional process was marked.

These states of mind were objectivized to a high degree, since they were already filtered through the demands made on the composer by the genre. Ultimately, it is in the composer's historical consciousness and his reflexive relationship to the works of tradition that the actually subjective experience becomes tangible. Schumann especially takes a prominent place in Tchaikovsky's confrontation with tradition, since he is at one with his life feelings of inner disunity. Schumann understood how to connect organically to the work of Beethoven. More important, he revealed an entirely new perspective that still had relevance for Tchaikovsky and his contemporaries. "Schumann's music reveals to us an entirely new world of musical forms, it touches chords within us that his predecessors have not yet touched. In him we rediscover the echo of all those deeply hidden processes in the lives of our souls, that doubt, that despair, those sudden impulses to strive for an ideal that moves the heart of contemporary man."[52]

An intellectual bridge was here built between Beethoven and Schumann and Tchaikovsky himself in the form of a musical psychodrama. The expositional outlines of the works of Beethoven and Schumann, which Tchaikovsky designated as contrasting, clarified the representation this particular formal disposition had for

Tchaikovsky's feeling about life. Thus he interpreted the classical-romantic sonata form as a result of characters whose rhythmic-motivic stylization he emphasized. Two rubrics of fundamental spiritual attitude appear almost stereotypically in his own notes as well as in the discussion of the works of others, particularly those of Schumann and Beethoven: sorrow, suffering, doubt, and mourning on one hand; happiness, joy, and looking forward to or reminiscing about an ideal on the other.

Even Tchaikovsky's internalized program for Opus 36 is influenced by this juxtaposition, whereby the first theme has the affect of dejection appointed to it. The second theme, which is transcribed as a rejection of reality, is in direct contrast to this. That which contains within itself contrasting moods of despair on one hand and the happiness of the world of dreams on the other is designated as *fatum*. This metaphor contains within it what Tchaikovsky observed in Schumann: contrasting character presented simultaneously in the closest thematic relationship. Tchaikovsky significantly concluded his attempt to give the addressee some help in understanding all this with an allusion to that Romantic topos of the unutterable: "Where words fail, there music begins."[53]

Tchaikovsky's consistent attempt to repress both motivic details and a melodic character that suggests the archaic, in favor of a pithily characteristic thematic that guarantees comprehensibility and plasticity of form, led in the first movement of the Fourth Symphony to a temporary solution to the problem of arranging symphonic procedure and character piece with each other. Six years of experience at composing apparently led him to the insight that "narrowly national" (Schumann) thematic premises are not suitable for shaping, in any original or generally comprehensible manner, expressivity that has no program but does use traditional sonata form.

Tchaikovsky's thoroughly individual concept in the first movement of the F Minor Symphony thus runs between Scylla and Charybdis in Russia. The form of the contrasting expositional outlines abstracted from the works typical of the genre (namely, the middle works of Beethoven) was filled in by a specific sequence of characters in such way that the outline of the sonata form was grounded by the aesthetic of the character piece, and vice versa. Thus the subject of the first thematic section remains, for reasons of the characteristic, within the framework of a particular rhythmic sequence that is presented in alternating rhythmic-diastematic motion. As opposed to the character piece, procedural thought of Beethoven-like origin reaches in this section towards a development curve directed against any stationary thought that would conform to lyrical objectivity. The sectional development is thereby so planned that characters are driven to a climax that drastically heightens the character contrast to the second theme. An expansion of the form is brought further into relief by a fusion of the climax of the development and the beginning of the recapitulation. This trick is found in many orchestral compositions written after the symphonic fantasia *Buria* (The Storm), and it gives a new meaning to the layout of the large format. In order to avoid making the alternation of character in the exposition nothing more than a disjointed potpourri, the form of the themes in Opus 36 is referred to the motivic-thematic center of the *Andante sostenuto*.

The *fatum* metaphor always suggested a direct parallel between Beethoven's Fifth Symphony and Tchaikovsky's Fourth Symphony. This relationship to the traditional topos of destiny has never been denied. On the contrary, Tchaikovsky himself referred explicitly to the imitation (*podrazhanie*) of what he called the "fundamental basic idea" (*osnovnoi idei*) of Beethoven's Fifth Symphony. At the same time, though, he distanced himself from the far too facile assumption that he also wanted to imitate the musical content, so that a motivic-thematic correlation between the introductory "themes" of both symphonies could not have been intentional. Tchaikovsky's own statement can also be cited to contradict such an interpretation: "The introduction is the *essence* of the entire symphony and doubtless its main thought."[54] For one thing, the fundamental idea is contained not only in the introductory six-measure phrase arranged across the bar lines, but in the entire introduction. For another, the metaphor of *fatum* could allude to a reception situation of the Beethoven symphony recurring, topos-like, in the readings of the nineteenth century, so the composer could, in light of the so-typical interpretation of this character, depend on universal comprehensibility. The traditionally authenticated musical character is thereby evoked in the imagination of the listener only at the beginning, without however resorting to quotation or, even worse, plagiarism. So the formulation of the main thought should be read much more as an interesting finger-pointing, indicating the musical process of the entire course of the introduction. If this can partially blunt the problematic ambiguity which, according to Carl Dahlhaus, is caused by the fact that the first theme is too feeble to comprise a "symphonic focal point," then an examination of this criticism could, under certain circumstances, emanate from the introductory section and its developmental curve. The premise of the consequent course of the movement, namely *en miniature*, is so presented that the cause of the alleged feebleness of the main theme is not to be sought in the theme itself, but rather in the material of the *Andante sostenuto*.

For a critic like Laroche or Hanslick, expressivity will more likely be strengthened than diminished through the connection of expressivity and comprehensibility. Tchaikovsky's middle path, however, may well have led to international recognition for those works that strove not for description, but rather for "inner musical expressive definition" (Dahlhaus). The question whether melodic character suggestive of archaic and quasi-modal formulations must play a leading role in the opus of a Russian composer can be answered in the negative, in so far as these elements can, but by no means must, contribute to the constitution of an original work. A comprehensive winnowing of the Russian reception would be meaningful because, until now, the impression derived from the reception-documentation was one of an impetus that brought the strictly national into relief, so that, historiographically, the national historic way of thinking was privileged. The exchange of opinions between nations about the aesthetic fundamentals of the Russian contribution to European music history rests on an offensive or defensive strategy that strongly encourages the formation of opinions by the artistic creator and by the recipient. This process, though, is only complete when one includes not only the Russian contribution and Russian reception, but also the foreign, non-national reception and tradition that provide standards to which the work of the Russian composer, or the journalism generated in response to it, can react. Otherwise, national schools would indeed be created that could only in truth slip to the periphery and, as Schumann pointedly remarked, isolate themselves in arrogance and fear.

NOTES

1. The exception to this would of course be the many reputable virtuosi and conductors who ensured the popularity of the solo concerti, the "program music," and lastly the symphonies, by making these works part of their repertoire.

2. "Etot final' (C-Dur), i po koloritu, i po masterstvu faktury, i po iumor—odno iz vazhneishikh proizvedenii vsei russkoi shkoly." Compare V. V. Stasov, *Dvadtsat' piat' let russkogo iskusstva* (published in *Vestnik Evropy*, 1882), in *Sobranie sochinenii Stasova 1847–1886*, Vol. 1 (St. Petersburg, 1894), 692.

3. "Po nature svoei, Chaikovskii-vysoko-darovityi simfonist." Compare again *Dvadtsat' piat' let russkogo iskusstva*, 692.

4. Hans Blumenberg, "Epochenschwelle und Rezeption" in *Philosophische Rundschau* 6 (1958), 94–120.

5. "Epochenschwelle und Rezeption," 102.

6. "Epochenschwelle und Rezeption," 102. To the question of the primal thesis out of which history produces and reproduces itself as problem history, Blumenberg further notes: "It is indeed not so, that ideas can be arbitrarily dropped anywhere in world history and need only to be met with credible reception in order to find fertile ground for themselves," at 106.

7. Carl Dahlhaus, "Das zweite Zeitalter der Symphonie," in *Die Musik des 19. Jahrhunderts*, (Wiesbaden, 1980) *Neues Handbuch der Musikwissenschaft*, Vol. 6, 221.

8. Siegfried Kross, "Das 'zweite Zeitalter der Symphonie,' Ideologie und Realität," in *Probleme der symphonischen Tradition im 19. Jahrhundert*. (Internationales Musikwissenschaftliches Colloquium Bonn, 1989, Tutzing, 1990), 20.

9. One reads, for example, in Sigrid Neef's *Die russischen Fünf: Balakirew–Borodin–Cui–Mussorgski–Rimski-Korsakow. Monographien–Dokumente–Briefe–Programme–Werke* (Berlin, 1992), 7: "The circle around Balakirev was the germ cell of Russian music on its path to European acceptance."

10. Compare Cesar Cui, *La musique en Russie* (Paris, 1880), 119.

11. "[. . .] nepreryvnogo, bezpredel'nogo mnogopisaniia i maloi kritiki avtora k samomu sebe," Compare V. V. Stasov, *Dvadtsat' piat' let russkogo iskusstva*, 693.

12. "Uchrezhdenie konservatorii i uspekh iskusstva vovse eshchë ne sinonimy." (The founding of a conservatory is by no means to be equated with progress in art.) *Dvadtsat' piat' let russkogo iskusstva*,, 662.

13. "V Germanii, velikaia muzykal'naia epokha *predshestvuet'* zavedeniiu konservatorii, i vse luchshie eë talanty vospityvalis' vne konservatorii . . . ." *Dvadtsat' piat' let russkogo iskusstva*, 662.

14. "Namerenie vozvyshat' i razvivat' russkuiu muzyku bylo, konechno, voobshche pokhval'no, no trebovalos' li podobnoe razvitie i vozvyshenie, kogda uzhe narodilas' u nas samostoiatel'naia, original'naia shkola—gluboko natsional'naia? V razsuzhdenii o russkoi muzyke pervyi vopros' dolzhen' byl sostoiat', konechno, v tom, shtob opredelit': chto takoe novaia nasha muzyka i shkola, v chem eë kharakter' i osobennost', i chto imenno nuzhno dlia dal'neishogo eë rosta i sokhraneniia eë samobytnoi osobennosti?" *Dvadtsat' piat' let russkogo iskusstva*, 661.

15. "Eti protivniki stali zvat' predstavitelei novoi shkoly—muzykal'nymi 'nigilistami,' 'radikalami,' 'muzykal'nymi slavianofilami,' pripisyvali im polnoe prezrenie ko vsei ostal'noi muzykal'noi Evrope (chego v deistvitel'nosti vovse ne bylo), pechatno uveriali publiku, chto novaia nasha shkola—vrag vsiakogo znaniia i ucheniia, chuzhdaetsia vsego vyrabotannogo Evropoi i zhelaet' vodruzit' na razvalinakh prezhnei muzyki odni tol'ko sobstvennyia svoi proizvedeniia, plod' nevezhestva samouchek." *Dvadtsat' piat' let russkogo iskusstva*, 680.

16. These expressions make it clear that the journalists who did not agree with Stasov's opinion (for example, Famintsyn or Rostislav) drew parallels with contemporary Russian literature. The nihilist reproach may be related to Evgenii Vasilev Baserov, the protagonist in I. S. Turgenev's novel *Fathers and Sons* (*Ottsy i deti*) (Moscow, 1862).

17. One year before Stasov wrote the article in German that was published in *NZfM*, he wrote a biography of M. I. Glinka, in which he pointed out that the "sliianiia i sochetaniia muzykal'nykh elementov drugikh narodov" was a typical characteristic of the "russkaia obrazovannost'." Compare V. V. Stasov, *Mikhail Ivanovich Glinka*, published by V. Protopopov (Moscow, 1953), 116 ff. Compare also Footnote 26.

18. In *NZfM*, Vol. 49, No. 1 from 1 July 1858, pp. 1–4, Number 2 from 9 July 1858, pp. 13–16, Number 3 from 16 July 1858, pp. 25–28, Number 4 from 23 July 1858, pp. 37–41 (Leipzig, 1858).

19. According to Stasov, the music critic Famintsyn conjectured that instrumental works with designations such as *Kamerinskaia, Serbskaia fantaziia* were rooted in, among other things, "some kind of hatred of the West and an exceptional affinity to all things Eastern" (kakaia-to nenavist' k Zapadu i neobyknovennaia simpatiia ko vsemu vostochnomu.) He further imputed to the members of the Petersburg circle of composers the notion "that musical Europe had surpassed its zenith and that progress could only be hoped for from Russian music" (chto muzykal'naia Evropa otzila svoi vek i chto tol'ko v Rossii muzyka mozhet nadeiat'sia na uspekh—Famintsyn quoted according to V. V. Stasov, *Dvadtsat' piat' let russkogo iskusstva*, 680). Famintsyn's assertion, most likely inspired by the popular dictum "Europe is falling to ruin" (Evropa gibnet), was much discussed in the literary circles of the 1830's and '40's as a result of the reception of Schelling and Hegel. In addition, Famintsyn was concerned about Stasov's claim to "the complete autonomy of thought and independence of ideas about that which has already been composed" (polnoiu samostoiatel'nost'iu mysli i vzgliada na to, chto sozdana do sikh por v muzyke, 646). Stasov based his insight into the "autonomy of the power of discernment" (samostoiatel'nost' der *Urtheilskraft*) on the "work of the brilliant philosophers of our century from Kant to Vischer" (rabota genial'nykh filosofov nashego veka, nachinaia s Kanta i do Fishera). Id., *Slovo sovremennika v otvet na dva izrechiniia tsukunftistov* (1859) *Sobranie sochinenii Stasova*, Vol. 3, 385.

20. *Über einige neue Formen der heutigen musik*, 2.

21. Stasov emphatically agreed with Marx's interpretation of the *Canzona lidica* from Beethoven's Opus 132, and directed his attention to Carl von Winterfeld's two-volume study of Giovanni Gabrieli.

22. V. V. Stasov, *Über einige neue Formen der heutigen Musik*, 2.

23. *Über einige neue Formen der heutigen Musik*, 2.

24. Friedrich Theodor Vischer (Karl Reinhold von Köstlin), quoted according to *Über einige neue Formen der heutigen Musik*, 2.

25. *Über einige neue Formen der heutigen Musik*, 28.

26. Stasov addressed this in his aforementioned 1857 biography of M. I. Glinka: "I maintain that Russian culture in general possesses this characteristic, as it carries within itself the prerequisites for a fusion and a connection with elements derived from other peoples. As the younger children of the European world, we employ the fruits of the culture of our predecessors by avoiding the extreme and choosing out the best of that which is compatible with our own national character. In time, this eclecticism should organically enrich the harmony of life in all of its aspects." (govoriu ia, russkaia obrazovannost' voobshche takogo svoistva, chto ona zakliuchaet v sebe vse usloviia dlia sliianiia i sochetaniia muzykal'nykh elementov drugikh narodov. Kak mladshie deti evropeiskogo mira my pol'zuemsia plodami obrazovannosti svoikh predshestvennikov, izbegaia krainostei i izbiraia luchshee, soglasno s nashei sobstvennoi narodnost'iu. Iz etogo eklektitsizma, neizbezhnogo v kazhdoi pozdnei tsivilizatsii, v kazhdom narode ili pokolenii, posle drugikh prishedshem, dolzhna so vremenem obrazovat'sia zhizn' organicheski stroinaia vo vse otrasliakh.) *Mikhail Ivanovich Glinka*, 116.

27. Eduard Hanslick, *Concerte, Componisten und Virtuosen der letzten fünfzehn Jahre, 1870–1885, Kritiken von Eduard Hanslick* (Berlin 3/1896), 174 ff.

28. *Fünf Jahre Musik (1891–95)* (The "Modern Opera," Part VII) *Kritiken von Eduard Hanslick* (Berlin, 2/1896), 303.

29. Carl Dahlhaus, "Die Idee des Nationalismus in der Musik," in *Zwischen Romantik und Moderne. Vier Studien zur Musikgeschichte des späteren 19. Jahrhunderts* (München; Berliner musikwissenschaftliche Arbeiten, Volume 7, 1974), 76.

30. Helga de la Motte-Haber, "Nationalstil und nationale Haltung," in *Nationaler Stil und europäische Dimension in der Musik der Jahrhundertwende* (Darmstadt, 1991), 51.

31. *Nationalstil und nationale Haltung*, 51.

32. Friedhelm Krummacher, *Gattung und Werk—Zu Streichquartetten von Gade und Berwald*, in id. and Heinrich Wilhelm Schwab (Editor), *Gattung and Werk in der Musikgeschichte Norddeutschlands und Skandinaviens*, Papers from the Kiel Conference 1980, Kassel 1982 (Kieler Schriften zur Musikwissenschaft, Vol. 26), 155.

33. Dimiter Christoff, "Grundlagen eines kompositorischen Nationalstils," in Helga de la Motte-Haber, *Nationaler Stil und europäischer Dimension*, 38.

34. *Grundlagen eines kompositorischen Nationalstils*, 39.

35. This case appeared in Josef Sittard's discussion of some of Tchaikovsky's works. Compare Josef Sittard, "Peter Tschaikowsky als Orchesterkomponist" (January 1888), in *Studien und Charakteristiken. Künstler-Charakteristiken. Aus dem Konzertsaal*, Vol. 2 (Hamburg and Leipzig, 1889). Sittard recommended to Tchaikovsky "and the school he represented" that they "fulfill with the elements of lovely temperance" (145) the "at times unbridled and wild imagination" (139). Sittard further explained the ethnological cause of this weakness: "They do not ascend those unfettered spiritual heights where the deepest sensibilities of the human soul fully and purely sound their last. Theirs [i.e., the works of the Russian composers] are to a certain extent separated by a spiritual barrier from German art, with its healthy and strong root in the deepest internal grasp of the universally human, valid for all time." (139)

36. This did not happen until around 1900, through Claude Debussy, to whom the symphonic developmental technique as the incarnation of German depth and thought was ascribed. Compare Wilhelm Seidel, *Nation und Musik. Anmerkungen zur Ästhetik und Ideologie*, in Helga de la Motte-Haber, *Nationaler Stil und europäische Dimension*, 12. This standpoint had been advocated thirty years earlier by Musorgsky. Compare the letter from M. P. Musorgsky on January 26/February 7, 1867 to M. A. Balakirev, quoted according to Hans Christoph Worbs, *Modest P. Mussorgsky in Selbstzeugnissen und Bilddokumenten* (Reinbek bei Hamburg, 1976), 32.

37. Rudolf Bockholdt names three features that characterize the classical in Viennese classical music: 1. maturity, 2. universal comprehensibility, 3. high expectation. Compare Rudolf Bockholdt, "Über das Klassische der Wiener klassischen Musik," in *Über das Klassische* (Frankfurt am Main; Suhrkamp Taschenbuch Materialien 2077, 1987), 225–229.

38. Rainer Warning, *Zur Hermeneutik des Klassischen*, in Rudolf Bockholdt (Editor), *Über das Klassische*, 90.

39. *Zur Hermeneutik des Klassischen*, 96.

40. Reinhart Koselleck formulated: "The concept [of the nation] contains a high degree of abstraction, since it makes possible a universal application, although its usage always included only real peoples." Compare *Geschichtliche Grundbegriffe. Historisches Lexikon zur politisch-sozialen Sprache in Deutschland*, edited by Otto Brunner, Reinhart Koselleck, Werner Conze, Vol. 7. (Stuttgart; *Verw-Z*, 1993), 1993. Despite historical changes with some constancy through the centuries, the *statement of opposition* appears

again and again as a structural characteristic. "External limitation for the purpose of internal constitution" is thereby always demanded. "Only through an individualizing nomenclature of other peoples will the concepts [people and nation] be asymmetrically opposing concepts," at 146).

41. "G. Chaikovskii nesravnenno blizhe k krainei levoi muzykal'nogo parlamenta, chem k umerennoi pravoi, i tol'ko to izvrashchennoe i lomanoe otrazhenie, kotoroe muzykal'nye partii Zapada nashli u nas, v Rossii, mozhet ob"iasnit', chto g. Chaikovskii nekotorym predstavliaetsia muzykantom traditsii i klassitsizma." G. A. Laroche, *Obshchaia kharakteristika tvorchestva P. I. Chaikovskogo*, in *Sobranie muzykal'no-kriticheskikh statei*, edited by V. Iakovlev, O P. I. Chaikovskom, Part 2 (Moscow-Petrograd, 1924), 39.

42. "[. . .] iz pustoi igry v akkordy, ritmy i moduliatsii." *P. I. Chaikovskii. S. I. Taneev. Pis'ma*, edited by V. A. Zhdanov, Letter number 32 from P. I. Tchaikovsky on March 27/April 8, 1878 (Moscow, 1951), 34.

43. "[. . .] chitaia poeticheskoe proizvedenie ili porazhennyi kartinoi prirody, kho-chet vyrazit' v muzykal'noi forme tot siuzhet, kotoryi zazheg v nem vdokhnovenie." Letter number 253 from P. I. Tchaikovsky to N. F. von Meck on December 5/December 17, 1878, in P. I. Tchaikovsky, *Perepiska s N. F. von Meck*, Vol. 1, edited by V. A. Zdanov and N. T. Zegin (Moscow-Leningrad, 1934), 531.

44. "I am of the opinion that the inspiration in the composing of a symphonic work can be of two different kinds: it can be either subjective or rather objective." (*Ia nakhozhu, chto vdokhnovenie kompozitore-simfonista mozhet byt' dvoiakoe: sub"ektivnoe i ob"ektiv-noe.*") Letter number 253 from P. I. Tchaikovsky to N. F. von Meck on December 5/December 12, 1878, 531.

45. "[. . .] samaia liricheskaia iz vsekh muzykal'nykh form." Letter from P. I. Tchaikovsky on March 27/April 8, 1878, in *P. I. Chaikovskii. S. I. Taneev. Pis'ma*, 34.

46. "V pervom sluchae on vyrazhaet v svoei muzyke svoi oshchushcheniia radosti, stradaniia, slovom, podobno liricheskomu poetu, izlivaet, tak skazat', svoiu sobstven-nuiu dushu. V etom sluchae programma ne tol'ko nenuzhna, no ona nevozmozhna." Letter Number 253 from P. I. Tchaikovsky to N. F. von Meck on December 5/December 17, 1878, 531.

47. Compare Carl Dahlhaus, *Lieder ohne worte*, in *Klassische und Romantische Musikästhetik* (Wiesbaden, 1988), 143: "Mendelssohn shared with Hanslick the belief that the aesthetic substance of music must be 'definite,' but that 'definition' of emotions through concepts represented an 'extra-musical' moment, that is, one useless to the foundation of a musical aesthetic. However Mendelssohn's aesthetic is an aesthetic of emotions: carried by the idea that the definition of the tonal structures that Hanslick juxtaposed to the definition of emotions are in reality their fundamental or corollary."

48. "[. . .] chto muzyka imeet nesravnenno bolee mogushchestvennye sredstva i bolee tonkii iazyk dlia vyrazheniia tysiachi razlichnykh momentov dushevnogo natroeniia." Letter Number 101 from P. I. Tchaikovsky on February 17/March 1, 1878 to N. F. von Meck, 216.

49. For more on the phenomenon of the "art of the experience" in the course of the subjectivization of aesthetics since Kant's *Kritik der Urteilskraft*, see Hans-Georg Gadamer, *Wahrheit und Methode*, (Tübingen, February 1965), 67.

50. Compare Hans-Heinrich Eggebrecht, *Zur Geschichte der Beethoven-Rezeption* (Mainz, 1972). He refers to Arnold Schmitz's examinations of the romantic Beethoven image, according to which Beethoven was perceived in Romanticism as "the art of

expression, association and experience" (at 15). Tchaikovsky, Stasov, and also Serov were in equal measure affected by this view of Beethoven.

51. "Te, kotorye dumaiut, chto tvoriashchii khudozhnik v minuty affektov sposoben posredstvom sredstv svoego iskusstva vyrazit' to, chto on chuvstvuet, oshibaiutsia. I pechal'nye i radostnye chuvstva vyrazhaiutsia vsegda, tak skazat', *retrospektivno*. Ne imeia osobennykh prichin radovat'sia, ia mogu proniknut'sia veselym tvorcheskim nastroeniem it, naoborot, sredi shchastlivoi obstanovki proizvesti veshch', proniknutuiu samymi mrachnymi i beznadezhnymi oshchushcheniiami. Slovom, artist zhivet dvoinoiu zhizn'iu: obshchechelovecheskoiu i artisticheskoiu, prichem obe eti zhizni tekut inogda ne vmeste." Letter Number 163 from P. I. Tchaikovsky on June 24/July 6, 1878, in *Perepiska s N. F. von Meck*, 371 ff.

52. "Muzyka Shumana [. . .] otkryvaet nam tselyi mir novykh muzykal'nykh form, zatragivaet struny, kotorykh eshchë ne kosnulis' ego velikie predshestvenniki. V nei my nakhodim otgolosok tekh tainstvenno glubokikh protsessov nashei dukhovnoi zhizni, tekh somnenii, otchaianii i poryvov k idealu, kotorye oburevaiut serdtse sovremennogo cheloveka." P. I. Tchaikovsky, *Vtoroi kontsert russkogo muzykal'nogo obshchestva*, published on December 6/18, 1871 in the *Sovremenaia letopis'*, in *Muzykal'no-kriticheskie stat'i*, edited by T. Sokolova (Moscow, 1953), 38.

53. "Gde konchaiutsia slova, tam nachinaetsia muzyka." Letter Number 101 on February 17/March 1, 1878 from P. I. Tchaikovsky to N. F. von Meck, in *Perepiska s N. F. von Meck*, 219.

54. "Introduktsiia est' *zerno* vsei simfonii, bezuslovno glavnaia mysl'." Letter Number 101 on February 17/March 1 1878 from P. I. Tchaikovsky to N. F. von Meck, 217.

Tchaikovsky's Tatiana

CARYL EMERSON

Tchaikovsky's *Eugene Onegin* has often been accused of betraying its literary source—yet the charge is baffling. Operatic transposition always demands adjustments. Alexander Pushkin's novel-in-verse, written in the 1820s and immediately recognized as a masterpiece, is hardly put in peril by the existence of a libretto illustrating its most "lyrical scenes." Tchaikovsky scrupulously preserved the poet's lines in all episodes of high emotional intensity. And unlike *The Queen of Spades*, the composer's second adaptation from Pushkin, the operatic *Onegin* remains very much Pushkin's story, the most famous Russian version of a familiar erotic plot: uncoordinated, unconsummated, yet ultimately symmetrical love.

The most common explanation for the infidelity charge is technical. Pushkin's novel, for all its familiar plot, is an unprecedented, untranslatable miracle of form. A narrative of some five-and-a-half thousand lines, it is written in the intricate, 14-line "Onegin stanza," an adaptation of the sonnet with three quatrains, each differently "spun" (AbAb, CCdd, EffE), capped at the end with a tart rhyming couplet of often ironic and subversive commentary. The highly inflected syntax of Russian offered Pushkin a multitude of flexible rhymes, employed effortlessly (his characters all manage to chatter naturally within these elaborate constraints). Even the most fastidious and gifted translation of Pushkin's novel—and there have been several into English, most recently and brilliantly by James Falen—does not, and cannot, pace itself as Pushkin does. This is because the Onegin stanza is both fixed and pliable: in places the rhyme groups are blurred, full stops are hopped over, the whole column of sound picks up speed—and readers find themselves disoriented, excited, and surprised each time the terminal couplet snaps the sonnet shut. In Russian, to recite *Eugene Onegin* is to treat oneself to a perpetually arousing, then consoling and relaxing, activity—in repeating 14-line segments. It has been called the closest that technical poetic form can come to inspiring in readers the temptations and unstoppable drives of love.

To touch this miracle of form, to flatten it out and then to inflate it into a libretto, could only mean a profanation—as Tchaikovsky well knew. His initial reluctance to touch the project, followed by his sudden conversion to it during the fateful year of 1877, is a staple of operatic lore. The composer was struck by Tatiana's futile letter to Onegin and by her unrequited love (surely both played a role in his own disastrous, short-lived marriage); he resolved, in a famous letter to Sergei Taneev, to "set to music everything in *Onegin* that demands music." That could only be a narrow extract of Pushkin's witty, abrasive, hyper-intelligent text; and, with some input from the sentimental poet Lensky, it was pretty much all Tatiana. To understand the ambivalence and even bad conscience expressed toward this opera, however, we must look beyond technical form. Here, three aspects of Pushkin's novel are crucial.

First, with the exception of her letter in Chapter Three and her reprimand to Onegin in Chapter Eight, Pushkin's Tatiana is almost wholly silent. We know and see almost nothing about her. The garrulous, gullible narrator—himself in love with Tatiana—jealously protects her from prying eyes and from any shock that might add to the hurt he knows is already in store. He is reluctant to share her letter: seventy-nine extraordinary freely-rhymed lines, written, the narrator assures us, in French and translated for us only grudgingly. Tatiana's primary characteristic is detachment from her surroundings. She has profound feelings, but no public outlet for them. In an episode from Chapter Four that Tchaikovsky did not set, Tatiana has a terrifying dream: pursued through snowdrifts by a huge bear, she is ultimately entertained at table by monsters whose master is Onegin. In another unset episode, Tatiana, still smitten, visits Onegin's deserted house, seeking in his library some clue to his strange character (leafing through his books, she asks herself: "Perhaps he is a parody?"). Pushkin's heroine reads, thinks, stores up impressions, passively waits; but except for the rash act of that one letter, she does not *act*. She is the Russians' Mona Lisa: a beckoning secret, the appeal of yet-unspent potential, of tensions in precarious balance. The very act of singing such a character would spend it and unbalance it— unless, of course, all songs for Tatiana were elegiac monologues or set pieces similar to the pastoral duet with her sister Olga that opens the opera. The operatic Tatiana begins in that mode. But Tchaikovsky, usurping the function of Pushkin's narrator with subtlety and enormous persistence, slowly reveals her inner self to us.

Second, Pushkin's novel is a lonely place. Many of its dramatic moments occur offstage or in dreams and fantasies; events are madden-

ingly delayed in the telling or happen to the heroes separately. We never
see the initial meeting of the lovers; the letters hang there unanswered;
the challenge to the duel is a private matter of terse notes, not a ballroom
scandal. In Pushkin, live people often slide by one another. Obviously,
any dramatization of this plot would have to bring the protagonists
together. Since many of Pushkin's best lines belong to the narrator, they
must be given to someone for singing. In Act I, it is the rather-too-dim
Lensky who analyzes the relationship between himself and Onegin as
"wave and stone, verse and prose, ice and flame"; both men sing out
their reservations about the duel while their seconds mark out paces; in
the opening of Act III, Onegin sings the history of his own travels. In
both recitative and aria, the characters become infinitely "smarter" and
more forthcoming about themselves than Pushkin's narration allows
them to be.

But most disturbing to Pushkin's plot is the fact that in the opera's
final scene the two lovers sing their respective monologues to one
another. Onegin performs snatches of his earlier love letter to Tatiana
(unanswered in Pushkin); Tatiana sings almost all of her reprimand to
Onegin (which in the novel also goes unanswered; Tatiana reproaches
him, rises, and leaves the room, leaving him dumbfounded on his
knees). By turning these two solitary love statements into one love duet,
pressure builds toward a scene where in Pushkin there was none. Or
rather, a conventional scene of love versus duty replaces Pushkin's much
more tantalizing ambiguity.

The precise tone and overtone of Tatiana's final words to Onegin in
the novel have long been a matter of dispute. That most famous of all
Russian renunciations, "No ia drugomu otdana; / Ia budu vek emu
verna" (But I have been given to another; / I will be eternally faithful to
him / it), also permits a literal (if only penumbral) reading along these
lines: "But I have given [myself] to another [i.e., to another person,
image, perhaps of Onegin or even of her own earlier self]"—and it is to
that image that Tatiana now desires to be true. To bring this ideal down
to the realm of mutual loving, to consummate it and enter it into real
time, would most certainly destroy it. Possibly Tatiana, an experienced
woman by the final chapter, has come to see Onegin's vices more soberly
and wants none of them (this is what Tchaikovsky's orchestration
suggests in his setting of this scene, with its hint of Lensky's theme); or
perhaps she now believes the words he had uttered to her in the country, that he is unsuited for the bliss of love. But that, too, we are not
given to know in Pushkin's novel. Tatiana tells us only that she still
loves Onegin and that she will be "faithful," which is to say, she will not
alter her present state. Action is simply suspended—and Pushkin,

abandoning his unfortunate hero as the clank of the husband's spurs is heard in the doorway, abruptly takes leave of his novel.

Such a dramatic suspension might have been possible for Musorgsky; the holy fool on stage alone at the end of *Boris Godunov* is just such an excruciatingly suspended tonality. But not for Tchaikovsky. He had chosen as his central theme Tatiana's lyric suffering, her desire, then her ultimate self-discipline—not her mystery. Pushkin, in contrast, structures his novel so that mystery is central: we do not know what Tatiana wants. In the words of the literary historian D. S. Mirsky, this "classical attitude of Pushkin, of sympathy without pity for the man and of respect without reward for the woman, has never been revived."

We thus arrive at our last point about the novelistic *Onegin*. It has to do with cultural eras. Although influenced by Romanticism, Pushkin remained a classicist—just as Tchaikovsky, for all of the realism that pressed in on him in the Age of the Russian Novel, remained a Romantic. Temperamentally an eighteenth-century aristocrat, Pushkin was not comfortable with public displays of embarrassment. He did not believe, as Dostoevsky and Tolstoy so earnestly did, that gestures of self-humiliation were proof of a person's sincerity. Such reticence was natural to a pre-realist age, one that took decorum and social codes very seriously. To avoid public shame, after all, was one important purpose of the duel of honor, an institution that was to claim Pushkin's life (he was killed in a duel at age thirty-eight, defending his wife's honor and his own). By refusing to fall and repent, sin and tell—easy and colorful paths, full of the juice of plot—Pushkin's Tatiana is a paradigm of energy under constraint, of inspiration itself. She is the perfect neoclassical Muse.

When Tchaikovsky made Tatiana the center of his opera, he had to open her to humiliation, uncontrollable impulses, self-expression in the presence of others, the lovers' duet. Precisely in this realm are the most irrational charges of infidelity lodged against Tchaikovsky's opera, even by those who appreciate fully his musical genius. The issue is not merely words; every libretto alters words. The blasphemy of the opera is one of psychology. It violates a personality beloved by Russians for its single act of compulsive exposure—which is then followed by silence, a commitment to privacy, a closed world that is rich but reluctant to express and define itself. For Pushkin's Tatiana is better than the rest of us: she does not even dream of playing out her fantasies. Paradoxically, by presenting the story from Tatiana's point of view and allowing her to struggle openly, sing back, be embraced, Tchaikovsky breaks the vessel he would most honor.

On the Role of Gremin:

Tchaikovsky's *Eugene Onegin*

KADJA GRÖNKE

TRANSLATED BY ALICE DAMPMAN HUMEL

Everyone knows Prince Gremin's great aria from Tchaikovsky's opera *Eugene Onegin*. It seems to outline and characterize the role completely; but that impression is deceptive. It is worthwhile to investigate the fundamental significance Tchaikovsky assigned, both dramatically and compositionally, to the role of Gremin.

The opera *Eugene Onegin* has as its source the verse novel of the same name by Alexander Pushkin. In it, the character whom Tchaikovsky calls Gremin in his libretto remains inextricably bound to the main female character, Tatiana.

She sees him for the first time at a ball in Moscow which Pushkin ridicules as the "marriage market" (VII/26).[1] He writes:

> Noise and laughter, haste and hurry,
> Galop and waltz . . . unnoticed,
> two old Aunties around her, a column
> guarding their backs, it cools and emboldens,
> Tatiana gazes into the tumult
> of the great world. [. . .] (VII/26)
> An imposing General
> has noticed her; the two Aunties,
> who immediately recognized Tania's chances,
> whisper excitedly into her ear:
> "Oh, look to the left, quickly, incline your head," [. . .]
> "Oh, look, now hurry up and look,

there, by the column over there, there,
where both of the others are standing now,
in uniform; look there, now. . ."
"Who, then? The fat General?" (VII/54)

"Kto? Tolstyi etot general?" (VII/54). Pushkin abruptly interrupts
his description of the "Moscow marriage market" (VII/26) with this
question. Not until the last chapter of his novel does he return to the
"fat general," presenting him as the worldly Prince and the husband
of Tatiana. By his side, Tania, the provincial maiden, has become a
lady of high society. The poet quite consciously skips over the inter-
vening period of time.[2] In his verse novel he repeatedly uses omissions and intimations, calling upon the reader to fill in such empty
places himself with the power of his imagination, and thereby to act as
a co-author of the "free novel" (VIII/50). Tchaikovsky takes this commission seriously. His stage work takes full advantage of the poetic
open-endedness that Pushkin offers.[3] Faithful to the poet's call to the
reader's imagination, the composer seeks his own explanation for the
open ending of the novel and the motivations for the actions of the
main characters. Thus the nameless figure of the "fat general"
(VII/54) becomes the operatic figure "Prince Gremin" (*kniaz'
Gremin*)—derived from the verb *gremet'*, which literally translated
means "to be well known," or "of good reputation." Tchaikovsky uses
his aria "Liubvi vse vozrasty pokorny" to negotiate between stages of
action in the opera widely separated in time.

• • •

The conclusive transformation of the "fat general" from Pushkin's
verse novel to the operatic figure of Prince Gremin was accomplished
in numerous steps. The composer's decision to set Pushkins's text to
music resulted in a scenario he described in a letter to his brother
Modest on 18 May 1877. This first spontaneous sketch describes
almost exactly the complete final version of the opera's course of
action. The only deviation concerns the appearance of Prince Gremin.
At this point Tchaikovsky still planned to include in the opera the
aforementioned ball in Moscow, and that first meeting of Tatiana and
her future husband that takes place there. "Moskva. Bal v Sobranii. [. . .]
Poiavlenie generala. On vliubliaetsia v Tatianu. Ona emu rasskazyvaet
svoiu istoriiu i soglashaetsia vydti za nego zamuzh," Tchaikovsky
sketched. (Moscow. Ball in Sobranie. The General appears. He falls in

love with Tatiana. She tells him her life's story and declares her willingness to become his wife.)[4] This scene, with its conversation between Tatiana and Gremin, was not included in the novel, and must have been replaced very quickly with the later ball in St. Petersburg, which introduces the third act in the final version of the opera. In a letter written as early as the fall of the same year, 1877, Tchaikovsky mentions the Prince's aria as belonging in the Petersburg ball scene; and the sixth scene was then also published in this form. His concept underwent no further changes.

The composition of the Finale was somewhat more complicated. In the scenario of 1877, the composer demands an additional appearance for Gremin, which slightly alters his literary model. In Pushkin's verse novel, the ending reads:

> "I love you, but I have also learned
> to control myself; and come what may:
> I remain faithful to my husband." (VIII/47)
> She is gone. As if struck by lightning
> Onegin stands motionless;
> and what a tempest do all his hopes
> stir deep within him!
> The jingle of spurs; footsteps;
> Tatiana's husband appears. (VIII/48)

In contrast to this, Tchaikovsky notes to himself: "Her husband appears. Duty wins the upper hand. Onegin flees in despair."[5] The fact that the Prince is supposed to enter is in keeping with Pushkin's original, but the actions of Onegin and Tatiana differ from it. The composer reasons that, "because of musical and staging demands I was forced strongly to dramatize" the final scene.[6] This decision brings problems with it, as Tchaikovsky admits in a letter to Konstantin Albrekht: "In my version, Tatiana's husband appears at the end and with a gesture commands Onegin to depart. Since I had to let Onegin say something, I gave him the following lines: 'O death, o death! It is you that I seek!'"[7] The Finale was published in 1880 in this second version, which exceeds the first by defining the Prince's entrance with a precise stage direction. "Prince Gremin enters; when Tatiana sees him, she cries out and faints into his arms. The Prince makes an imperious sign to Onegin that he should remove himself."[8] Tchaikovsky is, however, not satisfied with this solution. Onegin's last words strike him as unfitting[9]; finally, he decides on the definitive version "Pozor! Toska! O zhalkii zhrebii moi!" ("Shame! Sadness! [or indifference, boredom, hopelessness, longing—*author's note*] O, my lamentable fate!")

During the preparations for the premiere of his opera at Moscow's Bolshoi Theater (which took place on January 11, 1881) Tchaikovsky reluctantly acquiesced to certain additional changes suggested by his brother Anatolii, only one of which was ultimately performed: at the end of the opera, Tatiana leaves the room before Onegin sings his last words. "The General should not appear again."[10] Contrary to Pushkin's original, Tchaikovsky's opera relinquishes Gremin's entrance in the final version of his opera, but follows the novel concerning Tatiana's behavior, namely: "She is gone. As if struck by lightning / Onegin stands motionless."[11] Consequently, Tchaikovsky's concept of the role of Gremin has a first stage, in which Gremin is introduced at the ball in Moscow and enters once again in the Finale. In a second stage, the ball in Moscow is replaced by a ball in St. Petersburg; but the Prince still appears in the Finale. Only in the third and final version is Gremin's appearance restricted to the ball in St. Petersburg; unlike Pushkin's novel, Tchaikovsky's Finale has to get along without the Prince.

• • •

Gremin and Tatiana are portrayed at the ball in St. Petersburg as members of the privileged class. Onegin is also there. After long, aimless wandering, he has returned to his home. But the guilty conscience that has plagued him since the death of his friend Lensky in a duel has alienated him from himself and from fashionable social circles. The Princess Tatiana's appearance contrasts sharply with that of the outsider Onegin. In an exact reversal of the relationships, it is now she who completely embodies the social mores, who is completely *comme il faut,* (VIII/14) self-determining, while Onegin is as alienated from the world at large as Tania, the provincial maiden, once was (Act III, from Number 20[12]).

Tatiana's particularly grand entrance is emphatically set apart from all that has gone before by its tonality: after the clearly cadencing B-flat Major/E-flat Major tonal center of the Ecossaise, the music moves definitely into D-flat Major at the announcement "Kniaginia Gremina! Smotrite, smotrite!" (The Princess Gremina! Look, look!) and creates with this cross-relation (of D-flat to the D of the previous B-flat Major) an entirely new expressive dimension.

Against his will, Onegin becomes attentive. He tries to discover the identity of the person presumed unknown. In a conversation with the Prince he formulates his questions—which are simultaneously the questions of the opera audience. In the course of this game of question and answer, it becomes clear what has transpired in Tatiana's life during Onegin's absence: namely, that she has married the "fat General" from the ball in Moscow. Now, as Prince Gremin and Tatiana's husband, he stands bodily before Onegin. By means of this staging decision, Tchaikovsky succeeds in compressing the four brief mentions of the Prince from Pushkin's novel into one single appearance. The formal high point of this appearance is Gremin's big aria (Act III, Number 20a, Measures 1–40[13]).

• • •

Gremin's aria serves a central dramatic function that Asafiev sums up in the following way: "We recognize that the deeper meaning of this aria is in no way contained in the thesis pronounced therein, 'Every one knows love on earth [. . .],' but rather in Tatiana's outstanding characterization which appears in a new light to Onegin, but has long been evident to the listener from the letter scene and from her monologue before the chance meeting in the garden."[14] The identification of Tatiana with the "'ideal' of woman"[15] (as Ulrich Busch calls it) that takes Onegin completely by surprise, is not only attested to by the chorus of guests at the ball, but also by Prince Gremin. Onegin's re-evaluation of Tatiana is thereby doubly validated, objectified, and expressly reinforced.

The text of the aria does not originate for the most part in Pushkin's novel. Only the beginning is drawn from a verse (VIII/29) in which the author comments on Onegin's amorous longings. The fact that Tchaikovsky chooses precisely these verses endows them with a double meaning. While Tchaikovsky's Prince Gremin speaks only of himself and his love for Tatiana, those in the opera audience familiar with Pushkin's text will immediately connect these words to Onegin. What Gremin has to say about himself could therefore hold just as true for the title character of the opera. The aria gives a very private answer to Onegin's questions about life that he poses at the beginning of the act. Onegin must now recognize, by the living example of Gremin, that it is precisely the love he once spurned, "love as the surrender of the self,"[16] that could have shielded him from world-weariness and boredom, that might have given life meaning (Act III, Number 20a, Measures 41–94[17]).

The aria is identified formally as a simple A–B–A form; the closing A section repeats the beginning note for note and complements it at the end merely with inconsequential text repetitions. This apparent conventionality has a momentous function in the opera, even though it is the only passage in the score composed with such formal rigor. To be sure, the *lyrical scenes* (as Tchaikovsky literally subtitled his work, to differentiate between it and traditional operatic forms) have one big, aria-like musical number for each of the important characters. But Olga's solo in the first scene, as well as Onegin's "sermon on morality"[18] in the third scene, maintain a certain sense of freedom, despite a recognizably derivative framework. Even Lensky's aria before the duel does not necessarily adhere to a strict form. Tatiana's letter scene is not even designated by Tchaikovsky as an aria, and its development is unusually free.

In comparison to these numbers, Gremin's aria offers the only self-contained, practically academically conventional point of reference in the entire opera. This could indicate a bravura aria subsequently inserted for the sake of a particular singer, as Tchaikovsky informed Nikolai Rubinstein on 10/22 November 1877: "I have, it seems to me, written an affecting aria for Koriakin [a young bass who was intended for the premiere]."[19] This was, however, unequivocally contradicted by what Tchaikovsky confided to his brother Anatolii about his Fourth Symphony only one month later: "I am writing the Symphony in complete awareness that it is an *extraordinary* work and, from all my former scribblings, the most consummate in form"[20] (proizvedenie [. . .] naibolee sovershennoe po forme).

This value judgment of the form can doubtless be applied to Gremin's aria. The prominent, seemingly academic A–B–A form dare not be misunderstood as merely a relic of convention, but must rather be comprehended in terms of its dramatic import. The musical form unquestionably serves Gremin's characterization. In its precisely symmetrical layout, this aria describes a strong, self-contained personality. Gremin's sovereignty also imparts itself to Tatiana and is transferred to her. In the conversation with Onegin following the aria, she is able to demonstrate sufficient spiritual resolve to suppress her agitation. The memory of the unhappy love of her youth (which Tchaikovsky symbolically represents in the solo clarinet at the beginning of the letter scene) is quickly replaced by the little melody that characterizes Tatiana's entire appearance at the ball. It is also played by the clarinet and is clearly coupled with a return to the original key of D-flat Major, which Tatiana leaves during her inner monologue. At this meeting then, Onegin faces an externally whole, self-assured, seemingly unapproachable Tatiana, who seems surrounded by official music in the official tonality as if by "armor."[21] (Act III, Number 21, Measures 1–30.[22])

• • •

The fact that this external appearance is not an expression of some wholesale conformity to the moral code of the societal *comme il faut* on Tatiana's part (as Belinsky complains[23]), but is meant by Tchaikovsky rather to relate to Prince Gremin, is clearly illustrated by the Finale of the opera. The composer makes it perfectly clear by musical means that Tatiana owes her capacity for self-control to her husband. The last of the *lyrical scenes* remains under the influence of Gremin's entrance, although the General does not appear on the stage again. The opening of his aria—the cantabile melody to the words "Liubvi vse vozrasty pokorny"—is omnipresent in the prelude to the Finale and is later used to set Tatiana's words "Onegin! Ia togda molozhe, ia luchshe, kazhetsia, byla." This text (Onegin, I was younger then / and, it seems, better [VIII/43]) reveals that Tatiana remains true to her past, but looks back on this past now from the perspective of a mature woman. She identifies herself with the "loving," but "[by Onegin] unloved Tania"[24] from the beginning of the opera, demonstrating at the same time "that she has acquired the ability to control herself [and], aided by careful calculation, to fulfill the obligations of her society."[25] She thereby complies with the corresponding advice from Onegin's "sermon on morality"[26] from the third scene of the opera, "uchites' vlastvovat' soboi," (In joy as in sorrow / you must learn to control yourself at all times [IV/16]). The musical redress to Gremin's aria demonstrates, though, that the reason for this self-control has nothing to do with Onegin, but is rather completely and utterly conected with Prince Gremin.

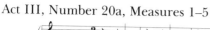

Music Example 1:[27]

Act III, Number 20a, Measures 1–5

Act III, Number 22, Measures 1–5:

Gremin's music influences the last scene of the opera in many ways. Both substantive orchestral rhythms in his aria continue throughout the prelude to the Finale—the two alternating quarter notes, emphasizing the duple meter of the A section, and the eighth–quarter–eighth syncopation from the B section.

Music Example 2:

Act III, Number 20a, Measure 1:

Act III, Number 20a, Measure 40:

Act III, Number 22, Measure 1/2:

Act III, Number 22, Measure: 25/26:

The prelude of the Finale corresponds to the beginning of Gremin's aria even in the emphasis on a predominating melodic voice only sparsely complemented by interjections from the violins at certain vocal phrases. On the one hand the orchestral interjection between the first and second lines of text in the aria appears again (despite the altered semitone structure) in the eighth measure of the prelude to the Finale (as an inversion of measure 4); and on the other hand, it influences that conversational treatment of individual voices characteristic of the first fifty measures of the prelude (Act III, Number 22, Measures 1–54[28]).

Music Example 3:

Act III, Number 20a, Measure 5/6:

Act III, Number 22, Measures 1–8:

The musical conception of the Finale, as well as the changes Tchaikovsky made in the text from the second to the third stage in the development of his concept of the opera, contribute to Gremin's significance. Indeed, he does not physically appear in the final version of the seventh scene, but the composer transforms the internally conflicted Tatiana from the earlier sketch of the libretto, drawn to Onegin, struggling with her fate, into an internally stable, sovereign woman who, as a matter of course, puts her duty above her desire. These text changes render a further appearance of Gremin dramatically redundant in the final analysis. It is not the concrete appearance of her husband that brings Tatiana to her decision. Much more to the point, she possesses within herself the inner strength to decide against Onegin's wooing and for her life as a married Princess.

Ulrich Busch states: "The actual reason for her rejection of Onegin is [. . .] that she herself, as the present Princess and the lost Tania, wants to endure with her current 'classical' sense of duty coexisting with her former 'romantic' amorous longing."[29] Tchaikovsky musically augments such an interpretation by placing a higher value on the inner attachment to Gremin: that weepy, fragile woman of the earlier concept has become the upstanding matron of the definitive libretto, and Tatiana's self-determining behavior remains immediately below the surface, in close connection to her husband's great declaration of love from the previous ball scene. Thus Tchaikovsky sets the verse novel to music in such a way that Pushkin's poetic multiplicity leads to interpretive singularity.

Despite the open-endedness of the opera, the composer approaches, in his view of Tatiana, the interpretation that Dostoevsky put forth in his legendary speech at the dedication of the Pushkin Monument in Moscow in 1880.[30] Indeed, Dostoevsky also emphasized Tatiana's inner strength equally with the unshakable ethical, moral ties to her husband: "Faithful to this old General, her husband . . . , whom she loves, who values her and is proud of her. . . . She herself has sworn faithfulness to him . . . and her unfaithfulness would . . . destroy his life. . . . What kind of happiness can this be, that is based on the unhappiness of others? [. . .] 'I do not wish to be happy at the expense of others!'"[31]

• • •

In summary, Tchaikovsky assumes the role of player in and co-author of Pushkin's verse novel. The composer follows the summons of the author to use the poetic open-endedness of the "free novel" (VIII/50) to create his own singular interpretation. "Whoever you may be, dear reader," says Pushkin "take for yourself what pleases you/ from my verses" (VIII/49). Through the figure of Gremin, Tchaikovsky finds the opportunity, to make a commentary on the fates of his characters beyond the limitations of action on the stage, and to explain the motivations for their behavior. Thereby the role becomes a catalyst by which the characters of Tatiana and Onegin are defined and their fates decided. Tchaikovsky uses that figure, completely settled in the wide open spaces of Pushkin's imagination, to give the stage action its unquestionable dramatic and musical turning point, and to realize his own interpretation of the verse novel. The part of Gremin offers an incisive key to Tchaikovsky's very personal understanding of *Eugene Onegin*.

NOTES

1. The quotations from Pushkin's novel will be designated by the number of the chapter (in Roman numerals), a diagonal line, and the verse (in Arabic numbers). The author employed the edition: Alexander Puschkin, *Eugen Onegin. Roman in Versen.* Translation from the Russian and epilogue by Ulrich Busch, Zürich 1981. Other translations of Russian quotations in this article are the author's.

2. See Pushkin's discussion with the critic P. A. Katenins in the foreword to the single printing of *Otryvki iz puteshestviia Onegina* (Fragments from Onegin's Journey). Compare A. S. Pushkin, *Sobranie sochinenii* Volume 4 (*Evgenii Onegin; Dramaticheskie proizvedeniia*), (Moscow, 1960), 184.

3. "Ia [. . .] nakhozhu, chto Puskin nekotorymi namëkami i nedomolvkami kak by daët pravo." (I find that Pushkin, through his allusions and intimations, actually validates [my interpretation]," the composer defends himself to his brother, Anatolii in a letter on 17 October 1880, quoted from K. Iu. Davydova, V. V. Protopopov, N. V. Tumanina, editors, *Muzykal'noe nasledie P. I. Chaikovskogo. Iz istorii ego proizvedenii,* (Moscow, 1958), 45.

4. Letter to Modest Tchaikovsky on 18 May 1877. Quoted from *Muzykal'noe nasledie*, 38.

5. "Iavliaetsia muzh. Dolg berët verkh. Onegin v otchaian'e ubegaet." Letter to Modest Tchaikovsky on 18 May 1877. Quoted from *Muzykal'noe nasledie*, 39.

6. "Ia prinuzden byl radi muzykal'nykh i stsenicheskikh trebovanii sil'no dramatizirovat' stsenu." Letter to Konstantin Al'brekht on 3/15 February 1878, Quoted from *Muzykal'noe nasledie*, 43.

7. "V kontse u menia poiavliaetsia muzh Tatiany i zhestom povelevaet Oneginu udalit'sia. Pri etom mne nuzhno bylo, chtoby Onegin skazal chto-nibud', i ia vlozhil v ego usta sleduiushchii stikh: 'O smert', o smert'! Idu iskat' tebia!'" Letter to Konstantin Albrekht on 3/15 February 1878, quoted from *Muzykal'noe nasledie*, 43.

8. "Vkhodit kniaz' Gremin, Tatiana, uvidev ego, ispuskaet krik i padaet v obmorok k nemu v ob"iatiia. Kniaz' delaet Oneginu povelitetl'nyi znak udalit'sia." Compare *ChPSS* 4, 533.

9. Letter to Konstantin Albrekht on 3/15 February 1878, quoted from *Muzykal'noe nasledie*, 43.

10. "General vkhodit' ne dolzhen." Letter to Anatolii Tchaikovsky on 17 October 1880, quoted from *Muzykal'noe nasledie*, 45.

11. Since Tchaikovsky did not personally enter his changes into the proofs of the score and the piano reduction, not all of the corrections were put in by the publisher. The earlier version with Gremin's appearance and Onegin's closing words "O Death, o Death! It is you that I seek!" is taken from the first edition of the score, which appeared in 1880, whereas the piano reduction published two years earlier reveals a combination version, that retains Gremin's appearance, but has the corrected version of Onegin's closing words "Pozor! Toska! O zhalkii zhrebii moi!" The final version without Gremin's last entrance first appeared in the second printing of the piano reduction in 1881.

12. *ChPSS* 4, 442–451.

13. *ChPSS* 4, 452–456.

14. B. W. Assafiev-Glebov, (Boris Asafiev), *Tchaikovskys Eugen Onegin. Versuch einer Analyse des Stils und der musikalischen Dramaturgie*, German by Guido Waldmann (Potsdam, 1949), 105ff.

15. *Onegin*, ed. Busch, 238.

16. Compare Ulrich Busch, *Puschkin. Leben und Werk*, (Munich, 1989), 28.

17. *ChPSS* 4, 456–461.

18. *Onegin*, ed. Busch, 239.

19. Letter to Nikolai Rubinstein on 10/22 November 1877, quoted from: Attila Csampai, Dietmar Holland, eds., *Peter Tschaikowsky. Eugen Onegin. Texte, Materialien, Kommentare* (Reinbek [bei Hamburg], 1985), 122.

20. Letter to Anatolii Tchaikovsky on 12/24 December 1877: "Simfoniiu ia pishu s polnym soznaniem, chto eto proizvedenie *nediuzhinnoe* i naibolee sovershennoe po forme iz svekh moikh prezhnikh pisanii." *Muzykal'noe nasledie*, 223.

21. Compare B. W. Assafiev-Glebow, 106.

22. *ChPSS* 4, 465–468.

23. Compare Visarion Belinski, *Sobranie sochinenii Belinskogo*, Vol. 2, (Kiev, 1911), 268 ff.

24. *Onegin*, ed. Busch, 33.

25. *Onegin*, ed. Busch, 238 ff.

26. Ibid, 239.

27. All musical examples were produced in Adobe Illustrator 88 by Don Giller.

28. *ChPSS* 4, 488–491.

29. *Onegin*, ed. Busch, 240 ff.

30. It is perhaps no coincidence that for Dostoevsky as well as for Tchaikovsky, Tatiana's husband awakens the impression of an old man, although his age is left unspecified by Pushkin. Vladimir Nabokov maintains, though, that he finds proof in the twenty-third verse of Chapter VIII of the novel that the Prince cannot be any older than his mid-thirties, since he shares childhood memories with Onegin. Pushkin's text does not reveal that common experiences are being discussed here, and Nabokov's argument does not seem compelling. Compare *Eugene Onegin. A Novel in Verse by Aleksandr Pushkin*, translated from the Russian with a commentary by Vladimir Nabokov, Vol. 3, (London, 1975), 191.

31. Fëdor Dostoevsky, *Puschkin—Eine Skizze*, quoted from: Institut für Auslandsbeziehungen (Editor), *All das Lob, das du verdient. Eine deutsche Puschkin-Ehrung zur 150. Wiederkehr seines Todestages*, Zeitschrift für Kulturaustausch 37/1, (Stuttgart, 1987), 185.

Nikolai Kashkin's Review of

The Maid of Orleans [1899]

TRANSLATED FROM THE RUSSIAN
BY MARINA KOSTALEVSKY,
NOTES AND COMMENTARY BY LESLIE KEARNEY

Tchaikovsky began his fifth opera, *The Maid of Orleans*, late in 1878, completing it early the following year. The libretto is self-composed, drawn chiefly from material found in Friedrich Schiller's play *Die Jungfrau von Orleans* (1801), which Zhukovsky had translated into Russian on the recommendation of Turgenev, who had seen the play in Leipzig in 1802. Tchaikovsky also consulted Auguste Mermet's opera, *Jeanne d'Arc* (1876), Jules Barbier's play by the same name (1869, 1874), and historical studies by Jules Michelet and Henri Wallon.[1] The opera premiered in Petersburg on 13 February 1881 at the Mariinsky Theater, Eduard Nápravník conducting. On this occasion the role of Joan was played by M. D. Kamenskaia, a mezzo-soprano with an especially rich low register and endowed with great musicality and artistry. To accommodate and enhance her range, Tchaikovsky transposed certain passages in the opera, notably in the two interactions with Lionel (Act III, No. 17 and Act IV, No. 22). Reporting on the premiere to his benefactress, Nadezhda von Meck, he wrote that "Kamenskaia was transcendent: she was even more excellent than she had ever been before" (16 February 1881). In spite of uninspiring costumes and decor that in no way represented the historical epoch, the public had a favorable response to the opera. Tchaikovsky notes that "My opera was a great success, I was called out twenty-four times."[2] The approbation was not shared by the critics, who were almost unanimously unimpressed; this was most vehemently expressed by Cesar Cui, who called the opera "a weak work of a fine and gifted musician, ordinary, monotonous, dull, and long . . . , with rare flashes of brighter, vivid music, and even those are echoes from other operas."[3]

The Maid of Orleans was not performed in Moscow until many years later, after Tchaikovsky's death, when the private opera company of S. I. Mamontov produced it on 3 February 1899. On that occasion E. A. Tsvetkova sang the role of Joan and a former colleague of Tchaikovsky, M. M. Ippolitov-Ivanov, conducted.[4] Nikolai Kashkin (1839–1920), one of Tchaikovsky's lifelong friends, reviewed the Moscow premiere. Kashkin was one of the first theory instructors at the Moscow Conservatory and, like Tchaikovsky, an early contributor to music theoretical literature in the Russian language.[5] In 1896 he published *Vospominaniia o P. I. Chaikovskom* (Reminiscences of Tchaikovsky). His review of *The Maid of Orleans* appeared on 5 February 1899 in *Moskovskie vedomosti* (Moscow News), No. 36, under the pseudonym of N. Dmitriev.

The Maid of Orleans by Tchaikovsky on the Stage of a Private Opera[6]

Although the name Tchaikovsky is universally praised, the average music lover does not seem overly eager to familiarize himself with the composer's works, even those that are major. *The Maid of Orleans* was written almost twenty, or at least nineteen, years ago, but in Moscow the opera was staged only this past February 3rd on the stage of the Russian Private Opera, which continues to fulfill its noble mission using its entire wherewithal and resources to acquaint the public with those Russian works that are truly great.

Tchaikovsky was very absorbed in *The Maid of Orleans* when he was writing it, but later his interest diminished.

The Maid of Orleans did not first appear at an opportune time. Tchaikovsky intended the leading role for a powerful soprano, but not necessarily one who would ostentatiously show off her ability to sing high notes. If we are not mistaken, the first production of the opera in Petersburg was not performed very many times; later on it was necessary to give the leading role to Ms. Kamenskaia and the composer reluctantly submitted to various changes, transpositions etc. in order to make the role possible for a low mezzo-soprano.

The publisher of *The Maid of Orleans*, P. I. Jurgenson, owns a copy of the original score with corrections by Tchaikovsky in case the opera were to be republished. In this edition, as far as we know, Tchaikovsky rejected the majority of changes in the second version. Nonetheless, a new edition has still not followed, and *The Maid of Orleans* had almost been relegated to the archives.

In Moscow people apparently knew only the aria from the first act of this opera, a world famous element in many concert performances, and the wonderful hymn from the very same act, often performed in the concerts of the Musical Society. Most of the rest of the opera was heard in Moscow for the first time on the stage of the Private Opera.

Right now we will not try to analyze in detail the music of this opera, for it would require more than the space of a newspaper column. We are not placing *The Maid of Orleans* on the same level as *Onegin*, *The Queen of Spades*, *Cherevichki*, or *Mazepa*; nonetheless, a work like *Maid of Orleans* could have a proud place in European musical literature. Yet we, acquainted by theatrical experience with much dross, are almost reluctant to recognize Tchaikovsky.

What appears less than sympathetic to us is the scene containing Agnes's ariosa and her duet with the king, by themselves very beautiful pieces, though they exude a sort of Franco-Italianate character that does not correspond to the prevailing character of the opera. The whole first act, though, is outstanding. Tchaikovsky fortuitously employed the myth of the heavenly voices heard by Joan, or perhaps borrowed this from Soumet's tragedy,[7] which he saw in Paris or perhaps only read. However, such voices can only be comfortably included in an opera.

Joan's [first act] aria is very good, as is the massive finale to the second act. We do not especially like the military-style introduction to the third act. The next scene with Joan and Lionel is considerably better and also significantly abridged in its performance. The following coronation scene is full of splendor and magnificence but demands tremendous resources to perform. One of the best spots in the opera is the introduction and the first scene of the fourth act, abridged as well. In the last scene, that of Joan's execution, Tchaikovsky himself wanted an abridgment, finding the visual impression too oppressive.

The Maid of Orleans demands resplendent performing capacity not only from the soloists, but also from the chorus and orchestra. One needs, however, to realize that this is the case in many operas, not to mention Wagner and most contemporary composers, and Meyerbeer demanded the same; on the other hand, the European public as a whole has gradually become accustomed to seeing these works staged on comparatively small stages as well. We can also reconcile ourselves to this with *The Maid of Orleans*, as long as the performance is given in a detailed and thorough fashion.

First of all, we must address the orchestra, quite difficult and tax-ing in *The Maid of Orleans*. It is a rare opera in which the vocal parts have such an overwhelming importance as here; therefore, the orchestra must not for a minute forget its accompanying role. The intentions of the composer will not be fulfilled if at any point the orchestra drowns out a voice. With respect to this, one need conduct not in formal accordance with instructions, like forte or fortissimo, but with respect to the balance of the voices and instruments, affording everywhere the most important role to the former. Granted, per-forming the opera in this manner is considerably more difficult, but in any case we must strive for this approach, an approach not to be found in February 3rd's performance, during which the orchestral playing contained an inordinate number of monotonous fortes, thereby losing the proper effect and muffling the singers.

Of all the performers, by far the best was Ms. Tsvetkova,[8] singing the main role, a role essentially incompatible with her natural gifts. Nonetheless, she showed that a gifted and intelligent artist can create a style of performance that rises above this incompatibility and gives the rendition a comprehensive character. For us, Ms. Tsvetkova pro-vided rare enjoyment with her singing and even her acting; one criti-cism: it is not a good idea to look excessively ill at the beginning of the opera.

Of the other performers, Mr. Olenin[9] in the role of Dunois and Mr. Shkafer[10] in the role of the king were not half bad, only occasion-ally dragging out the recitative. Moreover, many others seemed to share in this fault. It should be pointed out that we could simply call this an unfortunate manner of displaying the voice in recitative; we could then suggest that the proper style is that which is simpler, more genuine, which most approximates declamation or ordinary speech. Let singers drag out the recitative during concerts, if the singer and the public prefer it so. The more stage-oriented the opera, however, the more the dramatic interest is poisoned by a dull, colorless dirge. Indeed, Shaliapin sings on the stage of the Private Opera, and from him we could take lessons in how to sing a recitative; but it seems the Bolshoi Theater sets all standards in this area, and regrettably so.

One could write positive or negative reviews of all the other per-formers, be we do not want to make a final judgment based on a first performance. In all probability, everything will get better and we do not want to be rash, for that which is written is etched in stone. We intend to give a more detailed review at the end of next week, but for now we say that the cast of *The Maid of Orleans* was not flawless, but quite satisfactory.

The design, namely the decorations and costumes, was certainly better than one could have expected from a private stage. The theater was not completely full, but the opera definitely enjoyed success, and probably quite a lot. Much of the public expressed perplexity at the fact that such a Russian opera could remain obscure. It was our job simply to elaborate on this puzzlement, not to put it to rest.

NOTES

Notes 7-10 are paraphrased from the Russian source, Nikolai Kashkin, *Izbrannye Stat'i o P. I. Chaikovskom* (Selected Articles on P. I. Tchaikovsky) Moscow: Gosudarstvennoe Muzykal'noe Izdatel'stvo, 1954, 217–18, Notes 3–6.

1. See generally Henry Zajaczkowski, "On Čajkovskij's Psychopathology and Its Relationship with his Creativity," in *Čajkovskij-Studien I*, Thomas Kohlhase, ed. (Mainz: Schott Musik International, 1995), 307–28; Hans-Bernd Harder, *Schiller in Rußland* (Bad Homburg: Verlag Gehlen, 1969), 64–65; Alexander Poznansky, *Tchaikovsky: The Quest for the Inner Man* (New York: Schirmer Books, 1991), 385.

2. N. D. Kashkin, *Izbrannye Stat'i o P. I. Chaikovskom* (Selected Articles on P. I. Tchaikovsky) (Moscow: Gosudarstvennoe Muzykal'noe Izdatel'stvo, 1954), 216–17.

3. Quoted in Poznansky, *Quest*, 385.

4. Kashkin, *Izbrannye*, 216.

5. Ellon Carpenter, "Russian Music Theory: A Conspectus," in *Russian Theoretical Thought in Music*, Gordon McQuere, ed. (Ann Arbor: UMI Research Press, 1983), 21, 41.

6. Original text found in Kashkin, *Izbrannye*, at 80–84.

7. Alexandre Soumet (1788–1845) was a French poet and dramaturg, author of the tragedy *Norma*, the basis for Bellini's opera.

8. Elena Iakovlevna Tsvetkova (1872–1929), outstanding lyric-dramatic soprano; graduated from the Moscow Conservatory 1892, member of the Kiev Private Opera; 1896 became a member of the Mamontov company, where the young Shaliapin was beginning his operatic career; known for her great artistry and "beautiful execution," she sang the roles of Vera Sheloga (*Pskovitianka*), Natalia (*Oprichniki*), Oksana (*Charodeika*), Kuma (*Cherevichki*), Snegurochka, Iaroslavna (*Prince Igor*), Maria (*Mazepa*), and Tatiana (*Onegin*), as well as Joan. After the Great October Socialist Revolution, she took up musical pedagogy.

9. Pyotr Sergeevich Olenin (1874–1922), baritone and theater director, who began his career at the S. I. Zimin theater in Moscow, then the Bolshoi Theater. After the Great October Socialist Revolution, he became the head director of the Petrograd Academy Opera (formerly the Mariinsky Theater).

10. Vasilii Petrovich Shkafer (1867–1937), theater director and tenor, author of the book *Forty Years on the Stage of the Russian Opera. Reminiscences. 1890–1930* (published by the Kirov Opera and Ballet Theater, 1936). Shkafer writes about his work in Moscow at the Mamontov Opera, where he worked with Shaliapin (Shuisky in *Boris Godunov* by Musorgsky, Mozart in *Mozart and Salieri* by Rimsky-Korsakov). As director, Shkafer is associated with the first production of Rimsky-Korsakov's operas *Tsarskaia Nevesta* (in the Moscow Private Opera, 1899), *The Tale of the Invisible City of Kitezh and the Maiden Fevronia* (Mariinsky Theater, 1907), *The Golden Cockerel* (Moscow Bolshoi Theater, 1910), as well as productions of Tchaikovsky's operas (on the stage of the Moscow Private Opera): *Mazepa* (1899), *Charodeika* (1900), *Cherevichki* (1902). He was named an Honored Artist of the Republic.

Tchaikovsky Androgyne:

The Maid of Orleans

LESLIE KEARNEY

Understanding Tchaikovsky's artistic creations as reflections of his personal life is nothing new. In fact one can safely assert he has come in for far more than his fair share of this type of exegesis. His opera *The Maid of Orleans* seems to cry out for interpretation as a psychological autopsy.[1] In both the timing of the opera's creation (in the thick of a disastrous marital breakdown) and its content (a person of both male and female characteristics ostracized by society after falling in love with a man, although the precise cause-and-effect remains obscure) suggest unavoidable links to Tchaikovsky's life. If anything, the figure of Joan of Arc as autobiographical comment presents a target all too broad. Tchaikovsky himself invites such personal connection, with his well known and often quoted need to base operas only on "situations which were experienced or seen by me, which could move me to the quick."[2]

Tchaikovsky's homosexuality has been used first to paint him as a pervert and near-psychopath,[3] then to assert that this orientation was so normal as barely to require comment.[4] Not only does Tchaikovsky contradict both characterizations in too many instances to enumerate here, but neither reflects the complexity of human nature with any accuracy whatsoever. Both interpretations turn Tchaikovsky himself into a character that manages to be both exaggerated, yet unidimensional—in fact operatic. In this context George Steiner's interpretation of the blurring of sexual distinctions provides insight:

> The typologies of women's liberation, of the new politically, socially ostentatious homosexuality (notably in the United States) and of 'unisex,' point to a deep re-ordering or dis-

ordering of long-established frontiers. 'So loosly disally'd,' in Milton's telling phrase, men and women are not only manoeuvring in a neutral terrain of indistinction, but exchanging roles—sartorially, psychologically, in regard to economic and erotic functions which were formerly set apart . . . . A common formlessness or search for new forms has all but undermined classic age-lines, sexual divisions, class structures and hierarchic gradients of mind and power.[5]

Writing nearly a hundred years after Tchaikovsky's death, Steiner gives a good description of the society in search of redefinition in which the composer found himself. The fluid sexual boundaries, political uncertainties, and the "common formlessness" already present in society seem to have made Tchaikovsky somewhat uneasy. In a letter Soviet authorities later would have trouble with, he condemned the idea of socialism as a "senseless utopia, . . . contrary to human nature," of "material equality" that would make life "dull and colorless."[6] He feared the precise phenomenon that both Steiner and Jean-Jacques Nattiez would identify with the breakdown of defined social roles, especially sexual identity—a "denial of history, and freedom of interpretation"[7] that open up many possibilities but which are purchased at the cost of meaning, of a commonly understood societal coherence. The fact that Tchaikovsky might rather not have lived this social experiment does not preclude the possibility that he might have seen opera—an art form in which for him "everything is based on *pseudo* and where *truth* in the everyday sense of the word is altogether useless"[8]—as the perfect realm in which to explore the many interpretations and possibilities manifest in the androgynous persona. While Henry Zajaczkowski's attempt to explicate *The Maid of Orleans* in the context of something that Tchaikovsky dreamt may be built on shaky psychoanalytical ground and may fail to convince in its particulars, his placement of this opera in some kind of dream-state is suggestive. As Nattiez has pointed out, the link between Freud's dream theory and Lévi-Strauss' realization that "Beyond the rational there exists a more important and valid category. . . . The order which is thus introduced into a seemingly incoherent mass is neither contingent nor arbitrary."

What Freud found in dreams, Lévi-Strauss saw in myth, seemingly illogical information that nevertheless provides "a logical model capable of overcoming contradiction."[9] I suggest this is precisely the role *The Maid of Orleans* played in Tchaikovsky's output, but not to overcome the contradiction of either his own sexuality or his inability to deal with female sexuality, issues which the fiasco of his marriage must have decided for him unequivocally. Rather it would seem that, at this point in his life, Tchaikovsky found his place in society and his human relationships in general in need of reassessment, and perceived the androgynous, "outsider" figure of Joan as, if not exactly an alter ego, then the liberating artistic vehicle through which he might accomplish such a reassessment.

Although Tchaikovsky did not like to start a new composition before finishing one already in progress, he made an exception when he began work on *The Maid of Orleans* late in 1878; yet his excitement for the topic coexisted with feelings that he described to Nadezhda von Meck as "fear, trepidation, and a certain shyness."[10] As his research on the historical Joan progressed, Tchaikovsky experienced through her "such pity and pain for all humanity," emotion so violent as to cause insomnia, and ultimately the "mixture of intense pain coupled with pleasure [that] can really be compared with the pangs of childbirth, when you both suffer and joyously await your child."[11] After the opera's premiere more than two years later, when the work had met with popular success but critical failure, Tchaikovsky recalls the days of the opera's conception as " . . . both painful and sweet! . . . I feel so fine! But also sad for some reason! I want to weep, and I do not know what sort of tears they are: humiliation and gratitude and regret are all in them."[12] One might conclude that this artist who seems to have a foot in every camp, straddling the fences of east and west, romantic and classical, nationalism and cosmopolitanism, masculine and feminine, has achieved the ultimate ambiguity in *The Maid of Orleans,* a work for which even *he* seems to have felt ambivalence.

Ambivalence however, while perhaps presenting an intellectually interesting paradox, does not usually by itself "move one to the quick." So what did Tchaikovsky find in Joan that so affected him? A look at the terms in which Tchaikovsky approaches human relationships may help to clarify why Joan might have been just what he needed. One of the most well known eccentricities in the annals of Tchaikovskiana is the composer's long "phantom" relationship with Nadezhda von Meck. The image of their friendship—pursued through scores of letters, in which they address each other as "dearest friend," never "sullying" the friendship with the potential pettiness of close encounter—presents a romantic picture indeed. While Holden's biography of Tchaikovsky has been called, probably correctly, a "fantasy,"[13] his intuition that characterizes Nadezhda Filaretnova as "some bizarre kind of alternative spouse" seems accurate.[14] A look at Tchaikovsky's recorded attitudes shows, moreover, that this need to evade a flesh-

and-blood relationship resonates over and over throughout his life and has serious personal implications, concerning as it did people of both sexes, some of whom Tchaikovsky genuinely loved. This phenomenon of non-relationship takes several forms, most obviously avoidance of human contact, but also involvement with "non-persons." Both these predilections can be seen as an effacement of the other and, ultimately, a kind of effacement of the self.

One aspect of Tchaikovsky's taste in love-objects that has not been belabored is what might be called his affinity for the incompetent. Poznansky's research, along with other accounts of homosexual lifestyle in nineteenth-century Russia and Europe, paints a picture of societies in which casual sexual encounters with a variety of partners, many from "lower classes," constitute nothing unusual, much less pathological.[15] Beyond this behavior, however, Tchaikovsky consistently demonstrates a fascination for people who, at least in his own perception, seem to be incomplete or societally disenfranchised. His obsession with his servant Alësha, for whose sake he hung, disconsolate, around army barracks, hoping for a glimpse of the beloved after he'd been drafted, is a case in point.[16]

Given the composer's clear preference for men and the bizarre circumstances of his marriage, Tchaikovsky's lack of warmth for his wife comes as no surprise. The terms in which he describes her—or rather doesn't describe her—are telling:

> I won't tell you much about her, apart from the fact that she is thoroughly respectable and desperately in love with me, as I still don't really know her very well. . . . And I shan't be bringing her to see you in Kamenka until I get over my sense of shock that my nieces will call her "Auntie." As yet it seems to me audacious of her to have become the aunt of your children, whom I love more than any other children in the world.[17]

Not only does Antonina have no identity for Tchaikovsky, but this letter quite clearly implies that she is not even entitled to one; he thinks it "audacious" of her to assume the identity of aunt, a mere legalistic accident over which she has no control yet which unaccountably seems to taint his own love for his nieces. In another letter, this time to Nadezhda von Meck, Tchaikovsky describes Antonina as "of medium height," with eyes a "beautiful color but expressionless," having a manner "very affected, and there is not a single movement or gesture which is straightforward," with a complete lack of "that elusive charm that is a reflection of inner, spiritual beauty," and finally states

Her head and her heart are both completely empty; so in neither is there anything to describe. I can only swear to you that she has never once expressed a single idea or shown any feeling towards me. . . . I felt there was no real feeling beneath the caresses. It was something conventional, something she regarded as necessary, an attribute of married life. Never once did she display the least desire to find out what I was doing, what my work was, what plans I had, what I was reading or what my intellectual and artistic tastes were.[18]

Ultimately all one really knows of Antonina from this is that she was of medium height. Can any human being be so empty, so vacant, so absent as this nonentity Tchaikovsky describes? In this context an earlier letter is suggestive, in which he extols the joys of bachelor life, a life in which he is "almost happy," to Modest: "In moments like these I probably hate as much as you do that unknown, beautiful woman who will force me to change my habits and my friends . . . ."[19] In his letters about Antonina, Tchaikovsky is still talking about "that unknown beautiful woman," who, though she now happens to take up physical space, is no more real to him than before, but who has certainly inherited not only his hatred, but his contempt. One of the most positive things Tchaikovsky ever says about her is that "she will not constrain me in anything. I must not deceive myself: she is very limited, but that is even good. I should be afraid of an intelligent woman. But I stand so far above this one, I dominate her to such a degree, that at least I have no fear of her at all."[20] Here Tchaikovsky gets to the heart of the matter with a degree of candor to which we have become unaccustomed in our own time. Tchaikovsky can tolerate this woman he refers to as a "reptile" only as long as he can dominate her utterly.[21]

An associated phenomenon is Tchaikovsky's pronounced attraction to the very young, a subject on which scholarship, for all its fascination with his sex life, has remained curiously reticent, perhaps falsely assuming this to be part and parcel of the homosexual orientation. The complex triangle between Tchaikovsky and his younger twin brothers, to whom he felt like a "mother,"[22] presents an interesting example. While Modest, a homosexual himself, had a crush on Pyotr, Pyotr preferred Anatolii, who was not only heterosexual (perhaps neither evident nor relevant at that point), but "entirely average."[23] Possessing neither the artistic genius, temperament, nor eccentricities of his twin Modest, it is at least open to conjecture that at an early age Anatolii's attraction may have consisted in the blanker slate he presented to Pyotr. Another child who attracted Tchaikovsky's attention, Kolia Konradi, presents a disturbing example. This boy, under the tutelage of Modest, eight years old when he met Tchaikovsky, inspired passionate outpourings from the composer: "I adore him passionately and think of him every second"; and in a letter to the boy himself, "I kiss you warmly 1,000,000,000 times. Petia."[24] Besides Kolia's extreme youth, this child was also deaf and mute, a person whose powers of self-expression and whose very connection to the outer world were impaired and heavily dependent on intermediaries, naturally giving any hearing adult in his presence even more control than is the case in the average adult-child relationship.

Tchaikovsky did not always need to dominate, at least in theory. One of his more humorous letters expresses the wish that an actor named Boucher, to whom he felt attracted, would take his "precious hand [and] slap me across the face a hundred times!"[25] In a letter to Modest, newly available in its entirety, Tchaikovsky discusses one of his many infatuations, this time with a manservant *"whose boots I would feel happy to clean all my life long*, whose chamber pots I would like to take out, and for whom I am generally ready to lower myself in any way."[26] Instances of Tchaikovsky attending masked balls dressed as a woman, dancing a *pas de deux* with a male partner, and otherwise placing himself in an arguably submissive role are legion. Likewise Tchaikovsky had a clear penchant for identifying men with whom he had intimate relationships (even if not necessarily sexual) by feminine names and endearments, including identifying himself as feminine, in the most blatant example signing himself "Petrolina, your devoted and loving sister."[27] Yet submission is only the other side of dominance, and it seems clear that, for Tchaikovsky, intimacy was inextricably bound up in these roles. It is noteworthy that the terms in which he speaks of being slapped a hundred times echo his frequent expressions of desire to kiss someone or other "a billion times," "a hundred times," "all over," etc. The fact that the individuals on both sides of this equation are not only males, but feminized males, only makes the whole phenomenon all the more intriguing; ordinary male-female roles are not predetermined but can exist in a state of flux, constantly redefined to meet the demands of the relationship. Interestingly these men and boys, for whom he expresses genuine affection, often do not come across as any more three-dimensional than the despised Antonina. The immoderate gushing Tchaikovsky bestows upon them, even if somewhat typical of the style of the time, renders them caricatures; so does his tendency to fixate on isolated physical attributes, especially hands,[28] Anatolii's wart, and a nickname he applies to himself, Petu, which amounts to "penis;"[29] this habit reduces people to a series of disembodied parts.

Even though Tchaikovsky may have indulged in masochistic fantasies, in every "real" relationship cited he unquestionably occupies the dominant position, either by virtue of age, sex, education, or social status, and perhaps in a variety of ephemeral ways as well. It is probably no coincidence that he was extraordinarily reluctant to encounter Nadezhda von Meck, the woman who held the purse strings and thus exerted considerable control over his lifestyle and artistic freedom. Tchaikovsky carried this to the extreme of shuttering his house on her property when he discovered that she went past on her evening walks and often looked inside, a precaution that her nearsightedness rendered unnecessary.[30] Even within the stringent limitations of this "paper friendship" he held her at arm's length linguistically, declining her offer to employ the informal address (*ty*) in their letters.[31] The correspondence with Ms. von Meck also offers an interesting inversion of the gendered wordplay already observed. Two collections of their correspondence focus on the affectionate greeting with which most of the letters begin, "Beloved Friend," and "To My Best Friend."[32] What is lost in translation is the fact that Tchaikovsky invariably applies the masculine form of the word "friend," *drug*, not the feminine *podruga*. While Jakobson and others note that the masculine form in Russian is neutral, "unmarked" in linguistic terms,[33] Tchaikovsky's wordplay might suggest that this form of address has at least some significance. For example, a look at three typical letters written in quick succession shows Tchaikovsky addressing Kolia Konradi, a male with whom he was on very intimate terms, and Nadezhda Filaretnova with identical greetings on 9 May 1884, "Milyi, dorogoi drug moi!" (My dear sweet friend). A letter written a few days later (13 May) to his sister-in-law Praskovia Vladimirovna, however, actually opens by incorporating her nickname into a playful rhythmic "jingle," verging on babytalk, "Pania-milia pozabyla. . . ." (Pania-dearie forgot. . . .) The letter also closes in this vein: "Toliu, Taniu obnimaiu. Do svidan'ia, dushechka!" (Embrace Tolia and Tania. Goodbye, little soul [fem.]).[34] Extremely revealing, moreover, is a remark in Tchaikovsky's letter to Modest of 26 February 1879. Concerning the latest infatuation, with a homosexual prostitute to whom he had regularly referred as "she," Tchaikovsky calls this man's garret apartment "the focus of all human happiness," and then abruptly shifts to "he," explaining "I can't use the feminine pronoun talking about that dear person,"[35] a clear implication that once he starts to take someone seriously, that individual must be perceived as masculine. Considering the openness with which Tchaikovsky expressed himself to Nadezhda Filaretnova and the range of topics he felt free to discuss, it is arguable that one element of the "no-meeting policy" might have been the maintenance of a fiction that aligned her with his male—or, more accurately, androgynous—friends. Sibelan Forrester's fascinating study of lesbian poets' use of language suggests an obvious connection.[36] Poets like Sophia Parnok, Marina Tsvetaeva, and Zinaida Gippius, pursuing a lifestyle outside the mainstream, avail themselves of the rich possibilities the Russian language offers for gender manipulation to encode messages and feelings in subtle ways. Tchaikovsky's adept and creative way with words, not to mention his constant linguistic crossing of gender lines, would suggest a similar operation in process, an operation he understandably did not feel he could keep up in Nadezhda Filaretnova's physical presence.

Nor does the situation with Ms. von Meck represent the only such distancing. Over the course of his life Tchaikovsky made many allusions to his desire, verging on need, to avoid his fellow man. His meeting with Tolstoy in 1876 evidently so disillusioned him as to affect his relationship with Tolstoy's writing, and further to discourage him from meeting Turgenev when he had the chance in 1879, and to keep his meetings with Chekhov to a minimum.[37] This fear of disillusionment did not flow in one direction. Tchaikovsky expresses the opinion that if his passion for his friend Kotek were returned in full measure, he would "cool to him," feeling "disgust" that this young man would "stoop" to intimacy with the likes of him.[38] Even years earlier, informed that Vera Davydova, the sister of Tchaikovsky's brother-in-law Lev Davydov, was infatuated with him, causing the family to fear unpleasantness resulting from propinquity, Tchaikovsky reassured them in rather odd terms:

> It seems to me that if what you assume does in fact exist, then my absence is probably more harmful to her than my presence. When I am not around, my person can perhaps be imagined worthy of love, but when a woman who loves me confronts daily my far from poetic qualities, for example, my untidiness, irritability, cowardice, pettiness, vanity, secretiveness, and so on, believe me, the halo surrounding me when I am far distant vanishes very quickly—[39]

In other words, to know him is not to love him.

Perhaps the most powerful such statement comes in a somewhat different form regarding Tchaikovsky's nephew, Bob Davydov. This young man, who clearly touched Tchaikovsky in the deepest way, expressed to his uncle the fear that he was an empty vessel, a "container." Tchaikovsky responds, "You are by no means a 'container.' You have a great deal of content, only everything contained in the container is still heaped about in disorder. . . . Enjoy your youth and learn to value time. My dear, good, darling beloved! My adorable little container!"[40] One can easily imagine the pain Tchaikovsky experienced when Bob, whom he considered above "common mortals,"[41] spoke of himself in terms essentially equivalent to those his uncle had once used to describe his wife; empty, devoid of any worthwhile content. Bob was the exception to every rule of humanity that Tchaikovsky seemed to know, a person whom to know *was* to love.

Of course, refusing contact with another person constitutes the ultimate dominance. Regardless what impassioned outpouring or seeming candor may exist on a sheet of paper, the "relationship" only exists in the imagination, a fact that Tchaikovsky knew well and clearly demonstrated in his behavior and expressed attitudes; Tchaikovsky finds an impressive variety of ways to make the world go away, to reduce people, even people he loves, to manageable quantities, if necessary to nonentities. Lest this assertion become part of some portrait of Tchaikovsky as psychopath, I might add that the phenomenon identified here is one that Tchaikovsky shares with many, perhaps most individuals, differing only in degree, not in kind. The other important difference is naturally the sheer creativity, ingenuity and beauty of the ways Tchaikovsky sublimates his human relationships—in short, his artistry—enabling and fueling the romanticization of his idiosyncrasies. One might discern here a piece of the worldview that leads to the "truth or beauty" conflict between Tchaikovsky and Musorgsky. Musorgsky believed he could tell the truth about people by capturing their mode of expression, "defining" the speaker (along with the world his speech implies) by "saying things musically in such a way that they cannot be spoken differently."[42] Tchaikovsky seems to believe that, to see the real beauty of humanity, the last thing one should do is capture any part of it, but rather to abstract it into the realm of the imagination.[43] An overview of dramatic subjects he chose (not limited to opera) attests to this—*Undine, Romeo and Juliet, Snegurochka, Swan Lake, Eugene Onegin, Hamlet, The Enchantress, The Queen of Spades, Iolanta,* and of course *The Maid of Orleans*—a catalogue of near misses, impossible relationships, glimpses of ever unrealizable potential, or worse, punishment or even destruction if potential is realized. It is no accident that Tchaikovsky attains his heights of musical emotion precisely in the monologue, giving voice to the realization that outpouring of passion is far safer when the dreary reality of dealing with its object is not an issue. Nor does he exempt himself. It is entirely characteristic that the prosaic physical complaint of indigestion prompts him to experience an "indeterminate longing for something which seizes my entire soul with an unbelievable force and terminates in a quite definitive striving for nonbeing, *soif du néant!*"[44] In this light Taruskin's criticism of the many scholars who strive to appropriate Tchaikovsky, pulling him into each camp in fanciful and self-serving ways, is accomplished in interesting terms:

> In fine, in order for Chaikovsky to become the exemplary nineteenth-century composer it was first necessary for him to disappear, leaving a tabula rasa on which each participant in the ensuing symposium could inscribe whatever fantasies and prejudices he pleased about the nineteenth century, and about Russia.[45]

To some extent, this tabula rasa may be, consciously or not, precisely what Tchaikovsky wanted. The consistency with which his personality, life, death, not to mention his art, have been fictionalized, romanticized, and in general turned into a fairy tale, may be the greatest favor posterity could do for a man who felt he could only be loved if not really known.

If, in the stressful circumstances of late 1878, Tchaikovsky sought a vehicle through which to investigate the ambivalence of human relationships, he could not have chosen a better subject or literary model than Schiller's Joan. Although he consulted a number of sources about Joan of Arc, both fictional and historical, he quickly came to the conclusion that "although Schiller's tragedy doesn't tally with historical fact, it surpasses all other creative representations of Joan in the depth of psychological truth,"[46] an estimation that can be seen reflected on virtually every page of his opera. Tchaikovsky's observation that historical fact is not of the essence in this work is not only accurate, but constitutes a victory for Schiller, who informed Goethe that "Das Historische ist überwunden,"[47] a thing to be conquered. Yet, while dearth of historical fact is clearly evident in Schiller's *Jungfrau von Orleans*, the play may not quite so readily provide insight into the "psychological truth" that Tchaikovsky found there. Rather, like Tchaikovsky's opera, Schiller's play has puzzled people from its inception, a great deal of the confusion centered precisely in the strange flatness of a character from whom, at the very least, one might expect the passion borne of zeal.[48] Tieck notes that Joan expresses herself in "isolated declamations—indeed one can say—musical and concert pieces" (isolierte Deklamations—ja man kann sagen Musik- und Konzertstücke), which inspire Schiller's followers to emulate only his mistakes.[49] Hebbel sums up the general sentiment best in his judgment that "Schiller's *[Maid of Orleans]* belongs in a wax museum. . . . In history she lives, suffers and dies well; in Schiller's tragedy—she speaks well," (Die Schillersche *[Jungfrau von Orleans]* gehört ins Wachsfiguren-Kabinett. . . . In der Geschichte lebt, leidet und stirbt sie schön; in Schillers Trauerspiel—spricht sie schön).[50] Not only does Hebbel find Joan a lifeless mouthpiece, but he identifies her fundamental ambiguity in unsettling terms: "she makes the impression of an apple tree that is hung with grapes, but on which no grapes grow" (sie macht den Eindruck eines Apfelbaums, der mit Weintrauben behängt ist, auf dem aber keine Weintrauben wachsen).[51] Indeed, ambiguity does not adequately capture what Hebbel seems to imply. Schiller not only cloaks Joan in a persona not her own, but in a persona that cannot thrive—or grow—using her as a host; in other words, she is a creature lacking at least organicity, and at worst, integrity.

Such an assessment would surely have chagrined Schiller, for whom Joan clearly had special significance, but not, interestingly enough, as a historical reality. In his poem "Das Mädchen von Orleans," Schiller explicitly states "Dich schuf das Herz, du sollst unsterblich leben" (The heart created you, you should be immortal), vocabulary echoed in his description of the play, which "flowed *from the heart* and should speak *to the heart*" (floß *aus dem Herzen* und *zu dem Herzen* sollte es auch sprechen), in contrast to Voltaire's satirical treatment of Joan, which for Schiller indicates "Armut des Herzens" (poverty of heart).[52] This has been acknowledged as the means by which Schiller gets himself off the hook of historical accuracy;[53] but more than that, it seems a clear indication of the role Joan plays for Schiller, an entity not only created by the imagination, but which gives the imagination exceptional range and freedom, a kind of empty vessel that manifests the spirit of the artist who addresses himself to her. It is undoubtedly no accident that *Die Jungfrau von Orleans* provides the backdrop for Schiller's comment to Körner on the nature of tragedy: "Every material seeks its own form. . . . The idea of a tragedy must always be mobile and developing" (Jeder Stoff will seine eigene Form. . . . Die Idee eines Trauerspiels muß immer beweglich und werdend sein).[54] This might be seen as the artistic counterpart to a statement by Kant, in Schiller's estimation the nutshell of his philosophy, and than which "no greater word has ever been spoken. . . : define yourself from yourself" (kein größeres Wort [ist] noch gesprochen worden. . . : Bestimme Dich aus Dir selbst).[55] This idea seems to argue powerfully for a complete integrity of form and content on many levels, a manifestation of inner essence. What this means for Schiller, however, points only to further tension. Schiller's understanding of the term "nature" in itself bespeaks conflict, as Claude David finds in the poem "Der Spaziergang" (this is further taken up in Schiller's *Ästhetische Briefe*). David and others note Schiller's basic recognition that "nature is brutal and at odds with reason and culture."[56] By divesting Joan of the one thing that everyone knows about her—her martyr's death by burning at the stake—Schiller forces the reader to abandon all preconceptions and examine precisely the nature of this personality that does indeed defy reason and offend culture.

Joan offers abundant potential in such a role. An account of her in 1429 depicts a girl "powerfully built, with a somewhat dark skin, appear[ing] of uncommon strength, yet modest and hav[ing] a thoroughly feminine voice."[57] Here in this exceptionally concise description one finds the essence of Joan: a balancing act of masculine (power, strength) and feminine (modesty, feminine voice) traits, with perhaps the single most common sign of "otherness": dark skin, though one notes, only "somewhat" dark. When asked at her trial if she had an occupation, Joan specifically identifies her spinning and sewing as activities she shares with "every woman in Rouen,"[58] an ordinary womanly endeavor, which she later abandoned for sheepherding. Not surprisingly, a great deal of the questioning concerns the voices Joan hears, which in essence tell her to be a good girl, go to church, and, by the way, defend France against England. It is most interesting that, although she subtly evades clear answers in several cases, one question, "Who advised you to wear men's clothing?" provokes an aggressive refusal to answer. Joan "hesitates several times," finally responding "I will not burden any person with that!"[59] Out of this brief glimpse of Joan begins to emerge an ironic character who seems to act as an automaton during momentous historical events, but who remains strangely stubborn about assuming responsibility for her own personal ambiguity (only the most graphic manifestation of which is her male attire), imputing this decision neither to earthly nor to supernatural advisors. Both Schiller and Tchaikovsky may have achieved the greatest historical accuracy of all—if not the greatest dramatic vehicle[60]—when they created a central character who unequivocally represents nothing but ambivalence, and whose human motivation seems in every case obscure.

Schiller crafts the character of Joan with extraordinary care. His *tour de force* lies precisely in the degree to which he can saturate the play with her presence, expose her to the audience in scene after scene, yet reveal so little about her. Certainly Joan's contradictory nature is clearly recognized—so clearly, in fact, that it has elicited some rather touching apologias that strive to help her to "make sense" in human terms.[61] Ultimately, however, it would seem that maintenance of contradiction does not need to be explained away, but is rather the point, so aggressively does Schiller pursue his path of equivocation, spreading it ultimately beyond Joan to every character and situation. Schiller constructs several powerful dichotomies around Joan, all of which teeter back and forth, in virtually constant motion, throughout the play. A few examples will illustrate. Throughout the play Schiller deftly uses the word "Jungfrau"—which can mean either a generic virgin or young woman, or specifically the Virgin Mary—with uncertain referent, blurring the line between Joan and the Mother of God, implying her sanctity without directly addressing it. Similarly, the object Schiller specifically associates with Joan is a sword, a conspicuously masculine symbol, emblematic of the warrior for Christ, but embossed with lilies, one of the many symbols of Mary, the feminine aspect of God (Act II, Sc. 10, et al.). Schiller also reinforces Joan's links with nature in many ways, starting with her identity as a shepherd, but uses her lovely farewell monologue (Prologue, Sc. 4) as a transition away from the natural world, gradually associating her ever more with distortions of natural processes. For example, she promises to rescue Orleans before the moon changes ("eh' der Mond noch wechselt," Act I, Sc. 9, l. 59), aligning herself with forces of nature; yet she also assures the troops that, before France surrenders, "you will see the Loire run backwards," (Eh' siehest du die Loire zurücke fließen, Act I, Sc. 10, l. 120)—a perversion of nature. Incidentally, Tchaikovsky preserves this line. Schiller does not present these dichotomies as simple polarities, but rather embeds and entangles them with one another, so that the moment anything seems to point in a certain direction, it is immediately counterbalanced and redirected.

This process commences with the very first remark concerning Joan in the Prologue of the play (Sc. 2, ll. 13–22). Her father Thibaut informs us, in the strange disconnected manner in which he seems to speak to Joan, but in actuality talks past her, that

—Ich sehe dich in Jugendfülle prangen,
Dein Lenz ist da, es ist die Zeit der Hoffnung,

Entfaltet ist die Blume deines Leibes;
Doch stets vergebens harr' ich, daß die Blume
Der zarten Lieb' aus ihrer Knospe breche
Und freudig reife zu der goldnen Frucht!
O das gefällt mir nimmermehr und deutet
Auf eine schwere Irrung der Natur!
Das Herz gefällt mir nicht, das streng und kalt
Sich zuschließt in den Jahren des Gefühls.

I see you in the glory of your youth,
Your spring is here, it is the time of hope,
The flower of your body is unfolded;
Yet I wait in vain for the flower
of tender love to break out of its bud
and joyfully ripen into golden fruit!
Oh, this does not please me, and points
to a serious aberration of nature!
I don't like the heart that shuts itself up,
stringent and cold, in the years of passion.

Here Schiller establishes Joan's essence. First, he unequivocally associates her with natural forces and processes, while simultaneously undermining this association—she is a flower that refuses to bloom, bear fruit, etc.—climaxing with the explicit appellation "Irrung der Natur." Though he makes it quite clear that this aberration would be cured by marriage, the moment Joan's "stringent and cold" heart opens itself to love, she is undone, ostracized by society, and held up to public condemnation by, of all people, her father (Act IV, Sc. 11). Significantly, the first time that Thibaut addresses his daughter he calls her Jeanette, the solitary time in the play she is so named. On every level including the most basic, Thibaut has no comprehension whatsoever of his daughter's identity. Indeed, they do not even seem to inhabit the same physical dimension. Hebbel may identify Schiller's Joan chiefly as someone who "speaks well," but in the presence of her father she cannot speak at all. Both in their opening "interaction" and in the Act IV confrontation, Joan stands in eerie silence while Thibaut carries on a one-sided conversation that precludes, even as it demands, response.

While Tchaikovsky considerably tones down the poetic imagery of Thibaut's speeches, he retains and even exacerbates the disjunct dialogue. In fact, if this were a different kind of opera, it would be amusing that, whenever Joan is silent, her father demands that she speak, and whenever she speaks, he tells her to be quiet (see also Act I, No. 5). Thibaut's first three addresses culminate with questions to Joan that seem to require answers: "No ty molchish, ty otvarchaesh vzori?" (But you are silent, you avert your glance?); "O zachem ty mne prinosish odno lish' tol'ko gore i pechal?" (Oh, why do you bring me nothing but sorrow and weeping?); and most explicitly, "Otvetzhe, Ioanna, khochesh' ty otsa izpolnit voliu?" (Answer, Joan, do you want to fulfill your father's wish?). Joan interjects a remark after the second question (odd in itself, since it is the most rhetorical), but it is neither an answer nor is it addressed directly to her father. When she does attempt to answer the third question, saying "Mne sud'ba naznachena drugaia: volie neba podvlastna ia" (My fate is different: I have to obey the will of Heaven), the next word out of Thibaut's mouth is *molchi* (be silent). Tchaikovsky pursues and intensifes this impossibility of communication at the end of Act III, when Thibaut accuses Joan of allying herself with the powers of darkness. Over and over he demands that she answer and defend herself, a demand taken up by Raimond, the Cardinal, and the chorus' reproachful "Ona molchit!" (She is silent!). The only response is a "thunderous voice from heaven" (gremiashchi s neba glas), interpreted as a supernatural admission of guilt, another equation of Joan with some skewed force of nature. When Joan does speak, it is again a nonsequitur addressed to Lionel, not a response to the accusations of devilish alliance: "liuboi ty menia sgubi" (with love you have destroyed me).

Naturally, a crucial dichotomy Schiller manipulates throughout the play is Joan's polyvalent sexuality. He endows her not only with both male and female characteristics, but sometimes deprives her of sexuality—indeed humanity—altogether: "Schließ ich mich an kein Geschlecht der Menschen an und dieser Panzer deckt kein Herz" (I belong to no human sex and this armor conceals no heart; Act II, Sc. 7, ll. 31–32), while other times allowing her to feel passion. Schiller presents Joan in the context of two other female characters who act as foils for her in this regard, the comparatively uncomplicated Agnes, spokeswoman of femininity; and the woman every bit as adrogynous as Joan herself, Isabeau. One notes the masculine form of her name, also used by Auguste Mermet in his opera *Jeanne d'Arc*, but which could be rendered Isabelle or Isabella. Schiller's introduction of this character, in Act II, Sc. 2, again lays out the fundamental paradox that he will investigate throughout the play. Isabeau declares herself leader in the cause against England, explicitly placing herself in opposition to Joan: "Ein sieghaft Mädchen führt des Feindes Heer, / Ich will das eure führen, ich will euch / Statt einer Jungfrau und

Prophetin sein!" (A victorious girl leads the enemy troops / I will lead yours, I will be / in the place of the virgin and prophet; Act II, Sc. 2, ll. 70–72). She receives a disheartening response: her troops lose morale in her presence, they intend to win with weapons, not with women, and most pointedly—"Wir fürchten uns / Vor keinem Teufel mehr, sobald Ihr weg seid." (We fear / no *other* devil, as long as you are gone; [emphasis added] ll. 85–86) They reproach her for her inhumanity in betraying her own son, to which she responds "Ich darf ihn hassen, ich hab' ihn geboren" (I am allowed to hate him, I bore him; l. 118). Isabeau concludes with a lengthy self-justification, in which she attempts to humanize herself to her troops, assuring them that "Ich habe Leidenschaften, warmes Blut / Wie eine andre" (I have sorrows, warm blood / Like any other; ll. 133–34). Isabeau is some kind of evil twin to Joan. Both are androgynous, both are suspected of consorting with the devil, both have their humanity called into question; but Isabeau is ineffective both as male and female. Isabeau's troops reject her as a warrior, while Joan triumphs on the battlefield; nature has rendered Isabeau a monstrous mother, while Joan's affinity with nature and her nurturing instincts are exquisitely expressed in her farewell to her home and flock (Prologue, Sc. 4). Yet here again, Schiller does not leave matters in simple binary opposition. It is precisely the similarities between the two women that create the tension and, in an odd way, endow Isabeau with a certain credibility. When all others are still infatuated with Joan, Isabeau has the audacity to echo Thibaut's fear of his daughter's supernatural consortium, accusing her of deriving her powers from a "hirnverrückender Planet" (mind-twisting planet; Act II, Sc. 2, l. 2), by "Satans Kunst," (Satan's art; Act II, Sc. 2, l. 67), and in general trying to expose her as a fraud: "Sie eine Zauberin! Ihr ganzer Zauber / Ist euer Wahn und euer feiges Herz! / Eine Närrin ist sie" (She a magician! Her whole magic / Is your insanity and cowardly heart! / She is a fool; Act V, Sc. 5, ll. 24–26). In the absence of compelling information to the contrary, which of course is never forthcoming, one must admit that Isabeau makes a certain amount of sense. Indeed, because Schiller often describes the two women in such similar terms, Isabeau seems even to have some special insight into Joan—more, for example, than the smitten Lionel. Finally, because she shares both Thibaut's qualms about Joan and his unenviable position as a parent who betrays his own child, Isabeau stands in a bizarre kind of *loco parentis* to Joan, especially as she gains a brief but conspicuous authority over her.

In Tchaikovsky's opera Isabeau does not appear as a separate entity, but he pursues Schiller's equation of her with Thibaut by taking this to the logical extreme, conflating the two characters. For some reason, he feminizes her name to Izabella, which seems like a missed opportunity. He mentions her by name only once (Act I, No. 4), when Bertrand describes to Thibaut the capture of Orleans by the enemy,

> . . . burgunski gertsog,
> privël tuda svoi voiska,
> i broniei pokrivshis Izabella,
> mat' korolia, kniazei bavarskikh plemia,
> primchalsas v stan vragov i razzhigaet
> ikh khitrimi slovami na pogibel tovo
> kto zhizn' priial u nei pod serdtsem!

> the Burgundian duke,
> [who] summoned his troops there,
> and Isabella covered in armor,
> mother of a king, a clan of Bavarian princes,
> tearing into the camp of their enemies, inflaming
> them with sly words to the destruction of him
> who received life under her heart!

Here Tchaikovsky summarizes Isabeau's defining characteristics, clad like a man, mother of a prince whom she treacherously destroyed. The choral response disregards the Duke of Burgundy, focusing exclusively on Isabeau, and even more explicitly equating her with Jezebel, a Biblical woman responsible not for saving her city, like Joan, but destroying it:[62]

> srazi eë, prokliatem, Gospod'!
> Otstupnitsa, pogibnesh' ty,
> kak nekogda Iesavel' pogibla!

> strike her down, curse her, Lord!
> Apostate, you will perish,
> as once Jezebel perished!

When Schiller's Thibaut accuses Joan before the townspeople (Act IV, Sc. 11), he takes her by surprise and speaks only of her satanic powers, during which accusation (as well as the two subsequent scenes) Joan stands like a statue. After justifying herself to Raimond, Joan in essence turns herself over to Isabeau (Act V, Sc. 5), who ridicules and insults her, as we have seen; but although Isabeau orders her triply shackled, Joan breaks free like Samson, to whom she compares herself (Act V, Sc. 11). Thus Schiller continues to portray Joan as thoroughly passive *vis à vis* her father, but as assertive and effective in dealing with her alter ego, Isabeau. Tchaikovsky conflates elements of these scenes, putting Isabeau's vocabulary into Thibaut's mouth, calling her "nichtozhnaia" (worthless, nonentity) and attributing Joan's powers to the insanity ("bezumtsy") of the people. In the opera Joan flees from these accusations into the love scene, essentially from one man who *might* destroy her to another she *knows* will destroy her, as she tells us in her soliloquy (Act IV, No. 21). Significantly, the culmination of the love duet is not some kind of Wagnerian union, but a heavenly (choral) denunciation of Joan's behavior, reducing her to the same silent, staring, detached state she assumes in her father's presence, with Lionel, like Thibaut, asking "Zachem molchish' ty?" (Why are you silent?) It is also noteworthy that, while in Schiller's play a number of characters discuss Joan's possible provenance, with Isabeau spearheading the most vehement denunciation of her, in the opera only two characters accuse her of unholy alliance: her father Thibaut, and her would-be lover Lionel, who calls her "sozdanie Satany" (creation of Satan; Act III, No. 17).

Thus Tchaikovsky creates a number of interesting intersections and implications. He clearly sees Thibaut as connected with Isabeau, as a parent who sacrifices his own child, a child whom, in the final analysis, he never really knew. Similarly Tchaikovsky forges a strange link between Joan's father and her lover, vividly depicting both as impossible relationships. While Tchaikovsky allows for the interpretation that Thibaut acts out of love for Joan (Act III, No. 19), it is a love that can find expression only in condemnation. Lionel, on the other hand, while having no wish to condemn, is ultimately even more destructive. Thibaut's accusations prove ultimately empty and ineffective, but Lionel's love—which, as Tchaikovsky reminds us over and over, is only a dream (Act IV, No. 22)—calls down the retribution of heaven. Lionel destroys Joan not by anything he does, but simply by "being there." In this opera, to which Tchaikovsky turned after work on *Eugene Onegin*, he has created the ultimate manifestation of that Russian phenomenon typified by *Onegin*, the superfluous man.

Tchaikovsky not only draws parallels between Lionel and Thibaut, but also between Lionel and Joan, emphasizing their symbiotic characteristics both textually and musically. In their initial confrontation (Act III, No. 17), their equality becomes quite explicit. They are both armed with swords. After Joan disarms Lionel, he states "ne medli i porazhai tovo / kto sam srazit' tebia khotel" (don't delay to strike him

/ who wanted to strike you down). As Joan softens, she relinquishes her sword to Lionel, declaring herself unworthy of this holy symbol. In Schiller's play, Lionel tears the sword away from Joan ("entreißt ihr das Schwert"; Act III, Sc. 10, l. 53) and exits. In the next scene, Joan is bleeding. Schiller does not show any injury to Joan, allowing for the possibility that this is no physical wound, but rather stigmata or the feminine act of spontaneous bleeding, of which Joan is presumably capable now that she has lost what the sword represents. Tchaikovsky clearly interpreted the scene this way. In his version, Lionel mirrors Joan's relinquishing of her weapon, turning his own over to Dunois. Only at this point, the loss of *Lionel's* sword, does Joan bleed; moreover, since she has not left the audience's sight since the initial encounter with Lionel, no purely physical explanation for the bleeding is possible.

Musically, Tchaikovsky employs many of the conventions of French grand opera, including a basic structure of expansive *scenas*, each articulating a critical dramatic point or relationship. In this fairly slow-moving monumental style, the composer creates a dual tonal structure that mirrors the fundamental dramatic problem, associating sharp keys with Joan's spirituality, flat keys with her physicality. It seems that the more sharps or flats to the key, the more intense the emotional content. For example, the overture opens in G major, as does the first choral number, describing the joys of daylight and the terrors of darkness, when supernatural *rusalki* appear. Tchaikovsky clearly links this tonality with nature, the realm in which physical and spiritual most closely intersect. A chorus of "normal" girls in tune with the world around them sings about the balance that Joan will soon leave behind, reinforcing her difference. Joan will employ this key when she identifies herself to the king as "the daughter of a simple shepherd" (Act II, No. 15), but not in her first monologue, when she takes leave of the pastoral life she has known (Act I, No. 7). E major occurs far less frequently in this scheme, but its occurrences are highly significant. In this key Lionel expresses a feeling for Joan that he cannot decide whether to call love or pity (Act III, No. 17, m. 190 et seq.). Joan's visionary monologue (Act II, No. 15) concludes in this key, with her description of the Virgin Mary's ascent into heaven (m. 211–217). The tale understandably stirs her listeners, and a chorus ensues, fully endorsing Joan as one sent from heaven to lead France to victory (A major).

On the flat side, Joan's important first act aria (No. 7), in which she takes leave of the life she has known and takes up her crusade, is introduced with a mobile passage centering around A-flat, in which tonality she names herself (m. 11), but settles in D minor, the tonality most associated with her and in which key the opera concludes. Note that D minor is only one flat into the flat side and is the minor dominant of G,[63] the "nature" key, perhaps suggesting that Joan remains close to a state of grace. In D minor Lionel recognizes her power over him (Act III, No. 17, m. 50, where the tonality is approached from an A-flat–G pedal); at m. 100 Joan declares that Lionel's life is in her hands. D minor is also the key of Joan's execution, marking the beginning and end of her life as a martyr. On the other hand, A-flat will be worked out as the principal key of the love duet. (The necessary prelude to their love, Lionel's disarming of Joan, takes place in E-flat minor, preparatory to A-flat. [No. 17, m. 450].) Thus Tchaikovsky creates an important relationship between keys a tritone apart, D minor and A-flat, which, like the tritone itself, can be interpreted in two ways. Whether this suggests that Joan's love and martyrdom are mutually exclusive elements of her life, or that her love leads to her martyrdom as direct cause and effect, remains, like the tritone itself, ambivalent.[64]

Interestingly in this context, Tchaikovsky uses the key of A-flat minor and its relative major C-flat in two places. The key of C-flat, enharmonic equivalent of B major, necessitates seven flats and is visually confusing and alienating. Instances of this key occur when Joan quotes the Virgin Mary's charge to "take up [her] holy banner, take up [her] sword, and fearlessly destroy the enemy. . . ." (No. 15, m. 163, Example 1), the momentous statement of Joan's vocation that changes her life irrevocably. The other time Tchaikovsky uses the odd seven-flats notation is during Joan's public accusation, at the choral text "She bows her head, can it be we have been hearing her words through the powers of hell?" (Example 2). Joan's visionary monologue is in part underlain by a similar text, the chorus singing "Are your powers from heaven or hell?" although this accompaniment ceases during the passage concerning the Virgin Mary. It therefore remains somewhat unclear if the tonal connection between these two passages is meant to endorse Joan's vision as authentic; Tchaikovsky's portrayal of Joan's accusers is, as already noted, itself ambivalent, since they only *question* her legitimacy, rather than condemn her outright. This equivocation enables Tchaikovsky to locate Joan's guilt and punishment squarely in her "crime" of love, taking the question of satanic possession, anachronistic in the nineteenth century, out of consideration. The odd spelling may be meant to show that what Joan perceives as a spiritual vision is, in fact, the result of some kind of physical experience, such as hallucination. It may not be too fanciful

Example 1. Tchaikovsky, No. 15: The Virgin Mary's Command to Joan

Example 1. continued

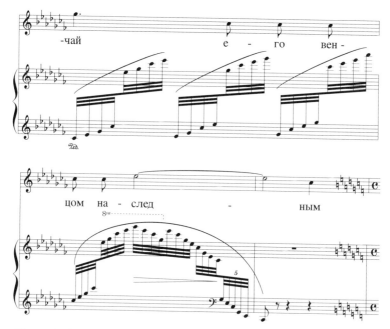

Example 1. continued

to suggest that the very strangeness of the notation, which graphically obscures the actual tonality, may be indicative of some spiritual *or physical* process (or both) gone awry. The key can also be seen as a kind of counterpart to G major, where the physical and spiritual intersect in nature. In A-flat minor–C flat/B major, the point at which sharp and flat tonalities merge, the *metaphysical* and spiritual seem to intersect; whether this intersection takes place in the supernatural, the transcendental, the surreal or even in paradise, and precisely what it may mean, remain incompletely understood.

A clue to what it may mean, however, is contained in Tchaikovsky's use of a reference to the eminently quotable *Tristan und Isolde*,[65] which not surprisingly takes place in the love duet. Tchaikovsky prefaces this duet with Joan's soul-searching soliloquy, which Lionel interrupts (Act IV, No. 21). The moment Lionel announces his presence, Tchaikovsky introduces a passage strongly evocative of music from *Tristan*, which provides a transition to the love duet itself. This reference consists of a phrase introduced and then developed sequentially in the famed prelude (Example 3).

Example 2. Tchaikovsky, No. 20: The Crowd Questions Joan's Provenance

In the duet itself, Tchaikovsky both fulfills and thwarts expectations. He presents the voices in symbiosis, echoing each other, completing each other, forming parallel thirds in the time-honored manner of operatic love. The text, however, reminds us repeatedly that this love is a "miraculous sweet dream" (*chudnyi, sladkii son*), harking back to Joan's first impassioned speech in an entirely different context (Act I, No. 5), in which she asserts that miracles (*chudesa*) are still possible, (this was seemingly borne out by the death of Salisbury, enemy of Orleans in Act I). Thus, like everything else in this story, things are called into question. Were France's victories the God-given miracles they seemed? Is this love a miracle and a reality, or a delusion?[66] Tchaikovsky creates a melody equally ambivalent, which teeters between major and minor at the end of the first full statement

Example 2. continued

(Example 4). He then uses this part of the phrase as a transition to another statement of the *Tristan* passage (Example 5).

In Tchaikovsky's work the passage provides a moment of E major in an otherwise A-flat tonal context; in *Tristan*, two passages of the utmost importance likewise take place in A-flat, the section of the *Liebesnacht* that states "stürben wir, um ungetrennt, ewig einig, ohne End" (we would die inseparable, eternally united, without end), and the beginning of the *Liebestod*, Isolde's statement of complete ecstascy of love and unification with Tristan. These moments pursue the dramatic and musical working out of processes initiated in the prelude,

Example 2. continued

including the sequencing of the ascending third. The *Liebestod* carries this development to completion, presenting a rhythmic diminution and intensification of the gesture (Example 6); the opera's final cadence is likewise approached by the last reiteration of the ascending third (Example 7).

The *Liebestod* also achieves the tonal progression from A-flat major to B major, the opera's ultimate tonal goal. We have already seen how

Example 3a. Wagner, *Tristan und Isolde*, Prelude

Example 3b. Tchaikovsky, No. 22, Transistion to the Love Duet

Example 4. Tchaikovsky, No. 22, Love Duet

Example 5. Tchaikovsky, No. 22, Love Duet

Example 6. Wagner, *Tristan und Isolde,* Liebestod

Example 7. Wagner, *Tristan und Isolde,* final measures

Tchaikovsky employs a similar tonal relationship, A-flat minor to B major, precisely at the two most critical moments of Joan's life—but not, significantly, in the love duet, which comes no closer than E major, one stop short around the circle of fifths. Joan experiences transcendence but, unlike Isolde, not through human love or intimacy, which in her case lead only to destruction. And while Isolde embraces her death and transfiguration, Joan explicitly fears hers ("mne strashno"). Wagner's use of this sequence, clearly associated with longing, obsessively worked out, leads ultimately to human connection and musical resolution. By contrast, Tchaikovsky's use of the passage does not attain musical closure, and leads Joan only to silence and isolation. Tristan and Isolde move toward union, while Joan and Lionel move toward estrangement.

Seen in the context of Wagner's unequivocal message, *The Maid of Orleans* expresses a devastating judgment on human connection, a judgment that arguably permeates all of Tchaikovsky's dramatic works. In an assessment clearly aimed to counter the "Tchaikovsky as psychopath" image, Taruskin sees many aspects of his work as an endorsement of "normality," of the status quo, best exemplified by a technique he attributes to Mozart's influence, the use of the dance. Dance provides a means to show people "at their most human . . . as members of groups—all right, *classes*—whose feelings and actions are mediated through social conventions."[67] It is of more than passing interest that one of the chief social conventions that dance represents is precisely socially sanctioned sex.[68] In the spirit of ambivalence that has pervaded this discussion, dance too can be seen as a societal ambivalence, providing a safe, somewhat chaperoned, public forum for an activity that sublimates another act usually deemed less acceptable.[69] And needless to say, dance is in most cases heterosexual by nature. Thus if Tchaikovsky does use dance as an encoding of social convention, even one of which he approves, it remains a convention which, at least in some fundamental ways, excludes him. The opera from which Taruskin draws most of his examples, *Eugene Onegin*, is indeed a work about the maintenance of propriety; but on another level, it is the story of human disconnection on a grand scale. Taruskin identifies the progression of "modest waltz to resplendent polonaise," which "would become a Chaikovskian paradigm."[70] This paradigmatic gesture precisely describes a progression from intimacy, the waltz danced eye to eye, in an embrace, to the aloofness of the ceremonial polonaise, danced side by side at arm's length. Nineteenth century explanations of the Taniec Polski, ancestor of the "blander" Polonaise, emphasize not only the restrained affect but the abstraction of this dance. Kazimerz Brodzinski (1791–1835) cautions, "This is not the place for a Lady to flirt. . . . [T]he expression is only one of a modest dignity. . . . [T]here is the impression of some kind of higher existence."[71] Karol Czerniawski (1860) sees the dance as a manifestion of the Slavic consciousness: "The large number of dancers (no limit to the number of couples) indicates the many Slavs with one leader."[72] Modern detailed instructions on the dancers' demeanor for authentic performance include:

> The eyes of a man may 'look' directly at a person but not harshly. The women's eyes 'gaze.' Her eyes are more downcast than upraised. Both the man and woman are conscious of their elevated social status and importance. . . . [The men] always accompany [the women], they constantly make way for her, giving her attention and comfort. She does not flirt; she knows her worth. Virtue is her worth. . . . Just as in the Mazur, the man turns to his partner often showing respect for her as a "thing" of Womanhood and Motherhood as represented by the Ideal of the Catholic Church and the Nobliness [sic] of the . . . community. Although the expression is happy it is not silly minded giddiness. It is one of contentment and proudness [sic] that they have the Honor to dance the Taniec Polski: the symbol of their (and human) cultural continuity. There is really only one basic couple position for the Taniec Polski. Partners are side by side, inside hands joined, held about chest high. The distance between partners for the Taniec Polski is as far as is comfortable so that forward motion is maintained. Couples do not stand shoulder to shoulder.[73]

The polonaise is indeed the dance equivalent of social status, cultural stability—and objectification of the woman. Powerful in its very awkwardness, this description could not make that fact any clearer— she is the "'thing' of Womanhood and Motherhood," not a flesh-and-blood human, but a sexless icon of the church, practically the Virgin Mary. This process from sensuousness and physicality to abstraction and objectification—in short, from intimacy to safe distance—may indeed be called the Tchaikovskian paradigm.

Although new and more accurate information is now counteracting the depiction of Tchaikovsky as hopelessly neurotic, one should resist the temptation to overreact in the opposite direction, seeing Tchaikovsky as the exemplar of "normality," whatever that may mean. Without going to the (probably self-serving homophobic) extreme of imputing guilt or self-loathing, much less suicidal ideation to

Tchaikovsky,[74] it is still possible to recognize a very human sense of "otherness," the voice of the outsider in both his correspondence and his art. He writes his twin brothers, "If there is the slightest possibility, try to be [normal]. This is very sad. At your age, one can still force oneself to love [a woman]; try at least once, maybe it will work out,"[75] a simple, poignant recognition that it is hard to go through life outside the mainstream of society, a hardship he wished to spare his brothers. Even more important is the controversial letter in which he states, "Do you really believe that the consciousness that [members of the family] pity and forgive me is not painful to me when, at bottom, I am guilty of nothing!" David Brown subjects this to the tortured interpretation that "I am guilty of nothing" means Tchaikovsky "had never actually had physical relations with another man," while Taruskin emphasizes the assertion of the absence of guilt.[76] Neither of these commentaries, however, mentions the pain of exclusion from his own family that Tchaikovsky clearly experiences, the lack of emotional connection, of true understanding of his personality by those who are supposed to be his intimates. Rather than constituting an aggressive self-justification, this resembles nothing so much as the sentiments embodied a few years later in Kafka's "Metamorphosis," a sense of being a "stranger and living in the midst of his family in exile, which [condition] Kafka calls 'Russian' in his diary."[77] A similar observation can be made to Modest's ecstatic realization, upon discovering Pyotr's homosexuality, that "I am not alone in my strange desires. . . . With this discovery everything became different. Mankind split into 'ours' and 'theirs.' . . . The earlier self-contempt changed into self-satisfaction, and pride to belong among the 'chosen.'"[78] Taruskin emphasizes that this does not constitute an example of protesting too much, not self-deception, but genuine self-validation, creating "a solidarity that . . . the famous composer [also] eventually found restorative and sustaining." Even so, could there be a more unequivocal expression of otherness? The very terminology of "the chosen" contains an implication of standing outside the norm, perhaps gaining an ineffable reward, but usually at the price of some special expectation, a heavier burden.

It is noteworthy that sometimes Tchaikovsky even feels the need to assert his own normality; in 1878 he assures Ms. von Meck that he is "Leaving foreign lands . . . as a completely healthy, normal person. . . ."[79] He seems to use his composition as well to assert "the normal," deliberately eschewing the "myth of the artist hero."[80] This very normality, however, takes on the utmost significance in the context of the work of an artist Tchaikovsky knew slightly and admired greatly, Leo Tolstoy. Gary Saul Morson observes,

In Tolstoy's view, ordinary and undramatic events are not just important; by their nature, they constitute the *only* important events in the chain of historical causality. Those who try to be heroic or self-sacrificing, and those who figure in narrative histories, are, in fact, unimportant in the chain of historical events precisely because they are exceptional. Indeed, characteristically, Tolstoy took this idea to its ultimate extension, postulating that a figure who did appear in histories could not possibly have been important. The really important events in history are those that no one notices because they are so common and because there is nothing dramatic about them. Anything that seems 'historic,' either to contemporaries or to subsequent writers, cannot be so. History is made, Tolstoy suggests, only by the countless, small daily actions, hidden in plain view, whose motives and cumulative operation we do not understand. 'Swarm life' is really what shapes history and, through the years, it is what has saved Russia.[81]

Normality becomes not the unspectacular, to be taken for granted, but the locus of history, and in itself a kind of heroism. This in turn has implications for Tchaikovsky's presentation of Joan, with its de-emphasis of her historical significance and accentuation of her psychology, her struggle with a human emotion that comes "naturally" to everyone else—and for his own perception of himself as one who stands outside the norms of society. His very investigation of personality, emotion, inner life, his seeming approval of the normal then, take on the quality not merely of complacent endorsement, but of aspiration. In his use of Joan as a vehicle for this process, he seems to have perceived Schiller's concept of the possibility of tragedy to reconcile tendencies at war in human nature, precisely the issue with which he was grappling at this time in regard to his own personal tendencies[82]:

Daher läßt uns das ästhetische Urtheil frey und erhebt und begeistert uns, weil wir uns schon durch das bloße Vermögen, absolut zu wollen, schon durch die bloße Anlage zur Moralität gegen die Sinnlichkeit in augenscheinlichem Vortheil befinden.

Thus aesthetic judgment leaves us free and elevates and inspires us, because through the sheer power to will absolutely, through our sheer relationship to morality, we find ourselves with an apparent advantage over the sensual.[83]

More simply stated, Tchaikovsky saw in Joan not only the difficulty of isolation, but a character who, located outside societal norms as she is, holds out the possibilty of transcending norms, of the androgynous persona who embodies the "consummate expression of inclusion."[84] The clear tragedy of *The Maid of Orleans* is that this inclusion remains out of reach.

NOTES

1. See Henry Zajaczkowski, "On Čajkovskij's Psychopathology and Its Relationship with His Creativity," in *Čajkovskij-Studien I,* Thomas Kohlhase ed. (Mainz: Schott Musik International, 1995), 307–28.

2. *P. Chaikovskii i S. Taneev. Pis'ma* (Letters), V. A. Zhdanov, ed. (Moscow, 1951), 223–24.

3. In *Tchaikovsky's Musical Style* (Ann Arbor/London, 1987), Ch. 1–2, and "The Function of Obsessive Elements in Tchaikovsky's Style," *Music Review* 43 (1982), 24–30, Henry Zajazckowski has taken this so far as to characterize Tchaikovsky's music as "suppressive propulsive." This phrase is obviously meant to evoke "obsessive compulsive," and suggests that the very music is "infected," a notion taken up by other scholars.

4. See for example the airy remarks of Tchaikovsky's sister-in-law Pania, "I stole a lover from him in Tiflis" and "No one wondered at anything in our milieu," quoted in Richard Taruskin, "Pathetic Symphonist," *New Republic,* 6 February 1995, 28.

5. George Steiner, *In Bluebeard's Castle: Some Notes Towards the Re-definition of Culture* (London: Faber and Faber, 1971), 66–67.

6. Letter to Nadezhda von Meck dated 16 April 1883, P. I. Chaikovskii, *Polnoe sobranie sochinenii; Literaturnyie proizvedehiia i perepiska*, (Complete Collected Works: Literary Works and Correspondence) (Moscow, 1953–81), vol. 12, 123–24.

7. Jean-Jacques Nattiez, *Wagner Androgyne* (Princeton: Princeton University Press, 1993), 272.

8. Diary entry dated 23 July 1888, P. I. Chaikovskii, *Dnevniki 1873–1891* (Diaries) (Moscow-Petrograd, 1923), 215.

9. See Claude Lévi-Strauss, "The Structural Study of Myth." In vol. 1 of *Structural Anthropology,* trans. Claire Jacobson and Brooke Grundfest Schoepf, pp. 206–31 (Harmondsworth: Penguin Books, 1977); and *Tristes Tropiques,* trans. John and Doreen Weightman (Harmondsworth: Penguin Books, 1976); both quoted in Nattiez, *Wagner Androgyne,* 248–49.

10. Letter dated 5/17 Dec 1878, Edward Garden, Nigel Gotteri (eds.), *'To My Best Friend.' Correspondence between Tchaikovsky and Nadezhda von Meck,* Galina von Meck, trans. (Oxford: Clarendon Press, 1993), 403.

11. Letter dated 10 Dec 1878, von Meck, 410.

12. Alexander Poznansky, *Tchaikovsky: The Quest for the Inner Man* (New York: Schirmer Books, 1991), 385.

13. See Alexander Poznansky, "Tchaikovsky—A Life Reconsidered," in this volume.

14. Anthony Holden, *Tchaikovsky* (London: Penguin Books Ltd., 1995), 198.

15. Poznansky, *Quest,* 465; see also Simon Karlinsky, *The Sexual Labyrinth of Nikolai Gogol* (Cambridge: Harvard University Press, 1976).

16. Poznansky, *Quest,* 381; Poznansky notes the irony of the elegant composer hanging around army barracks in this state of puppy love.

17. Letter to his sister Sasha dated 17 July 1877, quoted in Holden, *Tchaikovsky,* 128.

18. Letter to Nadezhda von Meck dated 25 October 1877, in Garden, Gotteri, eds. *'To My Best Friend,'* 50–52.

19. Letter to Modest dated 28 September 1876, Poznansky, "Unknown Tchaikovsky," in this volume.

20. Letter dated 8 July 1877 to Anatolii, P. I. Chaikovskii, *Pis'ma k rodnym* (Letters to relatives), V. A. Zhdanov, ed. (Moscow, 1940), 287.

21. Poznansky, *Quest,* 235.

22. Alexander Poznansky, "Modest Čajkovskij: In His Brother's Shadow," *Čajkovskij-Studien I,* 233–46, at 234.

23. Poznansky, *Quest,* 78; although in fact Anatolii distinguished himself greatly in the course of his life, probably constituting one of the few utterly stable safe havens for his older brother.

24. Quoted in Poznansky, *Quest,* 180. Poznansky notes the oddity of Tchaikovsky signing himself "Petia," an extremely informal and intimate way for an adult to identify himself to a young child.

25. Letter to Modest dated 7 January 1879, quoted in Holden, *Tchaikovsky,* 185. Poznansky identifies a sadomasochistic element to his relationship with Modest as well, *Quest,* 78.

26. Letter dated 9 September 1877, Poznansky, "Unknown Tchaikovsky," in this volume.

27. Letter dated 2 November 1872, to Modest (whom he addresses as "Modestina"), Poznansky, *Quest,* 140.

28. There are many references pointing to Tchaikovsky's obsession with hands; one of the more disturbing is found in his letter of 4 May 1877 to Modest, in which he attributes his cooling of affection for the violinist Kotek to his "disfigured finger," see Poznansky, "Unknown Tchaikovsky," in this volume.

29. See Poznansky, *Quest,* 76, 325, and in general.

30. Garden, Gotteri, eds., *'To My Best Friend,'* xxii–xxiii.

31. Garden, Gotteri, eds., *'To My Best Friend,'* xii. Although the mutuality of this non-contact is usually stressed, it seems clear that it was Tchaikovsky for whom it continued to remain important and who insisted on its maintenance. On 23 November 1878, nearly two years into the arrangement, he writes to Anatolii that " . . . the proximity of Nadezhda Filaretnova slightly disturbs me. She often drives and walks past my windows. What if we meet? What ought I to do? She does not seem to be afraid of it, as she has even sent me a ticket to the theatre for Saturday, where she is also going. She asks if I would like to come and have a look at her villa, saying that when I come not a soul will be there, but all the same I am a bit frightened." *TLP* vii. 479, quoted in *Best Friend,* 379. It is arguable that Ms. von Meck had tired of the situation, but safeguarded it in deference to Tchaikovsky's hypersensitivity about the whole matter.

32. Catherine Drinker Bowen and Barbara von Meck, *Beloved Friend* (New York: Random House, 1939); and Garden, Gotteri, eds. *'To My Best Friend,'* already cited.

33. Roman Jakobson, *Shifters, Verbal Categories and the Russian Verb* (Cambridge, MA: Harvard University Press, 1957), 6.

34. P. Chaikovskii, *Literaturnye Proizvedeniia i Perepiska,* Vol. XII, 370–74.

35. Poznansky, "Unknown Tchaikovsky," in this volume.

36. Sibelan Forrester, "Wooing the Other Woman: Gender in Women's Love Poetry in the Silver Age," in *Engendering Slavic Literatures*, Pamela Chester and Sibelan Forrester, eds. (Bloomington: Indiana University Press, 1996), 107–34.

37. David Brown, "Tchaikovsky and Chekhov," *Slavonic and Western Music: Essays for Gerald Abraham*, Malcolm H. Brown and Roland John Wiley, eds. (Ann Arbor: UMI, 1985), 197–205.

38. Letter to Modest dated 19 January 1877, Poznansky, "Unknown Tchaikovsky," in this volume.

39. Letter to Alexandra Tchaikovskova dated 8 August 1867, Poznansky, *Quest*, 102.

40. Letter dated 22 July 1891, Poznansky, *Quest*, 536.

41. Letter dated 11 July 1891, Poznansky, *Quest*, 536.

42. Letter dated 30 July 1868, Modest Musorgsky, *Pis'ma* (Letters) (Moscow: Muzyka, 1981), 68.

43. Ironically not only are these views not incompatible, they can ultimately amount to the same thing: a desire to render the personality in a form over which the artist has complete control.

44. Quoted in Poznansky, *Quest*, 286.

45. Richard Taruskin, *Defining Russia Musically* (Princeton: Princeton University Press, 1997), 263.

46. Letter dated 26 Dec 1878/7 Jan 1879, von Meck, 421.

47. Letter dated 24 Dec 1800, *Der Briefwechsel zwischen Schiller und Goethe*, Emil Staiger, ed. (Insel Verlag: Frankfurt am Main, 1977), 892.

48. See remarks of Clemens Brentano, Ludwig Tieck, A. W. Schlegel, among others, *Erläuterung und Dokumente: Friedrich Schiller, Die Jungfrau von Orleans* (Stuttgart: Philipp Reclam, 1984), 82 et seq.

49. Quoted in *Erläuterung*, 83.

50. Friedrich Hebbel, quoted in *Nachwort*, Friedrich Schiller, *Die Jungfrau von Orleans* (Stuttgart: Philipp Reclam, 1966), 128.

51. Quoted in *Erläuterung*, 91.

52. Letter to the publisher Göschen, 10 Feb 1802, *Schillers Briefe*, ed. F. Jonas, *Kritische Gesamtausgabe*, 7 vols. (Stuttgart, 1892–96), letter 1761.

53. Lesley Sharpe, *Friedrich Schiller: Drama, Thought and Politics* (Cambridge: Cambridge University Press, 1991), 274.

54. Letter dated 28 Jul 1800, to Körner (Jonas 1608).

55. Letter dated 18 Feb 1793, to Körner (Jonas 643).

56. Lesley Sharpe, *Schiller's Aesthetic Essays: Two Centuries of Criticism* (Columbia, SC: Camden House, 1995), 70.

57. André Maurois, "Der Hundertjährige Krieg (II)" in *Die Geschichte Frankreichs*, *Erstes Buch: Die Anfänge und das Mittelalter*. (Wiesbaden: Löwit, no year), 102–11. Incidentally, it is interesting that Schiller precisely reversed one aspect of this description, having Montgomery say to her "Furchtbar ist deine Rede, doch dein Blick ist sanft" (Your speech is terrifying but your gaze is gentle), Act II, Sc. 7, l. 24.

58. *Jeanne d'Arc. Dokumente ihrer Verurteilung und Rechtfertigung 1431, 1456.* Translated and with an introduction by Ruth Schirmer-Imhoff. (Köln: Bachem, 1956), 43–47.

59. Ibid.

60. The common criticism of Schiller's play; see *Erläuterungen*, generally.

61. See R. D. Miller, *Interpreting Schiller: A Study of Four Plays* (Harrogate: Wm. Harrison & Son, Ltd., 1986), 38–59, a study which seeks to rationalize things that prob-

ably would not even be at issue were Joan a male character, making clear that such matters remained problematic at least as late as 1986; see also Sharpe, *Friedrich Schiller*, 277.

62. It is also interesting that Jezebel's punishment is specifically to be eaten by dogs to the point of eradication, "so that no one will be able to say: 'This was Jezebel.'" II Kings 9:37

63. Both Tchaikovsky's and Rimsky-Korsakov's harmony textbooks describe tonal relationships in a manner that significantly undermines the major/minor distinction. See Ellon Carpenter, "Russian Music Theory: A Conspectus," in *Russian Theoretical Thought in Music*, Gordon McQuere, ed. (Ann Arbor: UMI Research Press, 1983), 18–28; Valerij Erohin, "An der Schwelle zum neuen Jahrhundert—Anmerkungen zu Čajkovskijs Harmonik," 103–10, and Tatjana Frumkis, "Zu deutschen Vorbildern von Čajkovskijs Harmonielehre," 111–26, in *Čajkovskij-Studien I.*

64. Tchaikovsky preserves the use of flat keys in the transposition necessitated by reworking the role for a mezzo-soprano; part of the initial encounter of Joan and Lionel is lowered a minor third, from F minor to D minor; part of the love duet is lowered a whole step, from A-flat to G-flat.

65. Although Arkadii Klimovitsky asserts that Tchaikovsky first saw *Tristan* only in 1882 in Berlin, this must mean that he first saw the opera in its entirety at that time (see "Tchaikovsky and the Russian 'Silver Age,'" in this volume.). Wagner programmed the *Tristan* Prelude, *Liebestod,* and *Verklärung* during his Russian concert tour in 1863, which Tchaikovsky attended. In a letter to Ms. von Meck, he mentions Wagner conducting "some Beethoven symphonies," one of which was programmed with the *Tristan* Prelude and *Verklärung*, on 26 February 1863 in Petersburg. Rosamund Bartlett, *Wagner and Russia* (Cambridge: Cambridge University Press, 1995), 23, 299.

66. Tchaikovsky's use of the chorus in *The Maid of Orleans* would constitute a study in itself. Like everything else in this opera, there can be no unequivocal understanding of exactly what the chorus represents. Sometimes it seems to function as an amplification of Joan's own voice and thoughts, at other times as the heavenly voices she hears, and still other times, as her accuser. The chorus' presence in the love duet first serves the interesting function of disrupting the meter, literally making the time "out of joint" (Act IV, No. 22, at m. 230). Tchaikovsky also creates two layers of text for the chorus, which carry subtly different meanings. Soprano I sings the text, "You have disobeyed the will of heaven, you have sinned, you have not fulfilled your duty, now you must seek forgiveness for your sin, and for your penance you will suffer imprisonment and death, but a blessing awaits you in heaven!" Soprano II and Alto sing "Broken is the command of heaven, you sinful one, you have experienced earthly love." This discrepancy would be insignificant if it did not encapsulate precisely the central problem of the opera; Tchaikovsky seems to imply that even the heavenly voices are divided as to whether Joan's love is itself the cause of her punishment.

67. Taruskin, *Defining Russia Musically*, 292.

68. A good discussion of this aspect of dance can be found in Anya Peterson Royce, *The Anthropology of Dance* (Bloomington: Indiana University Press, 1980), especially Chapter 9, "The Meaning of Dance," where she observes: "Touching also may be acceptable or encouraged in the dance context, while it is not allowed in nondance situations. . . . Dancing provided one of the most frequent occasions for tactile interaction, and people of both sexes put these opportunities to good advantage to size up potential marriage prospects," at 199.

69. This is traced to the very beginning of the couple dance at the time of the Crusades. "At this time a definite form of courtly dance different from that performed by the peasants is known to have been practised. It coincided with the establishment of

a code of social behaviour when, with the development of language, the significant gesture of the peasant would be substituted by a politer one. For example, the man's forward thrust of the body and his embracing and carrying off the woman became the dignified kneeling before the lady of his choice, and the delicate giving of hands as he led her down the room; or the girl's violent gesture of repulse and attempt to escape became the admonishing shake of a finger and a shy turn of the head; and the triumphant flinging of the girl in the fertility leap became the dainty twist under the man's arm." Joan Lawson, *European Folk Dance; Its National and Musical Characteristics* (London: Pitman Publishing, 1970), 14.

70. Taruskin, *Defining Russia Musically*, Note 103, 290–91.

71. Kazimierz Brodzinski, "O Tancach Narodowych" (1849) in Karol Czerniawski, *O Tancach Narodowych*, 1860.

72. Karol Czerniawski, *O Tancach Narodowych z Pogladem Historycznym i Estetycznym*, (Poland, 1860), 58–59.

73. Raymond Cwieka-Skrzyniarz, *The Great Polish Walking Dance, Sources of the Polish Tradition*, Vol. I, (Copyright 1983, R. Cwieka), 104. The author notes that in the nineteenth century performance of the salon polonaise, the position is the same but "the distance between them may not be as great," at 120.

74. Taruskin hits the nail on the head in this regard, when he observes that a great deal of Tchaikovskiana is attributable to the fact that "Many people, it seems, simply cannot bear the thought of a homosexual man enjoying life." "Pathetic Symphonist," 39.

75. Quoted in Poznansky, *Quest*, 76–77.

76. Quoted in Taruskin, "Pathetic Symphonist," 35.

77. Walter Sokel, *Franz Kafka: Tragik und Ironie* (Frankfurt am Main: Fischer Verlag, 1976), 86. " . . . [er ist] in der Familie ein völlig Fremder und lebt inmitten seiner Familie in dem Exil, das Kafka in seinem Tagebuch 'russisch' nennt."

78. Quoted in Taruskin, "Pathetic Symphonist," 40.

79. Poznansky, *Quest*, 297.

80. Taruskin, *Defining Russia Musically*, 261.

81. Gary Saul Morson, *Hidden in Plain View: Narrative and Creative Potentials in War and Peace* (Stanford: Stanford University Press, 1987), reprinted in Leo Tolstoy, *War and Peace*, the Maude translation, George Gibian, ed. (New York: W. W. Norton and Co., 1996), 1156.

82. P. I. Chaikovskii, *Pis'ma k rodnym*, 374. Letter to Anatolii dated 13 February 1878: "Only now, especially after the tale of my marriage, have I finally begun to understand that there is nothing more fruitless than not wanting to be that which I am by nature." See also Poznansky, "Unknown Tchaikovsky," in this volume.

83. *Schillers Werke* (Nationalausgabe), ed. J. Petersen, G. Fricke, H. Schneider, L. Blumenthal, B. von Wiese, N. Oellers (Weimar, 1943–), Vol. 21, 216.

84. Michel Serrès, *L' hermaphrodite* (Paris: Flammarion, 1987), 87.

The Coronation of Alexander III

RICHARD WORTMAN

A Russian coronation not only consecrated the Russian emperor, but also made known the image he intended to embody as monarch, setting forth what might be described as a symbolic program for his reign.[1] The coronation of Emperor Alexander III and Empress Maria Fedorovna in May 1883 was an elaborate display of the monarch's national character and the popular and religious sources of his power. It provided reaffirmation of the staying power of absolute monarchy, after the autocracy had been challenged by the rise of a revolutionary movement. The era of reforms, which had emancipated the serfs, and initiated major changes in the military, educational, and legal systems, had ended with the assassination of Alexander II on 1 March 1881. In the first months of the new reign, Alexander III, guided by his tutor, Konstantin Pobedonostev, had made clear that a new period of conservative, repressive rule had begun, including a set of "Temporary Regulations" aimed at the revolutionary terrorist group, "Will of the People," responsible for Alexander II's assassination. The government would defend the power of the autocratic Tsar on the basis of the religious faith of the Russian people. The coronation of 1883 presented and celebrated this concept of monarchy.

Although the revolutionary movement had been crushed in the first months of the new reign, fears about the security of the Tsar led to the delay of the coronation. As a result, the event took place more than two years after the accession—the longest interval in the history of the dynasty. Rumors circulated that there would be no coronation or that it would take place in secret. The manifesto announcing the coronation on 24 January 1883 promised that the celebration would put an end to "those monstrous rumors and gossip that have filled foreign newspapers in regard to Russia."[2]

Apprehensions mounted as the preparations began. The emperor's sojourn in the capital was to be brief—only two weeks; Alexander I's had been six weeks, Nicholas I's nearly two months, Alexander II's four weeks. "Everyone feared for the Tsar," Grand Duke Konstantin Konstantinovich wrote in his diary."[3] During the emperor's stay, he was surrounded by heavy guard, his departure times were kept secret, and crowds who approached him too closely were dispersed by bands of Cossacks.[4] The coronation manifesto on May 16 appealed for the reconciliation of "the entire disturbed order" as well as the strengthening of justice, the enlightenment of the people "in the truths of faith and the confirmation in each calling of loyalty to duty and law . . . ."[5]

But the coronation took place without incident, and the sweep, color, and animation of the festivities served as a demonstration of the recrudescence of the monarchy. The celebrations were to show to both Russian and foreign observers that the all-Russian emperor embodied the spirit of ancient Russia and enjoyed the support of his people. In staging the celebrations, the government drew on the formidable talents of Russian artists and musicians, displaying the creative resources the monarch could draw upon. It was in this context that Pyotr Tchaikovsky, the composer least given to the cause of Russian national music, was called upon to write music for a celebration of national monarchy. Tchaikovsky himself felt little inclination to write occasional music of any kind, and such a clamorous festival certainly offended his reclusive nature. But he needed money and felt indebted to the Tsar for gifts and encouragement. He contributed four pieces: an arrangement of Glinka's "Glory" Chorus from *A Life for the Tsar*, for performance at the Tsar's entry into Red Square; the Cantata "Moscow," to be sung during the coronation banquet; a "Coronation March" for a municipal celebration in Sokolniki Park; and the *1812 Overture*, to be played during the dedication of the Cathedral of Christ the Redeemer, which took place after the coronation. In these pieces, Tchaikovsky not only proved his ability to write in an idiom alien to his artistic nature, but disclosed some of that nature's bizarre possibilities.

Official publications presenting the coronation reveal the two sources of national appeal upon which the monarchy sought to draw. The coronation album, compiled for an audience of Russian and western elite, associated the monarchy with early Russia, emphasizing the Muscovite origins of imperial power.[6] The title and much of the text were printed in Slavic revival lettering. It was the first coronation album to contain artistic evocations of Muscovy. Russian folk-style illustrations depict the Tsar and boyars as burly bogatyrs—the heroic knights of Russian folk epics. The historical introduction identifies the

Orthodox Church as the bearer of the Russian national spirit, characterizing the coronation as "this sacred, solemn, and all-national act that expresses the historical union of the Tsar with his State, his precept with his church—that is with the soul and conscience of his people—and finally, the union of the Tsar and the people with the Tsar of Tsars, in whose hands rests the fate of tsars and peoples."[7] The church is thus "the soul and conscience of the people," and it is the church that bestows popular sanction. The people themselves are hardly mentioned in the album.

The color illustrations in the album are the work of exclusively Russian painters, including a number of the Itinerants (*peredvizhniki*), a previously dissident group of realists. Their contribution to the album makes clear Alexander's intention to encourage a national school of art.[8] Konstantin Savitsky (Fig. 1) presents the entry procession down Tver boulevard as a mass of guardsmen, a few Asian horseman, and the emperor, a commanding figure in his beard and Russian cap. The artist makes no effort to bring the spectators into the scene as Zichy had in depicting the entry procession of Alexander II. The entry appears as a triumphal show of force. In Vasilii Polenov's

Figure 1. Konstantin Savitsky, Alexander III's Coronation Entry to Moscow. Alexander III Coronation Album.

Figure 2. Vasilii Polenov, Welcome of Alexander III at the portal of Assumption Cathedral. Alexander III Coronation Album.

painting of the greeting at the Assumption Cathedral, Alexander is flanked by his brothers, also in beards and presenting strong martial images. (Fig. 2) The beards bring their appearance closer to that of the clergy, unlike their predecessors, whose sleek, clean-shaven faces had denoted the sharp difference between secular and ecclesiastical realms.

Indeed, the coronation album as a whole is a solemn statement of the might of the reign, of autocracy reborn through reconquest. The theme is expressed in the numerous depictions of military cere-monies, which appear for the first time in a coronation album. They show the emperor at the consecration of the standards of the Preobrazhensky and Semenovsky Regiments, the religious parade, the parade of the Semenovsky Regiment, and the feast for the regi-ments at Sokolniki.[9] The emperor dominates the scene in his distinc-tive military dress, on horseback and wearing Russian boots and hat.

He takes on the aspect of folk hero that could appeal to the national sentiment at the time.

The official popular account of the coronation was published by pan-slavist journalist and military general Vissarion Komarov, in his chauvinistic newspaper *Svet*, which had a circulation of over 70,000.[10] While sharing the Muscovite orientation of the coronation album, Komarov's volume emphasized the mass response to the coronation, and unity between Tsar and Russian people. Komarov as well as Russian and foreign correspondents dwelled on the wild acclaim that met the Tsar on the streets of Moscow, confirming the regime's claim to the support of the Russian people.

Eyewitness accounts convey the sense of mass enthusiasm that accompanied the traditional coronation entry on May 10, when the emperor, the guards regiments, and the imperial court marched down Tver boulevard past the people of Moscow. Charles Lowe, the correspondent of the *Times of London*, thought the roar of the crowd announcing the emperor's approach resembled nothing he had heard in England. "They do not strike the ear like sharp successive explosions of pent-up enthusiasm, but fall upon the sense like the steady, continuous roar of an ever-advancing sea. . . . every straining Slavonic throat utters deep and loud hoorahs," as the "two squadrons of ponderous cuirassiers"—the Cavalier Guards—marched before the Tsar himself.[11] Komarov interpreted the roar as the voice of the family of the Russian people welcoming their father and mother. "This family of one-hundred million is the basis of Russian state existence, the condition for its structure and life, the foundation of general equality before Tsar and law, the source and preserver of every living atom entering into the composition of the Russian people."[12]

After the traditional prayer at the chapel of the Icon of the Iberian Mother of God, the imperial family proceeded to Red Square, where they entered scenes of the seventeenth century. When they appeared on the square, a choir of more than 7,500 singers intoned the "Glory" chorus from Glinka's *A Life for the Tsar*, as arranged by Tchaikovsky. The chorus, sung at the conclusion of the opera when the Moscow population is awaiting the newly elected Mikhail Romanov, elevated Alexander into the theatrical world of legend, Glinka's stirring melody expressing the adulation of all for their new Tsar. Tchaikovsky had simplified the chorus and included a transition to the singing of "God Save the Tsar!" thus linking the presumed seventeenth- and nineteenth-century expressions of popular devotion.[13] Observers on the square exulted at the stirring response of the crowd to the Tsar. The *Novoe Vremia* correspondent wrote, "Only He, The Tsar of Russia, the Tsar of this people, which gathered not for the processions, but to see Him, to meet Him. Such shouts of rapture resounded that I have never heard."[14] Lowe concluded that, "as far as one can judge from the popular manifestations of this day, there is everything to show that the throne which he ascends on Sunday next is securely based on the love and devotion of his subjects."[15]

• • •

The people of Moscow represented the principal actor in Komarov's rendering of the ceremonies of coronation that took place on May 15. They appeared as "a vital force, concealing in themselves the presence of God," and not requiring the church as a link with their sovereign. The account expressed a physical sense of merger of people with sovereign. The key terms were *splosh'* (total) and variants of the verb *splotit'* (to fuse), etymologically connected with the word used to describe binding longitudinal sections of wood. The national rapture, *narodnyi vostorg*, submerged the individual in the mass:

> This national rapture, national unity seizing everyone, these ubiquitous gigantic crowds of the people, extending without limit as far as the eye can see, these cries of rejoicing, this sincere, heartfelt "Hoorah!" rising from the breast—all of this fused and united (*splachivali*) in one whole, all and everyone, and elevated and diminished each person.[16]

The organic metaphor was expressed in Afanasii Fet's coronation verse, printed in the frontispiece to Komarov's volume. The Tsar ascended his father's throne in the sun rays of "life-giving May."

> Diamonds glitter, crowns shine,
> And around the holy palace,
> Like a million young leaves,
> Hearts are turned to you.[17]

For Komarov, the people of Moscow embodied the spirit of Russia. Moscow was the embryo of Russia's state existence (*gosu-darstvennoe bytie*) and of Russian and Slavic unity. The Kremlin was the symbolic manifestation of the historical spirit that imbued the people of Moscow. The people of Moscow, "concealing in themselves the presence of God," were "crude, illiterate according to bureaucrats' statistics." But they had in them "something tender, sensitive, impressionable, a great heart in all cases of state life." The people of Moscow were suffused with "a feeling of conscious devotion to the Tsar and state."[18]

The coronation ceremony was also presented as a mass event. The Assumption Cathedral, to be sure, held only a small number of people. "The building," Lowe wrote, "does not at all correspond to the general idea of a cathedral, being rather a superb and exquisitely finished imperial chapel."[19] But the Kremlin square, holding the crowds that followed the progress of the ceremony by the tolling of bells and the cannon salute, opened out to Russia. It was as if the cathedral had no walls, Komarov wrote, "as if the coronation occurred on a boundless square, under an open sky, as an all-national (*vsenarodno*) event.

> It felt as if every word and every action in the cathedral were sensed by the entire people and were invisibly transmitted to [the Tsar], and acted on him and the excitement perceived by him went back into the cathedral and deepened the impression and the spiritual excitement. One organism, one thought, one being![20]

To show the prominence of the people, a delegation of peasants marched at the beginning of the procession to the cathedral, as they had at the 1856 coronation of Alexander II.[21] They appeared almost anomalous amidst the brilliant uniforms of the guards and courts. The description in the coronation album read, "*Volost'* [the smallest administrative unit, i.e. township] elders from all Russian provinces, communal heads (*gminnye voity*) from the Kingdom of Poland and the elder of the *belopashtsy* (descendants of Ivan Susanin, the peasant hero of *A Life for the Tsar*) stood out in the surrounding magnificence with their simple but varied attire."[22] Other accounts used similar terms. Komarov focused on the elder who represented Susanin's descendants, emphasizing that he would be one of twelve elders permitted to watch the ceremonies in the cathedral; in the 1856 coronation, all had waited in a nearby building.[23] The author described how the emperor was seized by the rapture of the crowd in the Kremlin as he was about to enter Assumption Cathedral: his benevolence was expressed as two great tears that wet his eyes—"the most majestic gift that Russia received." The tears were "the guarantee of the most majestic spiritual purity, good intentions and good will of the Tsar, the guarantee of the firmness of power, this blessedness of the heart, the pledge of love."[24]

During the rites of coronation, Alexander appeared as a model of dignity and strength. Komarov described the drama. The Tsar received the crown from the Metropolitan and placed it on his head "with unhurried, calm and smooth movement." The Adjutant-General, Edward Baranov, brought him the scepter, and Pyotr Valuev presented the orb, "with the low bow of a boyar." "Garbed in the crown and purple, holding the orb and scepter in his hands, the Sovereign Emperor presented a spectacle of extraordinary beauty. A feeling of spiritual contentment descended on all present." The empress approached the emperor and knelt before him while he placed the small crown on her head. Then he conferred on her the purple and gold chain of Andrew the First-Called. "All this was performed with great feeling and without the slightest hurry." He kissed her with "so pure and elevated a kiss, that spoke of endless, endless friendship and love." The Grand Duke Konstantin Konstanovich wrote in his diary "I cannot describe, cannot express how touching and tender it was to see these embraces of husband and wife and kisses under the imperial crown—this ordinary human love in the glitter and radiance of imperial majesty." The emperor and empress now sat on their coronation throne in full regalia, and the Protodeacon recited the full imperial title followed by a loud prayer for "many years" and a hundred-and-one gun salute. The Tsar then left the throne, fell to his knees, and pronounced the prayer of Solomon, asking for divine help in his "great service." Those present repeated the moving prayer to themselves. The Grand Duke Konstantin could not hold back tears. "How many warm prayers were raised at this moment!" he wrote.[25]

The paintings reproduced in the coronation album convey the overpowering presence of the emperor. Ivan Kramskoi's rendering of the moment of crowning is close up, focused completely on Alexander, who occupies almost two thirds of the picture (Fig. 3). The emperor dwarfs the clergymen at his side, his beard and balding head dominating the picture. The cathedral is a mere blur in the background. Alexander has an intimidating, crushing aspect, but his face is soft and pallid. The full page portrait by A. P. Sokolov of Alexander on his coronation throne in mantle, holding the orb and scepter, was the first of its kind in a coronation album. Sokolov's painting allows no distance between the viewer and the looming, impassive figure of the emperor.[26]

At the coronation, Alexander found his ceremonial persona. He towered over everyone; his size, his red hair and beard, his bright eyes, made for an impressive sight. "There is something grandiose in

Figure 3. Ivan Kramskoi, Alexander III at Crowning Ceremony. Alexander III Coronation Album.

him," the artist Vasilii Surikov remarked about his impression of Alexander in the cathedral; he was "a true representative of the people."[27] He seemed to fit, to express the notion of a national ruler. D. N. Liubimov, a secondary school student serving in the "Holy Guard" for the coronation, later recalled the great majesty of Alexander dressed in the imperial regalia. "This extraordinary garb that so befit the holy places of the Kremlin became him perfectly: his enormous height, his stoutness, his great beard. A truly Russian Tsar, of Moscow and all Rus'."[28] State Secretary A. A. Polovtsov wrote in his diary, "one felt that here it was not a case of an empty formality, but of a celebration having a national sense and taking place not without a fierce underground struggle." He noted that the courtiers attending to the

Tsar were nearly all from old Russian families, while the German noblemen were holdovers from the previous reign.[29]

In Komarov's description, the ceremony submerged individual feelings in a spiritual, political union. The key moment of fusion occurred after the Tsar had crowned himself, during the prayer for the Tsar. Then Alexander stood, and the entire assemblage knelt before him. At a signal, all those awaiting in the stands of the Kremlin also fell to their knees. Komarov claimed that he later heard that the people outside the Kremlin, along the Moscow river, did the same, as did the Asiatics among them. "This was so solemn a moment, during which the entire human being fused with an invisible world and ascended to the Creator." Again the people shed tears of gratitude and *umilenie* [emotion], but they were an expression not of love, but "of a unity and community (*obshchnost'*) of interests."[30]

After the anointing and communion, the emperor and empress in full regalia walked in procession across the Kremlin square to the Archangel and Annunciation Cathedrals accompanied by the loud hoorahs of the crowd. "A Hoorah that was unforgettable," Komarov wrote. He, like Lowe, described the Russian shout as distinctive. "Here was expressed all the people's love. All the nature of the Russian man, with his infinite kindness and selfless spirit of sacrifice unleashed that mighty inimitable cry. . . . That "hoorah" is unique in the entire world. That hoorah belongs only to the Emperor, to the leader of Russian might and glory, the bearer of the people's hopes and the people's beliefs." He described the Tsar's measured, imposing, gait. "The Tsar walked quietly and smoothly. With calm step, his head bowed slightly down, combining an expression of humility with firmness, he moved forward." The comparison now was with a believer going to a religious service, about to undergo a religious experience. "'The Tsar goes through a sea of sounds,' they said, but it would be more accurate to say that the Tsar walked with [the] same look and feeling as the first Christians went to take communion. So much clarity, purity, firmness."[31]

The imperial family followed the processions, which consisted of delegations from all estates, described conventionally as "all of Russia." After the services in the Archangel and Annunciation Cathedrals, the emperor and empress ascended the Red Staircase. They turned and the square fell silent. The couple stood side by side and the emperor bowed three times to the people. "From the first bow of the Tsar, tens of thousands of hats flew into the air and the mighty 'hoorah' resounded through the Kremlin and white-stone Moscow like rolling thunder."[32] *Sel'skii Vestnik* explained the political signifi-

cance of the bows and the joyous response of the people to their peasant readers: "These cries expressed the unlimited love of the Russian
people for their Anointed Tsar with consciousness that in him alone
resides the guaranty of national happiness and well-being."[33]
Koronovanie ikh Imperatorskikh Velichestv, a lower priced version of the
coronation album, described this "ancient Russian custom:" "The
exultation of the people then reached its apogee, and you will find no
words to express it."[34]

The historical national theme of the coronation held great appeal
for Slavophile circles. Ivan Aksakov believed that it marked the beginning of a new epoch.

> What a day! What a great historical day! It is beyond the pow-
> ers of a person to bear these titanic sensations fully if he expe-
> riences them as an individual. But no one lived the present as
> part of his individual life. All merged into one titanic body,
> into one trembling soul. All felt and understood themselves
> one Russian people, one in time and space. Two persons, two
> giants stood before each other today, Tsar and People, People
> and Tsar, and achieved the great historical deed. The land
> groaned from the people's rapture. It was she that spoke,
> Holy Rus'! These rolls of thunder drowning out the cannon
> shots and the tolling of the Kremlin bells, these are her rejoic-
> ing, her cries of love, her voice. [35]

Michael Katkov's influential *Moskovskie Vedomosti* gave a more
restrained assessment of the ceremonies. Katkov by now had adopted
the view, fostered by Konstantin Pobedonostev, that the Orthodox
Church embodied the spiritual union of Tsar and people. The coronation showed the entirely religious grounds of Russian autocracy,
which did not rely upon the rational egoism or contractual agree-
ments of the west. The crowning in the Assumption Cathedral consecrated what was for him "the unbreakable union between Russian
Autocracy and the Orthodox Church." The people joined in this
union by observing and sharing the feeling of *umilenie*, of humble joy
and sadness at the crowning of their Tsar.[36]

• • •

Post-coronation festivities evoked the dynasty's Muscovite past in
art, poetry, and music. The seventeenth-century interior of the Hall of
Facets, with the murals of Semën Ushakov, was restored for

Alexander's coronation banquet. The director of the Hermitage, Aleksandr Vasilchikov, had called for this restoration, hoping that "a new dawn will come for our native art." Artists from the Palekh shop of icon painters recreated Ushakov's figures so exactly, according to Komarov, that the fresh gilt and frescoes would "transport you far back into the historical past, to the very beginnings of Moscow."[37]

At the banquet, the emperor and empress occupied the same thrones they had sat upon in the Assumption cathedral, Komarov noted, and sat apart from the heir and other members of the family. "The symbolic meaning of the dinner was the unity and uniting (*edinstvo i edinenie*) of the Tsar with the state. Neither relatives, nor rank, nor foreign interference stands between the Tsar and the people." The emperor and empress were served by Alexander's brothers and the chief ranks of the court. The menu included Russian as well as western dishes: borscht and consommé, pirozhki, steamed sturgeon, veal, aspic, roast chicken, fowl, asparagus, kasha, and ice cream.[38] The menu was in old Russian style, painted by Victor Vasnetsov. Ornate floral decoration framed a scene of boyars bearing the Tsar's regalia to the feast, next to a shield and helmets draped in gonfalons. The reverse showed a priest and peasants bearing bread and salt, with the words of a popular drinking song.[39]

Then an orchestra, soloists, and chorus from the Bolshoi Opera performed Tchaikovsky's cantata, *Moskva*, with words by the panslavist poet Apollon Maikov. For the occasion, Tchaikovsky departed from his usual preference for classical forms and composed what one authority described as "his only work written in the archaic national style dear to Borodin and Rimsky-Korsakov."[40] At the previous three coronation banquets, choruses had sung the hymn "What Glory Now Shines!" with words of Lomonosov set to music by Giuseppe Sarti—a typical eighteenth century celebration of the brilliance and joy of the moment.[41] Maikov's cantata, which was reprinted in the coronation album, and Komarov's book used phrases and imagery from the medieval epics *Lay of the Host of Igor* and the *Zadonshchina* to extol Moscow's triumph in uniting Russia. The princes, experiencing the wrath of God, were disunited until the prince Moscow brought them together and overthrew the Tatar yoke. The Russian Tsar then appeared as bogatyr, representing the hope of all Slavic nations. The figure of this epic Russian knight combined the principle of armed force with Russian folk tradition and faith in the Providential mission of the Russian state as leader of all the Slavs. The people of "Eastern countries" apostrophize the Russian bogatyr:

For all eastern countries, You, now,
Are like the rising star of Bethlehem,
In Your Sacred stone Moscow!
The Lord loves and and has chosen You;
Fasten Konstantin's sword to Your side
And crown Yourself with the crown of Monomakh:
You are to be the defender of orphans,
The deliverer of captives,
The defender of true faiths!
There is this prophesy about Your Moscow:
"Two Romes Fell, The third stands,
There will be no fourth."[42]

The triumph of the Russian nation in the image of the autocrat was the theme of the two parts of the gala performance at the Bolshoi Theater on the evening of May 18. Rather than Donizetti's opera bouffe *L'elisir d'amore,* performed at Alexander II's coronation in 1856, the troupe presented the first and last scenes of Glinka's *A Life for the Tsar.* The opera created a ceremonial equivalence: 1613 became a historical setting for the coronation that had just occurred in 1883. The finale on Red Square, when Moscow witnesses the procession leading Michael Fedorovich on his way to the Kremlin, became a rousing hymn to the new reign. A chorus of almost 800 singers, accompanied by musicians playing old horns, sang the Slavsia chorus as row after row of soldiers marched in to bring the opera, and presumably the troubles of the early 1880s, to a rousing conclusion.[43]

After the intermission, the ballet company performed *Night and Day,* choreographed by Marius Petipa to music of Ludwig Mincus. If *A Life for the Tsar* celebrated the resurrection of authority, *Night and Day* allegorized Russia as the dominant nationality in a multinational empire. The ballet returned to the eighteenth-century theme of renovation. The traditional image of the sun represented the monarch who illuminated and gave warmth to everything. The spirits of night give way to glorious day, with birds, fountains and flowers ushering in the new reign. Butterflies burst from a hive and alit on flowers. "All the nationalities of the Russian empire (*Russkoe tsarstvo*) in holiday costumes"—Finns, Georgians, Don Cossacks, Siberian Shamans, Poles—"greet the rising light of day." Each group performed its own dance, then all joined a general Russian round dance at the center of which stood "the most beautiful and stoutest woman, that is, Rus'." At the conclusion, they came together while a chorus intoned glory to the "beautiful sun, our tsar on earth." The evening ended with the usual singing of the anthem.[44]

The people's feast on Khodnynskoe field on May 21 assumed a greater scope than previous events, as the monarchy tried to show its bond with the Russian people. Tables were set for 400,000, though the number attending reached 600,000, the highest until that time for a coronation feast. The people were treated to candies, cookies, figs, beer, and mead and received coronation mugs carrying the imperial seal and the year, 1883.[45] The feast also presented the most elaborate amusements. For the first time at a coronation, the entertainment included performances of the popular theater, the *balagan*, which had been attracting a growing audience during the 1860s and 1870s.[46] The entrepreneur and impressario M. V. Lentovsky, who had founded the Hermitage and Skoromokh theaters in Moscow, was recruited to organize the feast and entertainments. He proposed to the Coronation Commission that an event taking place in spring have as its theme "the rebirth and the dawn of spring, the glory of Russia and her peoples."[47]

Accordingly, the central event of the festivities was Lentovsky's spectacular "allegorical procession," "Spring," which took place in the central amphitheater on the field. The procession included popular folk heroes from *byliny* and *lubok* literature. The audience beheld a bewildering succession of floats, led in by heralds in "winged armor and spiked helmets," beetles on horseback and foot, grasshoppers, and frogs. The Queen of the Bees sat on a hive, followed by a float with the bogatyr, Mikula Selianovich, and a globe in front showing the boundaries of the Russian empire. Mikula wore the costume of a ploughman and was surrounded by figures of flies. He held a great golden plough, resting on the Russian land. He embodied, Komarov explained, "the power of the black soil." According to *Koronovanie ikh Imperatorskikh Velichestv*, Mikula enjoyed the greatest success among the people. A Russian peasant dressed in a red shirt and holding a birch branch came next, followed by the float "Spring," with a woman allegorizing spring and several butterflies. After the float came four bogatyrs leading captives. Behind them the bogatyr Dobrynia Nikitych rode on the back of the snake Gorinych, which he had slain in his legendary exploit. The final floats presented peasants celebrating. The float Intoxication held a carousing peasant seated next to a barrel. Then came a cart with a drunken young man, followed by four *skomorokhi*—the popular minstrels of old. The procession concluded with a goat, a bear, a crane, and a Russian chorus and dancers.[48]

The pageant connected the reassertion of authority with pagan sources of rebirth and fertility, and the government of Alexander III with the Antaean forces of the people, personified in the bogatyr. The forces of the Russian people had conquered their enemies, internal and external. The bogatyr Dobrynia Nikitych, representing the healthy forces of the Russian people, had struck down the serpent, "the annihilation of everything bad and evil." In the illustrated volume *Vesna Krasna* (Beautiful Spring), these figures were vividly depicted in watercolors by Fëdor Shekhtel. The concluding verse of the book condensed spring, the people, and the Russian monarch into a single image.

> Everything has returned to life;
> Thank God that you [spring] have breathed into us
> Justice, strength, power . . .
> So our native land and dear people,
> Like the ancient mythical bogatyr Mikula,
> Could be strong and full of vigor![49]

After the pageant and the departure of the imperial family, the merriment began—songs, round dances, carnival games, clowns, puppet shows. Komarov referred to the event as a carousal (*gul'bishche*). People devoured *pirozhki* and partook of beer and mead, which "poured forth abundantly from hundreds of carts." They spontaneously burst into song. Lentovsky arranged four shows with patriotic and national appeal: *A Russian Wedding at the End of the Sixteenth Century*, a play by Peter Sukhonin that had gained great popularity in Moscow, and several *balagan* productions—*Ivan-Tsarevich*, a folk tale in five acts by Vladimir Rodislavsky; a military pantomime, *Russian Eagles in the Caucasus*; and *The Resurrection of Harlequin*, in seven scenes. Komarov's account dwelled on the perfect order of the crowd. "All the foreigners were delighted with the calm of this awful mass of people, the order, the absence of pushing, noise and cries. In the course of the entire day, there were no drunks, fights, or scandals." The people had not come for the free drink or entertainment, Komarov asserted, but to have their Tsar among them, and be seen by him. He quoted one comment, "The Great Tsar is coming to us hearty fellows. To watch how we make merry."[50]

Lentovsky had ended his memorandum with the words, "More and more merriment! A person who makes merry thinks of no evil!"[51] Charles Lowe, making a similar point, described the people's feast as the Russian equivalent of bread and circuses.[52] But the feast was also intended to show the people's spontaneous feelings for the event, and to make the connection between the vigor of authority and the natural vitality of the people. The impression from the descriptions is of happy, childlike peasants, a scene from Brueghel. The festivity in Moscow was exemplary for all of Russia. A *lubok*, entitled "People's Fête in the Village on the Occasion of the Coronation of Their Majesty" showed an old peasant and a woman in folk costume dancing merrily to the strains of a balalaika, while a round dance goes on in the background. A boy on the side holds a sheet, perhaps the coronation manifesto. (Fig. 4)

The same day, on the grounds of the Petrovsky Palace in Moscow, the emperor gave a dinner for the peasant elders, numbering over six hundred, who had been selected to attend the coronation. This event, the first of its kind at a coronation, marked the peasants' inclusion as an honorable estate in the framework of Russian monarchy. But the elders also represented authority as custodians of order, and Alexander warned them in a speech to dispel the rumors circulating in the villages that the nobles' land was soon to be divided among the peasants. He thanked them for their participation and told them to thank all when they returned home as well. "Follow the advice and direction of your marshals of the nobility and do not believe the stupid and absurd rumors of a division of land, additions to household

Figure 4. Peasants Celebrating Alexander III's Coronation. *Lubok*, GARF.

land, and so forth. These rumors are spread by Our enemies. All Property, yours as well, should be inviolable."[53]

Komarov described the address of the Tsar to the peasants as a heroic act, a *podvig*. Alexander stood face to face with the peasants "and openly, directly, honestly delivered a speech to them, destroying the illusions and mirages and advancing law and justice." His speech affected them "with irresistible force." Alexander repeated the words "there will be no redivision" several times. Inspired and joyful, the peasants received the words of the Tsar "like a voice from above." Voices were heard, "We must not, we must not. We don't want that, we don't want that," and they vowed they would tell their fellow peasants the Tsar's words and obey the marshals. Then the imperial family passed by the tables, as the elders drank toasts to their health.[54]

Ilia Repin's famous painting of the scene makes clear the change in relationship between emperor and people occurring in the new reign. The emperor and the peasants are at the same level, they face each other as human beings, in contrast to representations of Alexander II standing above peasants who look up worshipfully to him. But the meeting of Tsar and peasants is uneasy. Repin conveys an awkward formality, Alexander standing uncomfortably before the bearded elders, their heads bared, obediently hearing his words. The peasants occupy the same space as the emperor, but they are passive recipients of his message, and the expressions on their faces are blank and unrevealing. The painting, meant for the Coronation Album, had been delayed because the authorities first insisted that Repin present Alexander III as Christ preaching to the people.[55]

• • •

The final two events of the celebration, the visit to Trinity Monastery and the dedication of the Cathedral of Christ the Redeemer, highlighted the central ceremonial and symbolic role of the Orthodox Church in Alexander's scenario. On May 22 the imperial family made the traditional post-coronation pilgrimage to Trinity Monastery, to venerate the relics of St. Sergei and to extol the saint and the monastery for their part in Dmitrii Donskoi's defeat of the Tatars at Kulikovo in 1380. After the ceremonies at the monastery, the family visited the hermitage of Gethsemane, which had been founded by the Metropolitan Filaret as a retreat for solitude and prayer. Alexander recalled a previous visit to the hermitage, and the imperial family took tea in Filaret's cells, which remained exactly as they had been at the Metropolitan's death. Then they venerated the Chernigov

Mother of God in the monastery's cave church. The visit provided an occasion to show the religious unity between Tsar and people. Komarov described the large numbers of worshipers greeting the emperor along the way and praying for him at the monastery cathedral. The response, he concluded, revealed the continued devotion of the rural population to the ruling house and to the state. The "common sense" and "firm character" of the Russian people had belied the revolutionaries' propaganda.[56]

The dedication of the Cathedral of Christ the Redeemer set the relationship between Tsar and church in the Providential narrative of the first half of the nineteenth century. Konstantin Thon's immense neo-classical rendering of Moscow-Vladimir church architecture had been built over a period of nearly a half-century to commemorate Russia's defeat of Napoleon. The cathedral stood as a symbol of the combined efforts of monarchy and church to realize Russia's destiny in creating a unified and powerful Russian state. The wall paintings, completed during the previous reign, placed the growth of the Russian state, assisted by the leaders of the church, in the context of sacred history.[57] The dedication took place on May 26, not the anniversary of the events of 1812, but the feast of the Ascension, which marks the entrance of Christ into glory. The ceremony associated the triumph of Russia with the triumph of Christ, endeavoring to recapture the Providential spirit that had been broken by the Crimean defeat in 1855.[58] The imperial manifesto on the dedication of the cathedral, written by Pobedonostev, incorporated the triumph of 1812 into the ancient union of tsar and people. The edifice, Alexander declared, was the fulfillment of Alexander I's vow to build a cathedral as an expression of thanksgiving to God for the salvation of the fatherland. The consecration of the church in the midst of the Russians gathered for the coronation attested to "how holy and fast is the centuries-old union of love and faith tying the Monarchs of Russia with the loyal people."[59]

The massive ceremonies, which spread over a large part of central Moscow, consecrated the transferal of sacred objects to the new cathedral.[60] The area was blanketed with processions of the cross bearing icons from numerous cathedrals and churches of the city. The processions established a succession from the Assumption Cathedral, ancient but minuscule, to the vast and towering new building that could hold nearly 10,000 worshipers and whose cupolas were visible across Moscow. This succession symbolized the spiritual continuity between Muscovy and Imperial Russia proclaimed in the new myth.

The processions began at eight in the morning, when the clergy from the Iberian Chapel and the Kazan Cathedral carried their icons to the Assumption Cathedral in the Kremlin. There they met a large cortege carrying icons from the Redeemer Cathedral. The processions filed between cordons of brightly dressed troops guarding the streets of Moscow. Komarov wrote, "The long endless row of gold vestments extended to the Kremlin from the Cathedral of the Redeemer like a golden river, along which gonfalons were held, like painted sails of a gigantic ship; icons, gospels, crosses, a mass of silver censors." The sun lit the entire scene, "the procession, the brilliant uniforms and countless crowds of people, these living walls of all this brilliance and splendor."[61] The processions then joined with the abbots of all the monasteries in the Moscow region in a massive movement to the Redeemer Cathedral. The clergy arrayed themselves around the cathedral, the priest of each church facing the building before the gonfalons. All awaited the arrival of the imperial family.[62]

At ten the emperor, wearing a general's uniform and mounted on a white horse, followed by the imperial family in carriage, made his way from the Kremlin palace to the cathedral. The bands along the way played "God Save the Tsar!" other military music, and Tchaikovsky's *1812 Overture,* which had been commissioned for the occasion.[63] After the sanctification of the altar, the imperial family, the suite, high officials, and foreign guests joined the clergy in the first procession of the cross around the cathedral, which completed the sanctification. The procession moved between the lines of the clergy and the standards of the regiments participating in the event. To the strains of the hymn "Kol' slaven" and the ringing of church bells, the artillery launched into a salvo that continued throughout the procession. The ceremony made clear the military significance of the event. "This solemn procession among the banners and standards, surrounded by troops, to the thunder of cannon fire truly recalled that a cathedral was being consecrated that had been erected in memory of the glorious deeds of the Russian army."[64]

The procession then returned to the cathedral for the first Mass. At the conclusion, the emperor kissed the cross, whereupon Bishop Ambrosii of Kharkov proclaimed that Alexander had completed the work of his forbears, "who sowed that others may reap." With the coronation, the bishop concluded, Alexander took up his labor of caring for the fate of "the great Russian people." Then, addressing the empress, he characterized the emperor as one with the laboring population. "The tiller of the soil, working in the field, weary and needing replenishing of his force awaits his food from his home, from his wife: may Your love, with all the treasures of the loving heart, be the bread replenishing the forces of the August Toiler of the Russian land."[65]

The dedication ceremony expressed the unity of the clergy and the military with the Russian tsar who, as August Toiler of the Russian land, established his identity with his people. The use of processions of the cross as mass spectacle marked the beginning of an era when such processions became the central, dominating display of the public ritual of Russian monarchy. The dedication incorporated the triumphs of earlier eras into a national myth that could overshadow the memory of recent setbacks and tragedies, including the disadvantageous provisions of the Treaty of Paris (1856), and the heavy casualties and generally demoralizing defeat in the Crimean War. In so doing, the monarchy appropriated the victory over Napoleon and presented it as a symbol of the recent triumph over the revolutionaries. Tchaikovsky's overture expressed the spirit of the solemnities, juxtaposing two national anthems that were not in use in 1812. The booming, triumphal cadences of "God Save the Tsar!"—composed only in 1834—play against the fanfares of the Marseillaise—banned by Napoleon as "a summons to rebellion" and thus regarded also by the tsarist government. Tchaikovsky himself had contempt for this work, which he had put together in less than a week and considered "very loud and noisy."[66] Like the Redeemer Cathedral, which he also disliked, the overture expressed the glories of the past in the ponderous idiom of late nineteenth-century patriotism. Thus, the most cosmopolitan and probably most proficient Russian composer of his generation created a work exemplary of the nationalist style of historical pastiche.

NOTES

1. For the inauguratory and programmatic role of the coronation, see my book, *Scenarios of Power: Myth and Ceremony in Russian Monarchy. Volume I: From Peter the Great to the Death of Nicholas I* (Princeton, NJ, 1995).

2. *Polnoe sobranie zakonov Rossiiskoi imperii* (henceforth PSZ), Sobranie, 3, No. 1330, 24 January 1883.

3. B. Kn. Constantine Konstantinovich, *Dnevnik, 5 marta–25 iulia, 1883g.*, Gosudarstvennyi Arkhiv Rossiiskoi Federatsii (henceforth GARF, 601-1-21), 61.

4. Grand Duke Alexander Mikhailovich, *Once a Grand Duke* (New York, 1932), 71; Tvardovskaia, V. A. Tvardovskaia Ideologiia poreformennogo samoderzhaviia (Moscow, 1978), 226.

5. PSZ, 16 May 1883, No. 1583.

6. *Opisanie sviashchennogo koronovaniia Ikh Imperatorskikh Velichestv Gosiudaria Imperatora Aleksandra tret'ego i Gosudaryni Imperatritsy Marii Fedorovny Vseia Rossii* (St. Petersburg, 1883). The album came out in an edition of five hundred copies, three hundred of which were in Russian, two hundred in French. It cost 92,376 rubles to produce the 500 copies, compared to 120,000 rubles for the 400 copies of Alexander II's album. *Koronatsionnyi sbornik i khudozhestvennyi al'bom*, Rossiiskii Gosudarstvennyi Istoricheskii Arkhiv (henceforth, RGIA), 472-65-113, 1. On the orientation to Moscow as imperial center in the late nineteenth century, see my article, "Moscow and Petersburg: The Problem of Political Center in Tsarist Russia, 1881–1914," in Sean Wilentz (ed.), *Rites of Power; Symbolism, Ritual and Politics Since the Middle Ages* (Philadelphia: Univ. of Pennsylvania Press, 1985), 244–74.

7. *Opisanie sviashchennogo koronovaniia*, 2.

8. On Alexander III's encouragement of the Russian realists see Elizabeth Valkenier, *Russian Realist Art. State and Society: The Peredvizhniki and Their Tradition* (Ann Arbor, Michigan, 1977), 123–27, 132–34; John O. Norman, "Alexander III as a Patron of Russian Art," in John O. Norman (ed.) *New Perspectives on Russian and Soviet Artistic Culture: Selected Papers from the 4th World Congress for Soviet and East European Studies, 1990* (New York, 1994), 28–33.

9. In addition, a special album was published containing the assembling, disposition, and responsibilities of the military units gathered for the coronation. *Opisanie sbora i zaniatii voisk pod Moskvoiu vo vremia sviashchennogo koronovaniia Ikh Imperatorskikh Velichestv v 1883 godu* (St. Petersburg, 1883).

10. V. Komarov, *V pamiat' sviashchennago koronovaniia Gosudaria Imperatora Aleksandra III i Gosudaria Imperatritsy Marii Fedorovny* (St. Petersburg, 1883); B–E, 30: 816. Komarov also published a brief, less detailed and evocative account in Moscow: V. Komarov, *Sviashchennoe koronovanie Imperatora Aleksandra III i Imperatritsy Marii Fedorovny* (Moscow, 1883). Komarov's publications clearly were subsidized by the government.

11. *The Times of London*, 23 May 1883, 5.

12. Komarov, *V pamiat' sviashchennago koronovaniia*, 57–58.

13. Alexander Poznansky, *Tchaikovsky: The Quest for the Inner Man* (New York, 1991), 420; Anthony Holden, *Tchaikovsky: A Biography* (New York, 1995), 226.

14. *Novoe Vremia*, 12 May 1883, 1. The text sung on the occasion follows:

Glory, Glory to our Russian Tsar!
Given us by the Lord a Sovereign-Tsar!
Moscow awaits you and our sacred Kremlin
Appear before the people our native father!

Glory, Glory, Holy Rus'!
Celebrate the festive day of your Tsar!
Rejoice, make merry, your Tsar comes forth
The people meets the Sovereign Tsar.

Greetings to the longed-for in his capital,
Greetings to your most beautiful Tsaritsa,
Greetings to the longed-for, given by the Lord
You are strong with the love of holy Rus'
You are the leader of Orthodoxy, God is with you
Greetings, Greeting, Hoorah! Hoorah!

15. *The Times of London*, 23 May 1883, 5.

16. Komarov, *V pamiat' sviashchennago koronovaniia*, 109–110.

17. Ibid., frontispiece.

18. Ibid., 110–11.

19. *The Times of London*, 28 May 1883, 7.

20. Komarov, *V pamiat' sviashchennago koronovaniia*, 111.

21. At the coronation of Alexander II, however, representatives of the state peasants had made up the opening delegation.

22. *Opisanie sviashchennogo koronovaniia*, 17.

23. Komarov, *V pamiat' sviashchennago koronovaniia*, 119–20.

24. Ibid., 125.

25. Ibid., 130–33; B. Kn. Konstantin Konstantinovich, *Dnevnik, 5 marta–25 iulia, 1883g.*, 68.

26. *Opisanie sviashchennogo koronovaniia*, Opp. 21, 22, 23.

27. V. A. Tvardovskaia, "Aleksandr III," in *Rossiiskie Samoderzhtsy, 1801–1917* (Moscow, 1994), 258.

28. D. N. Liubimov, "Russkaia smuta deviatisotykh godov, 1902–1906," Bakhmetev Archive, Columbia University, 93.

29. A. A. Polovtsov, *Dnevnik gosudarstvennogo sekretaria, A. A. Polovtsova* (Moscow, 1966), 1: 95. Among the Russians he mentioned Golitsyn, Gagarin, Iusupov, Meshchersky, Uvarov. Among the Germans, Nesselrode, Grot, Pahlen, and Sivers.

30. Komarov, *V pamiat' sviashchennago koronovaniia*, 133–34.

31. Ibid., 138.

32. Ibid., 138, 150.

33. *Sel'skii Vestnik*, April 3, 1883: 129.

34. *Koronovanie ikh Imperatorskikh Velichestv*, 136.

35. Ivan Aksakov, *Sochineniia* (St. Petersburg, 1896), 1:142. Printed originally in *Rus'* (1883), No. 10.

36. M. N. Katkov, *Sobranie peredovykh statei Moskovskikh Vedomostei 1881g.* (Moscow, 1898), 228, 234; *Moskovskie Vedomosti*, May 11, 1883: 2; May 16, 1883: 5.

37. The renovations of the Palace of Facets came to nearly one-half million rubles. "O vozobnovlenii Granitovoi Palaty, privedeniia eia v tot vid v kakom ona sushchestvovala v drevnee vremia i o raznykh rabotakh, otnosiashchikhsia do eia ubranstva," RGIA, 472-64-20, passim: Aida Nasibova, *The Faceted Chamber in the Moscow Kremlin*, (Leningrad, 1978), 13; Komarov, *V pamiat' sviashchennago koronovaniia*, 89–93.

38. Komarov, *V pamiat' sviashchennago koronovaniia*, 140–42.

39. The menu is reproduced in *Veseliashchiisia Peterburg* (St. Petersburg, 1994), 22–23.

40. André Lischke, *Piotr Ilyitch Tschaikovski* (Paris, 1993), 989–92.

41. E. P., "Koronovanie Gosudarei," *Russkii Arkhiv* 1 (1990), 62–63; see for example the account of Nicholas I's coronation banquet, "Istoricheskoe opisanie Sviashchennogo Koronovaniia," *Otechestvennye Zapiski* (1827), Vol. 31, 387.

42. Komarov, 143–47; A.N. Maikov, *Polnoe sobranie sochinenii* (St. Petersburg, 1914), 2: 413–20.

43. Komarov, *V pamiat' sviashchennago koronovaniia*, 307.

44. Ibid., 308–11.

45. Ibid., 333, 342. Two-hundred thousand had participated at Nicholas I's coronation in 1826. I have no figures for the 1856 coronation; however, since three times the number of tables were set in 1856 as in 1826, it is likely that the number in 1856 approached that for 1883.

46. A. F. Nekrylova, *Russkie narodnye gorodskie prazdniki, uveseleniia, i zrelishcha, konets XVIII-nachalo XX veka* (Leningrad, 1984), 158–60, 167–71; *Neia Zorkaia, Fol'klor, lubok, ekran* (Moscow, 1994), 49–56, 156–58.

47. M. V. Lentovskii, "Zaiavlenie v koronatsionnuiu komissiu o plane narodnogo praznestva v dni koronatsii [Aleksandra III], TsTM, 144-1-904, 1–6.

48. Komarov, *V pamiat' sviashchennago koronovaniia*, 341; *Koronovanie ikh Imperatorskikh Velichestv*, 195.

49. *Vesna krasna: allegoricheskoe shestvie ustroennoe na narodnom gul'iane v Moskve, 21 maia, 1883 g.* (Moscow, 1883).

50. Komarov, *V pamiat' sviashchennago koronovaniia*, 334–35, 342–43.

51. Lentovskii, 6.

52. Lowe, 75–76.

53. *Sel'skii Vestnik*, 1883, No. 23: 227–28. On the rumors circulating among the peasantry at the time of the coronation, see James H. Krukones, *To the People; The Russian Government and the Newspaper Sel'skii Vestnick* (Village Herald), *1881–1917* (New York and London, Garland Publishing Inc., 1987), 82–84.

54. Komarov, *V pamiat' sviashchennago koronovaniia*, 350–59.

55. See the interesting remarks by Elizabeth Valkenier, *Russian Realist Art* (Ann Arbor, Michigan, 1977), 126.

56. Komarov, 366–72; *Opisanie sviashchennogo koronovaniia*, 53–54.

57. Nicholas I had laid the cornerstone in 1837. See Volume 1: 384–86. On the paintings, see P. Iu. Klimov, "Zhivopisnoe ubranstvo khrama Khrista Spasitelia" in E. I. Kirichenko, *Khram Khrista Spasitelia* (Moscow, 1996), 73–132.

58. See the discussion of the rhetoric and ceremony of the event in E. I. Kirichenko, *Khram Khrista Spasitelia v Moskve* (Moscow, 1992), 140–42.

59. Komarov, *V pamiat' sviashchennago koronovaniia*, 445–46; PSZ, 3: No. 1602, 26 May 1883.

60. The ceremony is described in Kirichenko, *Khram Khrista Spasitelia v Moskve*, 144–48, and Komarov, *V pamiat' sviashchennago koronovaniia*, 429–45.

61. Komarov, *V pamiat' sviashchennago koronovaniia*, 432–33.

62. Ibid., 433–34.

63. The premiere of the work, however, was in a concert hall built for the Exhibition of 1881. Poznansky, 380; Holden, 203–04.

64. Komarov, *V pamiat' sviashchennago koronovaniia*, 436–41.

65. Ibid., 441–44.

66. Poznansky, 380; Holden, 203–05.

Tchaikovsky, Chekhov, and

the Russian Elegy

ROSAMUND BARTLETT

Silvery, nut-like October.
The tin glint of early frost.
The autumn twilight of Chekhov,
Tchaikovsky and Levitan.
"Winter Approaches"
Pasternak (1943)[1]

This article is not the first to address the subject of Tchaikovsky's relationship with Anton Chekhov. The mutual admiration felt by the composer and the writer has been often commented on, and has even
generated a slender bibliography of critical literature exploring its ram-
ifications. In 1962 Evgenii Balabanovich published the monograph
Chekhov and Tchaikovsky, whose revised third edition appeared in 1978,[2]
and this study had been preceded by articles and studies by other Soviet
critics such as I. A. Kremlev and L. P. Gromov.[3] Tchaikovsky's British
biographer David Brown produced the first English-language article on
Tchaikovsky and Chekhov in 1985, apparently written without knowledge of the previous literature.[4] While these studies contribute substantially to our knowledge of this brief yet important friendship, they
remain at the same time unsatisfying. The facts of Tchaikovsky's relationship with Chekhov have been firmly established (Balabanovich in
fact chronicles in exhaustive detail even tangential points of contact),
but the more interesting questions of why the friendship arose in the
first place, and what it meant to both composer and writer in terms of
their own creativity, have been less successfully analyzed. The rigor with
which Balabanovich explores the biographical context in the first eight
chapters of his study is not matched by his exploration of the more chal-

lenging question of shared traits in the work of Tchaikovsky and Chekhov, a discussion inexplicably limited to the final two chapters. Balabanovich identifies aesthetic views that he believes were shared by Chekhov and Tchaikovsky, and catalogues a series of styles and themes which he asserts are common to both of their oeuvres, namely symphonic realism, tragedy, idealism, lyricism, an interest in childhood, simplicity, heartfelt emotion, goodness, modesty and intense Russianness. His account remains at best a catalogue, however, and is marred by the hagiographic approach (of the "Chekhov and Tchaikovsky are the pride and glory of our people" ilk) which rendered so much Soviet criticism both superficial and unprofessional. Tchaikovsky and Chekhov emerge from his study as saintly artists and paragons of virtue, far removed from the complex human beings they really were.[5] David Brown in his article covers much the same biographical ground as Balabanovich, also leaving until the end his assessment of what fueled Tchaikovsky's and Chekhov's mutual attraction. His brief analysis, in which he considers the differences between writer and composer more than their similarities, is disappointing. For Brown, the introspective Tchaikovsky and the objective Chekhov were vastly different. Chekhov is classified as a writer with a huge range of characters representing all types of humanity, while Tchaikovsky, on the contrary, is a deeply subjective composer in whose works "there is no real hint of a creative personality other than his own."[6] In fact, the opposite could also be argued. In a brief but perceptive article, Gerard McBurney writes,

> Tchaikovsky is among the most centrifugal of composers. There is no single line of development in his music, no sense of the pursuit of an organically unified artistic vision. For Tchaikovsky a single genre could be the vehicle for a multitude of different intentions. The First and Second Piano Concertos, for instance, although they both *sound* like Tchaikovsky, seem, in the working out of their ideas, hardly to be written by the same mind. As for the symphonic music, each successive symphony, suite or symphonic poem seems to suggest a new beginning.[7]

Chekhov is similarly centrifugal, and the heterogeneity of his writing does not of course preclude the continuing presence of his own creative personality. In defining "a deep and very basic humanity" as the one trait both Tchaikovsky and Chekhov had in common, Brown is in the final analysis reduced, like Balabanovich, to making generalizations that leave the reader sensing there is something more to be said. The present article, therefore, seeks to delve a little deeper beneath the surface, by examining the relationship between Tchaikovsky and Chekhov from different perspectives and considering common traits in their work from new angles.

First, the circumstances surrounding Tchaikovsky's initial contact with Chekhov need to be reviewed. Chekhov appeared on Tchaikovsky's horizon in April 1887, when his story "The Letter" ("Pis'mo") was published in the Sunday supplement of the Petersburg daily newspaper *Novoe vremia*. At the time, Tchaikovsky was finishing the orchestration of his opera *The Enchantress* at Maidanovo, and his close friend Nikolai Kashkin was staying with him. Their evenings were spent in conversation, duet playing, or reading aloud. On the evening of 19 April, according to Kashkin, Chekhov's story was read twice over, because it made such an impression on them.[8] Tchaikovsky, in fact, was so taken with the story that he wrote to his brother Modest about it the following day, and decided to find out more about its author. Following inquiries made to the *Novoe vremia* music critic Mikhail Ivanov, he acquired Chekhov's first serious collection of short stories, *Motley Tales* (*Pestrie rasskazi*), published the previous year. His admiration evidently increased after reading this collection, for he then sat down to write Chekhov to congratulate him, although the letter apparently never reached its addressee.[9] As David Brown observes, Tchaikovsky was an avid reader, but, as a modest and retiring man (like Chekhov, in fact), he shunned direct contact with the Russian writers of his day.[10] It is surely all the more remarkable, then, that Tchaikovsky should have decided to write to the young writer directly, on the strength of reading a handful of his short stories. This point needs to be stressed. And it was surely something beyond a liking for the indubitable charm of these stories that attracted Tchaikovsky to Chekhov, as we will see. Also remarkable is Tchaikovsky's appreciation of Chekhov's talent, for the writer at this point was only at the very beginning of his career as a serious writer of fiction, and only twenty-seven years old. Having graduated as a doctor from Moscow University a few years earlier, Chekhov still regarded medicine as his main profession. Tchaikovsky, meanwhile, was forty-seven years old and finally enjoying great success as a composer, particularly following the triumphant production of *Eugene Onegin* in St Petersburg in 1884 and official recognition from Alexander III. He was also acquiring fame as a conductor of his own works abroad. In 1878, with financial support from Nadezhda von Meck, he had resigned his teaching position at the Moscow

Conservatory to devote himself to full-time composition, and was in the 1880s living outside Moscow. His prodigious output at this time included operas, ballets, orchestral and chamber works, as well as songs and sacred pieces.

It is true that many were beginning to recognize Chekhov's gifts in the mid-1880s, but few recognized the extent of those gifts the way Tchaikovsky did. Chekhov had begun his career writing extremely lowbrow humorous tales and feuilletons in order to provide for his impecunious family, was of provincial and lower class origins, and had no literary connections. Only in 1886 did Chekhov begin to sign his stories with his real name and start selling them to the major establishment newspaper *Novoe vremia*, on the proceeds of which he was able for the first time to rent a whole house for his family on Sadovaia Kudrinskaia street in Moscow (which now houses the Chekhov museum). It was also only in March 1886 that Chekhov began to take his fiction writing seriously, following an earnest plea from veteran writer Dimitrii Grigorovich. A drastic reduction in output resulted. In 1886–87, his most prolific period, he had published 166 stories and sketches; in 1888 he would publish only nine.

That Tchaikovsky's appreciation of Chekhov's talent in April 1887 was indeed far from arbitrary and actually highly informed can be ascertained from a letter he wrote to Iuliia Shpazhinskaia only a few weeks before (26 March). Here he expresses his frustration and disappointment with Tolstoy's latest work, the play *The Power of Darkness*, written primarily as a vehicle for the author's moral teachings. Tolstoy had just emerged from the spiritual crisis that engulfed him after the completion of his great novel *Anna Karenina*, and his new, mostly nonfictional writings were of a far more overt didactic cast than before. Tchaikovsky's letter to Shpazhinskaia reveals not only his sensitivity as a reader to the magical qualities of Tolstoy's literary genius, but also the sophistication of his critical judgment. For Tchaikovsky, Tolstoy was "the most powerful and profound genius which literature has ever known," "beyond all comparisons" and "as isolated in his unassailable grandeur as any Everest or Dhaulagiri amongst other summits." But in his opinion, the only merits of *The Power of Darkness* were its "mastery of language" and high level of artistic craftsmanship.[11]

Tchaikovsky's evaluation of Chekhov's story must be understood in the context not only of his knowledge of Tolstoy, but of his serious enthusiasm for Russian literature in general. When in May 1886, for example, Tchaikovsky met Pauline Viardot, who had been the great love of Turgenev's life, their conversation focused almost exclusively on the writer, who had died of cancer three years before. In particular, Tchaikovsky was fascinated to learn from Viardot how she and Turgenev together had written his late story "The Song of Triumphant Love."[12] In 1888, Tchaikovsky revealed his detailed knowledge of Russian poetry when he began discussing versification with Grand Duke Konstantin Romanov (himself a poet of some distinction), with whom he had previously entered into correspondence. Despite his avowals of dilettantism, Tchaikovsky's discussion of poetic craft is surprisingly detailed, and the articulation of his desire to see more rhythmic variety in Russian poetry shows how much he was attuned to the purely sonorous qualities of verse. It is also interesting that Tchaikovsky singles out for particular praise the poetry of Fet, precisely because of the musical qualities he perceived in it, at the same time acknowledging Fet's relative unpopularity amongst the Russian reading public when compared to Nekrasov, "whose muse crawls along the ground."[13] Tchaikovsky, then, had singular and well defined literary tastes, which, as with his initial response to Chekhov, did not always correspond with prevailing views.

The views Tchaikovsky expressed to Konstantin Romanov on poetic rhythm are interesting for the light they shed on what probably attracted him most to Chekhov's prose in the early stories he first read, namely, its musicality. The stories that make up the collection *Motley Tales* exemplify its title, in that they comprise a diverse assortment of pieces of fiction that look both backward to Chekhov's beginnings as a purely comic writer and forward to his mature, more elegiac style. Light-hearted and humorous stories like "Oysters" ("Ustritsy," 1884) and "Kids" ("Detvora," 1886), for example, are balanced by those such as "The Huntsman" ("Eger," 1885) and "Misery" ("Toska," 1886), which are altogether more serious, indeed elegiac, in both theme and structure. "The Letter" that so impressed Tchaikovsky in April 1887 is an example of a story that falls somewhere between those two poles, being at once poignant and extremely amusing. As David Brown summarizes, "it is the tale of a humble deacon who, observing that his son is not conducting his life according to the strict code in which he had been brought up, asks his pompous clerical master to devise a stern letter of reproof. After being persuaded against sending the letter by a poor and less-than-perfect priest, who advises instead that he should extend forgiveness, the father finally decides to dispatch it after he has added a gossipy, openhearted postscript which annihilates any effect the exhortation might have had."[14] The story is a masterpiece of Chekhovian irony, for it is suggested that the utterly dissolute and alcoholic Father Anastasii is in the end perhaps more of a model of Christian charity and forgiveness

than the upright and officious rural dean, Father Fëdor, with the vac-
illating deacon falling somewhere in between. Chekhov largely abandoned his religious beliefs after a particularly stern Orthodox
upbringing, but he continued to believe in the "importance of religious traditions and religious experience for the continuation of civi-
lization,"[15] and in the importance of having faith in something in
one's life. Many of his fictional characters are priests, but all are portrayed primarily as people with typical human flaws rather than as
representatives of the Christian faith—a typically subversive
Chekhovian approach. "The Letter" with its theme of human frailty
is a fine example.

For Brown, it is the "many human resonances" and simplicity of
this tale that appealed to Tchaikovsky,[16] while Balabanovich talks
about the story's verisimilitude and simplicity of narration, as well as
Chekhov's warmth and compassion.[17] Certainly all these qualities are
in evidence here, as well as Chekhov's rare ability to create intimate
portraits of human beings from very different walks of life.
Tchaikovsky's interest in "The Letter" was surely not only sparked by
the poignant and gently humorous content of the story, however, but
also by its form. As Donald Rayfield briefly comments in relation to
Tchaikovsky's attraction to "The Letter," it was musicians "who felt
most acutely the musical nature of [Chekhov's] prose in its rhythms
and the sonata-like structure, where the end recapitulates the beginning after a central development."[18] It was Shostakovich who first
divined the presence of sonata form in Chekhov's writing, in an article on Tchaikovsky published in 1943[19] (and it is "sonata form" rather
than "sonata" that Rayfield must have in mind here, an important distinction). It was a structural principle Chekhov began to develop precisely at the time of "The Letter." At the beginning of the story, the
characters of Father Anastasii and Father Fëdor are presented as dia-
metrically opposed to each other, like two distinct musical keys. What
Chekhov seems to be searching for in this story is the possibility of
some middle ground between the sterility of a life lived according to
the rules, and the depravity of a life lived without any rules. This
probing of the grey area between extremes is a perennial theme with
Chekhov, encapsulated in an oft-repeated remark in his notebooks:
"Between the statements 'God Exists' and 'There is no God' lies a
whole vast field, which a true sage crosses with difficulty. But a
Russian usually knows only one of these two extremes; what lies
between them is of no interest to him and he usually knows nothing
or very little."[20]

The central development in "The Letter" is provided by Father Fëdor's dialogue with the deacon about his son, which echoes the earlier conversation about Father Anastasii's failings, while Father Anastasii himself temporarily retreats into the background. Father Fëdor's views predominate here. The end of the story indeed then recapitulates the beginning, for Father Anastasii re-emerges to restore balance by urging the deacon not to send the harshly written letter, yet at the same time finally getting to drink the vodka he has craved all evening. What results is an untidy but far more palatable synthesis, so that the uncomfortable tension introduced at the story's outset is to some extent resolved by its gentle conclusion, although it is ultimately an unsatisfying conclusion that provokes the reader to ponder further what has gone before. The story thus exemplifies Chekhov's belief that the job of the artist is not to provide answers and solutions, but to ask the right questions.

Chekhov's two meetings with Tchaikovsky took place in 1888 and 1889, the first in St. Petersburg, the second in Moscow. It was Modest Tchaikovsky whom Chekhov first got to know, through mutual acquaintances, during his visit to the capital in December 1888. On this occasion, Chekhov read part of his story "A Nervous Breakdown" (his tuberculosis tended to make him lose his voice). Modest was also a fervent admirer of Chekhov's prose, and later got to know the author quite well; indeed, he often acted as a conduit of information between his brother and Chekhov. A few days later, on 12 December, Chekhov finally met Tchaikovsky himself (who was staying with his brother during his visit to St. Petersburg) and communicated to the composer his great admiration for his music. Tchaikovsky was also able to tell Chekhov in person how much he enjoyed his stories.[21] In the following months he recommended Chekhov to Iuliia Shpazhinskaia, declaring boldly (and quite correctly) that he was the "future pillar" of Russian literature, though the writer still had the majority of his fictional masterpieces ahead of him.[22]

The meeting with Tchaikovsky made a deep impression on Chekhov, and gave him the idea of dedicating his next collection of stories to the composer. In October 1889, he wrote to Tchaikovsky asking if he would agree to the dedication, in typically self-deprecating fashion describing the collection as "tedious and boring as autumn."[23] Chekhov had only once before dedicated a collection of stories to someone (the writer Grigorovich, who had written a famous letter to him in 1886), so the dedication to Tchaikovsky was of some significance. Tchaikovsky was in fact so moved by what he regarded as a great honor, that he decided to pay an impromptu visit to Chekhov in his Moscow home (he was still living in Sadovaia Kudrinskaia) to thank him personally. It was during this meeting that Tchaikovsky and Chekhov discussed the idea of collaborating on an opera (a "strong but intimate drama"), to be based on Lermontov's story "Bela," from his novel *A Hero of Our Time*. Chekhov informed Suvorin of this plan the following day, commenting that he loved Tchaikovsky's music passionately, especially *Eugene Onegin*.[24] The choice of a story from *A Hero of Our Time* is intriguing, for this novel was written under the heavy imprint of Pushkin's work, and Lermontov deliberately linked his hero Pechorin to Onegin by also naming him after a Siberian river. Both Chekhov and Tchaikovsky admired Lermontov's prose, and both had recently visited the Caucasus where the story is set, but the opera sadly never materialized. As David Brown comments, Tchaikovsky was always "running up against subjects which briefly inflamed his interest and then sank from sight."[25] He soon began work with his brother on *The Queen of Spades* instead.

During Tchaikovsky's visit, Chekhov presented him with an inscribed copy of the second edition of his latest collection, *Stories (Rasskazi)*, which had been published earlier that year. The volume contained eleven of the best stories written between 1886 and 1888, and several are notable for their rhythmic and musical structure. That Chekhov was aware of constructing his stories in a musical way is evidenced by his remark that his story "Fortune" ("Shchast'e," 1887) was a "quasi symphony." This lyrical story, which Donald Rayfield calls Chekhov's "first prose poem of steppe nature,"[26] published a few months after "The Letter" (also in *Novoe vremia*), is another particularly fine work from Chekhov's transitional period. Richly evocative, it is set at dawn on the steppe, where a flock of sheep is dozing. In some respects it follows the model of "The Letter" by again introducing three very different characters—a shepherd who is young, lying on his back gazing at the stars; another who is much older, depicted lying on his stomach; and a passing warden, who gets off his horse to ask for a light for his pipe. Their conversation centers on happiness. The old shepherd is preoccupied with the idea of treasure hidden in neighboring areas. He has always been convinced that finding it would be the answer to human happiness, but when challenged, cannot say what he would do if he found hidden treasure. The warden, of superior social standing and education, who had introduced the theme of hidden treasure, stands motionless and silent, merely punctuating the old shepherd's monologue, as do the sounds of nature surrounding them. His reticence communicates his skepticism at the idea that finding a fortune could be a guarantee of happiness, an idea which is, as it were, echoed by an ominous sound from a distant mine reverberating across the steppe. The young shepherd, meanwhile, who remains silent until after the warden has trotted off on his horse, finds the idea of looking for hidden treasure both unnecessary and incomprehensible, and ponders instead the elusiveness of human happiness. The story ends as silently as it began, with the two shepherds standing lost in wistful thought, at opposite ends of their flock. By likening this story to a symphony, Chekhov presumably had in mind his technique of developing the idea of happiness through contrast (the external stasis in the story is contrasted to the inner dynamism of the characters' thoughts), juxtaposition, and the rhythmic repetition of sounds and images.

"Fortune" can in some ways be seen as a prelude to Chekhov's first literary masterpiece, "The Steppe" ("Step'"), also included in *Rasskazi*. The publication of "The Steppe" in the prestigious literary journal *Severnyi Vestnik* in March 1888 marked Chekhov's debut as a serious writer, and his standing in the Russian literary fraternity was further consolidated when he was awarded the Pushkin Prize. Tchaikovsky and Modest had begun to read "The Steppe" aloud to each other on 31 May 1888. Modest was en route for the south, and was staying overnight with his brother in Frolovskoe, outside Moscow.[27] "The Steppe" was the most musical piece of prose Chekhov had yet written, and provides a classic example of a story written in sonata form. It was P. Bitsilli, author of a classic study on Chekhov's style, who first revealed how its particular rhythm is created: "by alternating themes—almost in a musical sense of the word—and by alternating tempos and harmonies."[28] As Bitsilli demonstrates, this story contains an "alternation of images and suggestions which, in terms of structure, approximates a purely musical development of theme and counter-theme, framed by supplementary themes. The repetitions of image-symbols, epithets, indications of movement, sounds and colors which create two complete images, correspond in musical terms to the recurrence of melodies, chords, harmonies, keys and tempos."[29] Bitsilli identifies a basic tripartite thematic structure in "The Steppe," which consists essentially of "statement," "reaction," and "conclusion," but stops short of taking his argument to its obvious conclusions and drawing a parallel with sonata form. "The Steppe" is a story about a young boy going on a journey to a new life. In this case departure itself, bringing with it the death of the boy's old life, provides the basic conflict, as P. Bitsilli points out, while the main body of the story develops the contrasting themes of life and death in myriad diffuse ways.

The steppe for example is arid, empty, flat and monotonous, while the boy is lonely, his traveling companion the priest is pompous and indifferent, and there are many instances of senseless violence, all of which are symbols of death, metaphorical and literal. Life, by contrast, is evoked by the frequent beauty and grandeur of the steppe, descriptions of moments where people in the story feel socially included rather than excluded, and where they participate rather than retreat into passivity. After slowly building to a crisis (in this case, a thunderstorm), arrival at the journey's destination brings apparent resolution and the official beginning of the boy's new life. It is followed, however, by a concluding scene in which there are numerous echoes of the ambiguous opening of the story, where the specter of death looms large. Just after the travelers started on their journey, they passed a graveyard, and the boy recalled that two five-kopek coins were placed on his grandmother's eyes when she died. At the end of the story, the boy's traveling companions give him ten kopeks; he is full of sadness as he realizes he will never see the old priest alive again, and his uncle speaks in a voice that suggests there is a dead body laid out in the room. The red shirt the boy wears at the beginning of the story is also recalled, through the image of a red dog barking at the end of the story. So the clash of opposing themes and their recapitulation is both something we can see physically on the page and something that operates at an entirely different level. Nothing is stated outright, but an elaborate thematic structure is created in the reader's mind through the various associations.

Gloomy People (Khmurie liudi), the collection dedicated to Tchaikovsky, was published in March 1890. It contained ten stories written between 1887 and 1889, and was, by the author's own account, painstakingly prepared. It contained several stories whose structure was consciously rhythmical, and it seems that Chekhov was attempting to communicate through them the impact Tchaikovsky's music had on his compositional technique. In a letter sent to Modest Tchaikovsky at this time, whileTchaikovsky himself was away in Italy, Chekhov wrote,

> I have long harboured an impertinent desire to dedicate something to [Pyotr Ilich]. This dedication, I thought, would be a partial, minimal expression of the huge critical respect which I, a scribbler, have acquired for his magnificent talent, and which, because of my lack of any musical gift, cannot commit to paper.[30]

Modest passed on these comments to Tchaikovsky in Florence, who was clearly touched ("You cannot imagine how pleasing *Chekhov's* words about me are") and promised to write personally to the author when his work on *The Queen of Spades* reached completion. Chekhov had by then departed on his journey to Siberia, which took him away from Moscow from April to December, but Tchaikovsky was still thanking the writer in the last letter he wrote to him at the end of 1891. It is interesting to note that Tchaikovsky felt as incapable of expressing what he so admired in Chekhov's prose as Chekhov found it difficult to articulate his particular reasons for liking Tchaikovsky's music:

> I was always going to write a long letter to you, even attempting to explain which particular qualities in your talent so captivated and bewitched me. But there was not the time for it—and, above all, *I had not got it in me*. It is very difficult for a musician to express in words what and how he feels in regard of this or that artistic phenomenon.[31]

Chekhov had begun his letter to Modest in 1890 by confessing he was in such deep awe of Tchaikovsky that he was ready to stand day and night as a guard of honor at the composer's door. He also comments that Tchaikovsky now occupied the second position in Russian art for him after Tolstoy, which is interesting in view of the opinion of Tolstoy Tchaikovsky expressed in the above-quoted letter to Iuliia Shpazhinskaia.

Two stories in *Khmurye liudi* stand out in particular for their musical qualities. Those in the story "Sleepy" ("Spat' khochetsia"), first published in 1888, in which an overworked and exhausted thirteen-year-old nursemaid kills the baby she is looking after and then at last falls asleep, have in fact attracted a certain degree of critical attention. Gleb Struve for example argues that, "if closely analyzed, 'Sleepy' can easily be broken up into musical phrases" in which anthropomorphic objects serve as "musical refrains." According to Struve, "the description of Varka's pastime between the morning, when the baby is fed, and the next evening, when she goes back to her nocturnal watch over it, is also musically organized with the aid of oral staccato orders which progress, crescendo, and punctuate the narrative into a series of brief, realistic descriptions of Varka's typically dreary and exhausting day."[32] H. Peter Stowell, meanwhile, has argued convincingly that the story is a

> fugue that is tight in its thematic unity, polyphonic in its juxtaposition of contrapuntal levels of reality, time, and space,

and dense in its overlapping fragments of perceptual experience. . . . The story breaks down into the six [sic] part fugue
structure of subject, answer, counter-subject, episode and
stretto.[33]

The story "An Attack of Nerves" ("Pripadok"), in which a young
student experiences a breakdown after visiting brothels for the first
time, is also musical, but in a different way. For P. Bitsilli, it was rhythm
that constituted the main element of Chekhov's musicality. Defining
his prose rhythm as arising from a harmonious combination of concise and protracted clauses in the sentences, Bitsilli describes, in reference to "An Attack of Nerves," how Chekhov "characteristically
strings together short, simple [clauses], ending in a long [clause] of a
more complex syntactic structure."[34] An example is given from the
opening of the story, arranged graphically to illustrate this technique:

The air smelled of snow,
the snow crunched softly under foot,
the earth, the roofs, the trees, the benches on the
    boulevards—
all was soft, white, young,
and this made the buildings look different from the
    day before,
the street lamps burned more brightly,
the air was transparent,
the carriages sounded more muffled,
and along with the fresh, light, frosty air a feeling like
    the white, young, fluffy
snow was aroused in one's soul.[35]

This passage in fact plays an important role in the complex symbolic
structure of the story Marena Senderovich has analyzed in some
detail, wherein rhythm is created on a thematic level.[36]

That it was the musical qualities of Chekhov's prose to which
Tchaikovsky responded most deeply is indicated by his particular
admiration for the story "Gusev," published in December 1890 in
Novoe vremia. It is surely no coincidence that another Russian com-
poser, Shostakovich, thought this story the "most musical prose in all
Russian literature" (and wanted himself to write music for it).[37] It was
"Gusev" which Shostakovich asked his wife to read to him on the
night that he died.[38] Since Tchaikovsky's references to Chekhov in his

letters are few and far between, his spontaneous exclamation to Modest that he thought "Gusev" was "lovely" is all the more resonant.

This unusual and highly poetic story, in which the language is particularly rhythmical, was inspired during Chekhov's journey home from Siberia by sea in 1890. A parable about nature's indifference to humanity (with faint echoes of one of Turgenev's recurring themes), it deals with the death of a Russian peasant soldier, Gusev, aboard the ship bringing him back home from duty in the Far East. The story ends with an extraordinary lyrical flight as Gusev's corpse is attacked by a shark while descending gently to the ocean floor, following burial at sea, the whole scene set against a backdrop of impartial and transcendent marine beauty. As Kenneth Lantz has pointed out, the story is built "on a series of polarities, and it is the alternation of these which provides the sense of dynamism in a work whose plot contains few incidents."[39] Gusev is contrasted, for example, with Pavel Ivanich, with whom he shares his cabin. Both are terminally ill; unlike Gusev, Pavel Ivanich is an intellectual and full of protest, whereas Gusev meekly accepts his fate. Day alternates with night, reality alternates with dream, death alternates with life in a regularity that matches the heaving of the ship as it continues on its journey.

Undoubtedly Tchaikovsky's feelings about "Gusev" were similar to those experienced by Shostakovich when he read the story. It was Shostakovich, in fact, who was probably the first person to draw an analogy between the creative worlds of Tchaikovsky and Chekhov, in a letter he wrote to Tatiana Glivenko in 1923.[40] The conviction and ease with which the seventeen-year-old musician draws parallels between creative worlds of a writer and a composer who (probably unbeknownst to him at that time) had great admiration for each other's work is remarkable. Shostakovich found that, his admiration of form in the works of Tolstoy and Taneev was followed by disappointment in their contents, whereas in the case of Chekhov and Tchaikovsky, all was "in place" regarding form and content. Chekhov indeed took great pains to insure that content, form, and sound should work together in his stories. According to his contemporary, Professor M. Chlenov, Chekhov once said that each of his works of prose fiction "should not produce an effect only with its content, but also with its form, and should not only convey an idea, but a sound, creating a distinct aural impression."[41] Tchaikovsky was certainly attuned to the tiniest details of Chekhov's technique. In his copy of "The Post," a story of 1887 included in the collection dedicated to him, he marked the rhythmical and onomatopoeic words "Kolokol'chik chto-to prozviakal bubenchikam, bubenchiki laskogo otvetili emu" (the bell jingled something to the little bells, the little bells replied warmly).[42] Meanwhile, Chekhov appreciated the same harmony of form and content in Tchaikovsky's works. He was particularly fond of the letter scene in *Eugene Onegin*, an opera he must have seen many times in Moscow.[43] The letter scene comprises the focus of the entire work (it was written before anything else), and is one of the many "vocal-symphonic poems which convey a vivid psychological portrait of character, and express intimate personal feeling and experience" and which, as Isaiah Berlin notes, have their counterparts to some degree in Chekhov's writings.[44] Gerard McBurney has described how closely Tchaikovsky matches his music to the text in this scene:

> He begins with the very language of the sentimental stuff [Tatiana] reads, the same clichés and mawkish vocabulary, and, line by line, deepens their meaning and endows them with astonishing power and resonance. He leads us from laughter to tears, and forces us to recognise that an experience that we might at first have thought silly and sentimental in fact contains within itself the seeds of a considerable tragedy.[45]

Shostakovich was to link Tchaikovsky and Chekhov again in an article about the composer published in 1943, in which he challenged the "commonly held belief" that Tchaikovsky "is akin to Chekhov and Levitan in his elegiac glorification of the Russian twilight at the end of the last century":

> This is unfair not only to Tchaikovsky, but also to Chekhov and Levitan, whose work is full of a strong life-asserting force. The three artists, do, however have much in common; their elegiac perception of Russian nature, their tender, emotional lyricism, and, most importantly, their total lack of indifference to the world. There is always passionate blood pulsing beneath the restrained outer form of their works.[46]

As Simon Karlinsky has observed, the "obvious superficiality" of the view that Tchaikovsky is Chekhov's musical counterpart, due to an "aura of melancholy that surrounds the art of both in the minds of many Russians," does not lessen the beauty of the final lines of Pasternak's poem "Winter is Approaching" (cited at the beginning of this article), in which Chekhov, Tchaikovsky, and Levitan are aligned. Pasternak's poem on autumn was written in 1943, and its last lines may well have been inspired by Shostakovich's article on Tchaikovsky, written earlier in the year.

Chekhov may indeed have dedicated the collection *Gloomy People* to Tchaikovsky, but, as his famous letter to Pleshcheev of April 1889 shows, the melancholy theme in his writings was always a means to an end, not an end in itself; it was precisely the painful gap between reality and the ideal that produced in Chekhov his elegiac perception of life:

> My goal . . . is to paint life in its true aspects, and to show how far this life falls short of the ideal life. I don't know what this ideal life is, just as it is unknown to all of us. We all know what a dishonest deed is, but who has looked upon the face of honor? I shall keep to the truth that is nearest my heart, and which has been tested by men stronger and wiser than I am. This truth is the absolute freedom of man, freedom from oppression, from prejudices, ignorance, passions, etc.[47]

Ever-sensitive to the contingency of being, the existential Chekhov shrank from imposing any kind of ideology on his readers, but Gurov's words in "The Lady with a Little Dog" neatly encapsulate a sentiment that seems to lie at the heart of his writing: "In essence, when one considers it, everything is really beautiful in this world—everything except what we think and do ourselves when we forget the higher aims of life and our own human dignity."[48]

Like Tchaikovsky, Chekhov probes the painful incongruities of life, leading us from familiar territory into the unfamiliar. For Tchaikovsky this might mean transforming an apparently sentimental melody into something altogether more sophisticated, while for Chekhov it entails presenting the reader with the absurdity of a world in which a dissolute, alcoholic priest is more truly a Christian than his pious superior (Chekhov, being of a younger generation than Tchaikovsky, was far more of a modernist). Shostakovich clearly understood the nature of the pathos in the writings of Chekhov and the music of Tchaikovsky, asserting that their "perception of the tragic" was the same, and drawing an analogy between Tchaikovsky's Sixth Symphony and Chekhov's story "The Black Monk" ("which is, by the way, one of the most musical works of Russian literature, written almost in sonata form").[49] Shostakovich challenges the misconception that Tchaikovsky's work is "'tinged' with the spirit of pessimism," and his thoughts on the nature of tragedy in Tchaikovsky help us understand how it is presented in Chekhov's work.

This misconception stems from the fact that certain contemporary researchers, like the majority of pre-revolutionary critics and musicologists, confuse pessimism with a vivid sense of the tragic. In all the centuries of world art, man's tragic conception of the world has never been better expressed than in the Greek tragedies. Yet no one would ever think of reproaching them for pessimism. Tchaikovsky has the same sense of the tragic, conflicting development of human life. With the perspicacity of a true philosopher, and the intuition of a great artist, he sensed the contradictory, dialectical path of world development, of the fate of man and mankind. But Tchaikovsky's work does not bear the stamp of fatalism or gloom. His most tragic works are moved by the spirit of struggle, and by the aspiration to overcome blind, elemental forces.[50]

In the Sixth Symphony, according to Shostakovich, the "dominant idea is not resignation but determination to overcome a tragic fate." In this symphony, which was always planned with a program in mind, the principle of polarity is clearer than in any other of his works, with extremes of dynamics matching its thematic extremes. Tchaikovsky describes such polarity in a note:

> Following is essence of plan for a symphony *Life!* First movement—all impulse, confidence, thirst for activity. Must be short (Finale *death*—result of collapse). Second movement love; third disappointment; fourth ends with a dying away (also short).[51]

Chekhov's "The Black Monk" (which incidentally contains a quotation from *Eugene Onegin*) is also a meditation on life and death, with the principles of polarity and paradox exhibited on every level of the story, which indeed appears to be constructed in a way that is similar to sonata form, as Shostakovich suggests.[52] The story strangely follows a similar program. Its central hero Kovrin, though exhausted, is inspired by his hallucinations of a mysterious black monk, and wants to devote his life to work. He falls in love with his guardian's daughter Tania, and they marry. His life begins to disintegrate, however, when she tries to cure him of his hallucinations. After leaving Tania, Kovrin contracts tuberculosis and dies. The many ambiguities inherent in this story make it difficult to agree wholeheartedly with Shostakovich's contention that it is, from the point of view of tragedy, a literary counterpart to the Sixth Symphony in every respect; it is impossible, for example, to identify fully with any of the characters. Nonetheless, the story is emblematic of the random, senseless, and comic nature of Chekhovian tragedy in general: the hallucination of the Black Monk that inspires Kovrin with such zest for life is in reality a messenger of death; he himself is far more attractive a human being when he is insane than when "cured"; his guardian (the famed horticulturalist Pesotsky) distorts his plants and trees as much as he nurtures them; his fiancee Tania seems to age ten years when she accepts his proposal of marriage, and so on.

While it is impossible to say to what extent Tchaikovsky and Chekhov might have influenced each other creatively, there is clearly a bond between their respective oeuvres that transcends mutual affection, similarities in personality, and historical contiguity. These two great elegists of the late 19th century seem to have felt instinctively that there was a fundamental artistic compatability between their works, in terms of both theme and technique. While interesting in and of itself, the story of Tchaikovsky's relationship to the writings of Chekhov may also have valuable potential as a key to unraveling some of the mysteries of the composer's life and work; but this must await detailed investigation.

NOTES

1. B. Pasternak, *Stikhotvoreniia i poemy,* ed. L. A. Ozerov (Moscow, 1965), p. 415.

2. E. Balabanovich, *Chekhov i Chaikovskii* (Moscow, 1978).

3. I. Eiges, *Muzyka v zhizni i tvorchestve Chekhova* (Moscow, 1953); I. Kremlev, "Chekhov i muzyka," *Sovetskaia muzyka,* 8 (1954); L. Gromov, "Chekhov i Chaikovskii," *Chekhovskie chteniia* (Rostov-on-Don, 1974).

4. David Brown, "Tchaikovsky and Chekhov," *Slavonic and Western Music: Essays for Gerald Abraham*, ed. Malcolm Hamrick Brown and Roland John Wiley (Ann Arbor, 1985), pp. 197–205.

5. For a more three-dimensional view, see Donald Rayfield's biography, *Anton Chekhov: A Life* (London, 1997) and Alexander Poznansky, *Tchaikovsky: The Quest for the Inner Man* (New York, 1991).

6. Brown, "Tchaikovsky and Chekhov," p. 204.

7. Gerard McBurney, *Sense and Sentimentality*, BBC Promenade Concerts Programme, 1993, pp. 19–22.

8. N. Kashkin, *Vospominaniia o P. I. Chaikovskom*, cited in A. P. Chekhov, *Polnoe sobranie sochinenii i pisem*, ed. N. F. Bel'chikov et al. (Moscow, 1960–74), vol. 6, p. 656.

9. Balabanovich, op. cit., pp. 64–65.

10. Brown, op. cit., pp. 197–98.

11. Letter cited in Alexandra Orlova, *Tchaikovsky: A Self Portrait* (Oxford, 1990), pp. 311–12.

12. See Orlova, op. cit., p. 296.

13. See Orlova, op. cit., pp. 336–339.

14. Brown, op. cit., pp. 198–99.

15. Simon Karlinsky, "The Gentle Subversive," *Anton Chekhov's Life and Thought* (Berkeley, 1973), p. 13.

16. Brown, op. cit., p.198.

17. Balabanovich, op. cit., p. 64.

18. Rayfield, op. cit., p. 156.

19. D. D. Shostakovich, "Mysli o Chaikovskom," *Literatura i iskusstvo*, 5 June, 1943. See my article "Shostakovich and Chekhov," *Shostakovich in Context*, ed. R. Bartlett (Oxford University Press, forthcoming) for further details.

20. Cited in Karlinsky, op. cit., p. 13.

21. See Balabanovich, op. cit., pp. 89–90.

22. Cited Balabanovich, op. cit., p. 97.

23. Cited in Brown, op. cit., p. 199.

24. Balabanovich, op. cit., pp. 101–104.

25. Brown, op. cit., p. 201.

26. Rayfield, op. cit., p. 155.

27. Balabanovich, op. cit., p. 85.

28. P. Bitsilli, *Chekhov's Art: A Stylistic Analysis*, tr. T. W. Clyman and E. J. Cruise (Ann Arbor, 1983), p. 87.

29. Bitsilli, op. cit., p. 101.

30. Cited in Balabanovich, op. cit., p. 118.

31. Balabanovich, op. cit., p. 120.

32. G. Struve, "On Chekhov's Craftsmanship: The Anatomy of a Story" (1961), reprinted in *Anton Chekhov's Short Stories*, ed. Ralph Matlaw (New York, 1979), pp. 330, 332.

33. H. Peter Stowell, "Chekhov's Prose Fugue: 'Sleepy,'" *Russian Literature Triquarterly*, 11 (1975), pp. 435–442.

34. Bitsilli, op. cit. p. 76.

35. Chekhov, *Polnoe sobranie sochinenii i pisem*, vol. 7, p. 200.

36. Marena Senderovich, "The Symbolic Structure of Chekhov's Story 'An Attack of Nerves,'" in P. Debreczeny and T. Eekman, eds., *Chekhov's Art of Writing: A Collection of Critical Essays* (Columbus, 1977), pp. 11–26.

37. See Elizabeth Wilson, *Shostakovich: A Life Remembered* (London, 1994), p. 170.

38. Conversation with Irina Antonovna Shostakovich, Moscow, June 1996.

39. Kenneth Lantz, "Chekhov's 'Gusev': A Study," *Studies in Short Fiction*, 15 (1978), p. 57.

40. Letter dated 29 November 1923, *Sotheby's London Catalogue: Fine Printed and Manuscript Music, including the Mannheim Collection*, 6 December 1991, p. 151.

41. Balabanovich, op. cit., p. 149.

42. Chekhov, *Polnoe sobranie sochinenii i pisem*, vol. 6, p. 335.

43. Balabanovich, op. cit., p. 108.

44. Isaiah Berlin, "Tchaikovsky, Pushkin and Onegin," *Musical Times*, cxxi (1980) p. 165.

45. G. McBurney, op. cit., pp. 20–21.

46. Cited in *Dmitry Shostakovich About Himself and His Times*, ed. L. Grigor'ev and Y. Platek, tr. A. and N. Roxburgh (Moscow, 1981), p. 105.

47. Anton Chekhov, *Letters on the Short Story, the Drama and Other Literary Topics*, ed. Louis. S. Friedland (New York, 1924), p. 60.

48. Chekhov, *Polnoe sobranie sochinenii i pisem*, vol. 10, p. 134.

49. Shostakovich, op. cit., p. 105.

50. Shostakovich, op. cit., p. 105.

51. Poznansky, op. cit., p. 558.

52. See my article "Sonata Form in Chekhov's "The Black Monk," *Intersections and Transpositions: Russian Music, Literature and Society*, ed. A. Wachtel (Northwestern University Press, forthcoming) for further details. See also L.M. Toole's discussion of complexity of the structural principles in "The Black Monk" in *Structure, Style and Interpretation in the Russian Short Story* (New Haven and London, 1982), pp. 161–79.

Tchaikovsky and the Russian "Silver Age"

BY ARKADII KLIMOVITSKY
TRANSLATED BY ALICE DAMPMAN HUMEL

Three years ago the world celebrated Tchaikovsky's 150th birthday, and today's anniversary has very quickly "caught up" to that one. The temporal proximity of these two so dissimilar memorials seems to embody the dramatic character of Tchaikovsky's fate, both as a man and as a composer. Even more: the closeness of the "round" remembrances, which can be quite shocking in its sinister uncanniness, reveals the unfortunate inseparability of life and death, to which Tchaikovsky and his art had a tormented relationship and which transformed itself into an ambiguous metaphor for his life and the historical destiny of his artistic heritage.

One hundred years separate us from Tchaikovsky's death. And these one hundred years encompass practically the entire twentieth century! I presume to state that we are closer to the great composer than his contemporaries were; what differentiates us from them is the knowledge of all the events that separate us and of all these hundred years contain. Historical experience has brought us closer to Tchaikovsky. What is most affecting to us about his music is not its unmitigated simplicity. We readily embrace a more complex insight into the music as a phenomenon that has revealed itself in the course of history and leads to ever new meanings. It is given to us to create a "new portrait" of Tchaikovsky from the vantage point of the close of our century.

The present article seeks to draw in some of the features of that new portrait, the most fundamental and essential of which are to be discovered in the Russian "Silver Age." One understands the significance of this discovery to its fullest extent only when one is aware of one of the most important cultural and historical paradoxes connected with Tchaikovsky: however enormous the socio-cultural reach of his music and its dissemination may be, in the destiny of his artistic heritage there have been some very dramatic developments.

This paradox was expressed in the amazing ease with which his contemporaries received Tchaikovsky's music as something of their very own—something about them and for them; thus it was demonstrated from the outset that the nature of the reception of this music was not comprehension, but consumption. His contemporaries contented themselves with a direct emotional response, quenching their thirst for the "spiritual" and the "psychological," with no desire whatsoever to delve into the intellectual aspect of the music. "Simplicity," "accessibility," and "truthfulness"—an insipid set of virtues that made it possible for the philosophical depth and the spiritual interest of Tchaikovsky's music to penetrate into the furthest reaches of the inner lives of those listeners who identified themselves with the ideal hero of music and were entirely content with that—served the tradition-laden awareness of a much extolled "common sense" as a paradigm of those ideas.

At the beginning of the twentieth century Tchaikovsky, ever present in the minds of the musical masses, was transformed into an object of emulation. The result was those imitators whom Gennadii Rozhdestvensky has pointedly called "little Tchaikovskys." They reflected the mighty emanations of Tchaikovsky's great talent in something of a distorting mirror. Also, for the audiences of the first decades of the twentieth century, the "old and past" was concentrated in Tchaikovsky's music. His art and the singularity of his musical language and orientation embodied a romantic ideology which proved a target for the sharp arrows of antiromanticism. His music also proved a prime target for the Russian cultural Bolsheviks. But soon Tchaikovsky was given the honor of a place on the pedestal reserved for the "classical great." This earned his music affection and good will, but no compelling interest. Since the totalitarian regime approved the subjective romantic experience as the standard measure of *Innerlichkeit*, it localized this experience into a series of official state "portraits," and included one of Tchaikovsky. All this led to an oppressive yet almost natural ubiquity of Tchaikovsky's music in everyday life, resulting in the estrangement of its musical language from the modern listener and an aesthetic devaluation.

The two decades around the turn of the century in Russia stand out from this otherwise bleak picture. This is the period when the original and true "Tchaikovsky cult" arose. The discovery of Tchaikovsky during this Silver Age was one of the most momentous occurrences in Russian cultural history, greatly stimulating the devel-

opment of Russian self-assurance and the unveiling of internal potential and additional prospects.

The turn-of-the-century Tchaikovsky cult had nothing in common
with the great popularity of his music among the general public mentioned above. This cult was far more the product of the cultural elite
and its eternal quest for new developments in all the arts. It captured
not only the established generation but, more importantly, the young—
those very people who would soon bear the reproof of the "oldsters"
who occupied positions of guardianship because of their devotion to the
modern and avant garde and their rejection of national tradition.
Today, from an observation point at the end of the twentieth century,
we can clearly see that the most prominent features of the new portrait
of Tchaikovsky were drawn by the Russian Silver Age.

Who first used the term Silver Age? Nikolai Berdiaev, R. Ivanov-
Razumnik, or Nikolai Ozup is considered the originator. The list
could undoubtedly be longer, but there is absolutely no doubt that
Anna Akhmatova was instrumental in the dissemination of the expression when she wrote, in her "Poem Without a Hero"

> The Galernaia Arch darkens,
> In the summer garden the weather-vane
> Sang in falsetto, and the silver moon
> Froze over the silver age.

Akhmatova's poem is riddled with real references to pre-World
War I Petersburg life, subjects and situations easily recognized by
those contemporaries forced into exile by the tragic circumstances. It
stirred up a storm of reverberation in utterances and memoirs in
which the term Silver Age was used quite naturally. In the literature,
the meaning of the expression was a singular one, as it was immediately connected with another metaphor firmly established in the col-
lective consciousness of the society: the age of Pushkin had been
known since the beginning as the Golden Age. As a concept in cultural
history, Silver Age has an even greater significance: right below the
surface shines the atmosphere of the Russian cultural renaissance of
the turn of the century, as Nikolai Berdiaev defines this epoch. The
time frame of this period extends from the last decade of the nineteenth century to the Bolshevik Revolution and the Civil War. The
Silver Age was represented in literature by prominent members of
many generations of the symbolists. Dimitrii Merezhkovsky, Zinaida
Gippius (Hippius), Konstantin Balmont, Fëdor Sologub, Innokentii
Annensky belonged to the older generation; Andrei Bely, Aleksandr

Blok, Jurgis (Iurii) Baltrushaitis, and Viacheslav Ivanov represented the young symbolists; their younger contemporaries and detractors Mikhail Kuzmin, Nikolai Gumilëv, Osip Mandelshtam (Mandelstamm) and Anna Akhmatova called themselves the Acmeists; and finally Maksimilian Voloshin must be mentioned. The group "Mir Iskusstva" (The World of Art) represented the Silver Age in painting. Igor Stravinsky and Sergei Prokofiev matured in the atmosphere of the Silver Age, too.

How was the Silver Age so enormously influenced by Tchaikovsky? For what is it indebted to this composer? Primarily one must bear in mind that the Tchaikovsky cult that came about as a result of the premiere of *The Queen of Spades* in 1890 revolved around a composer who was never numbered among the musical revolutionaries by his contemporaries, as were for example Beethoven or Wagner, Musorgsky or Scriabin, composers who knew how to stir up unrest in the social consciousness. Neither did this cult begin in the music world; in that world Tchaikovsky received love and recognition, but also criticism, as seen for example in the comments of Herman Laroche, who was quite close to Tchaikovsky.[1] The founders of the cult were rather poets, painters, and philosophers of the Silver Age. For them, Tchaikovsky embodied the "Petersburg mythos" in music.

The Petersburg mythos is a central theme in Russian culture. The city, its history and its daily life were endowed with a phantasmagoric air, and the expression "Petersburg Hoffmanniana" was born. The Silver Age brought the artists' enthusiasm for the Petersburg mythos to its zenith. One thinks in this context of *Petersburg* by Bely, "The Requital" and "Twelve" by Blok, and "Poem Without a Hero" by Anna Akhmatova. But the gestalt of Tchaikovsky is right there at the heart and soul of the Petersburg mythos.

Tchaikovsky was the link between Pushkins's Petersburg and the Petersburg of the Silver Age. Russian society reread Pushkin's tale "The Queen of Spades" and listened to Tchaikovsky's musical version of the same. The composer debated with the author, so to speak, and was victorious over him. Tchaikovsky allowed his contemporaries to forget the purposefully prosaic ending of Pushkin's story, but in return allowed them to believe in the natural reality of the scenes he had expanded in his opera and to see them as the only possible situations for the protagonists. The best example of this is the scene on the Simniaia Kanavka, the canal into which Liza throws herself in despair, and the scene of Hermann's suicide. Is this not the victory that Blok meant when he wrote about *The Queen of Spades*, "the Apollo

Pushkin tumbled into the abyss, where a right hook from Tchaikovsky, the magician and musician, landed him."[2]

Blok's metaphor impresses us not only with its expressive power, but with its ruthless precision: Tchaikovsky's victory over Pushkin in the matter of *The Queen of Spades* was undisputed, as can be seen in the many reminiscences about the opera in Bely's *Petersburg*, and in the poetry of Blok, Kuzmin, and Akhmatova. For these great masters, all of whom knew the works of Pushkin intimately, it was the opera *The Queen of Spades* that acquired definitive significance. In the name of the generation of the Silver Age, Boris Asafiev called Tchaikovsky a "historian of Petersburg."

Tchaikovsky's love for the eighteenth century provided Russia with a new realm of cultural and intellectual experience, first seriously cultivated in its twentieth century art. A cult of Mozart, the galant style, rococo art, and pastoral motifs were some of the characteristic features of the eighteenth century, foreshadowings of the painting of Benois and Somov and of the quest for "beautiful clarity" (M. Kuzmin) in the writings of the Acmeists. Without exception the adherents of the future Mir Iskusstva made a direct connection, as Benois later did, between their impressions of the premiere of *The Queen of Spades* and the deciding moment in the designing of the aesthetic platform of their organization. Sergei Diaghilev, Léon Bakst, Konstantin Somov, and Mstislav Dobuzhinsky all maintained a passionate love for Tchaikovsky throughout their lives, and found great inspiration for their own work in his music.

Other aspects of this relationship are connected with the ballet *The Nutcracker*. This time Tchaikovsky bridged the gap between E.T.A. Hoffman and "Mir iskusstva." Hoffman's idea of the alternation of the human and toy world so meaningfully brought out in Tchaikovsky's *The Nutcracker* attracted Blok, Bely, and Akhmatova in their writing, as well as Benois and Dobuzhinsky in their painting. In the ballet, Tchaikovsky expanded the scope of retrospective motifs to a much greater extent than in *The Queen of Spades*. This reference to the eighteenth-century world of the doll-like resurfaces in Russian turn-of-the-century art as little toy shepherds or marionette masks. In keeping with the spirit of the times, bold geometric forms and sharp hard lines were also integrated into the aesthetic concept. The flute parts in the Chinese Dance in *The Nutcracker*,[3] with their harlequinesque octave leaps, show definite early traits of neoprimitivism.

The Nutcracker was chronologically the first real ballet of miniatures. The Divertimento ("Confitürenberg") of Act II presaged the abstract ballets of the twentieth century and in fact prepared the way for the ballet reforms of Mikhail Fokine and the "Russian ballet season" of Sergei Diaghilev. If Tchaikovsky had not written *The Nutcracker*, then Stravinsky, Fokine, Benois, and Nijinsky could never have created *Petrushka*, the work that most effectively realized the ideals of Mir Iskusstva.

The loyalty of the representatives of Mir Iskusstva to Tchaikovsky's art was not restricted to the tastes and inclinations of individual members. The loyalty was of a much more objective nature, determined by developments in Russian culture. An anonymous little feature article with the heading "From the Past," in the newspaper *Theater*, provided paradoxical verification of this.[4] According to this article, Tchaikovsky was under the impression that the premiere of *The Queen of Spades* was a dismal failure and allegedly wandered the streets of Petersburg, alone and lonely. Suddenly he heard one of the "most compelling" parts in the opera, the duet between Liza and Polina,[5] being sung. The composer saw three young men in student garb, introduced himself to them, and asked them how they had managed to learn such a new piece of music so quickly. The young men then introduced themselves in their turn—Sergei Diaghilev, Alexandre Benois, and Dimitrii Filosofev. From that moment on—so the anonymous author concluded—the participants in that nocturnal meeting nurtured a close and intimate friendship, until the death of the composer.

It is unlikely that the three young men remained ignorant of the above-quoted piece, particularly as all three really did attend the premiere of *The Queen of Spades* after having procured the piano reduction and familiarized themselves with the music beforehand. And so this amazing meeting could truly have happened; none of those named ever contradicted the story.

There is another aspect that is far more important. Even if the anonymous author had invented his story, it proves that, in the sociocultural climate of the beginning of our century, the intellectual connection between Tchaikovsky and Mir Iskusstva was so immediate and generally validated that it had to become legend and mythology.

Tchaikovsky's relationship to Russian symbolism and its characteristic utopian views is typical of that of most turn-of-the-century Russian artists; he had a general and broad interest in the philosophical, moral/religious, and social questions of the time. In 1879 Tchaikovsky became smitten with and immersed himself in the writings of the Russian religious philosopher Vladimir Soloviev, the great authority in symbolist circles, as well as the writings of Boris Chicherin, whose philosophy was related to that of Soloviev. In 1884

Tchaikovsky composed two Romances on poems by Dimitrii Merezhkovsky—"Usni!" (Go to Sleep) and "Smert'" (Death), Op. 57, Nos. 4 and 5. Although they cannot be numbered among his masterpieces, their significance dare not be underestimated, as they are the first musical interpretations of poetry by one of the most renowned of the Russian symbolists.

The first real interaction with the emotional and psychical atmosphere of symbolism came in the opera *Iolanta*, Op. 69 (1891)[6] and in *The Nutcracker*. Both works possess characteristics of singular spiritualization, sublime intensification, and meaningful obscurity. In the opera as well as in the ballet there are situations with no external action, in which the primary focus is on previously unnoticed details of the emotional and psychical lives of the dramatis personae.

In both works Tchaikovsky designs a poetry of the "not spoken," the "intimated," the "penumbral," and at the same time of an ecstasy and a religious/pantheistic Utopia. For this he is certainly indebted to the Romantics. However, Russian Romanticism never really touched upon this area. It was given to Tchaikovsky to create a model of the emotional/spiritual experience lacking until then in Russian musical tradition, and consequently a system of the illustrative and the expressive, new to the national culture. It got its name only in connection with the work of the representatives of symbolist art, but the social consciousness recognized and acknowledged it in many respects thanks to Tchaikovsky: he prepared his countrymen for their encounter with symbolism.

Richard Wagner's role in Russian symbolism is well known. It was however not so much the composer's music that found resonance in Russian culture, but rather his philosophical/aesthetic ideas. The exceptionally strong resonance of Tchaikovsky's music in Russia's symbolist circles was due to the transformation through music of the listener's emotional/spiritual experience into an object of contemplation; this created an atmosphere in which Wagner's theoretical ideas did not seem to be abstracted from the world of sound that embodied them. (One remembers that the musical experience of most of the symbolists was very limited: they felt most secure with the abstract "music of the spheres.") When the Russian symbolists confronted Wagner, they leaned heavily on their experience with Tchaikovsky.

The late works adopted so enthusiastically by the symbolist circles were the ones in which Tchaikovsky juxtaposed himself to Wagner. Tchaikovsky's last opera, *Iolanta*, is a good example of this. While he was working on the opera, the composer wrote to I. V. Iakoviev, one of his old friends, "a subject matter has been found with which I will prove to the entire world that the lovers in the final scenes of operas should live, and that this is a real truth."[7] In this debate, Tchaikovsky called upon "the entire world" to reverse their belief in the opposite fate for the lovers in the final scenes of operas—particularly *Tristan und Isolde*, by Richard Wagner. Tchaikovsky experienced it for the first time in Berlin in 1882, and retained his dismissive attitude toward the work for the rest of his life. Nonetheless, Tchaikovsky's *Iolanta* reflected quite clearly impressions from Wagner's *Tristan und Isolde*. This can be seen in a comparison of nothing more than the orchestral introductions. They have in common a tonal ambiguity (in neither is there a key signature given, nor is there ever an identifiable tonic) and an entirely chromatically woven sound texture. Both are introduced by sequences, and in both, the following link in the chain of sequences begins with the highest of the concluding pitches from the preceding one. Finally, in both, movement is suspended by diminished seventh chords leading into the caesura between sequences in the series. Tchaikovsky's sequential motif is basically nothing more than an exact inversion of the chromatic motifs in the responses of the oboe and clarinet that conclude the sequential elements in the prelude of *Tristan*. Both encompass a minor third, but Wagner uses variation in timbre, whereas Tchaikovsky develops the motifs in one voice and one color as a solo line for the English horn. Furthermore, the upward motion of the minor third in Wagner's sequential elements corresponds to a downward movement in Tchaikovsky's.

One can definitely recognize in the *Tristan* Prelude the harmonic example found in the introduction to *Iolanta*, both as regards the expressivity of the unresolved and dovetailing dissonances, as well as the unusual harmonic richness of color. Furthermore, both introductions have the same time signature. The unusual colors in the introduction to *Iolanta*—English horn accompanied by woodwinds—are anticipated in the horn solo in the third act of *Tristan*, and the linear outlines of the cello motifs with which the *Tristan* Prelude begins (A–f–e) bear a formative impression on the very first measure of the introduction to *Iolanta*. All this indicates that, while he was working on his last opera, Tchaikovsky reflected upon Wagner's *Tristan*, either consciously or involuntarily; and he was referring to *Tristan*, perhaps without even being aware of it himself, when he made the polemic remark quoted above, that he wanted to present to the entire world his own concept of the proper representation of the fate of lovers on the operatic stage.

Tchaikovsky also confronts Wagner in *The Nutcracker*, but in an entirely different way. One thinks of two episodes that can be regarded to a certain extent as symphonic. The "Magic Spell" scene[8] is so heavily reminiscent of Wagner's richly colorful orchestral harmonies in the area of illustrative music that it borders on quotation. The episode entitled "The Growing of the Pine Trees"[9] is unquestionably an "endless melody," but composed in Tchaikovsky's own style, not in Wagner's.

The increasing strength of contemporary cultural movements as a factor in Tchaikovsky's Wagnerism can be seen as purely coincidental. However, one must think about Gustav Mahler's pertinent words about the essence of a composer: "One is oneself merely an instrument, so to speak, on which the universe plays."[10] According to Mahler's formulation, Tchaikovsky's Wagnerism was something unexpected that was only indirectly connected to Russian symbolism. (*Iolanta*, by the way, which took for its own so many impulses from *Tristan*, its medieval subject matter as well as its lyrical-philosophical density, anticipates much in Blok, including his drama *Rose and Cross*. And in a letter, Anna Akhmatova identified herself with *Iolanta*.[11]) Wagner influenced Russian symbolist philosophers, theoreticians, and artists primarily as a thinker. Tchaikovsky's image of the musician Wagner reflected in Tchaikovsky's own music gave the Russian cultural elite a more complete picture of their Bayreuth idol.

It was not the Wagnerian dimension in the sound of Tchaikovsky's late works that earned the applause of intellectuals. For the symbolists, the "Waltz of the Snowflakes" from the *Nutcracker*[12] was the real event: its novel tone-painting, connected with a metaphorical interpretation of the means of expression and a new imagery, was about an inexplicable unity of deeply-felt lyricism, unhealthy phantasmagoria, the finest impressionistic sound painting, and melancholy enigma. The semantic purview of the music encompasses Pushkin's "Snowstorm," as well as the future "Whirlwind" by Blok, Bely's "Goblet of Blizzards" and Akhmatova's "Ball." The elements of the waltz form an organic whole—a strict chaconne (eight variations over a retained harmonic pattern) symbolically represents a fatal reserve, the predetermination of the fates of the characters in the story, and the enchantment of the dance.

Tchaikovsky embodies an artistic pose otherwise not intrinsic to Russian musical culture: he was master of a number of different styles. Tchaikovsky himself took great pains to emphasize this—and his contemporaries were very conscious of whether their opinions of him were affected positively or negatively thereby. Tchaikovsky knew well the compositional principles of the circle around Balakirev and employed them, for example, in the eighth variation in the final movement of the Third Orchestral Suite, Op. 55 (1884)[13] and also to a certain extent in the final movement, "Tema russo," of the Serenade for String Orchestra, Op. 48 (1880).[14] The final movement, "Danse baroque," of the Second Orchestral Suite, Op. 53 (1883),[15] subtitled "In the style of Dargomyzhsky," is also indicative of this. Tchaikovsky imitates the strict style in Variation VII of the last movement of the Third Orchestral Suite;[16] deliberately and with some reserve, on the other hand, he imitates the Romantic style in the solo violin cadenza in Variation IX of that same final movement;[17] and early classicism in the *Rococo Variations*, Op. 33,[18] in the Orchestral Suites,[19] in *The Queen of Spades*,[20] and in *The Nutcracker*.[21] Through his example of working from a model, Tchaikovsky prepared the way for neoclassicism and presaged much of what Stravinsky and Prokofiev, influenced by the atmosphere of the Silver Age, did later in their own ways.

Tchaikovsky, who could have foreseen many of the cultural manifestations of the Silver Age, became himself an object of its interpretations. The image of Tchaikovsky as the author of unadorned and open music that had firmly rooted itself in the consciousness of his contemporaries gradually gave way to a new understanding of his art. Stravinsky was apparently the first to recognize, through the emotional outpouring of candor and heartiness of Tchaikovsky's distinctive way, a great master who possessed an enormous creative and intellectual will and whose artistic creative principles and simplicity extended far beyond the framework of a romantic ideal of the artist. The symbolists heard in Tchaikovsky's music apocalyptic and eschatological motifs. This was particularly true of Blok, who reacted with special sensitivity to the themes of despair and the end of the world: not in vain does he ominously rhyme the line from Tomsky's ballade in *The Queen of Spades*[22] with the word "fate" in the verses he wrote in 1905. Tchaikovsky's opera determines for Blok the name of the main character, Hermann, in his allegorical drama *Song of Destiny*. The opera also played a large determining role in the conception of Bely's *Petersburg*, the most significant novel of the twentieth century. There was much discussion of Tchaikovsky as perceived by Akhmatova and Kuzmin, who all heard "pre-symbolist" traits in his work. The representatives of Mir Iskusstva vehemently rejected, on the other hand, Tchaikovsky's classicistic aberrations, his creative treatment of the styles of the eighteenth century, which in many respects influenced the dance in Stravinsky and Prokofiev and anticipated the gavotte-like elements in the latter's music.

The Tchaikovsky of the Silver Age was spiritually eliminated in Bolshevik Russia; when an entire generation of this epoch was physically eliminated, so was their cultural milieu. One of the farewell blasts of the Silver Age in Tchaikovsky's honor was Vsevolod Meyerhold's renowned 1935 production of *The Queen of Spades*, which met with ruinous reviews and was also literally destroyed.

The ideas of Bely and Benois, Diaghilev, Somov, Dobuzhinsky, and others have recently resurfaced. After a delay of more than half a century, a book about Tchaikovsky written by the late Nina Berberova in 1936[23] has been published in Russia: finally the word about Tchaikovsky from the Silver Age can resound in his own homeland.

Today when we think about Tchaikovsky, we are compelled to corroborate that the portrait of the composer painted by the Silver Age does not display him as some precious museum piece, but rather as an artist capable of infinite development; and this portrait of Tchaikovsky is not only true to the original, it points the way into the future.

NOTES

1. See for example Hermann Laroche, *Peter Tchaikovsky, Aufsätze und Erinnerungen*. Selected, translated, and edited by Ernst Kuhn. With notes about Herman Laroche by Modest Tchaikovsky and Nikolai Kashkin, as well as an original contribution from Thomas Kohlhase (Berlin, 1993).

2. Aleksandr Blok, *Sobranie sochinenii v vosmi tomakh*, Volume 8 (Moscow-Leningrad 1963), p. 150.

3. Act II, Scene 3, No. 12v, Tea (Chinese Dance), *Chaikovskii Polnoe Sobranie Sochinenii* (hereafter CPSS), 136, pp 86–93.

4. Moscow, February 12–13, 1912, No. 1017, p. 13.

5. Act I, Scene 2, No. 7, *CPSS* 9a, pp. 187–95.

6. *CPSS* 10.

7. Elena Orlova, *Pëtr Ilich Chaikovskii*, Moskow 1980, p. 90.

8. Act I, Scene 1, Number 6, *CPSS* 13a, pp 142–82.

9. Ibid., pp. 165–82.

10. Gustav Mahler, *Briefe, Revidierte und erweiterte Ausgabe*, Hamburg, 1984, p. 165.

11. Letter to S. W. von Stein on February 2, 1907, in the periodical *Novyi mir*, 1986, Number 9, p. 203.

12. Act I, Scene 2, Conclusion, Number 9, *CPSS* 13a, pp 246–308.

13. *CPSS* 20, p. 148.

14. *CPSS* 20, pp. 347–66.

15. *CPSS* 19b, pp. 176–250, "Podrazanie Dargomyzhskomu."

16. *CPSS* 20, pp. 266–69.

17. *CPPS* 20, pp. 275–81.

18. *CPSS* 30b.

19. *CPSS* 19a, 19b, and 20.

20. *CPSS* 9a, b, and v.

21. *CPSS* 13a and b.

22. Act I, Scene 1, Number 5, *CPSS* 9a, pp. 129–44.

23. German edition: Nina Berberova, *Tschaikowsky. Geschichte eines einsamen Lebens*, translated from the Russian by Leo Borchard (Berlin 1938); revised French edition *Tchaikovski* (Arles 1987), German by Anna Kamp as: Nina Berberova, *Tschaikowsky. Biographie* (Düsseldorf, 1989).

Part III
Theoretical Writings

A Documentary Glance at Tchaikovsky
and Rimsky-Korsakov as Music Theorists[1]

INTRODUCED AND TRANSLATED
BY LYLE K. NEFF

With all of Tchaikovsky's popularity in the concert hall and the sensational aspects of his biography, it can easily escape the average enthusiast's notice or memory that during the decade or so when *Romeo and Juliet*, the first four symphonies, the three string quartets, the first piano concerto, the violin concerto, *Eugene Onegin*, and *Swan Lake* were composed, Tchaikovsky worked as a teacher of music theory, first starting in early 1866 in the classes given by the Moscow branch of the Russian Music Society and later that year on the staff of the new Moscow Conservatory. The subjects he taught over the years included harmony, orchestration, and composition. Among his significant former students were the music critic M. M. Ivanov,[2] the composer S. I. Taneev, and the conductor A. I. Siloti.

As a teacher Tchaikovsky seems to have given contradictory impressions to students. He thought himself an unfit instructor, but his Conservatory colleague N. D. Kashkin left a positive recollection, noting Tchaikovsky's diligence with the task despite frustration with the majority of students who looked on such course
work as a mere formality.[3] In 1871, while still on the faculty of the Moscow Conservatory, Tchaikovsky completed his *Rukovodstvo k prakticheskomu izucheniiu garmonii* (Guide to the practical study of harmony). Several ideas in this textbook, recognized as the first theory book modeled on Western practice and written by a Russian, became part of the pedagogical tradition at the Moscow Conservatory. As Ellon D. Carpenter notes, "Tchaikovsky's textbook significantly aided the development of a Russian theory of music. It provided a needed

Russian model for a practical, pedagogical textbook, a type of theory book that continued to dominate."[4] Although the *Guide* formed a convenient adjunct to his teaching load and its sales must have helped somewhat to boost his meager salary at the Conservatory, Tchaikovsky gave his primary rationale for compiling it in the modest but pointed prefatory remarks quoted here in full:

From the Compiler[5]

In setting about to compile the proposed guide, I intended least of all to introduce a new system, new views into musical science. Having satisfied myself that, with the developing musical talent of the public, the need for textbooks is growing more urgent with every day, I decided to help satisfy this need as far as possible.

Lovers of theoretical investigations and musico-philosophical reasonings will not find food for their inquisitiveness in my textbook; but I flatter myself with the hope that a generation of students will find there an aid on the path to a practical study of the art's technique. It does not delve deeply into the essence and cause of musically harmonic phenomena, nor does it endeavor to reveal the principles connecting in scientific unity the rules that bring about harmonic beauty; but it does set forth as logically as possible instructions, deduced by empirical means, for beginning musicians who seek a guide in their attempts at composition. From this I resolve not to call my modest, specifically pedagogical work by the fine-sounding name *theory*. If it is not doubted that musical science, as it gradually improves, will finally find the key to a theoretical elucidation of harmonic mysteries, one may be permitted to doubt that an acquaintance with present theories of harmony that are built upon sand can bring vital benefit to students. Nothing so confuses the beginner, nothing so weakens his energy and zeal for the study of music, as the diffuse, fine-sounding, verbose, though perhaps also witty expatiations on harmony that are encountered in some textbooks and used without effect by some teachers.

Thus, I repeat, my guide does not add one iota to the treasure-house of theories on music; I know that in the rich musico-pedagogical literature it would pass as an unnoticed phenomenon. But in Russia, which scarcely has just one good translated work in this field,[6] I dare to think that my work, which pursues serious practical goals in the matter of music, has some qualities that make it useful; it is called for by the obvious necessity for textbooks.

Nizy, August 2nd, 1871.

P. Tchaikovsky

With the advent of his patron, Madame Nadezhda von Meck, and the financial ease which ensued, Tchaikovsky finally resigned from the staff of the Conservatory in 1878 to pursue a full career in composition. This did not, however, mean an end to his activity as a sometime mentor in theory and composition. In the first letter given here, from 1883, we witness Tchaikovsky's response to a young would-be composer who sent him some fugues and "free" compositions to examine. Tchaikovsky prefaces his comments on the fugues with an explanation of counterpoint, particularly from a historical, developmental perspective, and then proceeds to discuss an overture and a quartet by the addressee.

Letter of P. I. Tchaikovsky to V. A. Pakhulsky[7]

Paris, April 10/22, 1883

Vladislav Albertovich! First of all, I will talk with you about your labors in counterpoint. What is counterpoint? This word sounds notorious, dreadful; and ignorant people fancy that this is some kind of musical gibberish. Meanwhile, there is nothing simpler. Counterpoint is the *consonant* combination of two or several voices. In its simplest form, between the high *voice* or high *voices* and the *fundamental* one, there is nothing except consonances, i. e., primes, fifths, thirds, sixths, octaves. In the more complex forms, which result from the melodic and rhythmic animation of the voices, dissonances, too, turn up in two forms: 1) syncope, i. e., dissonance on a strong beat (what is called suspension in the contemporary school), 2) dissonance on a weak beat, i. e., passing notes, auxiliary notes, cambiati, etc. All these dissonances impart inexpressible beauty and vitality to contrapuntal combinations, but on condition of a natural resolution to consonance. For a long time no other combinations of musical sounds were recognized. Later the dominant-seventh chord gained the right of citizenship and became so independent that the intervals that form it have obtained acceptance as if they were consonances, as a consequence of which *the tritone*, in both forms, the minor seventh and even its inversion, the second, have begun to be used without preparation, on strong beats of the measure, but with observance of the rules of resolution, i.e., the leading tone to the tonic, the fourth scale degree to the upper mediant. When counterpoint from the realm of vocal music turned to instrumental, chromaticism and the full freedom of modulations penetrated little by little into harmony. Counterpoint will not, should not go further than that. Yet it is happening in our time that we see contrapuntal works in which the fundamental principle of counterpoint is totally lost sight of. Dissonances are found in them not only in abundance, not only unprepared and unresolved, but held in such esteem and importance that it's as if everything were founded on them, and that natural combinations making consonance were only an inevitable evil the composers willingly would avoid completely, if it were possible. I will not say that your counterpoint was an example of a similar sort of exclusive predominance of consonances,[8]—but you are not far from that. At every step I meet in your fugues coincidences of voices that exceed my understanding. This is a kind of counterpoint for the *eyes*, not for the ears. Look . . . the voices possess the appearance of independent melodies, there is life and movement, and it is evident that your intentions were good— but when you begin to listen with an intrinsic ear, you very soon become tired, for the enormous quantity of dissonances, modulations, chromatic–enharmonic successions continually force you to stop in order to comprehend the *vestige* of a chord brought together by several voices as if alien to each other, and sometimes even the context doesn't help. In many such places I have placed question marks, but those places are far from the only ones that were incomprehensible and strange to me. If I made note everywhere of everything that seemed to me unnatural, forcibly put together, abrupt, ugly— then I would have to mark all over your whole manuscript, to the point of unrecognizableness. I don't know how to explain this phenomenon. Whether your teacher is to blame for being insufficiently strict to lead you along the path of contrapuntal subtlety, whether your nature is such that flexibility, healthy vitality, clarity and simplicity in harmony and voice-leading come to you with difficulty . . . but the only thing I can say is that your fugues in general cannot be called successful. In addition, they are all terribly long; they have a great number of interludes and inserted episodic parts, now too poor in modulation (i.e., the tonic predominates too much), now on the contrary stretched so far that an unnaturally quick return to the tonic and a forcible, unprepared ending must be made. It is evident that you meant to write them craftily, inventively—but this inventiveness and craft do not reach the goal, i. e., they do not delight, but they burden, they fatigue. How satisfied I'd be, if among your fugues there were at least a small one, with two or three more passages, but lucid, precise, simple, with irreproachable voice-leading (I even noted many *fifths and octaves* in your work, you know), with balanced form—well, in a word, a kind of fugue that befits a young person who is striving to refine his style and to learn, from the modest material of permitted and absolutely beautiful consonant combinations, to build a whole, fully finished form in sound. Of course, there are to be found in your fugues very nice, piquant, and beautiful episodes and details, and I don't want at all to say that everything is utterly bad—but I'd like you instead to study how to write in a masterly manner—simply; having looked through these fugues, I have experienced disappointment. The fugue with the inversion of the theme (F major) would be, perhaps, the most irreproachable from the technical side, but in it I've encountered *eleven dissonances in a row*, after which there is one fortuitous, consonant chord, and thereafter yet *4 dissonances*: in all sixteen consecutive combinations amoung which only one can be said to provide a place for the ear to rest on a chord!!!

I turn to the overture. Musically there is much in it that is very nice—for example, the first theme (in the spirit of Mendelssohn) is highly to my liking. The transition from the first theme to the second is too unwieldy. Much too soon have

you stated the first theme in all fullness, even furnishing it
with a concluding clause,

etc., and then, like something completely new, you begin the
second theme. Of course this is possible, for in music everything
is possible—but if you meant to write an overture in classic form,
this is a mistake. The ending, cast like Wagner, could have been
far more effective if the orchestration were not thick in the
extreme and, at the same time, insufficiently emphasizing the
primary idea. In general your orchestra is still alien. I would
very much advise you to practice writing for small orchestra
(without trombones), using the trumpets moderately as far as
possible. On the score I have made several remarks to which I
will ask you to pay attention. In places you write in a manner
that is *impossible* to play, you have even given notes to some
instruments that they don't at all possess. But the primary deficiency in the orchestration is the inordinate abundance of
details that disturb the attention, which is most strained, and
deprive your orchestra of strength and clarity. What disappointment would you experience if you heard in performance
the many places that are beautiful for the eyes—but which do
not satisfy the demands of the ear? This, however, is the fate of
all beginning composers. Only the very rare among them are
talented with such a flair for the orchestra that, almost without
having studied, they already display mastery. In the march the
orchestration is *much better*, although here, too, you don't treat
the brass with great consideration. For example, how crudely
this will sound, when two trumpets play the theme:

And how strangely you sometimes dispose the basses. For example, in one place the bass is thus:

Why is the 1st bassoon here playing a *solo* bass voice two octaves higher than the contrabass? No one will hear it, will they, and, besides, is this good? Next the string basses have a bass figuration, but the trombones are playing it at the same time in a simple manner, and they hinder each other to the point that, for example, on the strong beat of a measure one plays an E, the other a D#:

In the slow tempo of the march, this is very ugly. The *trio* of the march is good, but terribly short. At the end of it is a very unorchestral disposition of the harmonic voices. Is it possible that in the concluding cadence the triad on the dominant would be incomplete, without the third in the brass group?

Here it is:

In the orchestra, when the entire mass plays, it is precisely the middle that should be full!

As regards the quartet—of all the things you sent me, I like it much more than all the others; both with regard to inventiveness and in form, it is more mature and more solid. I've made such a lot of remarks to you that, in order not to spoil the impression of this last praise, I won't point out any mistakes in the quartet. And moreover it's so difficult in writing. God grant we see each other in the summer, and at that time it will be easy and pleasant for me to have a chat with you about all these screeds. And now I ask you, most kind Vladislav Al'bertovich, not to be embarrassed, not to be distressed, and not to complain of me for the great number of remarks that I've made, and in general for the fact that I seem to be scolding more than praising you. I know from experience how delicate a composer's feeling is, and I feel that I'm touching the sensitive strings of your composer's heart rather harshly. But, in order that my praises have worth, I *have* to tell the truth. Besides, why would you be in need of my compliments? I think that however brutal I may have been in my verdict, all the same this harshness is more useful than passing over the deficiencies in silence. However, I will say only this: be confident that I will be very, very glad when, in absolute honesty, it will be possible for me to approve some future composition of yours without any reservations. If you keenly feel within yourself the need to write, then don't for a minute lose courage, and patiently bear the captiousness of such a critic as I, who, the more severe I am, the more sincere is the friendly feeling that guides me when I have dealings with your attempts. I will immediately send to you with the dispatch of this letter all of the things you wrote. Forgive me for keeping them for such a long time.

Yours, P. Tchaikovsky

While Tchaikovsky was still a professor at the Moscow Conservatory, his textbook would serve to instruct none other than Nikolai Rimsky-Korsakov, who, after being invited in 1871 to join the St. Petersburg Conservatory to teach practical composition and orchestration, began assiduously his own study of harmony and counterpoint three years later, using Tchaikovsky's text, among others. He also employed Tchaikovsky's text in private theory lessons, although he expressed some dissatisfaction with it. With his appointment as assistant superintendent at the Court Chapel in February 1883 and inheriting of the harmony classes there, he "conceived the idea of writing a new textbook of harmony, according to a wholly new system as regards pedagogic methods and sequence of exposition" based, he claimed, on conversations with his Petersburg Conservatory colleague, A. Liadov.[9] Like Tchaikovsky's, Rimsky-Korsakov's textbook contributed to an identifiable method of teaching harmony at his Conservatory. As Carpenter notes, "despite the large number and variety of theory textbooks published in Russia during the next twenty years, none surpasses Tchaikovsky's or Rimsky-Korsakov's work in popularity or distinction."[10]

In the correspondence below, Tchaikovsky answers Rimsky-Korsakov's request to comment on the latter's newly lithographed harmony textbook and in the process reveals his own feelings about his past life as a theory teacher. Tchaikovsky's letter ends with reference to a clandestine proposal to have Rimsky-Korsakov become director of the Moscow Conservatory. Rimsky-Korsakov's response addresses some of Tchaikovsky's criticism of the textbook as well as the proposal; his own attitudes about his teaching career clearly differ from Tchaikovsky's.

Letter of P. I. Tchaikovsky to N. A. Rimsky-Korsakov[11]

Klin
Maidanovo
April 6, 1885

Dear most kind Nikolai Andreevich!

Since the time we saw each other,[12] I have had many pressing tasks (I've refashioned *Vakula the Smith*[13]) and much bustle of every kind, and journeyings, such that I could not properly devote myself to a survey of your textbook.[14] Little by little, though, I've been glancing at it and have been drafting my notes on special sheets of paper.[15] Today I finished surveying the first chapter and, having prepared to send you the above-named sheets, I have re-read what I wrote. A thought gripped me: To send them or not? The point is that, as it turns out, in my criticism of your textbook—completely independently of my will—can be detected some irritability, malice, captiousness, *almost* malevolence. I've become terrified that I would distress, offend you by the spite with which my criticism is saturated. Why this happened (i.e., the spite)— I myself don't understand. It seems to me that in essence my detestation toward the teaching of harmony makes itself felt there; a detestation that sprang from the recognition, on the one hand, of the unsoundness of existing theories and the inability to devise a new, well-grounded one, and, on the other hand, of the attributes of my musical temperament, of the unnecessary conditions which are demanded for conscientious teaching. For ten years I taught harmony and for ten years I loathed my classes, my students, my textbook, and my own self as a teacher. Reading your handbook revived in myself the *hatred* that had subsided; having vexed, embittered, and exasperated me, that hatred directed all its causticity and venom onto your textbook.

After long thought I've decided, though, to send you my notes all the same. You, of course, will at once notice their spitefulness, but, having been warned, will forgive me, I hope! In essence: on account of the conscientiousness, love for the cause, and aspiration in all ways possible to help the student— your handbook is very good. In much I don't agree with you, as you will see; I find the exposition rather negligent—but I cannot do fitting justice to the serious plan that is deeply well-considered with regard to small things. The main thing is to appreciate your preparedness and to remove any bewilderment, any difficulty to the student. However, if I'm not mistaken, you lavish too much on rules, you treat every detail too minutely and pedantically. If you are going to continue along this scale, your handbook will be colossal!!!

So then, most kind Nikolai Andreevich, once more I ask you to forgive me my captiousness and believe that no bad feeling has guided me, and certainly least of all a desire to make me feel that, as they say, "*my handbook is better.*" I consider my handbook *repulsive*; I'm saying this with complete frankness and sincerity and am not pretending in the least to be an authority in this matter.

If you won't become very angry with me, I will continue my survey further, trying to be less irritable and to restrain my tempestuous disposition.

Now I turn to you with a serious question that I ask you to answer not right away, but after thinking and talking *with Nadezhda Nikolaevna.*[16]

Is there the hope that in case they offer you the directorship of the Moscow Conservatory, you will not turn it down? Beforehand I will say that, in case this comes true, *I will take it upon myself to arrange things* so that there will be enough free time for you to compose and so that you won't be loaded with any, so to speak, "black work" (and there was much of that with Nikolai Grigorevich Rubinstein[17]); so that you would have only the highest supervision behind the musical side of affairs.

In my opinion, there is a guarantee of an excellent director in your straightforward, ideally honest character, in your excellent artistic and pedagogical qualities. I would consider myself fortunate if I could contribute to the realization of this plan. I would not dare turn to you with this question if I did not know that, on account of your family circumstances, you could not, like me, be free. You need employment, but the question is, what is better for you: to stay in Petersburg or to decide on moving to Moscow?

I haven't yet informed anyone of my idea, and ask you not to talk to anyone about this for the present.

Think about it, my friend, and answer me.

If I receive from you an answer that it's *possible* to make the request, I would then discuss it with the board of directors

(I am now one of the directors) and write to you all the details. In general, the whole business would be directed through my mediation.

I humbly give my regards to Nadezhda Nikolaevna; I shake your hand firmly.

Yours, P. Tchaikovsky

Letter of N. A. Rimsky-Korsakov to P. I. Tchaikovsky

[From April 15, 1885; response to the above]

Dear Pyotr Ilich, here it's been about a week since I received your letter, and only today have I read the *spiteful remarks*: there has been absolutely no time, but I wanted to read attentively. Many thanks to you for all the spiteful things and captiousness. The larger share of them, though, relate, so to speak, to the literary part (for example, the carping against the words *sviaz'* [connection] and *sviazyvan'e* [binding together], etc.) and also even to the philosophical side (a definition, what is a chord, etc.). I recognize that this whole portion of my textbook is very slovenly; I will take all your remarks of this type into consideration if I print the textbook. But I do not agree with many of your remarks that relate to the *essence*. *For example*: a) the minor subdominant triad is mentioned at the beginning, because it belongs to the principal triads, but the major triad on the 3rd scale degree in the minor mode will be mentioned later, when the matter of secondary triads is reached; b) the conjunction of triads of the IV and V scale degrees is touched on somewhat later for the sake of the student's becoming firmly established in the use of triads that are in a fifth *correlation*(!); c) hidden fifths and octaves in the outer voices are not talked about because these bad habits will easily fade away subsequently, and it is much more important to apply oneself to the sensible use of chords. For me an exercise that is overcrowded with hidden fifths and octaves, but has appropriate use of scale degrees, is much more agreeable than an exercise without hidden 5ths and 8ves but in which a triad on the III degree, or a chord on VI, or a subdominant after a dominant, etc., are found for no reason at all. However, one will not object to all this in writing. I

consider the teaching about leaps useful and not at all difficult; the point is that the student clearly conceive all *movements*
and the consequences of those [movements]. The goal of my
textbook is to train the student from the beginning first in the
harmonization of melodies, secondly in the harmonization of
an unfigured bass, and thirdly in the composition of his own
exercises, which will come in handy for him at a higher level
with modulation. For this I am giving him resources which at
first are very limited, but later on I keep broadening his horizon little by little. Likewise I recognize cases in which doubling of fifths and thirds is of use, but I insist on a doubling of
the fundamental tone in order not to generate in the student
many bad habits of which it will be difficult to break him, so
that he leaves hidden octaves and fifths behind. I know from
experience that students whom I assist by means of the methods propounded in my textbook have never brought me an
exercise that is overfilled with *pure nonsense*, and thus there is
fostered in them an understanding of the importance of the
principal triads and of the correlations of tonic, dominant,
and subdominant toward other chords. I don't know whether
I am expressing myself clearly at this minute.

Most kind Pyotr Ilich, I am not at all angry with your
spiteful things; "continue, it's pleasing to us!"[18] As a matter of
fact, only if you haven't been bored, do analyze my textbook
further and write to me. Everything which you will convince
me of I will take into consideration and will rectify as far as
possible, but in *essential matters* you will hardly shake me. And
I know that in particular the purely literary part in the textbook is weak, and over and above that there are also other
more important shortcomings, but that's why I decided only
to lithograph it and not to print it. *Incidentally*, "soedinennoe
garmonicheskoe (!) *trezvuchie* ["united *harmonic* (!) *triad*"] is a simple misprint; it needs to read "soedinennoe *garmonicheski
trezvuchie* ["*harmonically* united *triad*"].

Now about the other thing. Thank you for your friendly
assistance: you are offering to promote my selection as director of the Moscow Conservatory. On that I will tell you the following: 1) I consider the office of director completely *beyond
me*; musical affairs here will push me at once into the most
tangled relations with colleagues, and this is not how my disposition works. A director should be a tactician and a politi-
cian more even than a musician, I am convinced of this. 2)

Although I have little free time, I am tolerably well-to-do in a monetary respect, serving in the Chapel and the Petersburg Conservatory; in the office of director of the Moscow Conservatory I would likewise have little time *for myself*, but nowadays everything with me is calm and peaceful, and even if I don't adore the teaching part, I endure it and even rather like it. 3) To be director of the Moscow Conservatory while Erdmandsdörfer[19] is the conductor of concerts would be highly unpleasant. But if some day by some circumstance I am forced to leave the Petersburg Conservatory, moreover, if matters at the Chapel go badly (which I do not foresee)—in a word, when the world isn't large enough for me and there is nothing for me to eat, then it's another matter: then perhaps I would not turn it down, though it would in all probability be too late. But now I prefer to remain affiliated as I am.

Once more, many thanks for your friendly offer. According to your wish I will maintain strict silence.

I wait for further criticism of the textbook. I shake your hand.

Yours, N. R.-Korsakov
April 15, 1885

P. S. My wife sends you her regards.

Rimsky-Korsakov and Tchaikovsky shared more than friendship, similar careers, and harmony textbooks. Each of them also labored with works on orchestration: Tchaikovsky with his translation (1865) of F.-A. Gevaert's *Traité général d'instrumentation* on a commission from the music publisher Jurgenson, and Rimsky-Korsakov with his *Osnovi orkestrovki* (Principles of orchestration), variously sketched or rewritten in 1873–74, 1891–93, 1905, 1907–08.[20] Another common bond was the composition of stage works based on Ostrovsky's play, *Snegurochka (The Snowmaiden)*. Tchaikovsky's incidental music (Op. 12) for the premiere of the play dates from 1873. Rimsky-Korsakov's opera (1880–81), written with the playwright's approval, at first infuriated the older composer, but by the late 1880s Tchaikovsky made himself acquainted with the score and reversed his stance.[21]

Interestingly enough, in Rimsky-Korsakov's last years, a quarter of a century after its composition, *Snowmaiden* (his favorite opera[22]), would inspire him to undertake another musico-theoretical endeavor:

the *Razbor "Snegurochki"* (Analysis of Snowmaiden). The *Razbor* was written during the summer of 1905, when Rimsky-Korsakov's activities at the Petersburg Conservatory, and in musical life in general, were curbed by the political events of that year.[23] Unlike his autobiography and the orchestration textbook, however, the *Analysis of "Snowmaiden"* was left hopelessly incomplete. It seems clear that this document was not meant for publication in its unfinished and often sketchy state. Nevertheless Rimsky-Korsakov had great hopes for this work and enumerated his intentions in letters to his wife, an excerpt from which is quoted here:

> During the day I worked on the analysis of *Snowmaiden*, about which I wrote to you. I have already done the survey of all the themes of *Snowmaiden* that run through the whole opera, and I also analyzed the beginning of the Prologue, i. e., the introduction, recitative and aria of Spring. I don't know whether I'll finish doing a complete analysis of the whole opera. It is turning out to be very extensive, not at all like an article, rather like an entire work. The prologue, in any case, I do want to finish; then I'll see whether to continue further. I would like this to be a serious study, with even a pedagogical aim, by which it would be possible [to become familiar] with operatic forms in general through a text in which the author's purposes would be elucidated and their fulfillment examined. My work is intended to be read by persons who are familiar with my opera in general, and it should be read in conjunction with an examination of the full score, or at least a piano-vocal score, although in the text short examples of themes and motives are cited for explanation of motives derived from core motives. I suppose that the origin of motives one from another, and likewise the purposes for which motives are used at certain moments, may not be known by anyone better than by the composer himself, for I know very well the kinds of ridiculous mistakes critics fall into when they undertake an analysis of a musical composition. While indicating a method and finding successful application of it to the purposes of the composer, I do not mean to specify aesthetic value. For the reader with taste absolutely contrary to mine, my book cannot have any significance, as I will note in the foreword. My work, then, can interest the reader who likes my opera even a very little bit, and can open many eyes. To him who desires to learn, it will point out a whole

complex of problems and will force him to think about much in his own work. By accompanying the reading of my work with an examination of the score, the student-reader will learn much in the area of operatic form, use of voices, and operatic instrumentation. I would like my analysis to serve as a model for the proper analysis of other operas. I don't know if the thought of writing a work similar to mine has occurred to any other composer. I suppose not, and that my venture is original. I'm trying to be candid, not to show off. Twenty-five years have now passed since the time *Snowmaiden* was composed (1880), and for this reason I'm counting on the possibility of treating my own offspring objectively enough.[24]

The composer thus placed great pedagogical value on the *Razbor*, which was to provide not only an objective study of this particular opera, but also an objective and all-encompassing method for studying opera in general, specifically its forms and its use of vocal and instrumental forces. The study of instruments (and of voices to a certain degree) was realized, of course, in Rimsky-Korsakov's *Principles of Orchestration*, which uses as examples excerpts from his own works, primarily the operas. The study of operatic form, however, remained only fragmentary in the *Razbor*, which attempted to combine thematic, harmonic, and tonal analysis, with occasional remarks of an aesthetic or practical nature.

In less than two weeks, Rimsky-Korsakov recognized in another letter to his wife the unreasonable degree of detail in the work and hoped to improve the content:

I wrote the analysis of *Snowmaiden* through half of the prologue and stopped; but since you approve of my idea, I will continue, though, after finishing with the prologue, I will wait to go further or I will do part of the first act from a more concise viewpoint, for I am afraid I have penetrated into too much detail and that everything will come out too long.[25]

Here follows the last in this selection of documents, a portion of Rimsky-Korsakov's *Razbor "Snegurochki,"* specifically the overview of the characters and explanation of "thematicism" in the opera (the sketchy "Plan of the Foreword" and "Plan of the Introduction," which precede, are omitted). It gives a tantalizing hint as to how the composer discussed opera in his teaching.

Analysis of Snowmaiden[26]

[1905]

Snowmaiden—A Tale of Spring

The land of the Berendeyans. Prehistoric time. The cult of the Sun-God Iarilo.

The characters are partly mythical—personifications of eternal, periodically appearing forces of nature: Grandfather Frost, Spring Beauty, the Wood-Sprite, and Shrove-Tide (a strawman, representative of the established social and religious life of the human being).

The partly half-mythic/half-real characters are the girl Snowmaiden, Lel (a shepherd), and Tsar Berendei.

Snowmaiden is the daughter of Frost and Spring, charming but cold, having grown up in the dense forest; warmed by the feeling of love that has arisen in her through the rays of the burning Sun-God Iarilo, however, she melts and disappears without a trace. The wise Tsar Berendei[27] is the father of his people, who judges with a people's court. He has neither beginning nor end. The shepherd Lel, a singer of love songs and lady-killer to the female half of the Berendeyan kingdom, has apparently forever resided and will reside in the beautiful and melancholic land of the Berendeyans.[28] It is completely unknown when both the eternally old Tsar and the eternally young shepherd-singer were born and how long they will live. And, did the kingdom of the Berendeyens itself even have a beginning, and will there ever be an end to it?

The remaining portion of the characters are the real ones, who are born and who die, people of various callings: Mizgir is a merchant guest, Kupava is a young girl, Bobyl Bakula and Bobylikha are agents in the drama; Bermiata is a boyar, the two Heralds and a Princely Adolescent are additional characters, purely everyday agents.

Besides the Berendeyan people of both sexes and of every calling, besides the everyday representatives (blind gusli-players, shepherds, gudok-players, bag-pipers and *skomorokhi*), there are also representatives of nature in the capacity of Spring's retinue—the birds and flowers. These birds and flowers are prophetic, singing with human voices and in human language. There are also the voices of wood-sprites heard from the forest. Over all of this the supreme divinity, the Sun-God Iarilo, invisibly rules, the creative source who calls forth life within nature and the people. At the end of the play this divinity for a few moments becomes visible for the dramatis personae.

The spring tale is an extracted episode and an everyday tableau from the chronicle—without beginning and without end—of the kingdom of the Berendeyans.

Thematicism

The themes of the opera *Snowmaiden*—melodies, phrases, motives—should be subdivided into the following categories.

First category. A group of phrases and motives that are more or less large or minute, belonging to certain characters or to representations concommitant with them; likewise groups that correspond to certain representatives of everyday life and the life of nature. Such groups of phrases and motives are signified in the musical examples of the supplement by Roman numerals. They are

> I. The group of themes of the Snowmaiden.
> II. The group of themes of Frost, winter, snowdrifts, the snowstorm—severe, dismal.
> III. The group of themes of Spring.
> IV. The theme of the Wood-Sprite.
> V. The group of themes of Lel and the pastoral folk tunes.
> VI. The group that characterizes Kupava.
> VII. The group of themes of Mizgir.
> VIII. The group of themes of Tsar Berendei.
> IX. The theme of the boyar Bermiata.
> X. The group of themes of various powers in nature's manifestation. The group of themes of Bobyl and Bobylikha.
> XI. The group of bird tunes.
> XII. The theme of the Sun-God Iarilo.

The themes of the twelve groups in this category are true leading motives (leitmotivs) of the opera. Motives and phrases that form these groups are signified by the lower-case letters of the Latin alphabet, and the modifications of those same motives by letters corresponding to the signs.

The capacity of a motive, phrase, or melody to characterize a certain action or idea does not always depend on only one melodic contour of the motive. That same motive, but with rhythmic changes introduced into it, often assumes a completely different character and begins to serve different expressive ends. And a motive, while preserving a previous rhythm, may be completely modified by the tempo. Phrasing and the distribution of staccato and legato certainly influence the character of a motive; the nuances of dynamics (*f*, *p*, etc.) and, finally, the choice of sound—the instrumentation of the motive or the performance of it by the voice—contributes to the given motive its particular meaning. Thus one and the same fundamental motive, as a result of the influence of rhythm, tempo, phrasing, color, and nuances of dynamics, can exhibit numerous, almost innumerable modifications of its *root* form. The composer does not make use of all possible modifications; some modifications can turn out to be aimless and unnecessary for him, and many are anti-artistic. I cite motives and phrases of the present analysis and their modifications with tempo indications and, as far as possible, with phrasing, dynamic shading, and instrumentation. Only the principal and most characteristic modifications are cited.

The motives that make up the twelve abovementioned groups are those that chiefly figure in the course of the whole opera, a larger or smaller number of times in their root forms and in modifications; they accompany an appearance or presence on the stage, and also accompany the mention or mental representation of particular theatrical personages, concepts, and images of certain elements, appearing either independently or serving at the same time as material for musical elaboration.

The *second category* of themes is made up of more or less long melodies, for the most part with definite and clear endings that round them off. Melodies of this kind constitute attributes of the opera's purely lyrical moments—arias, songs, and dances. Such melodies usually appear only one time in the opera, but sometimes recur wholly or partially in the capacity of recollections (*réminiscences*) or on the occasion of analogous stage situations or moods. Sometimes the most characteristic motives extracted from these melodies are taken as material for an elaboration and weaving of the musical texture. Such long lyrical melodies for the most part are not cited here in the form of musical examples, but are designated by the initial words or verses of the song; but sometimes the beginning or some motive from the middle of a melody occurs as a musical example in the text with an Arabic numeral. Likewise, in the case of instrumental melodies.

The *third category* of themes is made up of phrases and motives that appear for a longer or shorter time at certain moments of the opera and do not recur subsequently. These themes are, as it were, passing, incidental, serving temporarily for the characterization of individual moments and not for general characterization of a theatrical personage or concept. And sometimes such passing motives serve only symphonic and not operatic goals constituting only material for treatment and structure of the musical edifice itself without referring to the general characterization of a personage or concept..[29] Themes of this category are referenced in the text of the present work and designated with Arabic numerals.[30]

NOTES

1. To the best of the translator's knowledge, none of documents chosen for translation here have been published in English until now. Some of the footnotes given here to the letters and the *Razbor* include information provided by editors of the printed sources employed. Paragraphing and punctuation are maintained as far as possible, except for the last selection. A portion of the narrative derives from an unpublished paper by the translator, "A Composer's Analytical Approach: Rimsky-Korsakov's *Razbor* 'Snegurochki'," presented at the South-Central Chapter Meeting of the American Musicological Society, Louisville, KY, Mar. 29, 1996. The reader is alerted also to a dissertation-in-progress on *Snowmaiden* by Gregory Halbe, Ohio State University, under the working title *Music, Drama and Folklore in Nikolai Rimsky-Korsakov's Opera "Snegurochka."*

2. Not to be confused with the composer M. M. Ippolitov-Ivanov, who originally shared the same name.

3. See excerpts from reminiscences by Kashkin and former pupils in David Brown, *Tchaikovsky Remembered* (London: Faber and Faber, 1993), p. 30–35.

4. Ellon D. Carpenter, "Russian Music Theory: A Conspectus," *Russian Theoretical Thought in Music*, ed. by Gordon D. McQuere (Ann Arbor: UMI Research Press, 1983), p.18–19. Carpenter evaluates and contextualizes Tchaikovsky's *Guide* and other such works along the continuum of their predecessors and successors.

5. P. I. Tchaikovsky, *Rukovodstvo k praktichestkomu izucheniiu garmonii* (Moskva: U. P. Iurgensona, 1872), p. [i–ii]. The preface is missing from the reprint of the English edition, *Guide to the Practical Study of Harmony*, trans. from the German version of P. Juon by Emil Krail and James Liebling (Canoga Park, Calif.: Summit Publ. Co., 1970); reprint of 1900 original. A few phrases from the introduction are translated in Carpenter, p. 18.

6. I am speaking about *Richter's Textbook of Harmony*. [Note by Tchaikovsky.]

7. Translated from P. I. Tchaikovsky, *Literaturnye proizvedeniia i perepiska. Polnoe sobranie sochinenii*, Tom XII (Moskva: Muzyka, 1970), p. 111–116.

8. Read "dissonances."

9. N. A. Rimsky-Korsakov, *My Musical Life*, trans. from the fifth revised Russian edition by Judah A. Joffe, ed. with an introduction by Carl van Vechten (London: Eulenburg, 1974; reprint Knopf, 1942), p. 115–16, 119, 150, 167, 273–74. The textbook, *Prakticheskii uchebnik garmonii* (Practical textbook of harmony), was written in 1884–85, during which time it was issued in two lithographed installments (under the title *Uchebnik garmonii* [Textbook of harmony]). The textbook was first printed in 1886

by A. Bittner. (See N. A. Rimsky-Korsakov, *Literaturnye proizvedeniia i perepiska. Polnoe sobranie sochinenii*, Tom VII [Moskva: Muzyka, 1970], p. 47, note 3.)

10. Carpenter, p. 26–27. While both texts have been highly regarded, Rimsky-Korsakov saw several editions of his tome issued during his lifetime, and after his death it was revised by former pupils Maksimilian Shteinberg and Jāzeps Vîtols (Withol). An English translation of the 12th edition, *Practical Manual of Harmony*, trans. by Joseph Achron (New York: Carl Fischer, 1930) includes Rimsky-Korsakov's prefaces to the first and third editions as well as an enumeration of changes made by the revisors. Tchaikovsky's *Guide* seems to have remained untouched by time, except for translations and his own issuance of a shortened version for musical amateurs, *Kratkii uchebnik garmonii* (Concise textbook on harmony), published in Moscow in 1874.

11. The two letters in this correspondence are translated from Rimsky-Korsakov, *Literaturnye proizvedeniia i perepiska. Polnoe sobranie sochinenii*, Tom VII, p. 45–49.

12. Probably in connection with a Mar. 30 concert of the Russian Music Society in Petersburg, where Tchaikovsky stayed Mar. 29–Apr. 1, 1885. The concert featured his orchestral fantasy *Francesca da Rimini*.

13. *Vakula the Smith*, Op. 14, was originally composed in 1874. The revised version of 1885 was called *Cherevichki* and has been known in the West under the titles *Oxana's Caprices* and *The Golden Slippers*.

14. Rimsky-Korsakov had sent the first installment of the lithographed edition to Tchaikovsky.

15. Unfortunately the "special sheets" of comments on Rimsky-Korsakov's textbook to which Tchaikovsky refers have not been discovered. Tchaikovsky's comments in the margins of a copy of the Rimsky-Korsakov's textbook survive and have been edited and printed in his (Tchaikovsky's) *Literaturnye proizvedeniia i perepiska. Polnoe sobranie sochinenii*, Tom IIIa (1957), p. 226–249.

16. Rimsky-Korsakov's wife.

17. N. G. Rubinstein, (1835–81), brother of Anton, was the first director of the Moscow Conservatory (1866–81).

18. "Prodolzhaite! Nam priiatno."

19. Maks Erdmansderfer (Max Erdmannsdörfer, 1848–1905), a German conductor, teacher and composer. During 1882–89 he conducted concerts of the Moscow branch of the Russian Musical Society and taught at the Conservatory. He was involved in some personnel conflicts.

20. A Russian edition: N. A. Rimsky-Korsakov, *Osnovi orkestrovki. Literaturnye proizvedeniia i perepiska. Polnoe sobranie sochinenii*, Tom III (Moskva: Gos. muz. izd-vo, 1959). English edition as *Principles of Orchestration*, ed. by Maximilian Steinberg, trans. by Edward Agate (New York: Dover, 1964; reprint of Edition Russe de Musique, 1922).

21. *My Musical Life*, p. 229, 243, footnote 8. Tchaikovsky's opera *Vakula the Smith* (1874) and Rimsky-Korsakov's *Christmas Eve* (1894–95, after Tchaikovsky's death), both based on the same Gogol story, constitute another *Snowmaiden*-type interplay between the two composers. (See *My Musical Life*, p. 343.)

22. E. M. Orlova, "Mysli N. A. Rimskogo-Korsakova ob analize muzykal'nykh proizvedenii," *N.A. Rimskii-Korsakov i muzykal'noe obrazovanie: Stat'i i materialy* ("Rimsky-Korsakov on Analyzing Musical Compositions," *Rimsky-Korsakov and Music Education*), pod redaktsiei S. L. Ginzburga (Leningrad: Gos. muz. izd-vo, 1959), p. 111.

23. *My Musical Life*, p. 412–14.

24. Letter of June 30, 1905 to Nadezhda Nikolaevna Rimskaia-Korsakova, published in Akademiia nauk SSSR, Institut istorii iskusstv, *Muzykal'noe nasledstvo. Rimskii-*

Korsakov. Issledovaniia, materialy, pis'ma, v dvukh tomakh (Moskva: Izd-vo Akademii nauk SSSR, 1953–54), Tom II, p. 104–05.

25. Letter of July 15, 1905 to N. N. Rimskaia-Korsakova, in ibid., p. 107.

26. This translation of the first part of Rimsky-Korsakov's *Analysis of "Snowmaiden"* is based on the following edition: *Razbor "Snegurochki." Literaturnye proizvedeniia i perepiska. Polnoe sobranie sochinenii*, Tom IV (Moskva: Gos. muz. izd-vo, 1960), p. 393–426 (p. 394–97 translated here). The Soviet editors seem to have retained the original paragraphing and punctuation, and include marginal notes and passages crossed out in the text. The translation here cites marginal notes relevant to the text and significantly readjusts the layout.

Other editions of the portion translated here as well as the thematic survey from the *Razbor* include those by M. Shteinberg, *"Snegurochka—vesenniaia skazka,"* *Russkaia muzykal'naia gazeta* No. 39–40 (1908), col. 804–16; N. N. Rimskaia-Korsakova, *Muzykal'nye stat'i i zametki (1869–1907)* (St. Petersburg: 1911); A. S. Ogolevets, *"Snegurochka—vesenniaia skazka,"* *Materialy i dokumenty po istorii russkoi realisticheskoi muzykal'noi estetiki*. Tom II (Moskva: Gos. muz. izd-vo, 1956); A. Solovtsov, *"Snegurochka (vesenniaia skazka)"* (Moskva: Muzyka, 1978); A. Lischké, "Les leitmotives de Snégourotchka analysés par Rimsky-Korsakov," *Revue de musicologie* 65/1 (1979), p. 51–75.

27. "A personification, as it were, of some wise form of government." [Marginal note by Rimsky-Korsakov.]

28. "As a personification of the eternal art of music." [Marginal note by Rimsky-Korsakov.]

29. "N.B. [Talk] about harmonic and characteristic leitmotives after motives and groups." [Marginal note by Rimsky-Korsakov.]

30. Rimsky-Korsakov's *Razbor "Snegurochki"* continues with a "Survey of Thematic Groups of the First Category" and an exhaustive analysis of the first half of the Prologue of the opera.

Index

Index of Names

List of Contributors

Rosamund Bartlett teaches in the Department of Russian Studies at the University of Manchester, England. She is the author of *Wagner and Russia* (Cambridge, 1995), coauthor of *Literary Russia: A Guide* (Picador, 1997), and editor of *Shostakovich in Context* (Oxford University Press, forthcoming).

Leon Botstein is President of Bard College, where he is also Professor of History and Music History. He is the author most recently of *Jefferson's Children: Education and the Promise of American Culture* (Doubleday, 1997).

Susanne Dammann trained in musicology, history, philosophy and Slavic studies in Hamburg and Kiel. Recent publications include *Gattung und Einzelwerk im symphonischen Frühwerk Čajkovskijs* (M & P Verlag, 1996).

Caryl Emerson is A. Watson Armour, III, University Professor of Slavic Languages and Literatures at Princeton University. She is co-translator (with Michael Holquist) of *The Dialogic Imagination: Four Essays by M. M. Bakhtin*, (University of Texas Press, 1981) and editor and translator of Bakhtin's *Problems of Dostoevsky's Poetics*. More recently, she is the author of *Boris Godunov: Transpositions of a Russian Theme* (Indiana University Press, 1986) and co-author (with Robert William Oldani) of *Modest Musorgsky and Boris Godunov: Myths, Realities, Reconsiderations* (Cambridge, 1994).

Kadja Grönke studied musicology, Slavic studies, and art history in Kiel. She has published extensively on Russian and Soviet music, most notably on Musorgsky, A. Rubinstein, and Serov in *Pipers Enzyklopädie des Musiktheaters*.

Alice Dampman Humel studied at the New School of Music, Depauw University, the Hochschule für Musik, Berlin, and the New England Conservatory. She has worked extensively as a free-lance musician in Europe and the United States, specializing in early music, and has recorded with the Boston Camerata and Schola Cantorum. Her translations include essays, *Lieder* texts, program and liner notes for the Akademie der Künste, the Berliner Festwochen, the German government, and various recording companies.

Leslie Kearney is Assistant Professor of Music History at Indiana University. She is the author of "Truth versus Beauty: Comparative Song Settings by Tchaikovsky and Musorgsky," in *Tchaikovsky and His Contemporaries* (Greenwood Press, forthcoming) and *Modest Musorgsky: Poetry, Opera and Song* (Cambridge University Press, forthcoming).

Janet Kennedy is Associate Professor of Art History at Indiana University, and author of *The "Mir Isskustva" Group and Russian Art 1898–1912* (Garland, 1976). She has published many articles on Russian art and theatrical design, including her recent contribution to *Petrushka: Sources and Contexts*, edited by Andrew Wachtel (Northwestern University Press, 1998).

Arkadii Klimovitsky is a leading scholar of the Russian Institute for Art History, and Professor at the St. Petersburg Conservatory, working on music theory, the history of European and Russian music, and the relationship between German and Russian culture. He is author of a monograph, *Tchaikovsky and Cultural Problems of the Twentieth Century*. He has also published essays on Tchaikovsky's Sixth Symphony and *The Queen of Spades*.

Marina Kostalevsky is Assistant Professor in the Division of Languages and Literature at Bard College, and author of the recent critically acclaimed volume *Dostoevsky and Soloviev: The Art of Integral Vision* (Yale, 1997).

Natalia Minibayeva is a doctoral student of music history at Indiana University. She holds a master's degree from Bowling Green University, and graduated from Kazakh Almaty State Conservatory, where she studied piano and music history.

Lyle Neff is a doctoral student of music history at Indiana University, and a member of the supplemental faculty of the University of Delaware (Newark). He holds a master's degree in composition, and has written a full-length opera, *Starbottle for the Plaintiff* (1981), as well as an English-language singing version of Rimsky-Korsakov's opera *Tale of Tsar Saltan*, performed at Indiana University in 1987. He is working on a dissertation, *Story, Style and Structure in the Operas of Cesar Cui*, and has articles forthcoming in *Opera Quarterly* and the *Pushkin Review*.

Alexander Poznansky is the leading authority on Tchaikovsky's life. He has published extensively on this subject, including *Tchaikovsky: The Quest for the Inner Man* (Schirmer, 1991) and *Tchaikovsky's Last Days* (Oxford, 1996). He works at Yale University's Sterling Library.

Richard Wortman is Professor of History at Columbia University. He is the author of *Crisis of Russian Populism* (Cambridge, 1967), the seminal work *The Development of a Russian Legal Consciousness* (Chicago, 1976), co-author of *The Making of Three Russian Revolutionaries* (Cambridge, 1987), and most recently author of *Scenarios of Power, Myth and Ceremony in Russia* (Princeton, 1995).